Folk-Tales of Kashmir

By

Rev. J. Hinton Knowles

Low Price Publications

Delhi-110052

First Published 1893
Reprinted in LPP 2004, 2025

ISBN 10: 81-7536-346-0
ISBN 13: 978-81-7536-346-5

Published by
Low Price Publications
A-6, Second Floor, Nimri Commercial Centre,
Ashok Vihar Phase-IV, Delhi 110 052
Phone: 011 4706 1936
e-mail: info@Lppindia.com
website: www.Lppindia.com

Printed at
Balaji Printers, Shahdara,
Delhi

PRINTED IN INDIA

PREFACE.

KASHMÍR as a field of Folk-lore literature is, perhaps, not surpassed in fertility by any other country in the world; and yet, while every year witnesses the publication of books on the subject from Bengal, Bombay, Madras, Panjáb, and other parts; and while each successive number of *The Indian Antiquary, Indian Notes and Queries,* and latterly *The Christian College Magazine* and *The Indian Evangelical Review,* presents to us articles more or less relevant, this field, ripe for the harvest, has remained almost ungleaned. No doubt its isolated position and the difficulty of its language have had something to do with this apparent neglect. I am the more glad, therefore, to have availed myself of the opportunities afforded me through a four years' residence in the valley.

The vocation of a missionary brings one into close and constant "touch" with the people, from whom, as I glide along in the boat, or walk by the way, or squat in the hut, or teach in the school, I have learnt many things. My primary object in collecting these tales was to obtain some knowledge of Kashmírí, which is a purely colloquial language; my secondary object was to ascertain something of the thoughts and ways of the people. Lately I have been contributing some of these tales to the pages of an Indian journal; and now, prompted by the advice of those whose advice I especially value, I venture to publish the whole collection in a book, and thus save them from the clutches of oblivion, to which they would otherwise have been consigned.

Many of these tales are, probably, purely Kashmírí in origin, while others are undoubtedly variants of popular tales current in India and other parts, which have been adapted and modified to suit the language, style of thought, and social usages of the country. To European Folk-tales, also, several of these stories will be found to have a great resemblance—notably the story of "The Two Brothers," to its counterpart, "St. George and the Dragon;" while many of the little stories mixed up in the tales, and quoted generally to explain the situation of the hero or heroine, will be recognised at once as variants of tales extant in France, Germany, Greece, Russia, England, and other countries.

It is not my intention here to attempt to trace the home of any of these stories. Whether they originated in the East or in the West I leave to more expert and learned minds to declare. "There can be no doubt that many Eastern stories were introduced into Europe by the Hans in the time of Genghis Khan. Many of these stories were translated into Persian, and thence into Syriac and Arabic." It is probable that the Arabs carried some of them into Europe, and that European invaders, like the Crusaders, imported fragmentary portions into their countries. These stories, as we know, became very popular in the West during the Middle Ages, when instruction through the medium of fables, so popular in the East in ancient times, was largely adopted by Western monks and other religious teachers for the sake of the impression thus made on the minds of illiterate hearers. "An apposite or well-told story would arouse attention where logical argument or abstract reasoning would fail to produce the slightest effect." These fictitious narratives, with their moral and religious applications, had a very considerable influence upon the literature of those days.

But, as Mr. Ralston remarks, it does not, of course, follow that, because a story is found both in Asia and Europe, therefore the Western version has been borrowed from the East. Europe has doubtless lent a fancy to Asia. One or two books of Western stories have been published in India. Greek fables are supposed to have exercised an influence on the Indian mind. European officials, missionaries, and others may have rendered a legend or story current in their districts. These and many other important facts have to be taken into consideration. The fields of philology and other sciences, too, have yet to be more thoroughly traversed before we can decide the origin of many tales. Folk-lorists must wait a while for the accumulation of more facts. From a disregard of this true and wise way many an absurd conclusion has been published, that threatens to bring the cause of Folk-lore into contempt in some quarters. It was only a little time ago that I read a most interesting article, wherein a certain professor's literary criticism fairly suggested that the Játaka form of a tale was older in point of time than the European version. I was almost convinced, till just afterwards I came across a paper in the *Contemporary Review* by another equally learned professor, who showed that the Chinese alphabet was derived from the Phœnician, and therefore the former professor's inference was evidently fallacious.

And if it is not my intention, even if it were within my power, to endeavour to trace the origin of any of these tales, much less shall I attempt to decide whether or not the root of any cycle to which these stories may belong is of a mythological nature, and also as to what was in either case its primal form and significance. Some Folk-lorists do not appear to hesitate a moment about the matter. "It is the story of the Sun and Dawn," says one; "Cinderella, grey and dark and dull, is all neglected when she is away from the Sun, obscured by the envious Clouds, her sisters, and by her stepmother, the Night. So she is Aurora, the Dawn, and the Fairy Prince is the Morning Sun, ever pursuing her to claim her for his bride." "It is the story of the Spring being released from the bonds of Winter, the Sun being rescued from the darkness of the Night, the Dawn being brought back from the West, the Waters being set free from the prison of the Clouds," some would say concerning the release of the fair Princess mentioned in the first tale of this collection. Not long ago a writer in the *Westminster Review* startled us by duly appropriating Rájá Rasálú, who has been called the King Arthur of the Panjáb, as a solar myth. Concerning this same Rasálú, Captain Temple says:—"I venture to submit that it is capable of historical proof that this man was a popular leader, on to whose name has been hung, as a convenient peg, much of the floating folk-lore of the Panjáb. At any rate, I hope to show that the particular tales, which went to prove beyond doubt in the mind of our Comparative Mythologist that Rasálú was a solar myth, are by no means confined to that hero, but are the general property of the heroes of India, told of this one or that as occasion arises. They are, moreover, as regards Rasálú himself, to a great extent only one local version out of many of his story." Truly many of the writers on popular Folk-tales seem to forget that this is a subject which requires the most dainty treatment and the most careful analysis.

However, I hope the reader will not consider that I suppose the science of Folk-lore should not include Comparative Mythology. On the contrary, I firmly believe that several tales must be attributed to a mythological origin. But I am also as firmly convinced that many tales must be attributed to a historical origin. "What seems to be demanded from every interpreter of old tradition, every explorer of the dark field of popular fiction, is a wariness that will not allow itself to be hoodwinked by any prejudice in favour of this or that particular theory. Every piece of evidence ought to be carefully tested and fairly weighed, whether it confirms the examiner's own opinion or not. If this be done, he will probably find that different classes of legends must be explained in divers manners. The more he becomes acquainted with popular tales, the less he will be inclined to seek for any single method of solving all their manifold problems." *

I would draw the attention of the Folk-lorist to the notes in connection with these different stories. They have been gathered and arranged with some care, in the hope that they may help the reader to turn up readily to variants of the tale, or of different incidents in the tale. All Kashmírí or Hindustání words have been fully explained—if they are special words, at the end of the page on which they occur; and if they are ordinary, in the Glossary at the end of the book. In nearly every case, too, the name and address of the narrator have been given. From these it will be seen that all classes of people have contributed to this collection—the officiating governor, the poor farmer, the learned Paṇḍit, the ignorant Musalmán, the physician, the barber, the day-labourer, the old man grey-headed, and the dirty little boy, all and every one of whom I can say, they were entirely free from European influence.

No apology will be needed for the presentation of this book to the public. The great interest and importance attaching to the Folk-tales of any people is manifest from the great attention devoted to them by many learned writers and others. Concerning the style and manner of the book, however, I would ask my readers to be lenient with me. I have sought not so much to present these tales in a purely literary form as to give them in a fair translation, and most of the work was done by lamp-light after an ordinary amount of missionary work during the day. However, such as it is, I sincerely hope it will prove a real contribution towards that increasing stock of Folk-lore which is doing so much to clear away the clouds that envelop

* Ralston.

much of the practices, ideas, and beliefs which make up the daily life of the natives of our great dependencies, control their feelings, and underlie many of their actions.

Several other short Folk-Tales of "The Happy Valley" are to be found in my *Dictionary of Kashmírí Proverbs and Sayings.*

J. HINTON KNOWLES.

KASHMÍR, 28*th April* 1887.

CONTENTS.

FOLK-TALES OF KASHMIR.

THE SEVEN-LEGGED BEAST.[1]

A CERTAIN king, who took especial pride in his troops and spent an enormous amount of money on them, wished to know thoroughly how strong and able they were. Accordingly he ordered the general in command to assemble the men in battle array on a large *maidán* without the city. On the day of review His Majesty, attended by his *wazírs* and *díwáns*, visited the place, and while they were watching the manœuvres, a beast having seven legs[2] suddenly appeared and prowled around near them. On noticing it the king was much astonished and wished to kill it; but the beast got away. The king rode after it as hard as his swift horse could carry him, and when he had thus pursued it for about two miles, the beast stopped, shook itself, and changing into a great and terrible *jinn*, turned round on His Majesty, slew him, and ate him.

The *wazírs* caused earnest search to be made for the king for eight days, and then, no tidings of him having been received, they fetched his son and proclaimed him king in his father's stead.

One day the young king was seized with an irrepressible desire to know the cause of his father's death. He forced the *wazírs* to tell him, and when he had heard everything he commanded another grand review of the

[1] Narrator's name, Shiva Báyú, Renawárí, Srínagar.

[2] *Satah-zung haiwán.*

whole army to be held in the same place where the review in his father's time had been held. On the appointed day he and all the court attended to watch the proceedings. They had not been present very long before the seven-legged beast came again, and growling fiercely at them, walked away. When the chief *wazír* saw this he laughed aloud.

"What is the matter?" asked the king.

"I laughed," replied the *wazír*, "because this is none other than the beast that allured your late father from our midst."

"Is it so? Then I must slay it, for I shall not have any peace till this enemy is killed." Saying this, the king whipped his horse and rushed after it. The beast led him on and on for some distance, as it did his father, and then stopping, shook itself, resumed its original shape, and prepared to spring. In his distress the king called earnestly on the great God to save him; and God sent an angel to direct him how to fight with the *jinn.*

"This is a most powerful *jinn,*" said the angel. "Should a drop of his blood fall to the ground, while life is in him, another *jinn* will be quickly formed therefrom, and spring up and slay you.[3] But fear not. Take this double-headed arrow and pierce the two eyes of the monster, so that he fall down and die." Then the angel departed.

Thus strengthened, the king dashed forward. He fought with the *jinn* for forty minutes. At last he plunged the double-headed arrow into both of his eyes, and thus slew him. When he saw that his enemy was dead the king drew his sword and cut off his head, and fixing it on his arrow, took it with him to the palace, where he placed it in one of the twelve thousand rooms of that building; and gave his mother the keys, bidding her not to open the doors thereof.

But as he did not tell his mother what he had so care-

[3] Cf. *Folk-Tales of Bengal*, pp. 85, 253; *Indian Fairy Tales*, p. 187; also a note on the "revivifying and healing powers of blood," in *Wide-Awake Stories*, p. 418.

fully locked up in the room, she supposed that it was some special treasure, and being very inquisitive, one morning went to the room and unlocked the door. Nothing, however, was to be seen, for the king had thrown the head into a corner; but a laugh was heard, and then a voice, saying, "Your son is a *jinn*. Beware of him. He is a *jinn*. Some time he will kill you, as he killed me, your husband. Get him out of the palace, if you wish to live."

"Whence comes this voice? What say you?" asked the king's mother.

"Pretend to be unwell, and beg your son to get the milk of a tigress.[4] Bid him to go himself and try to get this," said the head.

The next morning, with a sad and heavy heart, the king might have been seen wending his steps in the direction of a certain jungle, wherein tigers and other wild beasts were known to roam. He soon saw a tigress, with her two cubs basking in the sunshine. He climbed a tree and aimed at one of the teats of the beast. This teat chanced to be one in which she had suffered much pain for several days, owing to the presence of a nasty abscess near the place. The king's arrow broke the abscess, and the pain was at once relieved. Grateful for this relief, the tigress looked up and entreated the king to descend and ask whatever he would like her to get for him. His Majesty told her that he wanted nothing but a little of her milk for his sick mother, who had taken a strange fancy for it. The tigress readily filled the cup that the king had brought with him, and also gave him a tuft of her fur, saying, "Whenever you are in any difficulty show this to the sun, and I will at once come to your aid."[5] Taking

[4] Cf. *Indian Fairy Tales*, p. 178; *Indian Antiquary*, Part cxc. p. 367; *Bilochi Stories*, p. 27; and the story of the "Ogress-Queen" in this collection.

[5] A favourite device for summoning the absent. Notice that these things have generally to be shown to the sun or to the fire. Cf. *Wide-Awake Stories*, pp. 32, 271; *Legends of the Punjab*, vol. i. pp. 42, 43; *Indian Notes and Queries*, vol. iv. p. 49; and *Folk-Lore Journal*, vol. ii. 104, *re* charms placed in the fire; Russian tale of "Naznaiko" in Afanasief's collection (vii. No. 10): also tale of "Good King Hátam" in this collection. *Vide* also "Survey of Incidents in Modern Indian Folk-

the milk and the bit of fur, the king returned to his palace.

When his mother received the milk of the tigress she felt quite sure that her son was a *jinn*, and determined more than before to have him killed. She went to the room where the head was, and informed the speaker of everything, and heard again a voice saying, "Be assured thereby that this man is a *jinn*. None but a *jinn* could obtain milk from a tigress. Have him killed as soon as possible."

"But how can I get rid of him?" she asked.

The voice replied, "When your son visits you and inquires after your health, tell him that you still feel very weak and sick. The tigress's milk did not do you any good. But you have heard of a princess who lives alone in a castle on a certain high hill. If she could come and touch you, you would become well. Your son will go to this terrible castle, and be certainly killed on the way."

In the evening the king went to see his mother. "Are you better?" he asked.

"No," she said. "The tigress' milk has not benefited me in the least. But I saw in a dream a princess who lives in a certain castle, and heard that if she would come and touch me all would be well. Until she comes I shall never get strong."

"Be comforted, mother. I will fetch this woman for you, or forfeit my kingdom."

Early the following morning the king started on his perilous journey. He had not forgotten the bit of charmed fur. As soon as the sun appeared he showed the fur to it, and immediately the tigress and her two cubs came running towards him.

"What is the matter?" asked the tigress.

Tales" in *Wide-Awake Stories*, pp. 413, 414. There are some interesting notes on Hair and its wonderful properties in *Indian Fairy Tales*, pp. 268–270.

"I have to go and fetch the princess who resides in yonder castle."

"Fetch her! You cannot do it. Several people have tried, for the princess is very beautiful; but nobody ever succeeded in getting near her."

"I will try, though I lose my life in the attempt." Saying this the king left.

The tigress could not bear to have her benefactor thus leave her. So she ran after him with her two cubs, and begged him to ride on her.[6] They soon reached the castle.

"In this place," said the tigress, "there are three big doors, through which it is necessary to pass before a person can get to the princess. Near the first door is an immense block of iron, which must be broken by a wooden axe, or the door will not open. At the second door is an imitation cow, surrounded by real *jinns*. If any person can milk the cow, he will pass through; if not, he will be devoured by the *jinns*. By the third door sits the princess herself. If she is pleased with you, she will receive you; but if not, she will accomplish your death."

On hearing these words the king became very frightened, and begged the tigress[7] to help him.

"Very well," she said. "By a charm which I possess I will enter the block of iron, and when you strike with the wooden axe, I will cause it to divide into two pieces; and then the doorkeeper will think that you cleft the iron, and allow you to enter through the first door."

"And I," said one of the young tigers, "will cause the statue of the cow to give milk, and will keep the *jinns* who stand round it from hindering you in milking. Thus will you be able to pass through the second door."

[6] Cf. *The Orientalist*, vol. i. p. 27; *Indian Evangelical Review*. vol. xiii. p. 232; also tale of the "Wicked Queens" in this collection.

[7] Apparently a very grateful beast. Cf. *Indian Fairy Tales*, pp. 65, 156, 180; *Wide-Awake Stories*, p. 6; *Madanakamárájankadai* (The Dravidian Nights), Tenth Story; *The Orientalist*, pp. 181, 182, 250; also the *Pancha-tantra* (Appendix to Book I. Story 2).

"And I," said the other young tiger, "will put a charm into the eyes of the princess, so that when she looks on you she may think you to be bright and beautiful as the sun, and be so fascinated with the sight, that she will open the third door and do anything else you may ask her."

Faithfully they all three performed their promises. The king safely reached the princess, and she, overcome by his beauty and immense power, professed her great affection for him, and entreated him to make her his wife.

Then the tigress and her two cubs returned to their lair. In a few days the king took the princess home with him to his palace. "Mother," he said, "I have brought the princess. Oh! what a fearful place it was, and how difficult and dangerous the way to it! I should have perished on the way if a tigress and her two little cubs had not helped me. Praise be to God that I am here safe and well!" Some other conversation leading up to it, he told her also about the head of the *jinn*—how it had first appeared to him as a seven-legged beast, and led him away to a certain place where it changed itself back into its real character, a great and terrible *jinn*, and prepared to jump on him; and how he would have been slain and eaten up, as his father had been, if God had not sent His angel and helped him.

His mother was much surprised to hear this. "My son," she said, "I have been deceived. On the evening of the day when you borrowed the keys of the palace from me I went round several of the rooms, till I came to the one in which I heard the sound of laughing. On my inquiring the reason of this a voice said, 'Take heed lest your son, who is a *jinn*, slay you. I am the head of your husband. He killed me. Get rid of him, or he will kill you also.' My son, I believed the voice, and at its advice I sent you to fetch me the milk of a tigress, hoping you would be slain in the attempt. And I begged you to go and call the princess, knowing that the way to her abode was full of terrible dangers. But God has been with you, and He, who sent the angel to direct you, has also caused the tigress and young tigers to be your helpers. Praise be to His name!" Then she embraced her son, and wept bitterly.

Within a short time of these things the king married the princess, and spent the rest of his life in peace and prosperity.[8]

[8] Cf. article, "The Forbidden Chamber," in *Folk-Lore Journal*, vol. iii. pp. 193-242, for other stories presenting this prohibition; also *en passant*, vol. iv. p. 66 of the same journal.

THE CAT WHO BECAME A QUEEN.[1]

"Ah me! ah me! What availeth my marriage with all these women? Never a son has the Deity vouchsafed me. Must I die, and my name be altogether forgotten in the land?" Thus soliloquised one of the greatest monarchs that ever reigned in Kashmír, and then went to his *zanána,* and threatened his numerous wives with banishment if they did not bear him a son within the next year. The women prayed most earnestly to the god Shiva to help them to fulfil the king's desire, and waited most anxiously for several months, hoping against hope, till at last they knew that it was all in vain, and that they must dissemble matters if they wished to remain in the royal household. Accordingly, on an appointed time, word was sent to the king that one of his wives was *enciente,* and a little while afterwards the news was spread abroad that a little princess was born. But this, as we have said, was not so. Nothing of the kind had happened. The truth was, that a cat had given birth to a lot of kittens, one of which had been appropriated by the king's wives. When His Majesty heard the news he was exceedingly glad, and ordered the child to be brought to him—a very natural request, which the king's wives had anticipated, and therefore were quite prepared with a reply. "Go and tell the king," said they to the messenger, "that the Bráhmans have declared that the child must not be seen by her father until she is married." Thus the matter was hushed for a time. Constantly did the king inquire after his

[1] Narrator's name, Rází, a *panḍitání,* living in Srínagar. Collected by Pandit Ánand Kol of Zainah Kadal, Srínagar.

daughter, and received wonderful accounts of her beauty and cleverness; so that his joy was great. Of course he would like to have had a son, but since the Deity had not condescended to fulfil his desire, he comforted himself with the thought of marrying his daughter to some person worthy of her, and capable of ruling the country after him. Accordingly, at the proper time he commissioned his counsellors to find a suitable match for his daughter. A clever, good, and handsome prince was soon found, and arrangements for the marriage were quickly concluded. What were the king's wives to do now? It was of no use for them to attempt to carry on their deceit any longer. The bridegroom would come and would wish to see his wife, and the king, too, would expect to see her. "Better," said they, "that we send for this prince and reveal everything to him, and take our chance of the rest. Never mind the king. Some answer can be made to satisfy him for a while." So they sent for the prince and told him everything, having previously made him swear that he would keep the secret, and not reveal it even to his father or mother. The marriage was celebrated in grand style, as became such great and wealthy kings, and the king was easily prevailed on to allow the palanquin containing the bride to leave the palace without looking at her. The cat only was in the palanquin, which reached the prince's country in safety. The prince took great care of the animal, which he kept locked up in his own private room, and would not allow any one, not even his mother, to enter it.

One day, however, while the prince was away, his mother thought that she would go and speak to her daughter-in-law from outside the door. "O daughter-in-law," she cried, "I am very sorry that you are shut up in this room and not permitted to see anybody. It must be very dull for you. However, I am going out to-day; so you can leave the room without fear of seeing any one. Will you come out?"

The cat understood everything, and wept much, just like a human being. Oh those bitter tears! They pierced the mother's heart, so that she determined to speak very strictly to her son on the matter as soon as he should return. They also reached the ears of Párvatí, who at once went to her lord and entreated him to have mercy on the poor helpless cat. "Tell her," said Shiva, "to rub some oil over her fur, and she will become a beautiful woman. She will find the oil in the room where she now is." Párvatí lost no time in disclosing this glad news to the cat, who quickly rubbed the oil over its body, and was changed into the most lovely woman that ever lived.[2] But she left a little spot on one of her shoulders, which remained covered with cat's fur, lest her husband should suspect some trickery and deny her.

In the evening the prince returned and saw his beautiful wife, and was delighted. Then all anxiety as to what he should reply to his mother's earnest solicitations fled. She had only to see the happy, smiling, beautiful bride to know that her fears were altogether needless.

In a few weeks the prince, accompanied by his wife, visited his father-in-law, who, of course, believed the princess to be his own daughter, and was glad beyond measure. His wives too rejoiced, because their prayer had been heard and their lives saved. In due time the king settled his country on the prince, who eventually ruled over both countries, his father's and his father-in-law's, and thus became the most illustrious and wealthy monarch in the world.[3]

[2] Cf. *Tales of the West Highlands*, vol. ii. p. 274—a variant of story No. 41 in the same collection, to which also refer (p. 265).

[3] Undoubtedly belongs to the "Forbidden Chamber" cycle. Cf. note at the end of story of "The Seven-legged Beast" in this collection.

GOOD KING HATAM.[1]

THERE was once a poor man, who used to earn a few *páṅsas* by cutting and selling wood. It was a hard struggle to support himself and wife and seven daughters. Never a bit of meat touched his lips, never a shoe covered his feet, and only a rag covered his back.

One day, when not feeling very well, he lay down under a tree to rest. The lucky-bird Humá[2] happened to be flying about the place at the time, and, noticing the man's poverty and sickness, pitied him. So it flew down beside him and deposited a golden egg by his bundle of wood. In a little while the woodcutter awoke, and seeing the egg, picked it up and wrapped it in his *kamarband.*[3] He then took up his load and went to the *woni*, who generally bought it. He also sold him the egg for a trifle. He did not know what a wonderful egg it was; but the *woni* knew, and asked him to go and get the bird that laid it, and he would give him a rupee as a gift. The man promised, and on the following day went to the jungle as usual to prepare his load of wood. On the way back he sat down to rest under the tree where he had found the egg, and pretended to sleep. The bird *Humá* came again, and noticing that he was still as poor and as ill-looking as before, thought that he had not seen the egg, and therefore went and laid another close by him, in such

[1] Narrator's name, Qádir, a barber living by Amírá Kadal, Srínagar.

[2] A fabulous bird of happy omen peculiar to the East. It haunts the mountain Qáf. It is supposed that every head it overshadows will wear a crown. The Arabs call it *'anqá*, and the Persians *símurgh* (lit. of the size of thirty birds).

[3] Called also *hul* and *lungí*, a long piece of cotton stuff worn round the waist over the outer garment.

a spot that he could not possibly miss seeing it; whereupon the woodcutter caught the bird, and rose up to carry it to the *woni*. "Oh! what are you going to do with me? Do not kill me. Do not imprison me; but set me free," cried the bird. "You shall not fail of a reward. Pluck one of my feathers and show it to the fire, and you shall at once arrive at my country, *Koh-i-Qáf*,[4] where my parents will reward you. They will give you a necklace of pearls, the price of which no king on earth could give."

But the poor ignorant woodcutter would not listen to the bird's pleadings. His mind was too much occupied with the thought of the rupee that he felt certain of getting, and therefore he fastened the bird in his wrap, and ran off to the *woni* as fast as his load would permit. Alas! however, the bird died on the way from suffocation. "What shall I do now?" thought the woodcutter. "The *woni* will not give me a rupee for a dead bird. Ha! ha! I will show one of its feathers to the fire. Perhaps the bird being dead will not make any difference." Accordingly he did so, and immediately found himself on the *Koh-i-Qáf*, where he sought out the parents of the bird and told them all that had happened. Oh, how the parents and other birds wept when they saw the dead body of their beloved relative!

Attracted by the noise, a strange bird that happened to be passing at the time came in and inquired what was the matter. This bird carried a piece of grass in its beak, with which it could raise the dead.

"Why do you weep?" it said to the sorrowful company.

"Because our relative is dead; we shall never speak to it again," they replied.

[4] Another name is *Koh-i-Akhzar*, another *Koh-i-Zamurrad* (lit. the green or emerald mountain). The Muhammadans believe that these mountains encircle the world, and that they are inhabited by demons. They think that this mountain range of emerald gives an azure hue to the sky. Hence in Persian *az qáf tá qáf* means the whole world. The name is also used for Mount Caucasus. Cf. also *Wide-Awake Stories*, pp. 34, 37, 316.

"Weep not," said the strange bird. "Your relative shall live again." Whereupon it placed the piece of grass in the mouth of the corpse, and it revived.

When the bird *Humá* revived and saw the woodcutter, it severely upbraided him for his faithlessness and carelessness. "I could have made you great and happy," it said "but now get you back to your burden of wood and humble home." On this the poor man found himself back again in the jungle, and standing by the load of wood that he had prepared before he was transported to *Koh-i-Qáf*. He sold his wood, and then went home in a very sad frame of mind to his wife and daughters. He never saw the bird *Humá* again.

It has been mentioned that this woodcutter had seven daughters. These girls grew up to be big, and had to be married. But how was the woodcutter to arrange for their marriages? He barely earned money sufficient for their food; and nobody would be allied to such a poverty-stricken house as his. In the hour of his difficulty he sought the advice of a friend, who told him to go to Hátam, the noble-minded generous king, and ask for help.

Now in those days Hátam had become very poor, and was obliged to pound rice for a living. But although he was so reduced in circumstances, that there was scarcely a poorer man than he in the whole country, yet he had the same generous heart and was as desirous as ever of bettering others. When the woodcutter reached his country and happened to meet with him, we have a beautiful instance of his generous spirit. The woodcutter, not knowing who he was, related to him all his sad tale, and begged to be directed to King Hátam the Noble. The poor king advised him to stay there for the night and continue his journey on the morrow; to which the woodcutter consented, and walked with him to his house. That night Hátam fasted, in order to give something to his guest, and in the morning he informed him of the truth. "O friend," said he, "I am he whom you seek; but behold! I am as poor as yourself. Alas! I cannot help you. I cannot even give you another meal. But if you will accept my only daughter, you are welcome. You may be able to sell her, and thus get some money to marry your own daughters. Go, and God be with you."

"O king," replied the woodcutter, "your generosity melts my heart. I cannot thank you sufficiently for your kindness to me. May God reward you. Farewell!"

The woodcutter and the princess then left. On the way they had to pass through a very wild place, where they met a prince, who was hunting. The prince chanced to catch sight of the girl, and at once fell in love with her, and begged the woodcutter to accept him as a son-in-law. Of course the man agreed, and the marriage was celebrated. Henceforth money without stint flowed into the woodcutter's hands, so that he was able to resign his calling, to build for himself a beautiful house, and to marry his seven daughters into good and respectable families.

Meanwhile the prince was living very happily with his beautiful wife, under the idea that she was the woodcutter's daughter. One day, however, he discovered the truth of the matter. He had given an alms to a poor man in the presence of his wife, when she casually remarked that he had done a *hátamí*, meaning a generous act, a Hátam-like act;[5] whereupon the prince asked her how she knew anything about Hátam, and she told him everything—how the woodcutter had applied to her father for help, and how her father, not having anything else, gave her to him as a slave. The prince then sent for the woodcutter, and heard from him the same words, and all about the *Humá's* egg and the man's visit to *Koh-i-Qáf*. He was intensely surprised when he heard all these things. He immediately sent to King Hátam, begging him to come and rule the country in his stead, because

[5] *Hátamí* (Persian), boundless liberality. Cf. *arihiyat hátamíya*, liberality equal to that of Hátam (who was a man celebrated among the Arabs for his liberality). Hátam is a popular proper name in the valley.

he was too young and inexperienced to manage it properly. The retired woodcutter received a large pension in land; but the cunning *woni* was ordered to give up the golden egg to the king.[6]

[6] Compare whole story of "The Faithful Prince" in *Wide-Awake Stories*. The story of the charitable monarch, whose goodness and generosity are tried *ad extremum*, occurs in several tales. Kashmírís have a legend concerning Wainadat, an old king of the country, who gave up everything and worked himself, that he might not be chargeable to any person. Cf. *Indian Fairy Tales*, pp. 67, 85; *Buddhist Birth Stories*, p. 33; *Kathá Sarït Ságara* (Tawney's), vol. i. p. 244; *Kings of Kashmírá*, pp. 34, 51, 82; and the Tamil drama translated by the late Sir Mutri Coomára Swamy, *Arichandra, or the Martyr of Truth.*

METEMPSYCHOSIS.[1]

Once upon a time a young man left his home and country, and went to a wild desert place to meditate on religious subjects. He spent twelve years thus, during which he neither ate nor drank. When he thought he had perfected himself in religious matters and had discovered the end of things, he conceived a desire to visit a city about five miles distant. On the way he sat down under a tree to rest, and while he rested a crow came and perched on a branch just above him and let fall some lime on his head. He was very much annoyed at this, and turned towards the bird; and the bird died. When he had sufficiently rested, the holy man resumed his journey, and reached the city, where he entered the courtyard of a certain house, and begged for some food. A woman called to him from a window, and bade him to come in and wait till her husband arrived, when she promised to give him something to eat. The holy man was very angry at this reply, and was going to curse her, when she interrupted him by saying "I am not a crow, that you can burn me with your angry looks.[2] You had better come in and wait for my husband's return." The man did so, but he wondered how ever the woman had got to know of the crow incident. In a little while the master of the house appeared; whereupon the woman brought some warm water and washed his feet, and after that some food and

[1] Narrator's name, Náráyan Kol of Fateh Kadel, Śrínagar.

[2] Slaying, burning, or paralysing with a look is a power often attributed to holy men (Musalmáns and Hindús alike). Shiva is said to have reduced Kámadeva to ashes by fire from his central eye.

gave him to eat. Then she placed some food before their guest and gave him also to eat. When he had eaten as much as he wished, she ate her own dinner. Afterwards she prepared her husband's bed, and while he was reclining on it she shampooed his feet. Truly, she was a pattern wife! So thought the holy man, who observed everything, but said nothing.

"Tell us a tale," she said to her husband, while shampooing his feet; to which the man agreed, and began as follows:—

"In days gone by there lived a Bráhman, who for many years was praying to know something of the state of the departed. At last the gods complied with his request. Early one morning, while bathing according to custom,[3] his spirit left him, and went into the body of an infant, the child of a cobbler.[4] The child grew up, learnt his father's business, married, and became the father of a numerous family, when suddenly he was made aware of his high caste, and abandoning all went to another country. Now just as he reached that country the king died, and as there was no person to put upon the throne, the *wazírs* and others in authority had to resort to the popular custom of sending an elephant and a hawk round the place to elect a successor for them. Whomsoever the elephant and hawk acknowledged, the people also acknowledged. There was no alternative. Well, wonderful to relate, the stranger was chosen for this high office. The elephant bowed down before him, and the hawk perched on his right hand, and thus proclaimed him king in the presence of all the people. In the course of a few years his wife got to know of his whereabouts and went to join him. Then it

[3] In the early morning, both summer and winter, the religious H .dú is to be seen performing his ceremonial bathings in the river.

[4] Manu declares that the triple order of the passage of the soul through the highest, middle, and lowest stages of existence results from good or bad acts, words, and thoughts produced by the influence of the three Gunas—Sattoa, Rajas, and Tamas; and that for sins of act a man takes a vegetable or mineral form; for sins of word, the form of a bird or beast; for sins of thought, that of a man ˆ the lowest caste.—Monier Williams, *Hinduism*, p. 69.

somehow became known that he was a cobbler, and that his wife, also, was of that low caste. The people were in great consternation about it. Some fled, some subjected themselves to great penance, and others burnt themselves, lest they should be excommunicated. The king, too, burnt himself, when he heard what was happening, and his spirit went and reoccupied the corpse of the Bráhman, that remained by the river-side, and went home. 'How quickly you have performed your ablutions this morning!' said his wife; but the Bráhman answered nothing. He only looked very much surprised. 'Can this be the future state?' thought he. 'Have I really seen it? or was it only a dream?'

"About a week after this a man came into the Bráhman's courtyard, and begged for some bread, saying that he had not eaten anything for five days, during which he had been running away from his country as fast as he could, because a cobbler had been appointed to the throne. All the people, he said, were running away or burning themselves to escape the consequences of such an evil. The Bráhman gave the man some food, but said nothing. 'How can these things be?' thought he. 'I have been a cobbler for several years. I have reigned as a king for several years,—and this man confirms the truth of my thoughts; yet my wife declares that I have not been absent from this house more than the usual time; and I believe her, for she does not look any older, nor is the place changed in any way.'

"Thus ends my story, whereof the explanation is this: The soul passes through various stages of existence according to a man's thoughts, words, and acts, and in the great Hereafter a day is equal to a *yug*[5] and a *yug* is equal to a day."

On the conclusion of the story, the woman, wishing to sleep, turned to the stranger and inquired if he wanted anything more. He replied, "Only happiness."

[5] A *yug* or *yuga* is an age of the world or a great period.

"Then go and seek it in your own home," she said. "Go, return to your parents, who have wept themselves blind because of you. Go and put your hands on their eyes, and tell them that their son has returned; and they will see again.[6] Then shall you be happy. Happiness is to be sought for in the path of duty—in obedience to those whom the gods have set over us. It is the duty of a wife to seek the pleasure of her husband. It is the duty of a child to seek the pleasure of his parents. It is the duty of a citizen to seek the pleasure of his king. It is the duty of us all to seek the pleasure of the gods."

[6] For the recovery of sight by placing hand on eyes, cf. story "A Lach of Rupees for a Bit of Advice" in this collection.

THE CHARMED RING.[1]

A MERCHANT started his son in life with three hundred rupees, and bade him go to another country and try his luck in trade. The son took the money and departed. He had not gone far before he came across some herdsmen quarrelling over a dog, that some of them wished to kill. "Please do not kill the dog," pleaded the young tender-hearted adventurer; "I will give you one hundred rupees for it." Then and there, of course, the bargain was concluded, and the fool took the dog, and continued his journey. He next met with some people fighting about a cat. Some of them wanted to kill it, but others not. "Oh! please do not kill the animal," said he; "I will give you one hundred rupees for it." Of course they at once gave him the cat and took the money. He then went on till he reached a village, where some folk were quarrelling over a snake that had just been caught. Some of them wished to kill it, but others did not. "Please do not kill the snake," said he. "I will give you one hundred rupees." Of course the people agreed, and were highly delighted.

What a fool the fellow was! What would he do now that all his money was gone? What could he do except return to his father? Accordingly he went home.

"You fool! You scamp!" exclaimed his father when he had heard how his son had wasted all the money that had been given to him. "Go and live in the stables and repent of your folly. You shall never again enter my house."

[1] Narrator's name, Qádir, a barber, living by Amírá Kadal, Srínagar.

So the young man went and lived in the stables. His bed was the grass spread for the cattle, and his companions were the dog, the cat, and the snake, which he had purchased so dearly. These creatures got very fond of him, and would follow him about during the day, and sleep by him at night; the cat used to sleep at his feet, the dog at his head, and the snake over his body, with its head hanging on one side and its tail on the other.

One day the snake in course of conversation said to its master, "I am the son of Indrasharájá. One day, when I had come out of the ground to drink the air, some people seized me, and would have slain me had you not most opportunely arrived to my rescue. I do not know how I shall ever be able to repay you for your great kindness to me. Would that you knew my father! How glad he would be to see his son's preserver!"

"Where does he live? I should like to see him, if possible," said the young man.

"Well said!" continued the snake. "Do you see yonder mountain? At the bottom of that mountain there is a sacred spring. If you will come with me and dive into that spring, we shall both reach my father's country. Oh! how glad he will be to see you! He will wish to reward you, too. But how can he do that? However, you may be pleased to accept something at his hand. If he asks you what you would like, you would, perhaps, do well to reply, 'The ring on your right hand, and the famous pot and spoon which you possess.' With these in your possession, you would never need anything, for the ring is such that a man has only to speak to it, and immediately a beautiful, furnished mansion, and a charming, lovely woman, will be provided for him, while the pot and the spoon will supply him with all manner of the rarest and most delicious foods." [2]

[2] Cf. *Indian Fairy Tales*, pp. 34, 156; *Folk-tales of Bengal*, pp. 32, 34, 55, 282; *Old Deccan Days*, 174; *Wide-Awake Stories*, 199, 216; Portuguese story in *Young Ceylon*, of June 1850, which tale also exists in Tamil; the tale of "The Table, Ass, and Stick," in *Grimm's Household Stories*;

Attended by his three companions the man walked to the well and prepared to jump in, according to the snake's directions. "O master!" exclaimed the cat and dog, when they saw what he was going to do. "What shall we do? Where shall we go?"

"Wait for me here," he replied. "I am not going far. I shall not be long away." On saying this, he dived into the water and was lost to sight.

"Now what shall we do?" said the dog to the cat.

"We must remain here," replied the cat, "as our master ordered. Do not be anxious about food. I will go to the people's houses and get plenty of food for both of us." And so the cat did, and they both lived very comfortably till their master came again and joined them.

The young man and the snake reached their destination in safety;[3] and information of their arrival was sent to the *rájá*. His Highness commanded his son and the stranger to appear before him. But the snake refused, saying, that it could not go to its father till it was released from this stranger, who had saved it from a most terrible death, and whose slave it therefore was. Then the *rájá* went and embraced his son, and saluting the stranger welcomed him to his dominions. The young man stayed there a few days, during which he received the *rájá's* right-hand ring, and the pot and spoon, in recognition of His Highness's gratitude to him for having delivered his son. He then returned. On reaching the top of the spring he found his friends, the dog and the cat, waiting for him. They told one another all they had experienced since they

Makanakamárájankadai (*Dravidian Nights*), pp. 132, 154; the "Lad who went to North Wind," in Dasent's *Norse Tales*, which tale also appears in *Italian Popular Tales* (Crane); *Brentano Fairy Tales*, the story of "Ninny Noddy." Compare also Mahá-Bhárata, xii. 1769; Wolf, *Beiträge zur Deutschen Mythologie*, i. p. 12; *Dictionary of Kashmiri Proverbs*, pp. 179, 180. But, perhaps, the most ancient example of these tales is to be found in the Buddhist Játaka Book, Dadhiváhana Játaka (No. 186, Fausböll, also 291), *vide Buddhist Birth Stories*, pp. xvi.-xxi.

[3] *Nága* (Sanskrit), a snake. The race of *Nágas* is said to have sprung from Kadru, the wife of Kashyapa, for the purpose of peopling *Pátála*, or the regions below the earth, where they reign in great splendour. Cf. *en passant*, *Folk-Tales of Bengal*, pp. 20, 21.

had last seen each other, and were all very glad. Afterwards they walked together to the river side, where it was decided to try the powers of the charmed ring[4] and pot and spoon. The merchant's son spoke to the ring, and immediately a beautiful house and a lovely woman with golden hair appeared. He spoke to the pot and spoon, also, and the most delicious dishes of food were provided for them. As will be imagined, life went on very happily under these conditions for several years, until one morning the woman, while arranging her toilet, put the loose hairs into a hollow bit of reed and threw them into the river that flowed along under the window. The reed floated on the water for many miles, and was eventually picked up by the prince of that country, who curiously opened it and saw the golden hair.[5] On finding it the prince rushed off to the palace, locked himself up in his room, and would not leave it. He had fallen desperately in love with the woman, whose hair he had picked up, and refused to eat, or drink, or sleep, or move, till she was brought to him. The king, his father, was in great distress about the matter, and did not know what to do. He feared lest his son should die and leave him without an heir. At last he determined to seek the counsel of his aunt, who was an ogress. The old woman consented to help him and bade him not to be anxious, as she felt certain that she would succeed in getting the beautiful woman for his son's wife. She assumed the shape of a bee and went along buzzing.[6] Her keen sense of smell soon brought her to the woman, to whom she appeared as an old hag, holding in one hand a stick by way of support. She introduced herself to the beautiful woman as her

[4] Cf. *Madanakamárájankadai*, p. 27; the tale of "Aladdin, or the Wonderful Lamp," in *The Arabian Nights*; *Wide-Awake Stories*, p. 198; and the story of "The Robber and his Sons," in *Grimm's Household Stories*.

[5] Cf. *Evangelical Review*, "Santal Folk-Tales," vol. xiii. No. 51, p. 333; *Madanakamárájankadai*, p. 32; the Egyptian tale of "The Two Brothers;" also *Wide-Awake Stories*, pp. 60, 413.

[6] Cf. *Kings of Káshmírá*, p. 55; *Indian Notes and Queries*, vol. iv. p. 64; *Folk-Tales of Bengal*, p. 186; *Indian Fairy Tales*, pp. 56, 141; and *Indian Antiquary*, vol. xvi. p. 212.

aunt,[7] and said that she had seen nothing of her before, because she had left the country just after her birth. She also embraced and kissed the woman by way of adding force to her words. The beautiful woman was thoroughly deceived. She returned the ogress's embrace, and invited her to come and stay in the house as long as she could, and treated her with such honour and attention, that the ogress thought to herself, "I shall soon accomplish my errand." When she had been in the house three days, she mooted the subject of the charmed ring, and advised her to keep it instead of her husband, because the latter was constantly out shooting and on other suchlike expeditions, and might lose it. Accordingly the beautiful woman asked her husband for the ring, and he readily gave it to her. The ogress waited another day before she asked to see the precious thing. Doubting nothing the beautiful woman complied, when the ogress seized the ring, and re-assuming the form of a bee flew away with it to the palace, where the prince was lying in a very critical condition. "Rise up. Be glad. Mourn no more," she said to him. "The woman for whom you yearn will appear at your summons. See, here is the charm, whereby you may bring her before you." The prince was almost mad with joy when he heard these words, and was so desirous of seeing the beautiful woman, that he immediately spoke to the ring, and the house with its fair occupant descended in the midst of the palace-garden.[8] He at once entered the building, and telling the beautiful woman of his intense love, entreated her to be his wife. Seeing no escape from the difficulty she consented on the condition that he would wait one month for her.

Meanwhile the merchant's son had returned from hunting and was terribly distressed not to find his house and wife. There was the place only, just as he knew it be-

[7] Cf. *Indian Fairy Tales*, pp. 260, 262; *Orientalist*, vol. ii. pp. 94, 232.

[8] Cf. *Indian Antiquary*, vol. iv. p. 371; *Indian Evangelical Review*, vol. xiii. No. 50, p. 226; also story of "Aladdin, or the Wonderful Lamp," in *Arabian Nights;* and story of "True Friendship" in this collection.

fore he had tried the charmed ring, which Indrasharájá had given him. He sat down and determined to put an end to himself. Presently the cat and dog came up. They had gone away and hidden themselves, when they saw the house and everything disappear. "O master!" they said, "stay your hand. Your trial is great, but it is not irremediable. Give us one month, and we will go and try to recover your wife and house."

"Go," said he, "and may the great God aid your efforts. Bring back my wife, and I shall live."

So the cat and dog started off at a run, and did not stop till they reached the place whither their mistress and the house had been taken. "We may have some difficulty here," said the cat. "Look, the king has taken our master's wife and house for himself. You stay here. I will go to the house and try to see her." So the dog sat down, and the cat climbed up to the window of the room, wherein the beautiful woman was sitting, and entered. The woman recognised the animal, and informed it of all that had happened to her since she had left them.

"But is there no way of escape from the hands of these people?" she asked.

"Yes," replied the cat, "if you can tell me where the charmed ring is."

"The ring is in the stomach of the ogress," she said.

"All right," said the cat; "I will recover it. If we once get it, everything is ours." Then the cat descended the wall of the house, and went and laid down by a rat's hole and pretended she was dead. Now at that time a great wedding chanced to be going on among the rat community of that place, and all the rats of the neighbourhood were assembled in that one particular mine by which the cat had lain down.[9] The eldest son of the king of the rats was about to be married. The cat got to know of this, and at once conceived the idea of seizing the bridegroom and making him render the necessary help. Consequently,

[9] Rats have weddings, cf. *Wide-Awake Stories*, pp. 17–26.

when the procession poured forth from the hole squealing and jumping in honour of the occasion, it immediately spotted the bridegroom and pounced down on him. "Oh! let me go, let me go," cried the terrified rat. "Oh! let him go," squealed all the company. "It is his wedding day."

"No, no," replied the cat. "Not unless you do something for me. Listen. The ogress, who lives in that house with the prince and his wife, has swallowed a ring, which I very much want. If you will procure it for me, I will allow the rat to depart unharmed. If you do not, then your prince dies under my feet."

"Very well, we agree," said they all. "Nay, if we do not get the ring for you, devour us all."

This was rather a bold reply. However, they accomplished the thing. At midnight, when the ogress was sound asleep, one of the rats went to her bedside, climbed up on her face, and inserted its tail into her throat; whereupon the ogress coughed and urged violently, so that the ring came out and rolled on to the floor.[10] The rat immediately seized the precious thing and ran off with it to its king, who was very glad and went at once to the cat and released its son.

As soon as the cat received the ring, she started back with the dog to go and tell their master the good tidings. All seemed safe now. They had only to give the ring to him, and he would speak to it, and the house and beautiful woman would again be with them, and everything would go on as happily as before. "How glad their master would be!" they thought, and ran as fast as their legs could carry them. On the way they had to cross a stream. The dog swam, and the cat sat on its back. Taking advantage of the occasion the dog asked for the ring, and threatened to throw the cat into the water if it did not

[10] Cf. *Madanakamárájankadai*, pp. 40, 41. I have known rats to insert their tails into native inkstands in the hope of thus drawing up some dainty drop. A military gentleman told me the story of a rat who got at his wine in the same way.

comply; whereupon the cat gave up the ring. Sorry moment, for the dog at once dropped it, and a fish swallowed it.

"Oh! what shall I do? what shall I do?" said the dog.

"What is done is done," replied the cat. "We must try to recover it, and if we do not succeed we had better drown ourselves in this stream. I have a plan. You go and kill a small lamb, and bring it here to me."

"All right," said the dog, and at once ran off. He soon came back with a dead lamb, and gave it to the cat. The cat tore open the stomach of the beast, and took out the bowels, and then went inside and laid down, telling the dog to go away a little distance and keep quiet. Not long after this a *nadhar*,[11] a bird whose look even breaks the bones of a fish, came and hovered over the corpse, and eventually pounced down on it to carry it away. On this the cat came out and jumped on to the bird, and threatened to kill it if it did not recover the lost ring. This was most readily promised by the *nadhar*, who immediately flew off to the king of the fishes, and ordered it to make inquiries and to restore the ring. The king of the fishes did so, and the ring was found and carried back to the cat.

"Come along now, I have got the ring," said the cat to the dog.

"No, I will not," said the dog, "unless you let me have the ring. I can carry it as well as you. Let me have it, or I will kill you." So the cat was obliged to give up the ring. The careless dog very soon dropped it again. This time it was picked up and carried off by a kite.

"See, see, there it goes—away to that big tree," the cat exclaimed.

"Oh! oh! what have I done!" cried the dog.

11 *Nadhar* is a cormorant (?). Kashmíris have a saying *Nadharani naṭ*, Nadhar's fright, which they quote on occasions of any special fear. There is a small species of pelican in the valley, which closely resembles the cormorant in appearance. A skin of one of these was procured by the late Dr. Henderson, after whom it has been named.

"You foolish thing, I knew it would be so," said the cat. "But stop your barking, or you will frighten away the bird to some place where we shall not be able to trace it."

The cat waited till it was quite dark, and then climbed the tree, killed the kite, and recovered the ring. "Come along," it said to the dog when it reached the ground. "We must make haste now. We have been delayed. Our master will die from grief and suspense. Come on."

The dog, now thoroughly ashamed of itself, begged the cat's pardon for all the trouble it had given. It was afraid to ask for the ring the third time, so they both reached their sorrowing master in safety and gave him the precious charm. In a moment his sorrow was turned into joy. He spoke to the ring, and his beautiful wife and house reappeared, and he and everybody were as happy as ever they were.[12]

[12] Cf. whole of the second story of *Madanakamárájankadai*; also *Wide-Awake Stories*, pp. 196-206, and *Indian Antiquary*, vol. x. p. 347 *et seq.*

THE CROW-GIRL.[1]

One day two potters' wives went to the jungle to get a special kind of soil, which their husbands wanted for making some pots. They carried their little infant children with them a-straddle on their hips. When they reached the place where this earth was to be found, they put down their children, a little boy and a little girl, to play together, while they filled their baskets. A kite and a crow noticed what was going on, and swooped down upon the children and carried them off. The kite killed the boy, but the crow flew away with the girl to the hollow trunk of a tree in a distant part of the jungle, and there dropped her. Instead of crying the child thought it was great fun, and so laughed and played with the bird; and the bird got very fond of her, and brought her nuts and fruit, and scraps of bread and meat sometimes, whenever it could get them. The little girl grew up and became very beautiful.

One day a carpenter chanced to visit that part of the jungle for cutting wood. "*Salám*," said the girl to him. "I wish you would make me a spinning-wheel. I am here all alone, and I wish to do something."

"Why are you here? Where is your home? Have you no more clothes than the rag you are wearing?" asked the carpenter.

"You must not ask me any questions," replied the girl. "But please make me a spinning-wheel, and I shall be quite happy."

[1] Narrator's name, Lál Chand of Khunamuh in the Wular *pargana*. The story is known in the valley by the name of *Kávah-Kúr*.

The carpenter did so; and the crow stole a spindle and some cotton for the girl. So she had everything complete.

Not long after this the king of that part of the world was out a-hunting in the jungle, and as he passed by that way, his ear caught the sound of somebody spinning. "Who resides in this solitary place?" he said to one of his attendants. "I hear the sound of a person spinning. Go and see who it can be." After a long search the men discovered the girl sitting by her wheel in the hollow of a tree, and brought her before the king. His Majesty inquired everything about her; and was so interested in her story, and fascinated by her beauty, that he begged her to accompany him to the palace, and to stay there with him as his wife.

The king had six other wives. This crow-girl was the seventh. Each of the wives had a separate apartment and special attendants. One day His Majesty, wishing to try their skill and taste, ordered all of them to decorate their rooms as nicely as they could. The six wives went to work in the ordinary way; they bought several ornaments and pictures, and had the walls of their rooms washed with ottar of roses; but the seventh wife sought an interview with her beloved crow and asked his advice on the matter. "Don't be anxious," said the bird, and immediately flew off and brought back in its bill an herb, which it gave her, saying, "Take this herb and rub it all over the walls of your room, and they will shine like burnished gold." The girl obeyed, and her room shone so with gold—real gold, that one could scarcely look at it.

When the other wives of the king heard of this, they were very jealous. Notwithstanding they had washed their rooms with ottar of roses, and decorated them with the richest carpets and the most magnificent vases, yet they looked not one hundredth part as beautiful as the crow-girl's apartment. "What have you done to your room to make it so lovely?" they asked. But the crow-girl did not tell them.

When the king inspected the rooms of the six wives, he was much pleased with them, but when he came to the crow-girl's room he was overcome with astonishment and delight. Henceforth he made her his chief *ráni*, and seemed to forget all the rest.

This special notice from the king increased the hatred and jealousy of the other wives. They were wicked enough before; but now, maddened by the king's preference for the seventh wife, they plotted to bring about her speedy death. They soon found opportunity for accomplishing their wickedness. One day they were all going to the river to bathe, when it was decided to push the crow-girl queen into the water, and to inform the king that she had been accidentally drowned. Accordingly, when they reached a deep part of the river, they shoved the woman off the bank into the water.

The king's grief was intense when he heard the sad news. For a long time he gave up all business, shut himself in his room, and would not see any one. Fate, however, had not decreed the death of the *ráni*. She was not drowned, as everybody thought. Near to the part of the river where she fell, there happened to be a large tree growing out of an invisible island. She had floated to this island and climbed to the top of the tree, where she was constantly fed by her kind friend the crow.

One day some weeks afterwards, His Majesty chanced to go for an airing in his boat by the way of this tree. The crow-girl saw him, and shouting the words, "The king unjustly exposed me to danger.[2] Come, O beloved, come here," she discovered herself to him. On seeing his beloved *ráni* again, the king's joy knew no bounds. He immediately took her into the boat and carried her to the palace. There she told him all that had occurred, and when His Majesty heard the truth of the matter, he at once gave orders for the execution of the other wives.[3]

2 "The king unjustly bound me in a net," literally.

3 Compare variant in *Old Deccan Days*, pp. 79-93.

A LACH OF RUPEES FOR A BIT OF ADVICE.[1]

A POOR blind Bráhman and his wife were dependent on their son for their subsistence. Every day the young fellow used to go out and get what he could by begging. This continued for some time, till at last he became quite tired of such a wretched despicable manner of life, and determined to go and try his luck in another country. He informed his wife of his intention, and ordered her to manage somehow or other for the old people during the few months that he would be absent. He adjured her to be very diligent, lest his parents should be angry and curse him.

One morning he started with some food in a bundle, and walked on day after day, till he reached the chief city of the neighbouring country. Here he went and sat down by a merchant's shop and asked alms. The merchant inquired whence he had come, why he had come, and what was his caste, to which he replied that he was a Bráhman, and was wandering hither and thither begging a livelihood for himself and wife and parents. Moved with pity for the man, the merchant advised him to visit the kind and generous king of that country, and offered to accompany him to the court. Now at that time it happened that the king was seeking for a Bráhman to look after a golden temple which he had just had built. His Majesty was very glad, therefore, when he saw the Bráhman and heard that he was good and honest. He at once deputed him to the charge of this temple, and

[1] Narrator's name, Paṇḍit Chadh Ram of Habah Kadal, Srínagar.

ordered fifty *kharwárs* of rice and one hundred rupees to be paid to him every year as wages.

Two months after this, the Bráhman's wife, not having heard any news of her husband, left the house and went in quest of him. By a happy fate she arrived at the very place that he had reached, where she heard that every morning at the golden temple a golden rupee was given in the king's name to any *boná fide* beggar who chose to go for it. Accordingly on the following morning she attended at the place, and met her husband.

"Why have you come here?" he asked. "Why have you left my parents? Care you not whether they curse me and I die? Go back immediately, and await my return."

"No, no," said the woman. "I cannot go back to starve and see your old father and mother die. There is not a grain of rice left in the house."

"O Bhagawant!" exclaimed the Bráhman. "Here, take this," he continued, scribbling a few lines on some paper, and then handing it to her, "and give it to the king. It may be that he will give you a *lach* of rupees for it." Thus saying he dismissed her, and the woman left.

On this scrap of paper were written four pieces of advice —(1.) If a person is travelling and reaches any strange place at night, let him be careful where he puts up, and not close his eyes in sleep, lest he close them in death. (2.) If a man is in need, let him test his friends; but if he is not in need, then let not his friends try him. (3.) If a man has a married sister, and visits her in great pomp, she will receive him for the sake of what she can obtain from him; but if he comes to her in poverty, she will frown on him and disown him. (4.) If a man has to do any work, he must do it himself, and do it with might and without fear.[2]

On reaching her home the bráhmaní told her parents of her meeting with her husband, and what a valuable piece

[2] Cf. tale of "Three Maxims" in the *Gesta Romanorum*.

of paper he had given her; but not liking to go before the king herself, she sent one of her relations. The king read the paper, and ordering the man to be flogged, dismissed him. The next morning the bráhmaní took the paper, and while she was going along the road to the *darbár* reading it, the king's son met her, and asked what she was reading, whereupon she replied that she held in her hands a paper containing certain bits of advice, for which she wanted a *lach* of rupees. The prince asked her to show it to him, and when he had read it gave her a *parwána* for the amount, and rode on. The poor bráhmaní was very thankful. That day she laid in a great store of provisions, sufficient to last them all for a long time.

In the evening the prince related to his father the meeting with the woman, and the purchase of the piece of paper. He thought his father would applaud the act. But it was not so. The king was more angry than before, and banished his son from the country.

Alas! alas! how sad was the royal household when they heard of the king's cruel order! for the prince was a great favourite, and a young man of much promise, and, moreover, was heir to the throne. However, the king's order was urgent. So the prince bade adieu to his mother and relations and friends, and rode off on his horse, whither he did not know. At nightfall he arrived at some place, where a man met him, and invited him to lodge at his house. The prince accepted the invitation, and was treated like a prince. Matting was spread for him to squat on, the best of provisions set before him, and at night the host's daughter attended him.

"Ah!" thought he, as he lay down to rest, "I perceive the reason of the first piece of advice that the bráhmaní gave me. I will not sleep to-night."

It was well that he thus resolved, for in the middle of the night the man's daughter rose up, and taking a sword in her hand, rushed to the prince with the intention of killing him. The prince, however, averted the blow, and seizing the sword, said, "Why do you wish to slay me? Have I wronged you in any matter? Do I wish to wrong you? Put up the sword again, lest you bring sorrow on yourself, like that king who killed a favourite parrot by mistake."

"What king?" asked the girl.

"Listen," said the prince:—

"Once upon a time there lived a king who had a very beautiful parrot, which was very precious to him. This parrot lived in the royal *haram*, and the king always talked to it first before speaking to his wives. One day the parrot asked for one month's leave of absence to go and marry his son, which leave the king granted. The bird went, and the marriage was celebrated, and then the bird prepared to return. It brought back for the king the cuttings of two trees, one of which possessed the virtue of making a young man old, and the other of making an old man young. The cuttings were planted, and in due time flourished and bore fruit. But just as they were beginning to ripen a great storm passed over that country, and blew down the trees, and a monster serpent that was carried along by the waters took refuge in them, and covered their branches with its poison. This, however, was not noticed by any one. When the storm had subsided the gardener went and replanted the two trees and attended them with such care that they flourished again and bore fruit; and some of their fruit was taken to the king. Wishing to test it on an animal first, His Majesty threw some of the fruit of one of the trees to a dog. The animal ate it, and died immediately. On seeing this the king became very angry, and thinking that the parrot had been playing jokes with him, he ordered it to be killed. The following year the trees bore fruit again, by which time all the poison had exuded from their branches. One morning, when passing, an old man, being hungry, put out his hand and plucked one of the fruits and ate it, and immediately became young again. The report of this strange occurrence reached the king, who ordered some of the fruit to be brought to him. He gave some of the youth-restoring fruit to his old *wazír*, who ate it, and was at once changed into a strong young man, as people remembered him half a century before.[3] When the king saw this he was very sorry, and grieved much for the favourite parrot that he had so cruelly killed.

"Surely you would not do the same to me?" said the prince.

"No," she replied.

By the time the prince had concluded this story it was morning, and the other inmates of the house were about.

Thus was the prince saved. Of course he wished to depart, and would have immediately started, but the master of the house would not hear of it. He prevailed on him to stay that day also, and promised to allow him to go on the morrow. The prince was waited on with every attention, and fed in the same sumptuous manner as before, and at night was shown to the same room, whither the host's daughter also came to do his bidding. That night, too, the prince would not close his eyes in sleep. He was afraid what the girl might do to him. At midnight she arose, and taking a sword in her hand, was going to kill him, when he rose up and spoke.

"Do not slay me," he said. "What profit would you get from my death? If you killed me you would be sorry afterwards, like that man who killed his dog."

"What man? What dog?" she asked.

"I will tell you," said the prince, "if you will give me that sword."

So she gave him the sword, and the prince began his second story:—

"Once upon a time there lived a wealthy merchant who had a pet dog. By some unforeseen circumstance this merchant was suddenly reduced to poverty, and obliged

[3] Cf. *Folk-Tales of Bengal*, pp. 154–158; *Indian Antiquary*, vol. xiv. p. 109; *Orientalist*, vol. ii. p. 54.

to part with his dog. He got a loan of five thousand rupees on the animal from a brother merchant, and with the money commenced business afresh. Not long after this the other merchant's shop was broken into by thieves and completely sacked. There was hardly ten rupees' worth left in the place. The faithful dog, however, knew what was going on, and went and followed the thieves, and saw where they deposited the things, and then returned.

"In the morning there was great weeping and lamentation in the merchant's house when it was known what had happened. The merchant himself nearly went mad. Meanwhile the dog kept on running to the door, and pulling at his master's shirt and *páíjámas*, as though wishing him to go outside. At last a friend suggested that, perhaps, the dog knew something of the whereabouts of the things, and advised the merchant to follow its leadings. The merchant consented, and went after the dog right up to the very place where the thieves had hidden the goods. Here the animal scraped and barked, and showed in various ways that the things were underneath. So the merchant and his friends dug about the place, and soon came upon all the stolen property. Nothing was missing. There was everything just as the thieves had taken them.

"The merchant was very glad. On returning to his house, he at once sent the dog back to its old master with a letter rolled up in its ear, wherein he had written concerning the sagacity of the beast, and begged his friend to forget the loan and to accept another five thousand rupees as a present. When this merchant saw his dog coming back again, he thought, 'Alas! my friend is wanting the money. How can I pay him? I have not had sufficient time to recover myself from my recent losses. I will slay the dog ere he reaches the threshold, and say that another must have slain it. Thus there will be an end of my debt. No dog, no loan.' Accordingly he ran out and killed the poor dog, when the letter fell out of its right ear. The merchant picked it up and read it. How great was his grief and disappointment when he knew the facts of the case!

"Beware," continued the prince, "lest you do that which afterwards you would give your life not to have done."

By the time the prince had concluded this story it was nearly morning.

"Alas! alas!" said the girl, "what shall I do? Another hour and it will be day. My father strictly charged me to slay you before this, threatening to kill me if I did not do so. What shall I do? I am in your power."

"Show me the way out of this accursed place, and come with me," replied the prince; "we shall easily find a horse outside, and then we can ride off quickly without fear of pursuit. Come along."

Within an hour, when the other inmates of the house awoke from their sleep, the prince and the robber's daughter were several miles distant.[4] On, on they rode, till they came to some place, where one of the prince's friends lived, who gave him a hearty welcome, and made him stay in his house, and treated him in every way as his own brother for six months; and when he expressed a wish to leave, gave him jewels, and money, and horses, and servants, and every necessary for the way.

The prince then visited the country belonging to his brother-in-law. He disguised himself as a *jogí,* and sitting down by a tree near the palace, pretended to be absorbed in worship. News of the man and of his wonderful piety reached the ears of the king. He felt interested in him, as his wife was very ill; and he had sought for *hakíms* to cure her, but in vain. He thought that, perhaps, this holy man could do something for her. So he sent to him. But the *jogí* refused to tread the halls of a king, saying that his dwelling was the open air, and that if His Majesty wished to see him he must come himself and

[4] Cf. tale of "Two Brothers" in this collection.

bring his wife to the place. Then the king took his wife and introduced her to the *jogí*. The holy man bade her prostrate herself before him, and when she had remained in this position for about three hours, he told her to rise and go, for she was cured.

In the evening there was great consternation in the palace, because the queen had lost her pearl rosary, and nobody knew anything about it. At length some one went to the *jogí*, and found it on the ground by the place where the queen had prostrated herself. When the king heard this he was very angry, and ordered the *jogí* to be executed. This stern order, however, was not carried out, as the prince bribed the men and escaped from the country.

Clad in his own clothes, the prince was walking along one day when he saw a potter crying and laughing alternately with his wife and children. "O fool," said he, "what is the matter? If you laugh, why do you weep? If you weep, why do you laugh?"

"Do not bother me," said the potter. "What does it matter to you?"

"Pardon me," said the prince, "but I should like to know the reason."

"The reason is this, then," said the potter. "The king of this country has a daughter whom he is obliged to marry every day, because all her husbands die the first night of their stay with her. Nearly all the young men of the place have thus perished, and our son will be called on soon. We laugh at the absurdity of the thing—a potter's son marrying a princess, and we cry at the terrible consequence of the marriage.[5] What can we do?"

"Truly a matter for laughing and weeping. But weep no more," said the prince. "I will exchange places with your son, and will be married to the princess instead of him. Only give me suitable garments, and prepare me for the occasion."

[5] Cf. end of tale No. XIII. in *Baital Pachísí*.

So the potter gave him beautiful raiment and ornaments, and the prince went to the palace. At night he was conducted to the apartment of the princess. "Dread hour!" thought he; "am I to die like the scores of young men before me?" He clenched his sword with firm grip, and lay down on his bed, intending to keep awake all the night and see what would happen. In the middle of the night he saw two *sháhmárs* come out from the nostrils of the princess.[6] They stole over towards him, intending to kill him, like the others who had been before him; but he was ready for them. He laid hold of his sword, and when the snakes reached his bed he struck at them and killed them. In the morning the king came as usual to inquire, and was surprised to hear his daughter and the prince talking gaily together. "Surely," said he, "this man must be her husband, as he only can live with her."

"Where do you come from? Who are you?" asked the king, entering the room.

"O king!" replied the prince, "I am the son of a king who rules over such-and-such a country."

When he heard this the king was very glad, and bade the prince to abide in his palace, and appointed him his successor to the throne. The prince remained at the palace for more than a year, and then asked permission to visit his own country, which was granted. The king gave him elephants, horses, jewels, and abundance of money for the expenses of the way and as presents for his father, and the prince started.

On the way he had to pass through the country belonging to his brother-in-law, whom we have already mentioned. Report of his arrival reached the ears of the king, who came with rope-tied hands and haltered neck to do him homage. He most humbly begged him to stay at his palace, and to accept what little hospitality could be provided. While the prince was staying at the palace he saw his sister, who greeted him with smiles and kisses.

[6] Cf. *Folk-Tales of Bengal*, p. 100.

On leaving he told her how she and her husband had treated him at his first visit, and how he had escaped; and then gave them two elephants, two beautiful horses, fifteen soldiers, and ten *lachs* rupees' worth of jewels.

Thence he went to see his old friend who had treated him so generously. He pitched his encampment not far from his house, and then sent word to him to come and see him; but the friend would not go. On being asked the reason, he replied that the prince did not need his help. Accordingly the prince went and called on him at his house, and thanked him much for all his kindness in time of need.

Afterwards he went to his own home and informed his mother and father of his arrival. Alas! his parents had both become blind from weeping about the loss of their son. "Let him come in," said the king, "and put his hands upon our eyes, and we shall see again." So the prince entered, and was most affectionately greeted by his old parents; and he laid his hands on their eyes, and they saw again.

Then the prince told his father all that had happened to him, and how he had been saved several times by attending to the advice that he had purchased from the bráhmaní. Whereupon the king expressed his sorrow for having sent him away, and all was joy and peace again.

THE OGRESS-QUEEN.[1]

PEOPLE tell of a king who had seven wives that were all childless. When he married the first he thought that she would certainly bear him a son. He hoped the same of the second, the third, and the others; but no son was born to gladden his days and to sit on the throne after him. This was a terrible overwhelming grief to him.

One day he was walking in a neighbouring wood, and bemoaning his lot, when he saw a most beautiful fairy.

"Where are you going to?" she asked.

"I am very very miserable," he replied. "Although I have seven wives, I have no son to call my own and to make my heir. I came to this wood to-day, hoping to meet some holy man, who would intercede for me."

"And do you expect to find such a person in this lonely place?" she asked, laughing. "Only I live here. But I can help you. What will you give me if I grant you the desire of your heart?"

"Give me a son and you shall have half of my country."

"I will take none of your gold or your country. Marry me, and you shall have a son and heir."

The king agreed, took the fairy to his palace, and very quickly made her his eighth wife.

A short while afterwards all the other wives of the king became pregnant. However, the king's joy was not for long. The beautiful fairy whom he had married was none other than a *rákshasí*, who had appeared to His Majesty as a fairy in order to deceive him and work mis-

[1] Narrator's name, Paṇḍit Ánand Rám of Sunah Mashíd, Srínagar.

chief in the palace. Every night, when the rest of the royal household were fast asleep, she arose, and going to the stables and outhouses, ate an elephant, or two or three horses, or some sheep, or a camel; and then having satisfied her bloodthirsty appetite, returned to her room, and came forth in the morning as if nothing had happened. At first the king's servants feared to inform him of these things; but when they found that animals were being taken every night, they were obliged to go to him. Strict orders were at once given for the protection of the palace buildings, and guards were appointed to every room; but it was all in vain. Day by day the animals disappeared, and nobody could tell how.

One night, while the king was pacing his room puzzled to know what to do, the supposed fairy, his wife, said, "What will you give me if I discover the thief?"

"Anything—everything," the king replied.

"Very well. Rest, and by the morning I will show you the cause of these things."

His Majesty was soon sound asleep, and the wicked queen left the room. She went to the sheep-pens, and taking one of the sheep, killed it, and filled an earthen vessel with its blood. Then she returned to the palace, and went to the several rooms of the other wives of the king, and stained their mouths and clothes with the blood that she had brought. Afterwards she went and lay down in the room while the king was still sleeping. As soon as the day dawned she woke him, and said to him, "I find that your other wives have taken and eaten the animals. They are not human beings; they are *rákshasís.* If you wish to preserve your life, you will beware of them. Go and see if I am not speaking the truth."

The king did so, and when he saw the blood-stained mouths and garments of his other wives he was terribly enraged. He ordered that their eyes should be put out, and that they should be thrown into a big dry well which was outside the city; and this was done.

The very next day one of them gave birth to a son, who was eaten by them for food. The day after that another had a son, and he was likewise eaten. On the third day another was confined; on the fourth day another; on the fifth day another; and on the sixth day another: each had a son, who was eaten up in his turn. The seventh wife, whose time had not arrived, did not eat her portions of the other wives' children, but kept them till her own son was born, when she begged them not to kill him, and to take the portions which they had given her instead. Thus this child was spared, and through him in the future the lives of the seven queens were miraculously preserved.

The baby grew and became a strong and beautiful boy. When he was six years old the seven women thought they would try to show him a little of the outer world. But how were they to do this? The well was deep, and its sides were perpendicular. At last they thought of standing on each other's heads; and the one who stood on the top of all took the boy and put him on the bank at the well's mouth. Away the little fellow ran to the palace, entered the king's kitchen, and begged for some food. He got a lot of scraps, of which he ate a little, and carried the rest to the well for his mother and the king's other wives.

This continued for some time, when one morning the cook asked him to stay and prepare some dishes for the king, saying that his mother had just died, and he was obliged to go and arrange for the cremation of the body. The boy promised to do his best, and the cook left. That day the king was especially pleased with his meals. Everything was rightly cooked, nicely flavoured, and well served up. In the evening the cook returned. The king sent for him, and complimenting him on the exceedingly good food he had prepared that day, ordered him always to cook as well in the future. The cook honestly confessed that he had been absent the greater part of the day owing to his mother's death, and that a boy whom he had hired for the occasion had cooked the food. When he heard this the king was much surprised, and commanded the cook to give the boy regular employment in the kitchen. Thenceforth there was a great difference in the way the king's meals were served up, and His Majesty was more and more pleased with the boy, and constantly gave him presents. All these presents and all the food that the boy could gather he took daily to the well for his mother and the king's other wives.

On the way to the well he had every day to pass a *faqír*, who always blessed him and asked for alms, and generally received something. In this way some years had passed, and the boy had developed into a still more beautiful youth, when by chance one day the wicked queen saw him. Struck with his beauty, she asked him who he was and whence he came. Nothing doubting, and not knowing the real character of the queen, he told her everything about himself and his mother and the other women; and from that hour the queen plotted against his life. She feigned sickness, and calling in a *hakím*, bribed him to persuade the king that she was very ill, and that nothing except the milk of a tigress would cure her.

"My beloved, what is this I hear?" said the king when he went to see his wife in the evening. "The *hakím* says that you are ill, and that the milk of a tigress is required. But how can we get it? Who is there that will dare to attempt this?"

"The lad who serves here as cook. He is brave and faithful, and will do anything for you out of gratitude for all that you have done for him. Besides him I know of no other whom you could send."

"I will send for him and see."

The lad readily promised, and next day started on his perilous journey. On the way he passed his friend the *faqír*, who said to him, "Whither are you going?" He told him of the king's order, and how desirous he was of pleasing His Majesty, who had been so kind to him. "Don't go," said the *faqír*. "Who are you to dare to presume to do such a thing?" But the lad was resolute, and valued not his life in the matter. Then said the *faqír*, "If you will not be dissuaded, follow my advice, and you will succeed and be preserved. When you meet a tigress aim an arrow at one of her teats. The arrow will strike her, and the tigress will speak and ask you why you shot her. Then you must say that you did not intend to kill her, but simply thought that she would be glad if she could feed her cubs more quickly than before, and therefore pierced a hole in her teats through which the milk would flow easily. You must also say that you pitied her cubs, who looked very weak and sickly, as though they required more nourishment." Then, blessing him, the *faqír* sent him on his journey.[2]

Thus encouraged, the lad walked on with a glad heart. He soon saw a tigress with cubs, aimed an arrow at one of her teats, and struck it. When the tigress angrily asked him to explain his action, he replied as the *faqír* had instructed him, and added that the queen was seriously ill, and was in need of tigress' milk. "The queen!" said the tigress. "Do not you know that she is a *rákshasí*? Keep her at a distance, lest she kill and eat you!"

"I fear no harm," said the lad. "Her Majesty entertains no enmity against me."

"Very well. I will certainly give you some of my milk, but beware of the queen. Look here," said the tigress, taking him to an immense block of rock that had separated from the hill; "I will let a drop of my milk fall on this rock." She did so, and the rock split into a million pieces! "You see the power of my milk. Well, if the queen were to drink the whole of what I have just given you, it would not have the slightest effect on her. She is a *rákshasí*, and cannot be harmed by such things as this. However, if you will not believe me, go and see for yourself."

[2] Another reason is given in the story of "The Seven-Legged Beast" in this collection.

The lad returned and gave the milk to the king, who took it to his wife; and she drank the whole of it, and professed to have been cured. The king was much pleased with the boy, and advanced him to a higher position among the servants of the palace; but the queen was determined to have him killed, and debated in her mind as to how she could accomplish this without offending the king. After some days she again pretended to be ill, and calling the king, said to him, "I am getting ill again, but do not be anxious about me. My grandfather, who lives in the jungle whence the tigress' milk was brought, has a special medicine that I think would cure me, if you could please send for it. The lad that fetched the milk might go." Accordingly the lad went. The way led past the *faqír*, who again said to him, "Whither are you going?" and the lad told him.

"Don't go," said he; "this man is a *rákshasa*, and will certainly kill you." But the lad was determined as before. "You *will* go? Then go, but attend to my advice. When you see the *rákshasa* call him 'grandfather.'[3] He will ask you to scratch his back, which you must do—and do it very roughly."

The lad promised, and went. The jungle was big and dense, and he thought that he would never reach the *rákshasa's* house. At last he saw him, and cried out, "O my grandfather, I, your daughter's son, have come to say that my mother is ill, and cannot recover till she takes some medicine, which she says you have, and has sent me for it." "All right," replied the *rákshasa;* I will give it you; but first come and scratch my back—it's itching terribly." The *rákshasa* had lied, for his back did not itch. He only wanted to see whether the lad was the true son of a *rákshasa* or not. When the lad dug his nails into the old *rákshasa's* flesh, as though he wanted to scratch off

[3] Cf. *Indian Fairy Tales*, pp. 260, 262; *The Orientalist*, vol. ii. pp. 94, 232; Thorpe's *Northern Mythology*, vol. ii. p. 83; also a paper by Mr. Lewis before Ceylon Branch of the Royal Asiatic Society in 1884, but not yet printed; and Clodd's *Myths and Dreams*, p. 159.

some of it, the *rákshasa* bade him desist, and giving him the medicine, let him depart. On reaching the palace the lad gave the medicine to the king, who at once took it to his wife and cured her again. The king was now more than ever pleased with the lad, and gave him large presents, and in other ways favoured him.

The wicked queen was now put to her wits' end to know what to do with such a lad. He had escaped from the claws of the tigress and from the clutches of her grandfather—the gods only knew how! What could she do to him? Finally she determined to send him to her grandmother, a wretched old *rákshasí* that lived in a house in the wood not far from her grandfather's place. "He will not come back any more," said the wicked queen to herself; and so she said to the king, "I have a very valuable comb at home, and I should like to have it brought here, if you will please send the boy for it. Let me know when he starts, and I will give him a letter for my grandmother." The king complied, and the lad started, as usual passing by the *faqír's* place, and telling him where he was going. He also showed him the letter that the queen had given him.

"Let me read its contents," said the *faqír*. And when he had read it he said, "Are you deliberately going to be killed? This letter is an order for your death. Listen to it:—'The bearer of this letter is my bitter enemy. I shall not be able to accomplish anything as long as he is alive. Slay him as soon as he reaches you, and let me not hear of him any more.'" The boy trembled as he heard these terrible words, but he would not break his promise to the king, and was resolved to fulfil His Majesty's wishes though it should cost him his life. So the *faqír* destroyed the queen's letter, and wrote another after this manner:—"This is my son. When he reaches you attend to his needs, and show him all kindness." Giving it to the lad, he said, "Call the woman 'grandmother,' and fear nothing."

The lad walked on and on till he reached the *rákshasí's* house, where he called the *rákshasí* "grandmother," as the *faqír* had advised him, and gave her the letter. On reading it she clasped the lad in her arms and kissed him, and inquired much about her granddaughter and her royal husband. Every attention was shown the lad, and every delicious thing that the old *rákshasí* could think of was provided for him. She also gave him many things, amongst others the following:—A jar of soap, which when dropped on the ground became a great and lofty mountain; a jar full of needles, which if let fall became a hill bristling with large needles; a jar full of water, which if poured out became an expanse of water as large as a sea. She also showed him the following things, and explained their meaning:—Seven fine cocks, a spinning-wheel, a pigeon, a starling, and some medicine.

"These seven cocks," she said, "contain the lives of your seven uncles, who are away for a few days. Only as long as the cocks live can your uncles hope to live; no power can hurt them as long as the seven cocks are safe and sound. The spinning-wheel contains my life; if it is broken, I too shall be broken, and must die; but otherwise I shall live on for ever. The pigeon contains your grandfather's life, and the starling your mother's; as long as these live, nothing can harm your grandfather or your mother. And the medicine has this quality—it can give sight to the blind."

The lad thanked the old *rákshasí* for all that she had given him and shown him, and lay down to sleep. In the morning, when the *rákshasí* went to bathe in the river, he took the seven cocks and the pigeon and killed them, and dashed the spinning-wheel on the ground, so that it was broken to pieces. Immediately the old *rákshasa* and the *rákshasí* and their seven sons perished Then, having secured the starling in a cage, he took it, and the precious medicine for restoring the sight, and started for the king's palace. He stopped on the way to give the eye-medicine to his mother and the other women, who were still in the well; and their sight immediately returned. They all clambered out of the well, and accompanied the lad to the palace, where he asked them to wait in one of the rooms while he went and prepared the king for their coming.

"O king," he said, "I have many secrets to reveal. I pray you to hear me. Your wife is a *rákshasí*, and plots against my life, knowing that I am the son of one of the wives whom at her instigation you caused to be deprived of their sight and thrown into a well. She fears that somehow I shall become heir to the throne, and therefore wishes my speedy death. I have slain her father and mother and seven brothers, and now I will slay her. Her life is in this starling." Saying this, he suffocated the bird, and the wicked queen immediately died. "Now come with me," said the boy, "and behold, O king, your true wives. There were seven sons born to your house, but six of them were slain to satisfy the cravings of hunger. I only am left alive."

"Oh! what have I done!" cried the king. "I have been deceived." And he wept bitterly.

Henceforth the king's only son governed the country, and by virtue of the charmed jars of soap, needles, and water that the *rákshasí* had given him, was able to conquer all the surrounding countries. The old king spent the rest of his days with his seven wives in peace and happiness.[3]

[3] Cf. *Wide-Awake Stories*, pp. 98–111; *Folk-Tales of Bengal*, pp. 117–124; *Indian Fairy Tales*, pp. 51–63 and 173–193; and the *Indian Antiquary*, vol. i. p. 120.

THE GOLDSMITH AND HIS FRIENDS.[1]

ONCE upon a time there lived a goldsmith, who in addition to the ordinary vices of his class was a drunkard and great spendthrift.[2] Accordingly we are not surprised to find that eventually he was reduced to extreme penury. People said that he had not a *páṅsa* which he could call his own. While in this state of poverty his father-in-law came to his relief, and gave his wife one hundred rupees for household expenditure.

"If I had twenty-five rupees I could make such a piece of jewellery as would fetch one hundred rupees easily," said the goldsmith to her when the old man had departed.

"Could you really?" said she.

"Yes," he said.

"Then take the money and prove your words," she said, handing him twenty-five rupees.

The goldsmith went at once to his shop and made a bracelet with all the skill that he could command. It was a lovely piece of workmanship. "Ah, ah! this will bring me luck," he exclaimed as he looked at it admiringly. As soon as possible he went out to dispose of it.

On the way he met the son of one of the *wazírs*, who

[1] Narrator's name, Shiva Báyú, of Renawárí, Srínagar.

[2] The following references to tales that illustrate the suspicion with which goldsmiths are looked upon generally may interest some readers:—*Ceylon Journal of Royal Asiatic Society*, vol. vii. Part 3; *Orientalist*, vol. i. pp. 180, 184, 250; the story of the Bráhman Thephasavámi in Herr Adolf Bastian's German collection of *Siamese Tales;* a Panjábí tale in the Appendix to the Rev. Mr. Swynnerton's book on *Rájá Rasálú;* Sinhalese Pattinihilla, The History of Pattini; *Muntakha bát-i-Hindí*, vol. ii. p. 28; *Old Deccan Days*, pp. 249–270; the tale of the "Two Brothers" in *Grimm's Household Stories; Dictionary of Kashmiri Proverbs*, p. 207; and "Unjust King and his Wicked Goldsmith," and "The Cunning Goldsmith," in this collection.

saluted him, and said, "O friend! have you a nice bracelet to sell?"

"Yes," replied the goldsmith. "Here is one fit for your honour; and since you addressed me as a friend, I will give it to you."

On his return home he asked his wife to give him another instalment of twenty-five rupees, and promised to repay her with large interest in a short time. The woman gave him the money, and he quickly made another bracelet as beautiful as the first. He went out to dispose of this one also, and had not been out very long before he met the son of the *díwán*, who saluted him, and said, "O friend! have you a pretty bracelet for sale?"

"Yes," replied the goldsmith; "here is the very thing."

"How much do you want for it?" inquired the young man.

"Nothing," replied the goldsmith. "Since you treat me in such a gracious way, I also will treat you graciously. Take the bracelet, sir; it is yours."

Then he returned to his house, and entreated his wife to let him have another twenty-five rupees. But the woman was now getting a little suspicious about the success of her investment, and therefore demurred to his request. "What have you done with my money?" she asked. "You promised to get me one hundred rupees for twenty-five. But you have taken fifty rupees, and not given me a *páṅsa* as yet; and now you are asking for more."

"Do not be foolish," said the man. "I know what I have said and done. I have not lost your money. Give me a little time, and you shall see how much I shall gain by this business."

Moved by his earnest assurance, the woman gave him the money, with which he made another beautiful bracelet. When it was finished he went out to dispose of it as before; and on the road he chanced to meet with a celebrated thief, who also addressed him as a friend, and inquired if he had a bracelet for sale; whereupon the goldsmith gave him the bracelet, begging him to accept it as a present from a friend. Then he went back to his house, and informed his wife of all that he had done.

One day not long after this, when his wife had been bothering him for some money for household expenses, the remaining twenty-five rupees being almost exhausted, he thought that he would go and prove his friends. He put on his best clothes, and went first to the house of the *wazír.* He did not find him in. Then he went to the *díwán's* house, where he found them both, and was at once admitted to their presence, and treated in every way as a friend. During his visit the king's daughter chanced to come in. She sat down and talked with them, and in course of conversation asked if there was anybody there who would do her a great kindness. She wanted some of the fruit of a certain pear-tree in her father's garden; but she did not know how to get it, as the tree was surrounded by seven pools of powdered saffron, through which if any man walked he would certainly be stained with the colour, and thus be discovered. Of course, when they heard these words, the *wazír's* son, the *díwán's* son, and the goldsmith, all declared that they would try to fulfil her desire.

On leaving the *díwán's* house the goldsmith called on the thief, who was very glad to see him, and pressed him to stay to dinner. However, the goldsmith begged to be excused. "I have something special on my mind just now," he said.

"Indeed! Nothing of very great anxiety, I hope?" said the thief, rather inquisitively.

"Yes, very," answered the goldsmith. "I wish to get some pears from the tree in the king's garden for the princess. Canyou help me? I do not want to die over the business, if I can possibly avoid it."

"Do not be anxious," said the thief; "I will get some pears from this tree." And he did so; though how he accomplished it nobody can tell. Before a day had passed the beautiful pears were ready in a basket in the goldsmith's shop. As soon as possible a meeting was arranged between the *díwán's* son, the *wazír's* son, and the goldsmith; and the pears were presented. The princess at once desired to taste them; and so the *díwán's* son peeled one of them and divided it into little portions, and began to feed her, putting the pieces of pear to her mouth on the point of his knife. While eating it the princess unfortunately sneezed, and the knife pierced her throat and killed her.

"Alas! alas!" exclaimed the *díwán's* son, "I have slain the princess."

"Not so," said the *wazír's* son. "It was all owing to my fault."

"No, no," said the goldsmith; "it was I. She would not have been thus fed, if I had not got the pears. However," continued he, "we need not wait to be discovered. We had better get a *maṭ*,[1] and putting the princess into it, throw it into the river; otherwise the body will rise and be discovered, and we shall be executed."

Accordingly a *maṭ* was quickly obtained from a potter, and this was done. In the evening the princess was missed. Search was made in every place about the palace buildings and the different places that she was accustomed to visit, but no trace of her could be found. Then a royal proclamation was sent on all sides promising a very rich reward to anybody who could discover the princess's whereabouts. On the following morning a man appeared before the king, and informed him that he had seen a person throwing a *maṭ* into the river just after dark on the previous evening. On hearing this His Majesty immediately had the river dragged. The *maṭ* was found, and in it the dead body of the beautiful princess.

"Cause all the potters in the city to appear before

[1] A very large earthenware vessel, about three feet in height, for containing grain and beverages.

me," said His Majesty. "This affair must be thoroughly investigated."

So all the potters were assembled, and were asked if any of them had recently sold a *maṭ*. Whereupon one potter came forward and said that he had sold a *maṭ* on the previous day to the goldsmith.

Then the goldsmith was summoned to appear. "Why did you kill the princess?" said the king. "Speak, man."

But the goldsmith did not reply.

"His silence proves his guilt," said His Majesty. "Let him be executed within two days."

Accordingly the goldsmith was led away to the prison.

The king had ordered the execution to be delayed for a day or two, in order that he might ascertain the reason of this cruel murder (as it seemed to him). He disguised himself as a sentinel, and visited the prisoner at night. "You are to be executed to-morrow," he said to him. "Are all your affairs in order? Have you any relations or friends, who could help you at this time?"

"Thank you," replied the goldsmith. "I should like to see two or three of my friends before I die."

"Very well," said the sentinel; "come with me and visit them." The goldsmith first went to the house of the *wazír*, and had a talk with his son.

"O friend!" said he, "when I am led forth to execution, can you not do something for me?"

"Yes," replied the young man. "Be of good cheer. At the right time, I, the commander-in-chief, will give a sign to my soldiers and they will slay the king." The sentinel heard these words, and was very much surprised.

Then the goldsmith went to the *díwán's* house, and had a long conversation with his eldest son. "O friend!" said he, "what can you do for my release?"

"Be not afraid," replied the young man. "I shall not forget your kindness. At the proper time I shall arrive and slay the king with my sword." The sentinel heard this reply and trembled.

Then the goldsmith visited his other friend, the thief, whom he asked the same question as he had asked the others. The thief returned his greetings, and asked him to be seated for a while, as he had some very important work in hand just at that time. He had heard the goldsmith's words and seen his great distress, and determined to help him, even though it should cost him his life. He went off that very instant, and climbed the wall of the palace by the way of the window of His Majesty's bedroom, and having entered the room, beheaded the man who was sleeping there in the place of the king that night. "He will not fear anything now," he said to himself as he ran back to the goldsmith with the gory head in his hand. "Here you are, friend," he exclaimed, throwing the head down before the goldsmith and his sentinel. "Behold the end of your trouble! The king will not trouble you very much now."

After this the goldsmith returned with the sentinel to the prison. On the morrow he was led forth to execution in the presence of all the people and all the soldiery. As he approached the platform the *díwán's* son rushed forward with drawn sword to slay the king, and the *wazír's* son made sign to his soldiers to assist him in the deed. But there was no necessity for all this demonstration, for His Majesty had determined what to do, and cried out, "Let the goldsmith go free; let the goldsmith go free. He is pardoned; he is pardoned." Whereupon a great shout burst forth from the whole assembly, "Praise be to the king. May he live for ever."

THE TALE OF A PRINCESS.[1]

A KING had been defeated in battle with a neighbouring king, and was obliged to flee. He hastened as fast as he could to a little obscure village about twelve miles distant from the city. So hurried was his escape, that he forgot to take any money with him. Fortunately, however, the princess (the king's daughter-in-law) had eleven rubies,[2] one of which she gave to the king, as soon as they reached the village for the night, and begged him to go to the *bázár* and get some food. The king took the ruby, and went to the shop of a certain merchant and asked him to change it for a rupee's worth of food. Of course the man gladly consented, and told the king to go with him to his house, where he would give him the money.

But this merchant was a very wicked man. He might have paid the king there and then; but he wished to take him to his house, because in one of the rooms therein he had prepared a certain trap, whereby he ensnared several people. This trap was such, that whoever sat upon it was precipitated into a great pit, from which they could not escape till they had given and promised whatever the merchant might ask.

When several hours had elapsed, and the king had not returned, the princess took out another ruby, and giving it to her husband, asked him to go and get some food, and see what had become of the king. The prince, also, went to the wicked merchant's shop, seeing it was the biggest shop in the *bázár*, and begged him to buy the stone. "Very

[1] Narrator's name, Shiva Báyú, Renawárí, Srínagar.
[2] *Rattan* for *chauni*, in Kashmírí.

well," the merchant replied; "come to my house, and I will pay you. I cannot give you the money here." So he took the prince to his house, and made him also sit on the trap-door.

It being already dark, and neither king nor prince having returned, the princess took another ruby, and giving it to the queen, begged her to go and get some food. The queen went, and the same thing happened to her as happened to her husband and son.

The princess waited some time for her, and then began to suspect that some harm had befallen the king and queen and prince. Therefore she disguised herself in some of her husband's clothes and went to the *bázár*. Like the others, she walked straight to the shop of the big merchant and asked him to change her a ruby. "Very well," he said; "come to my house." On reaching the house he told her to enter the room in which was the trap-door, and there wait a few minutes while he went to fetch the money. The princess, however, was too sharp for him. She did not like the appearance of the man, and she thought it was very strange that he did not keep a few rupees regularly with him in the shop. Accordingly she declined to go inside. While she waited she heard sounds of human voices coming through the flooring. On going near she recognised her husband's voice, and then her father-in-law's and mother-in-law's voices. They were calling for help. She was astonished beyond measure. "O thief! murderer! where are you?" she shouted.

"What is it?" said the merchant, running towards her.

"What have you done with these people?" she asked. "Let them out of this place, wherever they may be, or I will go at once and complain to the king."

The merchant was afraid, and therefore set the prisoners free, and gave them back the rubies that he had taken from them. Then the king, queen, and prince left; but the princess (who, as we have said, was disguised as a man) accepted the merchant's invitation to dinner, and stayed.

The king and his wife and son returned quickly to the place where they had left the princess. "Alas! alas!" cried the prince, "some misfortune has happened to her. She has been stolen or killed."

"Not so," said the king. "Very likely she has gone in search of us, and will soon return."

However, it was many years before the princess returned to her husband and the king and queen. The following morning she departed, and walked on day after day till she reached another country. Here, disguised as a man, she pretended to be the son of a merchant, and that her name was Ganpat Rai. Attracted by her frank and ready manner, a wealthy merchant of the place gave her employment. This merchant had three wives, but no son. The reason of this was, that the night after any of his wives gave birth to a son a *ḍágin*[3] appeared and devoured it.

It happened that while Ganpat Rai was in the service of the merchant, a little boy was born to the merchant. "I wish," he said to Ganpat Rai, whom he quickly found he could trust with all his business, "I wish you would stay by the door of the bedroom this night and ward off the *ḍágin*. She will certainly come and attempt to seize the child."

"Very well," she replied.

At midnight the *ḍágin* came, and rushed to burst open the door, when Ganpat Rai prevented her. On this the *ḍágin* made a dash at Ganpat Rai, who seized her by the hair and threw her down. "Oh, spare my life, spare my life!" cried the *ḍágin*. "I promise you that I will never trouble this house any more. Spare me, and let me go. Here, take this handkerchief as a witness of my promise."

The princess complied, and the *ḍágin* went. The next morning, when the merchant heard what had transpired during the night, he was exceedingly pleased. "You have rendered me such service as I shall never be able to repay," he said. "You must remain in my house as long as you live. I will give you my sister in marriage."

[3] An ogress.

Ganpat Rai had not long been married to the merchant's sister, when the former expressed a wish to see her parents again, and entreated the merchant to allow her to depart with her wife. At first the merchant strongly demurred, but eventually he gave his sanction.

On reaching her own country Ganpat Rai searched far and wide for her husband and the king and queen, and at last found them in a small village begging. They did not recognise her, because she was dressed in man's clothes. One evening she put on her own clothes, and went to them. She was soon recognised then. "My darling wife!" exclaimed the prince. "My long-lost child!" exclaimed the king and queen, as they rushed forward to embrace her. "Where have you been? What has happened to you? We thought you were stolen or dead, and never expected to see you again." There was great joy in all their hearts that night. The princess took them all three to the house where she was staying with the merchant's sister, and introduced them to her. She then told them all that she had experienced since she had left them—how she had served a merchant in a certain country, and how *Alláh* had prospered her, so that she was now married to the sister of that merchant and possessed enormous wealth. Afterwards she discovered her real sex to the merchant's sister, and begged her not to be angry at this deceit, but to be married to her husband, who was a prince, and come and live together with them.

As soon as these private matters had been arranged, the princess gathered all the disbanded troops of her father-in-law, and, distributing much money amongst them, stirred them up to fight for the recovery of their kingdom and their liberty. A great spirit of enthusiasm was kindled among these soldiers. They were ready to do and dare anything for their king and country.

A battle took place, the citadel was taken, and the foreign king and his army were put to flight.

THE TALE OF A PRINCESS.[1]

A VARIANT.

A CERTAIN prince had been married. The day after the wedding the king, his father, sent to him, saying, "Tell your wife that the king sends his *salám*." The prince did so, and the wife simply replied, "Well!" In the evening the king came to inquire what answer the princess had given; and when he heard it he said, "Sorrow! I have lost the money spent on my son's wedding." In a little while the prince was married again, when, in the same manner, the king sent a *salám* to his wife. "Well, well," the princess answered, "thank the king for his kindness, and give him my *salám*." When the king heard this reply he exclaimed, "Alas! alas! my lot; I have lost the money spent on my son's wedding." A short time after this the king married his son for the third time, and tried the third wife in the same manner. Now this third wife was meek and modest and good. When she heard the king's notice of her, she begged her husband to say to His Majesty, "The princess says, 'Who am I that the king should deign to notice me?'" She did this, because she did not think it right either to treat His Majesty's *salám* with disrespect, or to receive it as if it were her due, like the other two princesses had done. On hearing her answer the king was glad, and said to his son, "This is a wise and good wife. I have not wasted any money over this wedding."

A few years after this third marriage a powerful king came with his soldiers and took the city, and put the king and his army to flight. The royal household was scattered. The king and queen and the prince fled to one country,

[1] Narrator's name, Shiva Báyú of Renawárí, Srínagar.

while the three princesses went to their own homes. Before leaving, the "wise and good wife" made seven loaves, and putting a ruby in each, she took them with her.

In the course of their wanderings the king, queen, and prince reached the country where the wise and good princess lived. Accordingly they went to her home, and related all that had befallen them since they had left their country. The princess had pity on them, and gave the king one of the loaves that she had made, saying, "This bread is very stale, but in the middle of it you will find a ruby, which take and sell in the *bázár*, and buy for yourself some necessaries." The king thanked the princess, and went at once to one of the great merchants of the place and asked him to buy the ruby. The merchant hesitated about the price; so the king said, "Very well; give me a rupee in advance, and I will come again to-morrow for the rest."

On the morrow, when the king went, the merchant said to him, "Go away, and do not waste my time with idle talk. There are lots of people like you going about pretending to have done this thing and that thing, thinking to deceive us busy people. But some of us have a better memory than others. When did you sell me a ruby? How could a poor man like you honestly obtain a ruby? I do not know anything about you. Go away, or I shall have to resort to force." Seeing that it was useless to press his claim, the unfortunate king turned away. "Alas! alas!" he exclaimed, "how can I go back to the queen and prince and princess with this reply? They will not believe me. Better for me to fly from the palace and dwell alone, than to meet their suspicions and reproofs." Accordingly the king went to a certain jungle, and there lamented his cruel fate.

When several hours had passed, and the king had not returned, the princess called her husband, and giving him another loaf, begged him to go to the *bázár* and dispose of the ruby that was in the middle of it. The prince took the bread, and went to the same merchant that his father had visited. He also was deceived by the wicked man, and like his father, thinking it better to live a life of solitude than to dwell with those who would always suspect him of having appropriated the money, he too went to the jungle. There he met his father, and recounted to him his sad tale, and heard that the same trial had happened to him.

Some weeks elapsed, and then the princess, thinking that the king and prince had deserted them, gave her mother-in-law some bread with a ruby in it, and asked her to go and try to sell it. Most unfortunately the queen also went to the wicked merchant, and was treated in just the same way; and she too, not caring to go back to the princess without the ruby or its equivalent in money, fled to the jungle, and there found her husband and son.

The princess waited several days. At last she disguised herself as a man, and mounting one of her father's horses, rode everywhere inquiring from the people whether they had seen any beggars wandering about in their neighbourhood. Nobody could give her any information of the missing ones. So she rode on and on till she came to another country. Here the king, as he was walking one day in the verandah of his palace, noticed her, and calling her to him, asked if she would like to take service in the palace. She readily consented, and at once was appointed to some special work. Her skill and wisdom and goodness soon obtained for her great favour with His Majesty, who often sent for her to talk with him or advise him on private as well as public matters.

While she was living in the palace a large *ajdar* appeared in the country and destroyed many lives. The whole country was in a terrible state of fear. Nobody dared venture far from his threshold. From the king down to the lowest subject there was daily expectation of death. In the hour of his distress the king sent for the princess, and begged her to say what ought to be done.

"I will go and slay the beast," she replied.

"Go," said the king; "and if you succeed I will give you my daughter in marriage."

The princess went and slew the *ajdar;* and as soon as she returned with the good news, the king married her to his daughter. At the princess's (his servant) earnest request, who said that she had been moved to do so by the advice of her *pír*, the king had a separate house provided for her, and another house for his own daughter. The house set apart for the princess (the king's supposed son-in-law) was situated in a place where two roads met. Sometimes, when she had not anything better to do, the princess used to sit by one of the lattice windows and watch the people as they passed by. One day she was startled by the sight of her husband and his father and mother. She beckoned to them, and inquired who they were, and where they were going, and what they were doing; and they, seeing that she was good and sympathising, told her everything. "Come into my house," she said. And then, when they had entered, she told them who she was. "See," she continued, "I am your princess. I knew not what had befallen you all, and therefore I disguised myself and went in search of you. Praise be to God, who has thus brought us together again! Wait here till the evening, when I will go with you. We will see this wicked merchant. He must be punished, and our property must be restored."

That evening the princess left the house in the company of the king, queen, and prince. They travelled as quickly as they could to the place where the merchant dwelt, and threatened him so severely, that the man, fearing the king would hear of the matter and order his execution, sold all his property and gave them the money.

Then the princess sent word to the king who had befriended her, and explained everything to him, and begged His Majesty to forgive her, and allow the princess, his daughter, to marry the prince, her husband. The king agreed. He also sent a large force of soldiers to help the princess's father-in-law to regain his kingdom. Another battle was then fought, and the country was regained; and henceforth peace and prosperity reigned in all its borders.

THE PRINCE WHO WAS CHANGED INTO A RAM.[1]

In a certain country there lived a king that had sixteen hundred wives, but only one son. This son the king very much wished to marry to a princess as beautiful as his son, and who was the only daughter of another king equal in honour with himself, and who also had the same number of wives.

The king who had the only son possessed a very wise and faithful parrot, whose counsel he very much valued, and whose help he generally sought on difficult occasions. Accordingly he sent for the bird at this time, and informing it of his wish, bade it go and seek for such a wife for his son. The parrot agreed, asked the king to fasten the likeness of the prince to one of its legs, and flew away. It soon reached one of the neighbouring countries, where, on account of the heavy rain, it was obliged to seek shelter in a wood. It espied an old hollow tree, and thought that it would be a most comfortable place to rest in; but just as it was flying into the hollow a voice came out therefrom, saying, "Enter not, for if you enter you will be deprived of your sight." So the parrot alighted on a twig that grew by the trunk of the tree, and waited. Presently a *mainá*[2] came out of the hollow and flew down beside the parrot, and entered into a long conversation, during which it spoke of the errand on which it was then going. Their meeting was most opportune, as will be seen. The *mainá* was looking for a beautiful prince, the only child of a

[1] Narrator's name, Shiva Báyú, Renawárí, Srínagar.

[2] Kashmírí word is *hár*, a species of starling.

great king, who had sixteen hundred wives, to try to arrange for a suitable match for the only daughter of his royal master, who also had sixteen hundred wives. Of course, the parrot replied that his master must be that king, and his master's only son the prince who should marry the princess. The parrot also showed the *mainá* the likeness of the prince.

Then they went both together to the country of the king with the only daughter. On their arrival a servant of the palace saw them, and informed the king that the *mainá* whom he had trusted had formed an alliance with a parrot, and was so taken up with its friend that it had altogether forgotten His Majesty's order. When the king heard this, he immediately ordered both the birds to be shot. For envy, the servants had thus maligned the bird's character. Expecting this, the *mainá* had flown down by the upper window of the assembly-room, and heard the king's cruel order. "Come away, come away; let us fly up out of reach of their arrows," it said to the parrot. "The king has been made angry against us on a false charge." So they flew together, and were presently out of reach and out of sight. The king's servants went about to kill them; but when they had spent several hours in vain search for them they returned, comforting themselves with the thought that the birds had been apprised of the royal order, and had betaken themselves to safer regions. For some days they waited, till they thought the matter was almost forgotten; and then one morning they both flew into the palace, and perched themselves, the parrot on the right knee of the king, and the *mainá* on his left knee. "Tell us," they said, "why do you wish to kill us? We are faithful. These people envy us; therefore have they lied against us. See, O king, and judge this thing that has come to pass. We both belong to kings famous in valour, in wisdom, and in wealth. Both of these kings have sixteen hundred wives. One of the kings has one only son, and the other king has one only daughter. These two kings, though they have never seen or heard of one another, yet wish their children to be united in marriage. The one king is seeking for such a daughter as the other king possesses, and the other king is seeking for such a son as the first king possesses. Behold, O king, the servants of these two kings before you. By divine will we met in a wood just outside Your Majesty's dominions, and have come to tell you this good news." As they said these last words the parrot held up to the king the likeness of the beautiful prince.

The king was as much astonished as he was pleased. At first he could hardly believe the birds, but the likeness convinced him. He took the beautiful picture, and sent it to the royal *zanána,* with the request that his sixteen hundred wives would look at it and say whether they approved of it or not. Some days passed. The likeness was not returned to the king. The princess was so fascinated with it, that she would not let it out of her hands. After a while an answer came, saying that the prince was unanimously accepted, and should be quickly called for the wedding, as the princess was dying to see him.

As soon as this answer reached the king, he ordered the parrot to depart and tell his master that a suitable princess had been found, and that he should send his son prepared for the wedding within four months. The parrot bowed reverently and left.

On arrival in its country the bird informed the king of its successful journey. The king was very glad. He immediately ordered arrangements on a grand scale to be got ready for the coming event. The most costly raiments were to be provided for the prince; the most magnificent trappings were to be made for the horses; the soldiers were to have a splendid uniform; presents of various kinds — the most costly jewels, the finest cloths, the rarest fruits, the most expensive spices and perfumes were to be prepared. Everything was remembered and ordered. The months soon passed. What with preparations and expectations the time seemed to fly. But a few days remained before the prince had to start, when alas! his father fell sick and died. It was a terrible trial, a tremendous disappointment. The prince was obliged to defer his departure; for to have started at such a time would have shown a great want of respect for his father. Accordingly he waited awhile.

As soon as the days of mourning for his father were accomplished the prince started. The parrot showed the way. It was not far, so that the wedding company quickly reached the princess's country. The prince pitched his tents in a garden near the palace. Would that he had never entered that garden, for there the parrot died! The faithful bird was shot by the gardener for throwing down dates to the king. And no sooner had this great trouble come upon him than the prince heard that the father of the princess had refused to sanction her marriage with him, now that his father was dead.

Some days after the prince had encamped in this garden, the princess was going for an airing in her *duli*, when she chanced to pass by that way, and looking into the garden, recognised the prince from the likeness that she had in her possession. She said nothing at the time, but at once had the *duli* turned round, and went back to the palace. She had seen her beloved. From that hour she began to get better. At meal-time that evening she ate only half her food; the other half she sent with the likeness to the prince. She ordered her maid to beg the prince to eat it, and if he would not, to ask him to thrust his finger into it. The maid obeyed. The prince declined to eat it, but had no objection to putting his fingers into the plate of food, on doing which he discovered his own likeness in the midst of the rice. "She loves me," he said to himself; and having wiped his hands, he wrote a letter to the princess, and sent it by the hands of the maid. When the princess read the letter, she was filled with an intense longing to go to the prince. At midnight she ordered her horse to be got ready, and taking some bags of *ashrafís,* she rode to the garden where the prince was encamped. The prince was surprised to see her. "Be not surprised," she said. "I love you, and therefore have escaped to you. The king, my father, will not sanction our marriage. Come, have your horse saddled, and fly with me to your own country. There nothing can harm us."

Presently two people might have been seen riding hastily along the great road that led out of that city. For some hours they proceeded at this swift pace, and then lay down under a tree to rest. The next morning, refreshed and strengthened, they continued their journey. They had not proceeded far before seven robbers mounted on horseback met them. "Let us flee," exclaimed the prince, "for we cannot fight them." On this they both whipped their horses and rode at a tremendous rate. But the robbers were well mounted also, and their horses were fresh. "It is of no use," cried the prince. "Look! they gain on us. What shall we do?"

"Then we must meet them," replied the princess. And saying this, she turned in her saddle, and discharged an arrow in their faces, and then another, and another, until she had shot seven arrows and killed the seven robbers.

Glad and thankful, they then resumed their journey, and that night reached a certain village where lived a *jinn,* who had a son with only half a body. The prince and princess halted by a pond in this village. While they were sleeping the *jinn* told her son to go quickly and slay the prince, and afterwards bring back the princess and the horses and treasure to the house. The wretched man went, glad at the prospect of shedding blood. Scarcely had he performed the cruel deed, when the princess awoke. Looking about, she saw the dead body of her lover, and the horrible deformed man standing over it. She laughed, and said, "I am so glad that you have killed him. Now take me, and make me your wife. First, however, bury the corpse, and then we will go. A grave was quickly got ready, and the princess was called to inspect it. "Too small," she said; "dig deeper." The man dug down another foot or so. "Still too small," she said. The man dug yet wider and deeper; but while he was bending down over his work the princess seized his sword, that was lying by, and cut off his head.

When she had avenged herself, she burst into tears. Her beloved was dead. She took up the corpse and carried it close to the brink of the pool, and there sat down beside it weeping and lamenting. It was a sad time for her. Fain would she have died.

While she was thus weeping, the wife of a very holy man who lived in that village passed the place. Seeing her great distress, the woman stopped and inquired what was the matter. The princess pointed to the dead body, and explained everything. "Have patience," said the woman. "I may be able to help you. Wait here till I come again."

On reaching home that evening, the woman told her husband the sad case of the princess, and begged him to restore the prince to life." "Sorrow, sorrow!" exclaimed the holy man. "Oh that the place were rid of this devilish woman and her dreadful son! I will go and comfort the princess by restoring the prince to life. He went, and found the princess most anxiously waiting for tidings of the help that had been half promised her in the morning. "I know your state," said the holy man, "and have come to help you. I will give you back the prince." Then he took the head of the corpse in one hand, and the body in the other hand, and pressed them together. The two parts reunited; life was restored to the cold corpse; the limbs moved; the eyes opened; the lips unclosed; the tongue spoke.[3] When the princess saw this she could not restrain herself: she rushed forward, fell on the prince's breast, and wept for joy. It was an exceedingly

[3] Cf. *Wide-Awake Stories*, pp. 56, 57; *Indian Fairy Tales*, p 84; also tale of "Strange Request" in this collection.

glad time, and not the least joyous of the three was the holy man who had done this thing.

That night the prince and princess went to another place. Here the life of the princess was in great danger. A *jádugaruni*[4] who lived in this place had a daughter, who on seeing the prince wished to have him for her husband. Accordingly she devised the following plan. She persuaded her mother to invite the prince and princess to their house, and while the prince was inspecting the rooms, she threw a cord round his neck and changed him into a ram. By day the ram followed her whithersoever she went, and at night, as soon as the cord was taken off its neck, it became a prince again, and slept with her. Several days thus passed. The princess was in great distress. She did not know what to suppose. Sometimes she thought that he had deserted her, and sometimes she thought that he had been slain. At last she could bear it no longer, and therefore disguised herself as a man, and went to the king of that country and begged for employment. The king was pleased with her appearance and speech, and appointed her one of his deputy-inspectors of police. The princess was especially rejoiced at this appointment. It was just what she had desired, because in this position she was best able to find the prince. Many secrets of many houses were known to the deputy-inspector, and the whole body of the police were sharp and ready servants at his pleasure. The deputy-inspector had only to explain the height and appearance of any person, and bid the police to search for such a one, when the whole country would be scoured until the man was found. The princess, however, could not discover anything about the prince, although she got to know that the woman in whose house she and the prince had stayed was a *jádugaruni*. Constantly she visited this house, and saw the ram running about,

[4] *Jádúgarní* (Pers.), a sorceress, a witch. Cf. note on "Witches," *Wide-Awake Stories*, p. 395.

but knew not that it was the prince, her beloved, and that the daughter of the *jádugaruni* had metamorphosed him. A great friendship sprang up between the deputy-inspector and this girl. Of course, the latter thought that the deputy-inspector was a real man. She became very fond of the deputy-inspector, and gave her several presents, among which was a piece of the most beautiful cloth that had ever been seen.

We shall now see what this piece of beautiful cloth had to do with the princess's future. One morning a servant from the palace happened to pass a window before which the deputy-inspector had hung some of this cloth. He was struck with its beautiful colour and texture, and, on returning to the palace sought an interview with the queen, and told her what he had seen. The queen desired very much to see some of the cloth, and so went to the king and begged him to speak to the deputy-inspector about procuring some of it for her. His Majesty did so, and the deputy-inspector sent him all the cloth that she had. When the queen saw it, she was fascinated with it and entreated the king to order some more.

"This is difficult. However, I will try to fulfil Your Majesty's wish," replied the deputy-inspector, when the king spoke to her of the queen's order. On leaving the king she went straight to the house of the *jádugaruni* to inquire where she could get some more of the cloth.

"Alas! I am afraid I cannot help you," said the *jádugaruni*. "My brother, who is a *jádugarun*, went a long time ago to a far country. He sent me this cloth."

"Then write and ask him to send you some more," said the deputy-inspector.

"I cannot," replied the *jádugaruni*. "He has slain every human being in that country, and now, excepting himself, only lions dwell there. My brother keeps these lions in a state of semi-starvation by feeding them with a kind of grass, which they do not much like. Consequently, when any person approaches the place, a lion is certain to burst forth from some thicket or from behind some rock and slay him. Several venturesome folks have thus lost their lives. How can I send any one—I dare not send any one on such a risky errand."

"Tell me," said the deputy-inspector, "where your brother dwells, and I myself will go, for go I must; otherwise the king will take away my life. There is no safety for me here unless I can get this cloth. I dare not stay here another day. So tell me where your brother lives, and I will go and see him."

"Stay," said the *jádugaruni.* "Since your state is thus, I must help you. I have here a small earthen vessel, with which my brother's life is bound up. As long as this earthen vessel continues safe in my keeping, he will continue well; but directly it is broken, he will be broken (*i.e.*, he will die). However, I will break it, for my daughter loves you." Saying this, she dashed the vessel on the ground. "Now go, and fear not. The lions will now eat grass, or whatever they wish, and will not need to slay every human being that comes near them. Go, and may you prosper."

Little did the *jádugaruni* think that the deputy-inspector was the princess, the betrothed of the prince whom her daughter had metamorphosed into a ram.

The following morning, having obtained leave from the king, the deputy-inspector started with a small company of soldiers. On reaching the country she at once sought for the *jádugarun's* house. This was soon found, and as was expected, was filled with piles of cloth. Lots of other treasure also were discovered. The deputy-inspector took everything, and hastened back to the king. His Majesty was so pleased with the success of the expedition that he loaded the deputy-inspector with presents and appointed her his successor.

A few years have passed. The old king is dead. The deputy-inspector reigns. She has got an inkling of what has happened to the prince, and accordingly orders all the rams in the city to be gathered before her. All the rams are driven together into one place, and she herself examines them, and speaks to each, but not one of the rams responds to her call or is recognised by her. Then she orders the police to go and search diligently and see whether there are any that have disobeyed her order. Some policemen come to the *jádugaruni's* house, and find that she has not sent her ram. They seize the ram by the cord and lead it away to the king. The *jádugaruni* tries very hard to keep possession of the charmed cord, but in vain. The police will not allow her to have it. Away they go, leading the ram by the piece of cord. The king notices their coming, and goes forward a little to meet them, when lo! the cord suddenly breaks, and a prince, young and beautiful, stands before her. "Surely," she exclaimed, "this *jádugaruni* must be a very wicked woman. Such a woman ought not to live. Let her be executed to-morrow at dawn. Concerning the prince, let him stay in the palace."

The rest of the story will now be easily imagined. The princess (the king) explained her real character. She summoned a general assembly of her people, and spoke to them the following words:—

"Behold, O people, your king is a woman. To find the prince, my husband, was my object in disguising myself. That object has now been accomplished. Henceforth regard my husband as your king and me as your queen." [5]

The people approved with loud shoutings and rejoicings, and all proceeded happily ever afterwards.

[5] Cf. the conclusion of the story, "How the Princess Found her Husband," in this collection.

SAIYID AND SAID.[1]

THERE was a poor villager who managed to make a scanty living by cutting and selling wood. In the early morning he used to cut the wood and bind it into bundles, and in the evening he went to the nearest *bázár* and sold it. This poor man got married, and two sons were born to him, the elder of whom he named Saiyid, and the other Said; but while the boys were yet young their mother died, and their father married again.

The second wife proved more energetic than the first. One day she said to her husband, "Why do you not ask me and your two sons to help you in collecting wood? We are living very meagrely now; but if I and the two boys worked, we should be able to earn more money and live better than we do."

The man replied, "Very well."

Accordingly they all four went to the jungle every day, and worked so diligently, that in a few months they had saved much money, besides having collected a large quantity of wood, sufficient to maintain them all through the winter. This wood they piled up in great stacks near their house.

A few days after they had arranged this wood it began to rain very heavily, and three travellers, who happened to be passing through the jungle at this time, took shelter in the hollow of a big tree. The rain had chilled the air, and so the travellers took some of the wood that the woodcutter had collected and made an immense fire. For two whole days these people stayed there, and kept up

1 Narrator's name, Makund Báyú, of Suthú, Srínagar.

such big fires all the time, that there was scarcely any wood left. When the rain abated they resumed their journey. The woodcutter, too, went out to look after his wood. Great was his grief when he saw nothing but a pile of ashes. Presently his wife and two sons arrived at the place.

"It is not God's will that we should prosper," he said to them. "What shall we do? What shall we do?" and as he spoke he moved his staff among the ashes with an air of despair.

"What is that?" said his wife, pointing to something bright and shining in the ashes. "Yes, look! what is it? Look there, too, and there!"

On this they searched all over the heap of ashes, and found several pieces of silver. Fearing lest they should meet any person on the way, they put their treasure into their *kángars*,[2] and covering it with charcoal, returned to the house.

In order that suspicion might not be aroused, the woodcutter gradually discovered his wealth to his friends and neighbours. After a while he left off woodcutting and commenced trading as a merchant. In this he obtained much success. At length he was accounted a very rich man. Meanwhile his two sons went to school and became learned.

One day, as the merchant and his sons were returning from a *melá*, they saw a *zamíndár*[3] carrying a cage, in which was a most beautiful bird, that sang very sweetly. When the boys saw the bird and heard its sweet song, they entreated their father to buy it. "How much do you want for the bird?" the merchant asked. "Two *muhrs*," was the reply. "Take them," said the merchant, "and give the bird to my sons."

Saiyid and Said thanked their father very much for the present. They got very fond of the bird. Every day, on

[2] Cf. *Indian Antiquary*, vol. xiv. pp. 264–266, vol. xv. p. 57, vol. xvi. p. 61; also *Dictionary of Kashmírí Proverbs*, pp. 128–130. This little portable brazier is generally called *kángrí* by Europeans and Panjábís.

[3] *Grúst* (Kashmírí), a cultivator of soil.

returning from school, they used to play with it. After a while the bird laid an egg, which was watched most anxiously by the two sons, as they wished very much to have another bird like their present one. One day the cage was carried to the river-side to be cleaned, and in order that this might be done properly, the bird was taken out and kept in the hands of Saiyid, and the egg was carefully deposited on a stone. While the cage was being cleaned a man, who was bathing on the other side of the river, saw all that was done; he saw, too, what the merchant and his son had, for some reason, failed to notice, namely, that the stone whereon they had placed the egg had been transmuted into silver. He was much astonished at this, and thought that the egg possessed the property of changing everything which it touched into silver. He had heard of such things, and never believed them, but here was plain proof. He determined therefore in some way or other to get the egg.

"Hie! hie!" he shouted to the merchant. "Will you sell me that egg? I wish to make some medicine from it."

The merchant answered, "No; I am not so poor that I need sell it. I would willingly give it to you, if my sons were not so anxious to have another of this kind of bird."

But the man was in earnest. "Let me have it, please," he said; "I will give you one rupee for it."

"No," was again the reply.

"I will give you five—ten—twenty—a hundred—a thousand rupees for it," continued the man, finding that the merchant would not easily be persuaded.

"No," replied the merchant; "but if you will give me ten thousand rupees, you shall have it."

"Very well," he said; "for if I do not get this medicine I shall die." So the bargain was concluded. They all walked back together to the house of the merchant, where the money was paid and the egg given up.

As will be supposed, the man who had bought the

egg took the earliest opportunity of going to the bank of the stream and removing the stone that had been turned into silver. But he had not much need of doing this, as he afterwards proved; for every stone that he touched with the egg was transmuted into that precious metal.

Some time after this the man was visited by a *jogí*, who, noticing the egg, said, "That is a most valuable egg. But where is the bird that laid it? Try and get that bird, if possible; for whoever will cut off its head, cook it, and eat it will be the richest king in the world. The head of the bird will remain in the chest of the person that eats it; and when that person rises in the morning, he will find ten thousand *muhrs* underneath him. He will also understand the speech of birds and of animals. The breast of the bird, too, is of special virtue. Whoever will cook and eat it will become a king; but he will not be as great as the other king."

When the man heard these things from the *jogí*, he at once sent to the merchant and begged him to sell the bird. He promised to pay any price that might be asked for it. The merchant, however, sent back to say that on no account would he part with the bird—no, not even if the whole world were offered in exchange. But the man was quite as determined to get the bird as he had been to get the egg. When he heard the merchant's answer, he said to himself, "I know what to do. Through this man's wife I will get it. I will immediately seek an interview with her." Hereupon he sought the aid of an old wise woman in this matter, and promised her a very handsome present if she could arrange for him an introduction with this merchant's wife. The old wise woman consented. She went to the house of the merchant, and finding that he was not at home, she entered, and commenced conversation with his wife. The woman was very glad to see her, and asked her to come again. In this way a thick friendship sprung up, till at last the merchant's wife asked the wise old woman to come and stay altogether with her. During this time the old woman had constantly spoken in the most glowing terms of the man who had employed her, and thus excited the curiosity of the merchant's wife to that extent, that the poor stupid woman expressed a great wish to see him. Of course the old hag then told how anxious the man also was to see her. The promise of an interview was then given, as soon as the merchant's wife could make quite certain that her husband would be out of the way. In order to accomplish her purpose the more easily, she advised him to carry out his long-thought-of intention and go abroad for a time. "What vast treasure you might amass!" she urged. "What great sights you would see! And, moreover, this is expected of you."

"I will," he replied. "It is foolish of me not to have done this before." In a few days he, accompanied by a suitable retinue, started on his travels.

"Go now," said his wife to the old woman, "and tell this man who wishes to see me, that I shall be ready to meet him at twelve o'clock to-morrow morning."

The woman went, and the merchant was very glad to hear the news. "Give her my best respects," he said, "and beg her, if she is thinking of making a feast for me, to cook the beautiful bird and to set it apart especially for me. Tell her that I have set my heart on eating this bird, and shall be terribly disappointed if it is not prepared and kept for me."

Before twelve o'clock on the following morning the bird and other viands were ready, and the merchant's wife was in a state of great expectation, wondering what manner of man this great stranger might be, and why he should thus desire to know her. Just at this time Saiyid and Said came home from school, and being hungry, as usual, they rushed to their mother for something to eat. She told them to go to the dining-room and take what they liked from any dish, except from that on which the beautiful bird had been served, and a few other dishes, that she had specially prepared for the expected guest. The boys ran off to the room and looked at the various dishes, and, boy-like, they wanted every dish that they had been explicitly told not to touch. They went directly and thrust their fingers into the several dishes, and finding some of them more savoury, ate up all their contents. The dish containing the precious bird was amongst the number. Saiyid ate the head, and Said ate the breast. When they had done this, they thought that their mother would be very angry with them and beat them, and therefore they determined to run away.

At last the guest arrived. After some conversation the merchant's wife led him to the room where all the dishes had been arranged, and bidding him sit down, she placed some food before him. "I am not very hungry," he said. "It is very kind of you to take all this trouble, but if you will please bring me the bird about which I spoke to you I shall be quite satisfied. I think I could eat that." Accordingly the woman set before him the dish that contained the remainder of the beautiful bird. "What have you done?" he exclaimed. "Not half the bird is here. Who has eaten the head and breast?"

"I do not know," she replied, much alarmed.

"Somebody has been touching the food," said the merchant, and left the house in a great rage.

The merchant's wife was very much grieved at his sudden departure. Was this the man whose visit she had looked forward to for many a day!

Saiyid and Said walked far and fast till they reached the middle of a big plain. Here they determined to spend the night, although the place was dreaded by every one, because of the many wild beasts that were said to prowl about there. These two youths feared nothing, for they were emboldened by eating the head and breast of the beautiful bird. They were totally ignorant of the wonderful virtues of the bird, but they felt within them a power inspiring them to do and to dare anything.

That night they slept sound and safely, and in the morning when they arose Saiyid, the elder brother, saw ten thousand *muhrs* in the place where he had lain. Great was their delight when they saw this. They loaded themselves with the golden pieces, and resumed their journey. On reaching the other side of the plain they found themselves in a place where two roads met. Pointing in the direction of one of the roads was a big stone, whereon were inscribed these words, "Do not go this way, or you will repent it." Saiyid, however, who was the bolder of the two, on account of his having eaten the head of the bird, wished very much to try this dangerous road, and urged his brother to venture with him. But Said would not agree. "No," he replied; "I do not care to meet death thus rashly. I shall not go that way." But Saiyid was resolute, and so the brothers parted. One went the dangerous road, and the other went the regular road.

SAID'S FORTUNES.

Said, the younger brother, eventually reached some city by the sea, and was there employed by a great merchant and shipowner. Not long had Said been in his employ before he was asked if he would like to go to sea for a while. Said replied in the affirmative, as he was most anxious to travel and see something of the world. On the appointed day, the weather being suitable, the ship sailed steadily out of the harbour. For several days everything proceeded most happily, and there seemed every prospect of a bright and prosperous voyage, when one morning a nasty wind suddenly sprung up, and increased so violently that the ship was tossed hither and thither, and finally was wrecked. All on board were drowned except Said, who escaped by means of one of the timbers to a desert island. Faint and hopeless, he threw himself down on the shore and cried, "Oh, why was I born? Why did I eat the forbidden food, and so was obliged to fly from home? Why did I leave my brother to go alone? It would have been better to have died with him than to perish by a lingering death in this wretched place. Ah me! Ah me!" Presently sleep, the panacea for all ills, came to him, and night with its thick curtains covered him. He slept till the morning, when, as he rose to look around him to see what sort of place he was in, he noticed a ship passing near. He shouted, and waved his hands most madly to apprise the people of his presence there; and fortunately he was seen. The captain of the vessel brought the craft near and took him in.

The ship reached her destination in safety, and Said wished the captain and the sailors farewell. For some time he wandered round the city, inquiring about the country that he had left and his father and brother, but nobody could give him any information. Not thinking it worth while to remain in that city, he started for the adjoining country, concerning which he had heard many wonderful things.

In a few days he reached the place, and found it wonderful indeed. The capital of the country was bounded by four high insurmountable walls, and was entered by one door, which was kept shut and most carefully guarded. Why it was so we will explain. It had been the custom in that city for the ministers to appoint somebody as their king by day and to slay him by night. In consequence of this wicked custom the people had fled in crowds, and therefore the ministers had met together in solemn assembly to discuss plans for the future, in order that the city might not be entirely deserted. They decided to repeal the custom, and notices had been sent in every direction ordering the people to return and elect for themselves a king, who should reign over the land till death called him away. There was a mighty concourse of people in the city just as Said had arrived at the door.

"O people!" said the chief minister, coming forward, "seeing the old custom of appointing and slaying a king every day is obnoxious to you, we have determined to do away with it. And now we call on you to choose for yourselves one who shall always reign over us. The matter is in your hands. Say who shall be our king."

"Close the doors," they replied, "and let the man who now first comes up to the city be our king." This they did, because each were afraid to suggest any one out of their own company, lest others should be offended and kill them. Said was the man chosen for this high office. While he was standing outside the great door of the city the people came with the *wazírs*, and seeing him there, they led him to the place of honour in their great hall of assembly, and cried, "Behold the king! Long live the king!"

SAIYID'S FORTUNES.

Saiyid, the elder brother, pursued his way, nothing daunted by the dreadful warning that he had read. Every morning he found ten thousand *muhrs* in the place where he lay, so that he became very rich. He was obliged to engage several coolies to carry his wealth.

Nothing had happened to him so far, and he was beginning to think that the inscription on the stone was only a hoax, when he arrived at the entrance to a most beautiful garden, stocked with all kinds of rare and lovely flowers. On entering the garden he saw a splendid house also. The walls were made of silver, and its pillars of gold, and it shone so brilliantly in the sunshine that one could scarcely look at it.

"Who lives here?" he inquired from an old woman whom he met in the garden. "Who lives here? An angel, a holy man?"

The old woman replied, "A beautiful woman lives here, and I am her *dáí*. You seem astonished at the magnificence of the place. My mistress has several other houses and gardens quite as good as this."

"Is your mistress at home? Can I see her?" asked the youth.

"Oh yes, you can see her. Any person may see her that can pay ten thousand rupees for the visit."

"Very well," he said, "I will pay the money. Lead me to your mistress."

On seeing the lovely woman Saiyid was so much surprised that he could hardly speak. He had never before seen so lovely a woman.

"Welcome," she said, taking him by the hand, and asking him to sit down. "The *dáí* will have acquainted you with my terms. Every day you come to see me you must pay me ten thousand rupees, and when all your money is exhausted you will be killed."

"Agreed," he replied. "Nay, I will give you ten thousand *muhrs*;" for he was intoxicated with her beauty.

Hearing this, the woman was very glad, and allowed him to stay in her house a long time. Every day the ten thousand *muhrs* were forthcoming, and duly given to the woman. After a while the woman began to wonder what kind of man he must be who could pay her so well and so regularly. She thought that he must surely be a wizard or suchlike. Accordingly she watched him. The secret of his wealth was soon discovered. "He has swallowed the head of the golden bird," she said to herself, when she saw the *muhrs* on the bed, from which Saiyid had just risen. She could tell this because she was a witch. From the moment of this discovery she determined to destroy her paramour.

One day she said to him, "Come and let us taste some wine that I have just received;" whereupon she went and fetched some wine and cups, and placed them before him. Saiyid drunk heartily. She too drank, but only a little. This wine was of a most potent quality; consequently Saiyid, who had imbibed much of it, soon began to feel giddy and giddier, till he became quite mad. It also created an intense burning thirst within him. "Give me some water! give me some water!" he shrieked. She brought him some juice of a water-melon, and a few grapes. He snatched them eagerly, and no sooner had he drunk the juice of the melon and eaten the grapes than he was violently sick. He vomited everything that was in his stomach, and then went to sleep.

Now the head of the bird that Saiyid had swallowed had not descended to the stomach, nor had it decomposed like other food. Consequently when Saiyid was sick this too appeared. The woman expected this, and hastily seizing it, put it into one of her secret boxes.

When Saiyid rose the next morning he was terribly surprised not to find the *muhrs* as usual. He did not know what to do. The woman had threatened to kill him if he could not obtain them by the evening. All that day he was in terrible distress, and when evening arrived he shut himself in his room and locked the door. The woman waited some time, and then sent for him. But he replied that he was not feeling well that evening, and therefore wished to be excused. Finally, however, he was obliged to go to her. "I have nothing to pay you," he said, when she reproached him with want of affection. "I know not how it is I have not any money. I cannot explain my sorrow to you. I have so grieved over this matter to-day that I can scarcely walk."

"I too am sorry," said the woman; "but matters cannot be mended. However, since you have paid me so liberally, I will revoke my order concerning your death and let you go. Depart, and do not show yourself to me again till you are a richer man." Saiyid thanked her and left.

"Sorrow, a thousand sorrows!" he exclaimed as he went out by the garden gate. "Oh that I had listened to my brother's earnest entreaties and not ventured on this path! In vain for me now to retrace my steps. Let me go straight on and see whither the hand of fortune will lead me." On the way he passed through a jungle and over a great plain, and as he was leaving this plain he met three men hotly disputing with one another over the distribution among themselves of four things that their master, a *faqír*, who had just died, had bequeathed to them.

"Why do you thus wrangle?" he asked. "Show me these things."

The three disputants unfastened their loads and set before him a *badra-píṭh*,[4] a *thál*,[5] a box of collyrium, and an old ragged garment.

"Well," said Saiyid with a laugh, "these things do not appear of such value that you need quarrel over them."

"You do not know their value," they replied. "Listen, this *badra-píṭh* will carry anybody who sits in it to the place where he would be, no matter how far or how inaccessible the place may be; this *thál* will at all times supply its owner with all kinds of food; this collyrium has only to be applied to the eyes and it will render the person on whom it is placed invisible, while that person can see everything and everybody; and this old garment has four pockets; one pocket supplies as many *páṅsas* as the man requires, another supplies silver, another gold, and another precious stones."

"Most interesting! most valuable!" said Saiyid, when these men had finished their explanation. "Now conclude your quarrel. I will tell you what to do. Be not disturbed by the last article. Give that to me. You take the *badra-píṭh*, you the *thál*, and you the box of collyrium."

"No, never," they all replied. "This we can never do, for we have made a vow not to part with any of these things. On this condition our father (meaning the *faqír*) gave them to us. No, let us alone. Our only hope is that one of us will soon die, and then there will not be any difficulty about sharing the things. Four things can very easily be divided among two people."

"But why wait till one of your party dies?" said Saiyid. "To all appearance each of you will live to a very old age. My advice is, decide at once. One of you take two things, and the other two one thing each. Look

[4] *Bhadra-píṭha* (Sanskrit), a beautiful chair, a splendid seat, a throne.
[5] A tray or large dish.

here, will you agree to this? I will throw these three arrows as far as I can. One arrow I will throw in front of me, another on this side, and the third on that side. You each run after one of these arrows at a given signal from me. You run after the one thrown in front of me, you after the one thrown on this side, and you the one thrown on that side; and the man that returns first with his arrow will have two things."

"Agreed!" they replied. So Saiyid threw the three arrows and the men started. While they were running Saiyid took up the *thál*, the box of collyrium, and the old ragged garment,[6] and seating himself in the *badra-píṭh*, wished to be transported to some place where the three men could not reach, and immediately disappeared.

When the three men returned with the arrows they were terribly distressed to find the stranger and their precious things gone. They wept and lamented their lot. "Our teacher was angry with us," they said, "because we quarrelled, and therefore he came in the person of this man and took away our treasures."

Saiyid was carried away a great distance from the place where he left the three men. When he had satisfied himself with all kinds of food from the *thál*, he remembered the beautiful woman, and wished to see her again. So, putting his things into the *badra-píṭh*, he sat in it, and soon found himself on the roof of the magnificent gold and silver house. Here he first hid his treasures, and then descended the steps that led down into the yard. There he saw the *dáí*, whom he asked to go and inform her mistress of his arrival.

When the beautiful woman saw him she knew that he had got some more money. Accordingly she gave him a great welcome and showed him much honour, and asked him about his travels since he had left her.

"I have been to my own country to get some more money for you," he said. "I could not stay away from you."

[6] Cf. *Indian Fairy Tales*, pp. 34, 156, 157; *Wide-Awake Stories*, pp. 281, 289.

This was a falsehood, but he did not wish the woman to guess the source of his wealth. Every day he went to the old ragged garment, and got as much money as he required. The days passed happily for a month or so, till Saiyid began to suspect that he was watched. Once he heard something like a footfall behind him up the steps, and another time he thought that he saw some one on the roof. Consequently he determined to sleep on the roof, and told the woman so. "My darling," he said, "I intend to sleep outside to-night on the roof. You also come." She consented, and they slept together in the open air for several nights, till Saiyid's suspicions were further aroused. "Supposing," he said to himself, "that this garment and other things were stolen from me, what should I do? I will leave the place this very night, and try to get the woman to go with me."

That night, when they went up on the roof, he showed her the *badra-píṭh*, and asked her to sit in it with him. She did so, and then Saiyid wished to be carried to some place where they would be free from all other society; and they were at once carried to a beautiful uninhabited island.

"Here let us dwell together, my love," he said to the woman, when the *badra-píṭh* stopped.

"Your will is mine," she replied. "I care not so long as I am with you."

Saiyid was much rejoiced at these words, because he thought that the woman really meant what she said. By-and-by he got so thoroughly persuaded of her affection that he confided to her the secrets of all his treasures.

"How do you get such splendid food every day?" she asked.

"God gives it to me," he replied. "I have only to take this *thál* and wish, and the food wished-for is at once provided."

"Whence do you obtain money in this uninhabited spot?" she inquired.

"From this old garment," he replied. "I put my hand into these pockets, and *páṅsas,* silver, gold, and precious stones come at my will."

"How does this *badra-píṭh* bear us about in the air, as though it were a bird?" she said.

"I cannot explain," he replied, "by what means it does this. All I know is, that I simply sit on it, wish to be somewhere, and I am immediately borne to the place that I wish to reach. But there is another thing that you have not seen: I have got some collyrium, which when rubbed on the eyes renders the person invisible, while that person can see everything that is going on."

"O my beloved! how glad I am that you have told me of these precious things!" she said. "How rich we are, and how fortunate I am in having you! Why did you not make me acquainted with your good fortune before? Now I shall give up all desire of returning to my house."

Sweet words indeed! They fell like nectar on the ears of the simple Saiyid, but they were not sincere. The woman's object was to disarm him of all suspicion concerning her. She never loved him, and never once wished to stay with him. On the contrary, she wanted to bamboozle him out of his wealth, and then to slay him. Henceforth, therefore, she tried to obtain possession of the four precious things. She had not to wait long for an opportunity. One morning, while they were walking together on the sea-shore, she expressed a wish to bathe, and asked Saiyid to first go into the water and try the depth. He complied, and while he was swimming about she took up the *thál,* the pot of collyrium, and the ragged garment, and running to the *bádra-píṭh,* sat in it, and wished herself back again in her magnificent house.

Poor Saiyid, how terribly duped he felt! Naked, cold, and hungry, he ran about the island bemoaning his fate. As evening drew on he began to think what he should do for the night. If he had neither clothes nor food, still he might put up a shelter from the wind. Perhaps, too, he might sight a ship on the morrow. Thus he tried to comfort himself. He at once commenced to break down branches from the trees, and while he was doing this his attention was drawn to three birds who were seated on three different trees, and were answering one another most lustily. Presently he began to comprehend what they were talking about.

One bird said, "My tree is of great virtue. If any person will peel off the bark, pound it very fine, and then work it into a ball, the ball will be found to be most efficacious in cases of headache. The sufferer has only to take a good smell at it, and the headache immediately disappears."

"Very good, very good!" said the second bird; "but listen to me. My tree is much more valuable than yours. If any person will peel off the bark, pound it, mix the powder with some of the juice of its leaves, and then work it into a ball, it will be found to act like a charm; for any person who smells it will be turned into an ass."[7]

"Wonderful, wonderful!" said the third bird; "but not so wonderful as the tree on which I am sitting. If any person will do the same with the bark of this tree, and then give it to that, or any other, ass to smell, it will at once transform the beast into a man."

Saiyid understood every word of the birds' conversation. He was able to do this because he had once swallowed the head of the golden bird. How glad he must have been at the good news! As will be imagined, he lost no time in preparing three balls from the three different trees, as the birds had directed. He carefully marked each of them, lest he should forget which was which, and then lay down and went to sleep. In the morning he rose with a very sad heart. "O God, save me, save me!" he cried; and his prayer was heard. A great bird came flying over the place where he was, and so frightened him, that he ran to a big hollow tree for safety. The

[7] Cf. *Orientalist*, vol. ii. p. 151.

bird, however, did not leave, but kept on circling round and round, and looking now and again at Saiyid most earnestly.

"What can the creature mean to do?" thought Saiyid. "Does it want to eat me?"

While he was thus meditating, the bird alighted on the ground just opposite the hollow tree, and looked at him. "A man has come to this island," it said. "He is in great distress, and will die if he does not listen to me. I am most anxious about him. Oh that he could understand my speech and would lay hold of my leg! I should then fly away with him to some more habitable spot."

Saiyid understood every word of what the bird said, and to show that he did, he caught hold of one of the bird's legs with both hands. At once the great bird spread its wings and flew away. Miles and miles it travelled, until it reached a famous city. There it left Saiyid and disappeared. Attracted by the bird, many of the inhabitants of the place soon gathered round and began to ask numerous questions, "How did you reach this state? What is your name? Where is your home?" all of which Saiyid fully answered; and his account so touched the sympathies of the people that they brought him clothes and food, and invited him to lodge in their houses till he had arranged his plans.

Some few days after his arrival it happened that the daughter of the king of that country fell violently sick with headache. All the physicians in the city were summoned to attend at the palace and prescribe for her, but nothing they did availed. The dreadful headache continued. At length the king, fearing that his daughter would die, issued a proclamation to all the people of his country to this effect—that if anybody could find some remedy for the princess, he should have her hand in marriage and half the kingdom. Saiyid was delighted to hear these words. He now saw before him the way to honour, great power, and glory. He immediately wended his steps in the direction of the palace, and told the man at the gate to apprise the king of the arrival of a person who could cure the princess of her headache.

"Send the man to me," said the king, when he heard the message. Saiyid approached, and the king said, "Can you, O man, find a remedy for my daughter's headache? Several physicians in my country have tried to cure her, but alas! in vain. What hope have you of doing better than they?"

Saiyid replied, "Much hope, Your Majesty. Please, call the princess, and within five minutes she shall be well."

"God grant it!" exclaimed the king, and called his daughter.

The princess appeared, moaning bitterly, and looking very thin and worn. "Smell this," said Saiyid, giving her the little ball of pounded bark, that the bird had said was good for headaches. The princess did so, and was immediately relieved. Great was the astonishment of the king and the princess and every one present. The king inquired who Saiyid was, whence he had come, and why he was in the city; and when he had heard his story, he felt so thoroughly interested in him, that he at once gave orders for rooms to be prepared for him in the palace. In due time, also, he married his daughter to him, and handed over to him half of his kingdom as a wedding dowry. However, Saiyid really reigned over the whole kingdom, because the king was getting old, and wished very much to retire altogether from public life.

In his great honour and prosperity Saiyid did not forget the beautiful woman who had treated him so wickedly. He wished very much to be revenged on her, till at last this thirst for revenge so overcame him, that he went to his father-in-law and begged to be allowed to go and punish some robbers who had seized all his property on his way thither. The king at first hesitated to give his sanction, but eventually was constrained to do so by Saiyid's earnest entreaties.

Saiyid left with a great retinue and much treasure, and marched straight to the house of the woman that had deceived him. "My darling," he exclaimed on meeting her, "how I have sought for you! Why did you leave me thus to perish? If God had not had mercy on me I should not be here."

The woman answered, "It was my great sin. I was foolish and afraid, and did what I now thoroughly repent of. Forgive me, I beseech you." The woman uttered these words tremblingly, for she was afraid of him. She thought to herself, "I have been saved twice, but who knows what he will do to me now?"

One night while she was asleep Saiyid took the ball whose virtue was that it could change a person into an ass, and put it by the woman's nose. Presently her face and whole body gradually changed into the face and body of an ass; and scarcely was this accomplished, when she woke up and began to bray.[8] Saiyid was delighted to see and hear this. Now he had his revenge. He found all the keys of the house, and opened all the rooms, *almairas*,[9] and boxes in the place. The four precious things were discovered, also the head of the bird. Tying them up into bundles, he gave them to his servants, and ordered them to prepare to march the next morning. The ass, too, he gave into their charge.

"Why are you leaving so soon?" asked the old *dáí*, when she saw him leaving early the next day.

"Your mistress has robbed me of all my money," he replied, "and run away. What have I to stay for?"

"Never," said the *dáí*. "Some other person must have done this thing. Or if my mistress has taken this money, she has done it in joke, and no doubt will soon return.

[8] Cf. *Indian Antiquary*, vol. xiv. p. 109; *Bilochi Stories*, No. XIII.; Mongolian story in *Folk-Lore Journal*, vol. iv. p. 24.; *Grimm's Household Stories*, p. 385.

[9] Kashmírí *kut*, a cupboard chest of drawers. "The word *almárí*" (Hindust.), says Forbes, "is of European origin; for example, the old English term is "almarie;" and the Scotch word "awmrie," or "aumrie," is in common use to this day.

Do not go, I pray you. My mistress will be very angry when she comes and finds you have left."

"I cannot help it," he replied. "I must go."

By noon that day Saiyid had finished his march, and was encamped under some large trees beside a pretty little stream. "Bring me some of that water," he said to one of his servants standing by.

While the servant was going for the water one of the villagers shouted, "Don't give that water to your master. It is rank poison. Your master, or any one, would not long survive a draught of it. Go a little distance up the stream, and you will get water fit to drink." The servant did so.

Not knowing the reason of the delay, Saiyid was very angry and impatient. "Why have you been so long?" he inquired.

"I was warned not to take water from the part of the brook opposite you, because it is very poisonous; and so I went higher up the stream, where I was told there was good water."

"Strange, very strange!" exclaimed Saiyid. "Call one of the people of the village and inquire the reason."

Lots of people were called, but nobody was able to explain it. All that the villagers knew was, that from a certain spot the water of the brook was very poisonous. Accordingly Saiyid ordered the spot to be well dug and cleared. He got some coolies from the village to dig about the place, and had the soil carried away on the ass's back to a distant spot and buried. By this means the stream was made pure; and the people were very glad.

"Why do you give me this menial work to do?" asked the ass. "Is it not enough to have degraded me to the beasts? Why add this extra burden to my lot?"

Saiyid answered her not a word. On the morrow he continued his journey, and tarried not till he reached the country of his father-in-law. There was much rejoicing in the city when he arrived; for he governed wisely, and was very popular.

In a little while, when he thought that he had obtained such honour and power as would certainly captivate the beautiful but wicked woman, he determined to restore her to her original form. Accordingly he gave her another of the balls to smell, and she became a beautiful woman once more.

"O my beloved, why did you treat me thus?" she asked.

"Because I wished to teach you a lesson," he replied. "Learn now my power, how useless it is to try to oppose me. See, too, my affection. I have prepared a suitable house for you. Dwell there, and whatever you require shall be supplied."

The woman acceded, and henceforth remained faithful to her paramour.

SAIYID AND SAID MEET AGAIN.

Saiyid now exerted every effort to find his younger brother. He sent many messengers into all parts of the world, and promised them great rewards if they were successful. By the hand of good fortune one of these messengers arrived in the country over which Said was ruling. He discovered him in this way. One night he tarried in the hut of an old widow, who was one of the many recipients of Said's charity.

"How do you contrive to live, mother?" he asked.

"Well you may ask," the old woman answered. "I am not able to do anything; but our king is very just and good. He regularly distributes alms to many poor, old, and sick people in the city. If it were not for his charity, several of us would perish. Praise be to God for our king! Praise be to God!"

"Who is your king? Is he one of this country? Where do his parents live?" the messenger asked.

"I do not know," she replied. "Report says that he came from far, and that during his travels he was separated from his brother, of whom he was very fond. He has despatched messengers in all directions to try and discover some news of him, and of his father also."

"Can I get an interview with your king?" said the messenger.

"Oh yes," she replied. "The king's ear is open unto all. Whoever wishes can go and speak to him at all times."

Accordingly, early the next morning, as soon as he heard that the king had risen, he went to the palace and begged to be shown before the king. Thinking that he had come on urgent business, the servant led him into the king's private room. "O king," said the messenger, falling down before him, "Saiyid, your brother, has sent me to you, to inquire of your welfare. God has prospered him exceedingly, and raised him to be ruler over a great and mighty kingdom, but he cannot rest day or night till he knows of your estate."

When Said heard these words he was so startled that he could scarcely speak. After some conversation with the messenger, he sent for one of his *wazírs*, and ordered him to clothe the man in splendid apparel, and to see that he had everything he wanted. He also told him that he had heard of his long-lost brother. Saiyid was ruler over such-and-such a kingdom, and he wished to go and see him immediately. Arrangements were to be at once made for the journey. The *wazírs*, however, demurred to this journey, as there were several countries intervening, whose rulers were inimical to the king. Therefore they begged him to give up the idea, and to send word to his brother Saiyid, who appeared to be more powerful than he was. So Said, very much disappointed, though he felt that his *wazírs* were wise, bade the messenger to return as quickly as possible and inform his brother of his affairs, and come and bring him word again.

After resting a day or two the messenger left. He reached his country safely, and informed his royal master of all that he had seen and heard of his brother. Saiyid was very much rejoiced, and richly rewarded the messenger.

He immediately arranged a plan for conquering all the countries that intervened between his and his brother's kingdoms. He sent word to his brother to fight with the few countries on his side, while he would fight with the countries on his side. They were both rich and powerful, he said, and ought to overcome. And they did overcome them.

Oh! who can tell the joy in which these conquering heroes met one another again?[10]

[10] Compare the story of the "Two Brothers" in this collection.

THE CRUEL MERCHANT.[1]

ONCE upon a time there lived a merchant who was very cruel to his servants. When anybody applied to him for service, he agreed to employ him on the condition that the servant's nose should be cut off if he at any time showed himself abusive or angry. Now, since servants are no better than the majority of their masters, we are not surprised to hear that several servants quitted this merchant's service *minus* their noses. One of these servants was a poor farmer, who had been obliged to take service on account of a failure in his crops. The man lived up in the hills, where nothing except *makáí*[2] can be grown; and that year but little rain had fallen, so that his labour and expense were all wasted. He was of a most amiable and willing disposition. If any man had a chance of continuing in the merchant's service, it was he. But, alas! he too failed. One day he was very much troubled about a matter, when something his master did or said—and the merchant used to say and do some very nasty things—provoked the farmer, so that he spoke angrily; whereupon the merchant rushed at him and cut off his nose.

This farmer had a brother, who grieved to see him in this noseless condition, and resolved to avenge him of this cruelty. So he went to the merchant and offered himself for employment.

"Very well," said the merchant. "I will give you work, but only on the condition that your nose is cut off if you ever show yourself abusive or angry."

[1] Narrator's name Makund Báyú, of Suthú, Srínagar. [2] Maize, Indian-corn.

"I will agree to this if you too will be bound by the like condition," said the man.

"All right," said the merchant.

"If the plan worked well for one party, it might also work well for the other," thought the man.

It did work well for a long time. Both master and servant were so very careful over their words and actions, that they both preserved their temper. One day, however, the merchant ordered his servant to go and put on his son's clothes quickly. The man went, and while dressing the boy pulled him about here and there to make him run. The boy, naturally not liking such treatment, roared, "O father! O mother!"

"What are you doing?" asked the merchant.

"The boy will not run about while I am dressing him, but wants to sit down," he replied.

Now the master had ordered him to dress the child quickly, and thus he would have been understood by nineteen out of twenty people; but the words might possibly be construed to mean, "Run about and dress the child;"[3] so the servant chose to understand them thus, thinking thereby to provoke his master to anger; and he almost succeeded.

On another occasion the merchant, accompanied by all his family, went to stay for a few days in some place where a big *melá* was accustomed to be held. He left the house in charge of this servant, and before leaving, especially ordered him to keep his eye on the doors and windows. The man promised faithfully. His master, however, had not long departed when he too felt an intense desire to attend the *melá*. Accordingly he collected the furniture and things of the house and stored them away in a big pit. He then called several coolies, and loading them with the doors and windows of the place, started off for the *melá*. The astonishment of the merchant, when he saw his servant, followed by a long string

[3] *Gatshit tshun nĕchivis poshák náli ṭukán ṭukán.*

of coolies bearing his doors and windows, will be imagined. "You fool!" he exclaimed, "what have you done?"

"I have simply obeyed your order," replied the servant. "You told me to look after the doors and windows. So, when I wished to leave the house and come to the *melá*, I thought it would be safer to bring them with me. The furniture, too, is quite safe. I have hidden it all in a great pit."

"You consummate fool!" said the merchant, and struck him a blow across the face.

"Ha! ha!" said the man, seizing him by the back of his neck and cutting off his nose, "we are quits now. I will go and tell my brother."[4]

[4] Cf. *Orientalist*, vol. i. pp. 131, 132; and *Indian Antiquary*, vol. xvi. p. 296.

THE MAN FROM SHÍRÁZ.[1]

A LONG time ago a Shírází visited Kashmír, and called on an old friend, and stayed with him for three days. This friend, who prided himself on his hospitality, prepared a great feast for his guest. During dinner he naturally looked for some expression of approval from him, and the Shírází, seeing that he was expected to say something complimentary, after a little while remarked that the dinner was good, very good, but not for a moment to be compared with the feasts given in his country. Other conversation followed, and then the company dispersed.

The host, however, was so disappointed at the Shírází friend's modified commendation of the dinner that he could not sleep. All through the long night he was endeavouring to smother his feelings, or planning for a still larger and more extravagant dinner on the morrow; and long before daylight he ran and called the cook, and gave him such an order, and explained everything so minutely to him, that his guest might at least say that the dinner was equal to the meals prepared in his country. If it was a success he promised to give the cook ten rupees *bakhshish.*[2] But it was not a success. All the expense and all these preparations were again in vain. The feast was declared to be inferior to those in Shíráz.[3] Not that it was owing to any fault of the cook. On the contrary, no feast could have been cooked or served up better than this one.

[1] Narrator's name, Mihtar Sher Singh, officiating governor, Srínagar.

[2] Generally pronounced *bakshâish*, a gift, gratuity.

[3] A city in the south of Persia.

The Kashmírí, now suspecting that his *cuisinier* was not so skilful as he thought him to be, engaged another servant in his place, whom he ordered to prepare a still more elaborate meal for the following day, and promised the man twenty rupees if the dinner was thoroughly approved of by the guest. However, there came the same reply—"My dear friend, your feasts cannot match those which are served up in my country."

Some years elapsed, and the Kashmírí, being a traveller as well as his guest, found himself in the city of the Shírází, and seeking out his old friend's house, called on him. He received a very hearty welcome, and was asked to tarry there for three days, with which he complied. After ablutions and a change of garments he sat down to smoke the pipe of friendship and peace, while dinner was being prepared. He waited with much expectation and curiosity to see what kind of a dinner it would be. "I shall now see," thought he, "in what respect these Shírází feasts are superior to ours." At last dinner was served. Imagine the chagrin and surprise of the Kashmírí when he saw simply a large tray of boiled rice, dotted here and there with bits of vegetable, placed before him. At first he thought it must be a dream, and rubbed his eyes to make quite certain that he was awake. Still the same tray of rice and vegetables was before him. He rubbed his eyes again; he cracked his fingers; he stretched his legs. Still there was the same tray. There was no doubt about it. These rice and vegetables were all that his host had prepared for that evening's meal. Perhaps this meagre display was owing to the lateness of the hour of his call, and that on the morrow a grander dinner would be provided. The morrow came, and the third day, and still the same fare was provided. During the last meal the Kashmírí could not refrain from asking the reason of his friend's remark concerning the inferiority of Kashmírí to Shírází feasts. The host replied, "Well, we here in Shíráz are very plain folk. We welcome you to our country and homely fare. You see us.

You have dined with us. Yesterday, to-day, and for ever this is our manner of life. But the feast you provided in honour of my coming (I thank you for it) was special, only for a day. Man could not always live at that rate; for the pocket of the host would soon be emptied and the stomach of the guest impaired—the result to both would be most unpleasant. Hence my remarks, of which I am quite certain you will perceive the truth."

SHABRANG, PRINCE AND THIEF.[1]

A CERTAIN king of Kashmír was very fond of hunting. One day, when he went to some distant jungle to shoot, he saw an animal that gave him such a chase as he never had before or after. He shot at it again and again, but missed. Determined to get it, however, he pursued the beast more swiftly. A long long way he ran, leaving his attendants far behind out of sight and hearing. At length he could not run any more, and therefore stopped. He found himself in a large well-kept garden, along one of the paths of which a beautiful girl was walking unattended.

"Ha, ha!" said the king, going up to her. "Certainly! A wife like you, whom after marrying I could put aside here in this jungle!"

"Of course," retorted the maiden, "I'd marry somebody like you and get a child; and the boy should marry your daughter!"

Surprised at her clever and ready reply, the king left the garden. He found his way back to the palace, and there inquired about the beautiful girl. Nobody could tell him anything, and so he despatched a messenger to make a thorough and full inquiry. It appeared that the maiden was a princess, and was accustomed to go to the garden where the king had seen her, because of its beautiful flowers, crystal fountains, and delightful shades.

On hearing this the king of Kashmír said, "I must marry her," and ordered the most skilful and experienced go-betweens[2] to start at once and arrange for the match.

[1] Narrator's name, collected for me by Pandit Makund Báyú, of Suthú, Srínagar, who heard it from an old shepherd at Krĕndih, near Bijhibárá.

[2] *Manzimyor.*

The go-betweens left, and as soon as they reached the kingdom of the princess's father they obtained an interview with His Majesty. Prostrating themselves before him, they said, "Our king has sent us to you on a special errand, of which we care not to speak before all the people. We pray Your Majesty, if it seem convenient, to grant us a private reception, when only Your Majesty and the chief *wazír* may be present." The king consented, and immediately ordered the clearance of the assembly-hall, and then, when nobody but the king and chief *wazír* were present, the embassage again prostrated themselves and said, "O great king, live for ever! May peace and prosperity abide in your kingdom, and may all its enemies be scattered. O king, we have been sent to you to arrange for the marriage of your daughter, the fame of whose beauty has reached all countries, with our good and noble king of Kashmír. He knows her beauty and excellent virtues, and cannot rest day or night till he is certified of your good pleasure concerning this his wish. Our king's goodness and power and wealth are not hidden from Your Majesty. We beseech you, therefore, to sanction this most desirable union, and dismiss us."

"I have heard," the king said after a brief pause. "To-morrow I will give you my reply."

On the morrow, therefore, he consulted his wife and his *wazír*, and they both having accepted the match, he called the embassage and told them to go and inform their king that the offer was approved, and that in due time arrangements would be made with him for the wedding.

When the king of Kashmír heard from his go-betweens that the other king would give him his daughter in marriage he was exceedingly glad, and gave large presents to the go-betweens.

In a little while the king sent for him. A convenient day was at hand, and the message to him was to come at once. Accordingly, attended by his most wise ministers and courtiers, the flower of his army, and a large company of gaily dressed servants and richly caparisoned horses bearing gifts, the king of Kashmír started. He reached his destination without any mishap, and was heartily welcomed by the other king.

Within a day or two the wedding took place. It is not necessary to speak of the magnificent arrangements of everything—how that the palace seemed one blaze of jewels; and gold and silver, like so much rice, were distributed to vast crowds of beggars who came from all parts; and the bride and bridegroom looked very beautiful. All these will be supposed. Everything was splendidly done, and everybody was exceedingly happy.

On arrival in his own country after the wedding, the king of Kashmír put his new wife, with the rest of his wives, in the royal *haram*. But, strange to say, these first days passed without his ever seeing her or speaking to her. In a little while her father sent for her, according to custom. So she went back to her father's house, and there remained; but she said nothing to any one, except her mother, about her husband's strange behaviour to her. To her mother, however, she explained everything. She told her of the garden episode also, and added that she supposed it was on account of her retort that the king of Kashmír thus treated her.

"Never mind," said the queen. "Don't worry. Matters will right themselves again. Only wait."

When three years had elapsed, and the king of Kashmír had not sent for or inquired after his wife, she went to her father and expressed her great desire to travel, and begged him to allow one of his *wazírs* and a cohort of soldiers to accompany her, in order that she might travel in a manner befitting her position.

"What do you wish to do? Where do you wish to go?" said the king.

"I wish to see something of other countries, and especially your feudatories; and in order that I may do so with ease and pleasure, I beg you to give me help."

"But you are a woman," said the king, with an astonished air, "and young and beautiful. How can *you* travel? People will wonder to see you going about unattended by your father or mother. No; I don't think that I can grant your wish. I should be wrong if I did."

"Then I must go altogether alone," she said; "for I am determined to carry out my wishes."

"Ah me! if it is so, I suppose I must give my consent. It will only be adding trouble to trouble to hear of your death as well as your disgrace. But I ask you not to go very far—only in the surrounding countries."

"I promise you," she replied, and left the room.

Then the king summoned a *wazír*, one in whom he had special confidence, and ordered him to attend the princess in her wanderings. His Majesty also gave him charge of all the money and jewels and other valuables which his daughter would require on the journey.

In a few days the princess departed, attended by the faithful *wazír* and a large company of soldiers and servants. Her first visit was to a petty king who held a small tract of country in fief under her father. Hearing of her coming, this king went forth to meet her, and received her with great honour, and caused a great feast to be made in her name. She remained there a few days, and then continued her journey. In this way she saw nearly all the adjacent countries, and learnt very much of their rulers and their ruled.

At length she arrived near her husband's country of Kashmír. She naturally wished very much to see it—its court, its *bázár*, and its commerce, and everything concerning it. Accordingly she sent a letter to the king saying that she was the daughter of a certain king to whom he paid tribute, and that she was now waiting outside the walls, and wishing much to see the city within them. When the king of Kashmír had read the letter he summoned his *wazírs* and others, and at once went forth to the princess's camp, and conducted her to his palace. There everything that could minister to the illustrious visitor's comfort and pleasure was ordered and got ready. A special suite of apartments were set apart for her, the walls of which were hung with the most beautiful cloths, and the floors covered with the richest carpets; the most sumptuous food was provided; and the royal minstrels were bidden to be always present. These excellent arrangements charmed the princess, who at the end of the day thanked the king for his attention, and promised to remember him to her father.

The next day, in the course of conversation, she said to the king of Kashmír, "I have something to say to you privately. Please come into the room."

Thinking that she had a special message for him from her father concerning his country, he did so. It happened, however, that she loved him, and had called him aside into that room in order that she might tell him so, and entreat him to allow her to stay there as long as she liked, and to come and see her constantly.

Overcome by her beauty and entreaties, the king of Kashmír consented, and was often in her society. Many many months thus passed, till the princess revealed her intention of leaving for her own country. Her excuse was, that she had other cares, and wished to be at home again. However, she promised to return as soon as possible, and giving the king her ring, asked him for his ring and handkerchief[3] in exchange, in token of this promise and of their affection for one another. The king did so, and kissed her.

The princess then left Kashmír, and returned to her own country as soon as she could. Everybody was very glad to see her back. The king, her father, was much interested in the account of her travels, and professed that he was now glad that she had visited the different

[3] In Indian Folk-tales the identity of hero or heroine is often proved by a ring, but less frequently by a ring and handkerchief. Cf. *Indian Fairy Tales*, pp. 133, 199, 200; the Norse tale of "The Widow's Son."

countries. The queen, her mother, was intensely pleased to hear of her expectations of a child, and began to concoct all sorts of plans for the bringing together of the husband, wife, and little one.

At the appointed time a son was born, and they called him Shabrang.[4] When the king heard of his birth he was much enraged, for he thought that his daughter had done wrong. "This comes," he cried, "of sanctioning her wild request! Oh that I had not been such a fool, and allowed her to go! Her character is ruined; her husband will never have anything to do with her; and my name is brought to reproach. Alas! alas! better to die than to suffer this!"

"Not so," said the queen, who had been attracted by the king's loud voice. "You have not asked who is the father of the child. He who ought to be the father is the father; and nothing has happened to damage either our daughter's reputation or your name. While travelling the princess visited her husband's country; and feigning herself to be another, she was admitted to her husband's palace, and there quickly won his affections, so that he grieved exceedingly to part with her; and now she has given birth to a son by him. To accomplish this end was her only reason for asking your permission to travel."

On this explanation His Majesty's anger and grief entirely disappeared. The thought of a son having been born into his family filled him with joy, and he praised his daughter for her affection and cleverness.

As the boy grew he became wise and learned. Every instruction was given him, so that he had knowledge of almost every art and science then extant. He was also brave and skilful with the sword. The king was exceedingly proud of his grandson, and declared his readiness to make him one of the chief *wazírs*, and in a few years to

[4] *Shab-rang* (Persian), black, dusky, obscure. Any especially wicked, cunning boy is often called Shabrang by his companions, after the hero of this tale.

deliver up the throne to him, if his father, the king of Kashmír, would not acknowledge him.

His mother, however, was bent on Shabrang becoming a thief. She thought that by such a training he would become proficient in all manner of trickery and cunning, and thus be a great help to her in the accomplishment of her wishes. Accordingly, the most clever master-thief in the country was sent for, and ordered to take Shabrang and educate him in all the secrets of his art, and he was promised a very handsome present when the youth should be judged perfect. The thief said that he would try to teach him thoroughly, and he had no doubt that in a few months Shabrang would become an incomparable thief. Within three months the master-thief returned with the lad, and said that he had learnt remarkably quickly and well, and that the princess would not find him wanting in any respect.

"Well," said the princess, "I will examine him to see whether it is as you say. If Shabrang can climb yonder tree (which was an immense *buni*[5]), and can take away the hawk's egg from the nest without disturbing the hawk, I shall be pleased."

"Go," said the master-thief, "and do your mother's wish."

Away went Shabrang, climbed the lofty tree in a trice, and so skilfully inserted his hand into the nest and underneath the hawk, and took away the egg, that the bird did not notice anything, and remained quiet and still long after Shabrang had descended and given the egg to his mother.[6]

"Clever! well done!" she said. "But go you now,

[5] Persian, *Chindr*, the Oriental plane-tree, which was introduced into the valley by the Musalmáns from the West. Cf. Elmslie's *Kashmírí Vocabulary*, p. 100.

[6] A dangerous game, *vide* the interesting episode narrated in the late Rev. Charles Kingsley's *Memoirs*, vol. i. pp. 14, 15. Cf. *Grimm's Household Stories*, the story of "The Four Accomplished Brothers," p. 380; the same incident is also recorded in Shekh Núru'ddín's Life, as told in the *Rishináma* (the principal original work of the country).

Shabrang, and take that man's *paijámas* from him." She pointed at a labourer who was on the way to his house.

Shabrang at once left, and running round a field, got some distance in front of the man, and then sat down by the path and looked most earnestly up at a tree. Presently the labourer came near, and being very curious about what did not concern him, like the majority of ignorant people, he asked, "What are you looking up there for?"

"O wretched fellow that I am!" replied Shabrang, assuming a most pitiful expression. "My beautiful coral necklace is on the top of this tree. I was playing with it, and accidentally slung it up there. Will you please fetch it for me? I promise to give you two rupees *bakhshish*."

"Oh yes," said the labourer, and immediately swung himself on to the lowest branch of the tree, and climbed higher and higher in the direction indicated by Shabrang. Shabrang thought that he would surely have taken off his *paijámas* before climbing; but the labourer refused to do this, saying that there was no need. So now Shabrang knew not what to do. He could not return to his mother empty-handed. His wits, however, did not fail him. He found a reed, and putting one end of it by an ant-hole, soon had it filled with those insects. Then, taking the reed, he climbed the tree after the labourer, till he got within a yard or two of him. The labourer did not notice him, because of the dense foliage and the noise of the wind and birds. Seeing his opportunity, Shabrang put the reed to his mouth, and blew with all his strength against the man's *paijámas*. In a minute or two the poor labourer was itching terribly, and looking down, saw that the whole of the lower part of his body was covered with ants. He supposed that he must have rubbed by one of the holes of these insects in climbing. At all events they were there, and he had to unfasten his girdle, and pulling off his *paijámas*, throw them out on to the ground.

Happy Shabrang! As quickly as possible he descended, picked up the *paijámas*, and went to his mother.

The princess was astonished. "You have been well taught. I do not fear for you now," she said; and then turning to the master-thief, she gave him a handsome present and dismissed him.

One morning, not long after this, while Shabrang was playing with other youths in the palace-garden, one of the company twitted him about his illegitimate birth. Very much surprised and annoyed, Shabrang immediately left the game and ran to his mother. "Mother, mother, tell me of my father," he cried, almost breathless.

"My boy," she replied, "you are the son of the king of Kashmír, to whom I was duly married, but by whom I have been most cruelly deserted." [7]

"Dear mother," said Shabrang, "why did you not tell me this before? And why doesn't my grandfather avenge this insult at the point of the sword?"

"Be not hasty," the princess answered. "To wound and to slay are not necessary, if other means are at hand. You are a sharp and clever boy. Go to your father's country, and so ingratiate yourself in the king's favour that he will promote you to high office, and offer you his own daughter in marriage. When matters reach this stage send for me, and then I will give answer to the king whereby he will be convinced of his wrong, and perhaps restore his banished wife and place his brave and clever son on the throne."

"Good," said the youth; "I will struggle hard to do this."

As quickly as possible Shabrang started for Kashmír. On arrival the first thing he did was to make friends with the king's doorkeeper.[8] This friendship increased, until the doorkeeper liked Shabrang so much, that he would do anything for him. One day he asked him whether he

[7] Cf. story of Núru'ddín 'Alí and Badru'ddín Hasan in *The Arabian Nights*.

[8] A most important personage, *vide* note to "Gullálá Sháh's" story.

wished for employment in the state, and how he would like to serve in the king's palace. Shabrang thanked him, and replied that he should be very happy to undertake some definite work. And so the doorkeeper introduced his friend to the king, and spoke most eloquently of his skill and wisdom and general fitness for any important work that His Majesty might be pleased to grant him. The king was satisfied with Shabrang's appearance and manner and speech, and at once appointed him one of the royal attendants, in which position Shabrang quickly prospered, and became most popular with the king and every one.

After a time he thought he would put to the test the training which he had received from the master-thief. So every alternate night, and sometimes every night, he went on stealing expeditions. He stole here and there about the city, wherever he found opportunity, and hid all the ill-gotten things in a pit in a field. However, this did not interfere with his regular work. Every morning he was always most punctual at his post.

By-and-by so many people losing their money and valuables, and no traces of the thief being discovered, a public petition was got ready and presented to the king, praying him to use all endeavours for the discovery and punishment of the thief.

His Majesty was much grieved to hear this news. He called the deputy-inspector,[9] and severely upbraiding him for the inefficient state of the police, ordered him, on pain of the royal displeasure, to find the offender. The deputy-inspector said that he was very sorry, and promised to do all he possibly could.

That night he made special efforts for the capture of the thief. Policemen were stationed in every street and lane, and were given strict orders to watch; the deputy-inspector, also, spent the night walking about. Notwithstanding all these arrangements Shabrang went to three or four places, stole as much as he had a mind to, hid

[9] Called *koṭwál* or *kuṭawál*, the chief police-officer in the city.

what he had stolen in the pit in the field, and then returned to the palace.

The following day the people belonging to these three or four houses went to the king and complained that they had lost certain goods during the night. The king was much enraged. When the deputy-inspector saw His Majesty's great anger, he fell down on his knees and begged for mercy and justice.

"Be pleased to listen, O king, to your servant's words. I and all the police spent the whole night on patrol. Not one of us has slept for a moment. Every street and every corner of the city have been thoroughly guarded. How, then, can these things have happened?"

The king was much astonished. "Perhaps," said he, "the people have a grudge against you, or perhaps some of your men are thieves; or it may be that some servants in the different houses have arranged among themselves to do this thing. Howsoever it may be, I expect you to discover the offenders, and to bring them before me; and I give you a full week for this business."

During these seven days and nights the deputy-inspector tried all manner of means to get some clue of the thief. He disguised himself in various dresses; he had several of his men disguised also; he offered great bribes for any information; he promised the thief or thieves the royal pardon if they would confess and desist; and he advertised in all places that the State would honour and protect the man who should discover the thief, so that no person might fear to reveal the matter. But all was in vain. The thief was not discovered, although he was stealing all this time, and even more than before. These extra measures for his capture put Shabrang rather on his mettle, and excited him to dare yet greater things.

The city was much disturbed. Everybody, from the king himself down to the most menial subject, was in constant fear of being robbed. By day and by night, although every one kept a most careful watch over his property, yet nobody felt safe.

"What can be done?" inquired the deputy-inspector on the evening of the seventh day. "No person can do more than has already been done."

"True," replied the king; "but take you the army also, and order them as you will."

So on the seventh night soldiers as well as the police were posted at near distances from one another all over the city, and ordered to watch as for their own lives. The deputy-inspector also walked about the whole night supervising matters. In the midst of his peregrinations he saw a figure moving stealthily along in a garden by the river-side. "A thief, a thief!" he shouted, and rushed up to it.

"Nay, nay," was the reply; "I am a poor gardener's wife, and have come hither to draw water."

"Strange time to fetch water," said the deputy-inspector. "Why did you not get it before?"

"I was too busy," was the reply.

Then said the deputy-inspector, "Have you seen or heard anything of the thief?"

"Yes, yes; but I was afraid to give any alarm, lest the man should strike me. He has just been along here and taken a lot of my *hák.*[10] If you can wait a little you may catch him, as he is most likely to come by here again. He came from that quarter, and he has gone over there."

"Good news, good news, good news!" said the deputy-inspector; "but how can I catch him? There is not a bush here to hide one; and seeing me, he will run off."

"Put on my old *pheran,*[11] and pretend you are drawing

[10] Vegetables.

[11] *Pheran* (Pers. *Píráhan*) is the chief garment worn by the Kashmírí, male or female, Pandit or Musalmán. Its shape is not unlike a stout night-gown, but with sleeves very often half a yard wide and two or three yards long. The women's sleeves are generally larger than the men's. These *pherans* are made in all colours and in all kinds of cloth. Kashmíris have a story that the Emperor Akbar, enraged at the brave and prolonged resistance offered by them to his general, Qásim Khán, endeavoured to unman and degrade the people of this country. And so he ordered them, on pain of death, to wear *pherans*, which have effeminated them, and hindered them in battle and in all manly exercises. Before Akbar's time they all wore coats, vests, and trousers, like we do. Bates' *Gazetteer*, I believe, has a short article on the subject. Cf. also Vigne's *Travels in Kashmír*, vol. ii. p. 142.

water. He is almost certain to come and take the rest of my *hák,* and then you can go up to him and seize him."

Now the deputy-inspector did not like the idea of "going up" to a man of that character. However, he took the *pheran,* and asked to be shown how to draw water. The gardener's wife tied him to the weighted end of the beam, which acted as a lever for drawing up the water, and then told him to pull the string that was attached to the other end.[12] He did so, and as will be supposed, was carried up some twenty feet into the air. Then the gardener's wife fastened the down end of the beam to a peg in the ground, and taking up his clothes, left him.

"Oh, oh!" exclaimed the deputy-inspector.

"Be quiet," said the gardener's wife on going away, "or the thief will hear you and not come this way. Keep quiet. You need not fear. The beam will not come down of itself. When the thief is coming I will let you down, and then you can catch him."

Within half an hour Shabrang (the gardener's wife!) was sleeping in his bed. Within half an hour, also, there being no sign of a second visit from the thief that night, the deputy-inspector asked to be let down. But he received no answer.

"Oh, let me down!" he shouted, thinking that the gardener's wife had fallen asleep; "let me down, for the thief is not coming here again to-night. Let me down; the wind is blowing cold. What am I doing here, while the thief is probably stealing in another place?" Still no answer.

Then he shouted again, and threatened the gardener's wife with heavy punishment, pretending that he knew her name and her house. But still there was no reply.

"Alas!" he cried at last, "what trickery is this? The wife of the gardener can be no other than the thief, and the blackguard has fastened me up here!"

[12] *Tul* is a contrivance consisting of a long wooden pole, so placed upon another fixed perpendicular pole that one end shall be nearly equal in weight to the other end, with a vessel full of water. It is employed in raising water out of a stream or well.

Early the next morning other people complained to the king that their property had been stolen. His Majesty sent for the deputy-inspector to know what he had done during the night; but the deputy-inspector was not at home, and had not been to his house since the previous evening. So the messenger went all over the city hunting for him. At length he came by the garden where the deputy-inspector had unfortunately entered, and there found the poor wretched man, dressed in a woman's *pheran*, sitting across the raised end of a well-beam, and almost frozen with the cold. Lest the king should not believe him, he begged His Majesty to come and see for himself what had happened to the deputy-inspector. The king went, and when he saw the man he could not refrain from laughing—his position was so ridiculous.

As soon as the deputy-inspector's feet touched the ground, he explained to the king how it had all happened, and entreated him to take away his life, as he did not care to live.

"What shall we do?" inquired the king of his chief *wazír*. "A great and terrible calamity will happen to our country if it is not soon rid of this thief. How can it be averted? The people will not suffer the loss of their goods much longer. Rather than live in this dreadful uncertainty they will quit the country."

"This cannot and shall not be," replied the *wazír*. "If Your Majesty will allow me, I will go this night and search for the disturber of our peace."

The king assented. Just as it was beginning to get dark the *wazír* mounted his horse and set out. Shabrang, the thief, also went out, and in a little while appeared as a poor *musalmání*, wearing a ragged *pheran* and a greasy red *kasába*,[13] over which a dirty *púts*[14] was carelessly thrown. He sat at the door of a mud hut, and ground

[13] *Kasába*, a small red cap worn by Kashmírí musalmánís.

[14] *Púts*, a piece of cotton cloth which is thrown over the head, and is allowed to hang almost down to the heels of Kashmírí musalmán women.

maize by the dim light of a little oil lamp, that was fixed in the wall just behind. It came to pass, as Shabrang quite expected, that the *wazír* arrived at the place, and attracted by the sound of the grinding, drew up his horse, and asked who was there.

"An old woman," was the answer. "I am grinding maize;" and then, as if observing for the first time that the rider was the *wazír*, she said in a most piteous tone, "Oh, sir, if you could catch the thief! A man has just been here and beat me, and taken away nearly all the maize which I had ground for my dinner."

"A thief—what!—where! Tell me who it is. In what direction has he gone?"

"There, down there," pointing to the bottom of the hill.

The *wazír* rode off and explored the neighbourhood, but found not a trace of the thief, and therefore came back again to the old woman to inquire further.

"I have told you everything," she replied; "but what is the good? Dressed as you are, and riding on a grand horse, you will never catch the thief. Will you listen to the advice of an old woman? Change places with me. Change clothes with me. You stay here, and I will go quietly in search of the fellow. You remain here and grind some maize. He may come by again, and then you can catch him."

The plan seemed good, and so the *wazír* agreed.

Presently Shabrang, dressed as a grand *wazír*, and mounted on a most beautiful horse, might have been seen riding through the *bázár* of the city. An hour or so after he might have been seen talking with some other of the king's attendants in the court of the palace.

The next morning several other people came weeping and complaining to the king about the loss of their property. Some had lost money, others jewels, others grain.

"Sorrows, a hundred sorrows! What shall we do? Call the *wazír*," cried the king.

A messenger was at once despatched to the *wazír's*

house, where it was heard that the *wazír's* horse had arrived without its rider; and, consequently, the whole family were almost mad with anxiety, supposing that the *wazír* had met with the thief and had been slain by him.

When His Majesty heard this he was terribly grieved.

Ordering his horse, he bade some of his attendants—Shabrang among the number—to accompany him at once in search of the *wazír*. "It cannot be," he added, "that one so wise and faithful should perish in this way." In an hour or so, as the company were passing the little mud hut, they found the missing *wazír*, dressed in all the dirty, greasy rags of a poor *musalmání*, and weeping most pitifully.

"Your Majesty, please go, please go," he cried. "Look not on my shame. I can never lift up my face in this country again!"

"Not so," said the king. "Courage! We shall yet find the man who has thus disturbed our country and disgraced our *wazír*." His Majesty then ordered the *wazír* to be taken to his house.

For the next night the *thánadár*[15] offered to superintend arrangements, and notwithstanding his subordinate position, was accepted by the king.

That night Shabrang disguised himself as the *wazír's* daughter, and waited in the *wazír's* garden, hoping that the *thánadár* would reach the place some time during the early part of the night. He was not disappointed. Just before *khuphtan*[16] the *thánadár* passed that way, and, seeing somebody walking about the garden, he inquired who it was.

"The *wazír's* daughter," was the answer. "What are you looking for?"

"The thief," said the *thánadár*. Yesterday he disgraced your father, and before that the deputy-inspector; and now to-night I am trying my fortune."

15 The chief magistrate of a *pargana* (a district).

16 *Khuphtan* (Pers. *khuftan*, to sleep), 9 P.M.–10 P.M. Bedtime.

"Well, what would you do with the man if you got him?"

"I'd put him in the prison in chains, and flog him every day as hard as the blackguard could bear it."

"Oh, let me see the prison!" said the girl. "I've often wished to see it, but my father never would let me. Now is my opportunity. It is not far. I should so like to see the place!"

"You must wait for another time. I haven't leisure now. And besides, your father would be angry if he knew that you were outside the garden at this late hour."

"He will never know," replied the girl. "He is ill. He was brought home ill yesterday. Make haste. I am coming!"

Thus constrained, the *thánadár* led the way to the prison. Only one policeman was on guard there, as all the rest had been ordered out to find the thief. At the girl's request the *thánadár* showed her everything. He even put on the chains, and went within the cell and showed her how the thief would fare if he were caught and put in the prison. Then Shabrang (the *wazír's* daughter!) gave the *thánadár* a push and sent him toppling, and closed the door of the cell; and taking off the girl's dress, he put on the *thánadár's* turban and fastened the *thánadár's* belt round his waist, and went straight to the *thánadár's* house. Speaking hurriedly to the *thánadár's* wife, he said, "Give me some money and the jewels. I must leave the city and seek a living elsewhere. I have failed to find the thief, and therefore the king will no more favour me. Let me have these things and go. I will send you word where I am, and how and when you are to come to me."

The woman immediately gave him the jewels and several hundred rupees in cash. Shabrang then kissed her and went.

The following morning the king sent for the *thánadár*, and not finding him at home, caused search to be made for him throughout the city. Great was His Majesty's astonishment when he heard that the *thánadár* had been put into chains and placed within the innermost prison, and that the thief had visited the *thánadár's* house and obtained all the family jewels and the greater part of their savings. He called an assembly of all the wise men in his country to confer with them as to what should be done under the present distress. "You see," he said, "that it is useless to try and catch the thief. We may as well try to lay hold of the wind. The whole of the police and the greater part of the army have been watching for several days. Everybody has been on the alert. For the last week several in each house have always been awake. Greater precaution there could not have been, and yet the people are robbed. Our *wazír* and deputy-inspector and one of our *thánadárs* have been made laughing-stocks in the city. What can we do? If any person can help us, or if the thief himself will confess and promise to eschew his evil ways, we will give him our daughter in marriage and the half of our country."

On this Shabrang stepped forward and asked His Majesty's permission to speak. "O king, you have promised before all the great and wise in your land to give your daughter and the half of your country to the thief if he will only confess and desist from stealing."

"Yes," said His Majesty.

"Then know you, O king, that I am the thief; and to prove my words, let Your Majesty be pleased to command all those who have lost any money or property of any kind during the last few weeks to attend at a certain place outside the city on the morrow, and I will give them back their goods."

The whole assembly was electrified with astonishment. People stared at Shabrang as though he were a god. Some thought that he was mad and knew not what he said. At length, after some moments' dead pause, the king spoke and said, "It is well; it shall be so. Shabrang, attend me."

The king left with Shabrang, and the assembly was dismissed. In private His Majesty repeated his promise, and said that arrangements for the wedding and for the handing over of half of the country would be made as soon as possible.[17]

On the morrow all who had been robbed of anything gathered together in a large field by the wall of the city, and there, in the presence of the king and his *wazírs*, Shabrang restored all the money and jewels and clothes that he had taken. Everybody went away pleased, and there was peace again in the land.

On returning to the palace Shabrang begged the king to permit him to send for his mother, that he might get her counsel and help concerning the marriage. The king agreed, and Shabrang's mother was sent for.

She arrived as quickly as she could, and at once had an interview with the king. His Majesty received her most graciously, and expressed himself as most glad to be able to give his daughter to one so clever and handsome and well-bred as her son.

"Your Majesty speaks kindly," she replied, "but this marriage cannot be. It is not lawful to marry one's son with one's daughter. A brother cannot marry his own sister."

"I do not understand you," said the king.

"And no wonder," was the reply, "for you do not remember me; but this ring and this handkerchief will remind you of me. Take them, please, for they are yours, and give me back the ring which I gave you in exchange."

She then told him everything—how that she was his lawful wife; and how that, because he had forsaken her, she had visited him in disguise; and how that Shabrang

[17] Cf. "The Clever Thief," in *Tibetan Tales*, p. 43. In a story also told by Herodotus (Bk. II. ch. cxxi.), the king promises his daughter's hand to the robber, who reveals himself and receives the princess.

had been born to him; and how, when he had grown up, she had prevailed on him to go to the Kashmír court. Now was fulfilled what she spoke to him that day when they first met in her father's garden—"A boy should marry his father's daughter."

Then and there the king of Kashmír was reconciled to his wife, and Shabrang was acknowledged as prince and heir to the throne. Henceforth all three lived together for many many years in great joy and happiness." [18]

[18] Cf. the twelfth story of the *Madanakamárájankadai* (*The Dravidian Nights*) for a parallel tale; the commencement of the thirteenth tale of the *Baital Pachísí*; the story of "The Master Thief" in *Norse Tales*; *Tibetan Tales*, p. 43; *Orientalist*, vol. ii. Part iii.-iv. p. 48, and Part ix.-x. p. 167. The tale probably came from Herodotus, *vide Orientalist*, vol. ii. p. 168.

Kashmíris tell many such tales of Láiq *Tsúr*, and his companion Kabír *Tsúr*, and pupil Mahádev Bishta, who is now alive in Srínagar jail. Compare also several incidents in the history of She*kh* Núru'ddín as given in the *Rishináma*.

THE TROUBLESOME FRIEND.[1]

A MUQADDAM[2] became very friendly with another man of his village, who eventually proved to be such a mercenary individual that he determined to get rid of him. But this was easier said than done, for a very close friendship had sprung up between them, and he did not wish to seriously offend the fellow, as he had revealed to him too much of his own private affairs.

At last he hit on the following plan:—"Wife," said he, "this man will certainly call just as we are sitting down to dinner, in the hope that he also will get something to eat. I will go out now, but will come back later on to eat my food. You have a little, and put the rest aside, and when he comes tell him that we have finished our meal. If he says, 'Never mind. You can cook something else for me,' tell him that you dare not do so shameful a thing without your husband's permission. Be very civil to him, but do not give him any food."

When the man came the woman did as her husband had advised. "I am sorry, sir," she said, "that the *muqaddam* is out. If he were here he would undoubtedly kill a cock for you."

"Why are you sorry?" he said. "It does not matter if your husband is out. I am here, and I am not ashamed to kill a cock."

"Never," said the woman. "If my husband heard of such a thing he would be very angry with me. Please do

[1] Narrator's name, a shawl-weaver living in Srínagar.

[2] The chief man of a village. These *muqaddams* and the officers immediately above them are the real oppressors of the people in the valley.

not bother; but go, and come again at some other time when the *muqaddam* is in."

However, the man was not to be put off so easily. "Bother!" said he. "Believe me, I shall really like to do a little work. Come now, let me kill a cock while you prepare a fire to cook it for me. I will explain matters to the *muqaddam* when he returns." Saying this, he walked out into the yard where the fowls were kept, and taking one of the finest cocks he could catch, proceeded to kill it.

"Oh, please do not," cried the woman. "My husband will be here soon, and will get some food for you."

But the man was not to be put off. He at once killed a cock, and handing it to the woman, asked her to cook it for him. Seeing no way of escape out of the difficulty, the woman obeyed, but before the meal was ready the *muqaddam* returned.

"*Salám, salám*," he said to his friend, and after the few usual questions concerning his health and affairs, rushed to the kitchen and asked his wife what she had done. She told him everything.

"Very well," he said. "It is not of much consequence. We will get the better of this man yet. Listen,—when the cock is ready, mind you give him only a little, but give it in the copper pot.[3] Give me the rest, but set it before me in the earthen pot."

As soon as the meal was ready the woman did so. However, the man was too sharp for them. He noticed the meagre quantity placed before him, and the abundance that was set before the *muqaddam*. "No, no," he said. "Do you think that I am going to eat out of this copper pot and you out of that earthen pot? Never! This cannot be." Thus saying, he seized the *muqaddam's* pot, and put the copper one before him instead. In vain all remonstrance from the *muqaddam*. The latter might as well have held his breath.

[3] Kashmírí, *trám*, a copper vessel out of which the Musalmáns eat. Hindús do not make use of vessels made of this metal.

Seeing the state of affairs, the *muqaddam* looked most significantly towards his wife, and said, "For several days a *dev* has haunted our house. Once or twice he has appeared about this time and put out all the lights."

"Indeed," said the visitor.

The woman took the hint, and at once extinguished the lamp. When all was in total darkness the *muqaddam* put out his hand to take the earthenware pot from his friend; but the friend perceived the movement, and placing the pot in his left hand, seized the lamp-stand with the other and began to beat the *muqaddam* most unmercifully.

"Oh! oh!" exclaimed the *muqaddam.*

"What are you doing to my husband?" shouted the woman.

"The *dev* is trying to steal my food," said the man. "Be careful. Be careful!" he shouted to the supposed *dev,* and each time he struck him as hard as he could with the lamp-stand. At last the lamp-stand was broken, and the man ran out of the door, taking good care to carry the earthenware pot and its contents with him.[4]

[4] Compare the story of "Vidamundan Kodamundan" from Madras, *Indian Antiquary*, vol. xiv. pp. 77, 78. Cf. also Sinhalese story in *The Orientalist*, vol. ii. p. 147.

THE WICKED STEPMOTHER.[1]

One day a Bráhman adjured his wife not to eat anything without him lest she should become a she-goat. In reply the Bráhmaní begged him not to eat anything without her, lest he should be changed into a tiger. A long time passed by and neither of them broke their word, till one day the Bráhmaní, while giving food to her children, herself took a little to taste; and her husband was not present. That very moment she was changed into a goat.

When the Bráhman came home and saw the she-goat running about the house he was intensely grieved, because he knew that it was none other than his own beloved wife. He kept the goat tied up in the yard of his house, and tended it very carefully.

In a few years he married again, but this wife was not kind to the children. She at once took a dislike to them, and treated them unkindly and gave them little food. Their mother, the she-goat, heard their complainings, and noticed that they were getting thin, and therefore called one of them to her secretly, and bade the child tell the others to strike her horns with a stick whenever they were very hungry, and some food would fall down for them. They did so, and instead of getting weaker and thinner, as their stepmother had expected, they became stronger and stronger. She was surprised to see them getting so fat and strong while she was giving them so little food.

In course of time a one-eyed daughter was born to this wicked woman. She loved the girl with all her

[1] Narrator's name, Shiva Báyú, Renawarí, Srínagar.

heart, and grudged not any expense or attention that she thought the child required. One day, when the girl had grown quite big and could walk and talk well, her mother sent her to play with the other children, and ordered her to notice how and whence they obtained anything to eat. The girl promised to do so, and most rigidly stayed by them the whole day, and saw all that happened.

On hearing that the goat supplied her step-children with food the woman got very angry, and determined to kill the beast as soon as possible. She pretended to be very ill, and sending for the *hakím*, bribed him to prescribe some goat's flesh for her. The Bráhman was very anxious about his wife's state, and although he grieved to have to slay the goat (for he was obliged to kill the goat, not having money to purchase another), yet he did not mind if his wife really recovered. But the little children wept when they heard this, and went to their mother, the she-goat, in great distress, and told her everything.

"Do not weep, my darlings," she said. "It is much better for me to die than to live such a life as this. Do not weep. I have no fear concerning you. Food will be provided for you, if you will attend to my instructions. Be sure to gather my bones, and bury them all together in some secret place, and whenever you are very hungry go to that place and ask for food. Food will then be given you."

The poor she-goat gave this advice only just in time. Scarcely had it finished these words and the children had departed than the butcher came with a knife and slew it. Its body was cut into pieces and cooked, and the step-mother had the meat, but the step-children got the bones. They did with them as they had been directed, and thus got food regularly and in abundance.

Some time after the death of the she-goat one morning one of the step-daughters was washing her face in the stream that ran by the house, when her nose-ring unfastened and fell into the water. A fish happened to see it and swallowed it, and this fish was caught by a man and sold to the king's cook for His Majesty's dinner.[2] Great was the surprise of the cook when, on opening the fish to clean it, he found the nose-ring. He took it to the king, who was so interested in it that he issued a proclamation and sent it to every town and village in his dominions, that whosoever had missed a nose-ring should apply to him. Within a few days the brother of the girl reported to the king that the nose-ring belonged to his sister, who had lost it one day while bathing her face in the river. The king ordered the girl to appear before him, and was so fascinated by her pretty face and nice manner that he married her, and provided amply for the support of her family."[3]

[2] Cf. story of "True Friendship" in this collection.

[3] Cf. Servian story in *Vuk Karajich*, No. 32; a Greek variant of the story (Hahn, No. 2); the Sicilian tale (Pitré, No. 41). This story evidently belongs to the "Cinderella" cycle. *Vide* Professor Ralston's interesting paper in the *Nineteenth Century*, xxxiii. pp. 832–854. One of the most significant features of these stories is that which refers to the dead mother's guardianship of her distressed children. "The idea that such a protection might be exercised is of great antiquity and of wide circulation."

TRUE FRIENDSHIP.[1]

A KING and his chief *wazír* were in great trouble. Neither of them had been blest with a son.

A like trouble had bound the king and *wazír* very much together. They appeared happy only in one another's society. Very rarely were they to be seen separate. Where the king was, there the *wazír* also would certainly be; and where the *wazír* was, there the king also would assuredly be found. One morning they went hunting together in a jungle, where they came across a *gosáín* squatting before a fire and evidently worshipping, for he did not look up or in any way notice his illustrious visitors.

"Let us speak to him," said the king. "Maybe the good man will do something for us." Accordingly they both prostrated themselves before the man and told him all their trouble.

"Grieve not," replied the *gosáín*, still bending down his head, "grieve not. Take these two mangoes, and give one to one wife, and the other to the other wife, and bid them eat. Then they each shall bear a son."

Thanking the *gosáín*, the king and the *wazír* returned and carried out his instructions; and in the course of nine months and nine days their wives gave birth to two fine boys. What rejoicings there were in the palace, and in the *wazír's* house, and in the city, and in all the country round when these two boys were born! Gifts were lavished without measure on the bráhmans, the poor were feasted everywhere, and all prisoners were re-

[1] Narrator's name, Shiva Báyú, Renawárí, Srínagar.

leased. Never was there such a time known in the land before.

As will be supposed, great care was bestowed on the young scions of such noble houses. While they were infants they were attended to by several experienced *dáís*, and when they were of an age to learn they were instructed by the best masters. No pains or money were spared to make them proficient in every way; and so much did they profit with all these advantages, that they both became prodigies in learning and prowess and art.

Like their fathers, they too became much attached to one another, and were generally to be found together. One day they went together to a certain jungle to hunt. They rode about the place for several hours, till the prince becoming very tired and thirsty, they dismounted. The horses were fastened to a tree, and the prince sat down by them, while the *wazír's* son went in quest of water. He quickly found a stream, and forgetting the prince, started off to discover its source. He went on a mile or so, till he came to a little spring, where he beheld a lovely fairy reclining beside a great lion. He noticed, too, that the beast seemed afraid of the fairy. Surprised at this strange sight he immediately turned and ran back to the prince as fast as he could, taking with him a little water on the way.

"Where have you been so long? Why do you look so? What has happened?" inquired the prince when the *wazír's* son appeared.

"Oh! nothing," replied the *wazír's* son.

"But something has occurred," persisted the prince. "I can see it in your face."

"O brother," replied the *wazír's* son, "I have seen the most lovely creature in the world, and a lion was by her side, and the animal seemed afraid of her,—such was the power of her beauty."

"I also would like to see this woman. Come along, take me to her," said the prince.

The *wazír's* son agreed. So they both went together to the place, and found the lion asleep, with its head in the fairy's lap.

"Don't be afraid," said the *wazír's* son. "Let us go right up and seize the woman while the beast is sleeping."

They both went close up, and the *wazír's* son raised the lion's head and laid it on the ground, while the prince took the fairy's hand and led her away. The *wazír's* son remained.

When the lion awoke, and saw nobody there except the *wazír's* son, it said, "What has become of the fairy?"

"My friend has taken her away," replied the *wazír's* son.

"Your friend?" repeated the lion. "Is he your friend who has left you to die alone? Surely such a one is your most bitter enemy. No real friend would act like this. Listen to me, and I will tell you a story of some true friends:—

"Once upon a time there were three friends; one was a prince, the other was a bráhman, and the third was a carpenter.[2] Each of them had some special gift. The prince was well qualified in settling hard and difficult disputes; the bráhman could raise the dead to life again; and the carpenter could make a house of sandal wood that would go here and there at the command of its owner.

"One day the bráhman was banished from his home. Something unpleasant had cropped up between him and his parents; so the latter turned him away. In the hour of his distress he sought his two friends, and told them everything, and entreated them to depart with him to some distant country. The prince and the carpenter both agreed. Accordingly they all started together. They had not gone far, when the prince for some reason or other stopped. The others, however, proceeded on their way. After a while the prince hastened forward, thinking to overtake them; but he unfortunately followed a wrong path, and did not find them. On and on he went, how-

[2] Cf. *Wide-Awake Stories*, pp. 48, 256; *Bilochi Stories*, p. 33.

ever, hoping to reach them, and wondering why they were walking so fast. Meanwhile the bráhman and the carpenter were going on very slowly and wondering why the prince lagged behind, till at last they gave him up, thinking that he had become home-sick and returned to the palace.

"In the course of his wanderings the prince arrived at an immense plain, in the midst of which was a grand and lofty building. 'Who lives here?' thought he. 'Some mighty potentate most assuredly. I will go and inquire.' On entering the building a most beautiful woman came forward to meet him.

"'Come in,' she said in a most kindly tone, and began to weep.

"'Why do you weep?' he asked.

"'Because,' she replied, 'your beauty and your youth excite my compassion for you. In your ignorance you have wandered to the gates of death. Oh! why did you not inquire before venturing on this journey? Knew you not that a *rákshasa* resides here, who has eaten every human being for many a mile around? Alas! alas! what shall I say? I am afraid that you too will be devoured by him.'

"'No, no,' said the prince. 'Speak not so despondingly. Advise me, please, and I shall be saved.'

"'But I really do not know what to do for your safety,' said the woman, and sobbed. At length, however, she led him to a room at the back of the house, and shut him up in a big box that was there. 'Now remain here quietly till I come again,' she said, 'and may Parameshwar preserve you.'

"In the evening the *rákshasa* returned. His keen sense of smell soon detected the presence of another human being in the place. 'Another person is here besides yourself,' he said. 'Who is it? Tell me quickly. I am hungry.'

"'You cannot be very well to-day,' replied the woman.

'No person has been here. Who do you suppose would dare to approach this place, which has become the terror of all the world?'

"On this the *rákshasa* was quiet; and the woman, seeing the effect of her words, gained confidence and played with him, and among other conversation asked him to inform her of the secret of his life. 'You leave me every day,' she said; 'and when you go I know not when you will return. I sometimes fear that you will never come back, and then I—what shall I do? whither shall I go? The people hate me for your sake, and will come and kill me. Oh! tell me that there is no cause for fear.'

"'My darling,' said the *rákshasa*, 'do not weep. I shall never die. Except this pillar be broken,' pointing to one of the massive pillars that supported the front verandah of the building, 'I cannot die. But who is there that knows this thing to do it?'

"The following morning the *rákshasa* went forth as usual, and directly he was out of sight the woman went and released the prince, and related to him all the adventures of the night. The prince was very glad when he heard what had happened. 'Now is the time,' said he. 'I will immediately destroy this pillar, and rid the land of the monster.' Thus saying, he struck the pillar again and again, till it was broken into several pieces; and it was as if each stroke had fallen on the *rákshasa*, for he howled most loudly and trembled exceedingly every time the prince hit the pillar, until at last, when the pillar fell down, the *rákshasa* also fell down and gave up the ghost.

"The prince stayed with the beautiful woman in the grand house, and people came in crowds to thank him for slaying the *rákshasa*. Henceforth peace and plenty reigned in the country. The surrounding land was again cultivated, villages were again inhabited, and the air was again filled with the songs of a happy and prosperous people. But true happiness does not flow on in even course for ever. One day the woman was arranging her hair by a window of the house, when a crow flew down and carried off the comb that she had placed on the sill. The bird carried it far away to the sea and let it drop. There it was swallowed by a big fish, and this fish chanced to be caught by a fisherman, and being a fine fish, was carried to the palace to be prepared for the king. In cleaning the fish the comb was found. Thinking it very curious, the cook showed it to the king. When His Majesty saw the comb he expressed a great wish to behold its former owner. He despatched messengers in every direction to try to find the woman, and promised an immense reward to any person who would bring her to him. After a while a woman was found who recognised the comb, and promised to introduce the owner of it to the king as soon as she could conveniently do so. She visited the wife of the prince, and quickly contrived to ingratiate herself in her favour. She got an invitation to come and stay at the house altogether, which she accepted. When she saw that she could not possibly accomplish her purpose so long as the prince was alive she poisoned the prince, and bribed the *hákím* to declare that he had died a natural death. Oh how the wife of the prince grieved when he died! People thought that she too would die. She would not give up the corpse, but had it placed in a big strong box and kept in her own private room. She had often heard of her husband's two friends, and what they could do, and hoped much to see them some day and get her husband restored to life.

"At the earliest opportunity the wicked go-between persuaded the woman to leave the house, the scene of so much trouble, and to come and reside with her for a time. The woman agreed. As soon as she had got her into her house the go-between sent to the king and secretly informed him of her success, whereupon His Majesty came and took the woman away by force to his palace and entreated her to live with him as his wife. She said that she would, but asked him to defer the marriage for six months, because her religious adviser had persuaded her to do so. The king was intensely happy in the thought of her affection, and waited anxiously for the day. He had a little palace built expressly for her near the roadside, and allowed her to live alone in it. Meanwhile the woman was praying and longing for some news of her deceased husband's friends. She was inquiring everywhere, and was watching from her window every day, lest peradventure they should pass that way.

"One day she saw two men coming along together in the direction of the house. 'Who are you, and whence do you come?' she asked.

"'We are travellers,' they said, 'and after much journeying have reached this place. We have lost our prince and friend, and are looking for him everywhere.'

"'Come in,' she said, 'and rest a while. Come in and tell me more of your friend who is lost. Perhaps I can help you to find him.'

"'Show us,' said they, 'where the prince is, and we shall be happy.' So they both entered the palace, and sitting down with the woman, told her all their history.

"'Praise, praise!' she exclaimed. 'I can tell you what has become of your friend; but, alas! he is dead.'

"'Never mind,' said the bráhman; 'I can restore him to life again. Thanks, a thousand thanks, that we have reached this place! May Parameshwar bless you, lady, with all that heart can desire! Show us the body of our beloved friend once more.'

"'But stay,' said she. 'We must act with great caution. The king of this country is deeply in love with me. I have plighted myself to him. Nearly six months has he waited for the marriage at my request, and now the day is near when he will come and fetch me. We must be very careful, because His Majesty has surrounded me with servants, who give information of all that transpires here.

Without doubt he has already been informed of your presence in this place. How can we escape?'

"'Fear not, lady,' said the carpenter. 'If you can procure me a little sandal wood, I will construct for you a house that will remove from place to place at the owner's pleasure.'

"'Very well,' said the woman; 'I will try to get it for you.'

"Presently a messenger was speeding to the king's palace with a letter written after this manner:—'O king, I have betrothed myself to you. The day of our wedding draws nigh. Be pleased, I pray you, to send me three hundred maunds of sandal wood.' The king complied at once with her request. When the house was quite ready the woman sent another letter to the king after this manner:—'O king, most gracious and good! The day of our wedding is at hand. Be pleased, I pray you, to allow my sister-in-law and the wife of my brother-in-law to come to me without delay. There are some matters on which I wish to have their counsel.' The king complied with this request also.

"As soon as the two women reached the sandal wood house, where the woman and her friends were waiting for them, the carpenter ordered the building to transport them to the *rákshasa's* palace, where they would find the prince, and be able to enjoy themselves, and be safe from all attacks of the king. Away the house went, and so quietly, that the women knew not what was happening. They were talking to one another and admiring the beauty of the structure, when suddenly they found themselves looking at the lovely palace of the dead *rákshasa*. There the bráhman was shown the corpse of the prince, whom he restored to life again by touching his hand.

"Now all was joy and gladness again. The prince was formally married to the lovely woman, who turned out to be the daughter of one of the mightiest kings of that time; and his two friends the bráhman and the carpenter were married to her sister-in-law and brother-in-law's wife. And they all lived happily together to the end of their days in the *rákshasa's* palace.

"*O wazír's* son!" said the lion on finishing the story, "such men as the bráhman and the carpenter are friends. Speak not of the prince, who has gone off with the fairy and left you here to perish alone—speak not of him as a friend. However, you shall not perish. I will not harm you. Depart to your house, and may peace be with you."[3]

[3] Compare variant in *Indian Antiquary*, vol. x. p. 228 ff.; also tale of "The Shipwrecked Prince" in this collection.

THREE BLIND MEN.[1]

"O NÁRÁYAN, grant me, I beseech thee, one hundred rupees, and I will give ten of them in thy name to the poor." Thus ejaculated a poor bráhman one day as he walked along the *bázár*, wondering how he should get the next meal. Náráyan had pity on him, and heard his prayer. The bráhman at once received the money, part of which he kept in one hand open, ready for distribution among the poor, and the remainder he held in the other hand, tied up in a handkerchief. Presently he came across a blind man begging, and gave him ten rupees, as he had promised in his prayer.

Astonished at such unwonted liberality, the blind man inquired, "Why have you given me this money?"

The bráhman replied, "Náráyan has just sent me one hundred rupees on the condition that I give ten of them in his name to the poor."

"May you be blessed!" said the blind man. "Please show me all the money. I have never felt a hundred rupees all together in my life. Do please let me feel them."

Nothing suspecting, the bráhman readily put the handkerchief into the beggar's hand. Foolish man! he must have been simple to do so. Of course the blind man immediately pretended that all the money was his, and when the bráhman remonstrated with him and laid hold of the handkerchief again, the fellow shouted with all his might, "Help, help! This man is a thief, and is

[1] Narrator's name, Shiva Rám, Banah Mahal, Srínagar.

trying to take away all that I possess. Seize him, O people! I have not sufficient strength to hold him any longer."[2]

"What has he done?" cried they all.

"He has taken my money," was the reply. "See! he has it here in his hand—ninety rupees altogether. Count them, and prove my words."

The people seized the bráhman, and counted the rupees; and finding the money to be the same as the blind beggar had said, they naturally believed him, and gave him the money. In vain the bráhman protested. The people would not believe him. His tale seemed most unlikely. Accordingly he left the place, and walked home as fast as he could.

"What a fool you were to show the money!" said his wife, when she heard what had happened. "Have you not yet discovered the cunning of these blind men? Go now and follow up this fellow, and watch where he puts the money."

The bráhman soon discovered the blind beggar. He was slowly walking towards a mosque, on reaching which he entered and sat down. "Nobody is here," he said to himself after a brief pause. However, to make quite sure, he felt with his stick all over the place. "Yes, the place is quite empty," said he; "I am quite safe." Then he went to a corner of the mosque and removed an inch or so of the earth, and put the hundred rupees into an earthen pot which he had secreted there. "Thank God!" he exclaimed. "I had only one thousand rupees this morning; but now I have eleven hundred. Thanks be to God!"

When the bráhman heard these words he was very glad. As soon as the beggar came out of the mosque he went in, and quickly took out the earthen pot of rupees and carried it to his house.

On arrival his wife praised him, and said, "Now you

[2] Cf. *Old Deccan Days*, p. 264.

must go again, and see what the blind man will do. Keep your wits about you."

The bráhman went. All the next day he steadfastly followed the beggar, until he again found himself in the mosque, where the man had gone as usual to deposit the few *páṅsas* that he had received during the day.

Great was the grief of the blind man when he found the earthen pot and all his treasure taken away. He beat his face and breast, and made such a noise that the *malah* went in to see what was the matter. Now this *malah* also was blind, and a great scamp.

"What are you doing," he asked, "disturbing the neighbourhood and desecrating this place? Out with you. You will bring a curse on us and the mosque. Be off at once, or I will call the people, and you will suffer for this behaviour."

"Oh, sir," cried the beggar, "I have been robbed of everything that I possess. Some thief has visited this place and taken every *páṅsa* of mine. What shall I do? What shall I do?"

"You are a great fool!" said the *malah*. "Stop your crying and learn better for the future. Who ever heard of a man keeping eleven hundred rupees in an earthen pot hidden just under the ground of a public place like this mosque, where people are accustomed to come and go at all hours of the day? If you had managed as I have done this would never have happened."

"How do you manage?" asked the poor beggar.

"Listen," replied the *malah*. "I have a big hollow stick, in which I keep all my money. This stick I always have by me. See, here it is;" and he touched the beggar on the foot with it. "Go and get another stick like it, and you shall have no fear about your money."

On hearing this the bráhman carefully watched the blind *malah*, in the hope of getting his money also. He cut a big hollow stick, something like the *malah's* stick; and as soon as he found opportunity he changed the sticks.

The *malah* always put his stick into the ground when he prayed, and as he prayed frequently the bráhman was not kept waiting very long.

His wife again praised him when she heard what he had done and saw the piles of rupees that he had brought back with him. "Go again," she said to him, "and see what this *malah* will do. May be that you will discover more treasure."

The bráhman obeyed, and found the old *malah* sitting by another blind *malah*, and weeping bitterly over his great loss.

"Curses be on you," said the other blind *malah*, "for your foolishness! Listen, and I will tell you what I do with my money. All my money I keep sewed up in my clothes. Who can take it from me? I advise you to do likewise."

When he heard these words the bráhman went and bought a hive full of bees. This hive he placed at the bottom of a large earthen jar, and over the hive he spread a thick layer of honey. "Ha, ha! this will frighten him," said he, as he walked disguised as a *musalmán* to the house of the other blind *malah*, to present him with the jar full of honey (?)

The *malah* was very pleased with the gift, and blessed the man. Then the bráhman left. But he only went a short distance, for he wished to keep near the house till the *malah* had finished the honey.

As soon as the man had left the *malah* began to take out the honey and to put it into smaller vessels, as he did not wish to be seen with so much of the good thing in his possession at one time. He filled one or two small pots, and began to poke the hive about to get out some more, when the bees, not liking such rough treatment, flew out and stung him.

In vain he ran about and beat himself; the bees were most determined, and had no mercy. There was no help for it; the blind *malah* was obliged to take off his cloak and throw it aside, and then to escape into his house. All the bees followed him. Poor man! he would have been stung to death by them if his wife had not arrived with a thick branch of a mulberry-tree, and beat them off.

Meanwhile the bráhman had carried off the cloak. On reaching home his wife praised him more than ever. "We are very rich now," she said, "and shall not need anything more for the rest of our lives."

As soon as the *malah* recovered from the stings, and knew that his precious cloak had been stolen, he was much distressed. He went and told his trouble to the other blind *malah*, and they both went together and informed the blind beggar. After a while the three blind men determined to get an interview with the king, and to ask him to cause strict search to be made for the thief.

His Majesty listened most attentively, and was exceedingly interested in their stories, and wished very much to know who it was that could thus deceive three such shrewd, clever men. He ordered proclamation by drum to be made throughout the city, that whosoever had done this thing, and would confess it, should obtain free pardon from the king, and be abundantly rewarded.

Accordingly the bráhman went and explained everything to His Majesty, and the king said, "*Shábásh!*[3] But have you done this of yourself, or has another advised you?"

"My wife prompted me, Your Majesty," replied the bráhman, "and I did so."

"It is well," said the king, who gave him many presents, and then sent him away.[4]

[3] A well-known exclamation, meaning "Bravo!"

[4] The sharpness of a woman's wits forms the theme of scores of tales in the East. *Vide* "All for a *Páṅsa*," "The Stupid Husband and Clever Wife," and "Why the Fish Talked," in this collection.

ALL FOR A PAŃSA.[1]

THERE lived in the valley a very wealthy merchant, who had an exceedingly stupid and ignorant son. Although the best teachers were provided for the lad, yet he learnt nothing. He was too idle, too careless, too thick-headed to exert himself or to profit by what he heard; he preferred to loll away his time instead. One does not wonder, therefore, that his father gradually got to despise him; but his mother, as was natural, hoped for the best, and was always making excuses for him.

When the lad had reached a marriageable age his mother begged the merchant to seek out a suitable wife for him. The merchant, however, was too much ashamed and grieved to have anything to do or say about his stupid son, and in his own mind had fully determined never to have him married. But the mother had set her heart on this. It was the one thing that she had been looking forward to for years. To have the lad remain a bachelor all his life would be an intolerable disgrace; it would also be contrary to all religion and practice. She would not consent to this for a moment. And so she urged other excuses on her son's behalf. She professed to have now and again noticed extraordinary traits of wisdom and intelligence in him. This sort of speech only aggravated the merchant. "Look here," he said to her one day, when she had been eulogising her son, "I have heard this many times before, but never once proved it. I do not believe there is a particle of truth in it. Mothers are blind. However, to assure you, I will give the fool another trial.

[1] Narrator's name, Makund Báyú, Suthú, Srínagar.

Send for him, and give him these three *páṅsas*. Tell him to go to the *bázár*, and with one *páṅsa* to buy something for himself, to throw another *páṅsa* into the river, and with the remaining *páṅsa* to get at least five things—something to eat, something to drink, something to gnaw, something to sow in the garden, and some food for the cow."[2]

The woman did so, and the boy left.

He went to the *bázár* and bought a *páṅsa*-worth of something for himself, and ate it. He then came to the river, and was on the point of throwing a *páṅsa* into the water, when he suddenly perceived the absurdity of so doing, and checked himself. "What is the good of doing this?" he said aloud. "If I throw the *páṅsa* into the river I shall have only one left. What can I buy with one *páṅsa*—to eat and drink and be all the other things my mother asks for? And yet if I do not throw this *páṅsa* away I shall be acting disobediently."

In the midst of this soliloquy the daughter of an iron-smith came up, and seeing his distressed countenance, asked what was the matter. He told her all that his mother had ordered him to do, and that he thought it extremely stupid to obey. But what was he to do? He did not wish to disobey his mother.

"I will advise you," she said. "Go and buy a water-melon with one *páṅsa*, and keep the other in your pocket. Do not throw it into the river. The water-melon contains all the five things you need. Get one, and give it to your mother, and she will be pleased."

The boy did so.

When the merchant's wife saw the cleverness of her son she was very glad. She really thought that he was exceedingly wise. "Look," she said to her husband as soon as he came in, "this is our son's work."

[2] The Kashmírí words used were: *Khyun, chun, tah trakun, tah wárih wawun, tah gov kyut khurák.* This is also a riddle, of which the answer is *Hĕndawĕnd*, a water-melon.

On seeing the water-melon the merchant was surprised, and replied,[3] "I do not believe that the lad has done this of himself. He would never have had the sense. Somebody has been advising him." And then, turning to the boy, he asked, "Who told you to do this?"

The lad replied, "The daughter of an ironsmith."

"You see," said the merchant to his wife. "I knew this was not the work of that stupid. However, let him be married—and if you agree and he wishes it—to this ironsmith's daughter, who has so interested herself in him, and seems so very clever."

"Yes, yes," replied the woman; "nothing could be better."

In a few days the merchant visited the ironsmith's house, and saw the girl that had helped his son. "Are you alone?" he inquired.

"Yes," she replied.

"Where are your parents?"

"My father," she said, "has gone to buy a ruby for a cowrie, and my mother has gone to sell some words. But they both will be here presently. Please to wait till they come."

"Very well," said the merchant, much perplexed by the girl's words. "Where did you say your parents had gone?"

"My father has gone to get a cowrie's worth of ruby, *i.e.*, he has gone to buy some oil for the lamp; and my mother has gone to sell a few words, *i.e.*, she has gone to try and arrange a marriage for somebody."

The merchant was much struck with the girl's cleverness; but he reserved his thoughts.

Presently both the ironsmith and his wife returned. They were astonished to see the great and wealthy merchant in their humble abode. Giving him a most respectful *salám*, they inquired, "Why have you thus honoured our house?"

[3] Cf. *Madanakamárájankadai* (*The Dravidian Nights*), p. 63.

He informed them that he wanted their daughter as a wife for his son. Of course, the offer was readily accepted. A day was fixed for the wedding, and the merchant returned to his house.

"It is all right," he said to his wife. "The people have agreed to the marriage, and the day has been arranged."

The wind carried the news everywhere, and people began to talk among themselves concerning the supposed severity of the merchant in marrying his son to one so much lower in rank than himself. Some busybodies even went so far as to prejudice the merchant's son against the girl. They advised him to warn her father that if he continued to sanction this unsuitable union, and the marriage really took place, he would beat the girl seven times a day with a shoe. They thought that when the ironsmith heard this, he would be frightened and break off the engagement. "However," they added, "even supposing that the man is not frightened and the marriage is celebrated, it will be a good thing if you thus treat your wife at first. She will in this way learn obedience and never give you any trouble."[4]

The stupid fellow thought this was a splendid plan, and acted accordingly.

The ironsmith was very much disturbed. As soon as he saw his daughter he informed her what the merchant's son had said, and begged her to have nothing to do with the man. "It were better," he said, "never to be married, than to be joined to one who would treat you like a dog-thief."

"Do not be distressed, dear father," she replied. "Evidently this man has been influenced by some wicked persons to come to you and say this thing. But be not troubled. It will never be. There is a wide gap between what a man says and what a man does. Do not fear for me. What he says will never come to pass."

On the appointed day the marriage was celebrated. At

[4] Cf. *Dictionary of Kashmírí Proverbs and Sayings*, p. 35; also Persian "Story of Beating the Cat."

midnight the bridegroom arose. Thinking his wife was fast asleep, he took up a shoe and was about to strike her, when she opened her eyes. "Do not so," she said. "It is a bad omen to quarrel on one's wedding-day. To-morrow if you still desire to strike me, then strike me; but do not let us quarrel to-day." The following night the bridegroom again lifted his shoe to strike her, but she again begged him to desist, saying, "It is a bad omen when husband and wife disagree during the first week of their marriage. I know that you are a wise man and will hear me. Defer this purpose of yours till the eighth day, and then beat me as much as you think proper." The man agreed, and flung the shoe on one side. On the seventh day the woman returned to her father's house, according to the custom of all muhammadan brides.

"Aha! aha!" said the young man's friends when they met him. "So she has got the better of you. Aha! what a fool you are! We knew it would be so."

Meanwhile the merchant's wife had been planning for her son's future. She thought it was quite time he occupied an independent position. She said, therefore, to her husband, "Give him some merchandise, and let him travel."

"Never," replied the merchant. "It would be like throwing money into the water to give it into his hands. He would only squander it away."

"Never mind," persisted the wife. "He will learn wisdom in this way only. Give him some money, and let him visit distant countries. If he makes money, then we may hope that he will value it. If he loses the money, and becomes a beggar, then we may hope, also, that he will value it when he again gets it. By either experience he will profit. Without one of these experiences he will never be fit for anything."

The merchant was persuaded, and calling his son, gave him a certain amount of money and some goods and servants, and bidding him be careful, sent him away. The young merchant set out with his wife and a great company of servants. The caravan had not proceeded far before they passed a large garden, which was completely surrounded by thick high walls. "What is this place?" asked the young merchant. "Go and see what is inside." The servants went, and came back and informed their master that they had seen a grand, lofty building in the midst of a beautiful garden. Then the young merchant himself went and entered the garden. On looking at the grand building he saw a lovely woman, who beckoned to him to come and play a game of *nard*[5] with her. This woman was an inveterate gambler. She was acquainted with all manner of tricks for getting her opponent's money. One of her favourite tricks was this: while playing she kept by her side a cat that she had taught at a given sign to brush by the lamp and extinguish the light. This sign she always gave when the game was going against her. In this way, of course, she obtained immense wealth. She practised the cat-trick on the young merchant much to his loss. Everything went—his money, his merchandise, his wife, his servants, himself; and then, when there was nothing left, he was put in prison. Here he was treated with great harshness. Often he lifted up his voice and prayed that God would take him out of this troublous world.

One day he saw a man pass by the prison-gate. He hailed him, and inquired whence he had come. "I come from such-and-such a country," replied the man, mentioning the country where the young merchant's father lived.

"It is well," said the prisoner. "Will you do me a great kindness? You see I am shut up in this place. I cannot get free till I have paid a great debt that I owe. I want you to deliver these two letters to my father and wife. Here is the letter for my father, and this is for my wife. If you will do this for me I shall be eternally grateful to you."

[5] Chess, draughts, &c. Any game played with counters.

The man consented, took the two letters, and went on his way.[6]

In one letter the young merchant told his father all that had happened; and in the other for his wife he dissembled matters, saying that he now had a large amount of money, and would soon return and beat her head with the shoe, as he had forewarned her.

As soon as the man had transacted the little business which he had to do in that place, he went back to his country and delivered the two letters; but, being ignorant of writing, he gave the letter which was intended for the father to the wife, and that which was meant for the wife to the father! On reading the good news the father was exceedingly glad. He could not understand, however, why the letter was addressed to his daughter-in-law and not to himself, and why his son threatened her with a severe beating on his return. When the daughter-in-law read her husband's letter, telling of his misfortune and distress, she became very sad, and wondered why he had sent the letter in her father-in-law's name and not in her own. In her perplexity she went to her father-in-law. The surprise of both will be more easily imagined than described, when they compared the two accounts. It was a mystery.

After a little conversation the daughter-in-law—wise, brave woman like she was—determined to go and see her husband, and, if possible, to set him free. The old merchant also sanctioned her going, and gave her some money for the expenses of the way.

Disguised as a man, the brave woman started, and reached the place where the lovely woman dwelt. She informed the gambler that she was the son of a wealthy merchant, and knowing something of the game, wished to try his skill with her. The gambler readily consented. In the evening they were to play. Meanwhile the would-be merchant's son visited the wicked woman's

[6] Cf. *Wide-Awake Stories*, pp. 277–279 and 427.

servants, and begged them to acquaint her with the trickery by which the woman won so much money. At first the servants demurred, but when they saw the piles of *ashrafís* and the beautiful things that the young merchant temptingly placed before them they were persuaded, and informed her of everything. Moreover, they told her that their mistress would probably try the cat-trick again that evening. Then the would-be merchant's son left. By the evening, when she arrived and sent in her *salám* to the woman, she had provided herself with a mouse, which she kept concealed in the folds of a sleeve of her jerkin.

The play commenced. Being an exceedingly good player, the would-be merchant's son soon began to win. Noticing this, the wicked gambling woman gave a sign to her cat. The cat moved towards the lamp, when the would-be young merchant let the mouse run free. Away went the mouse quickly, and away went the cat after it, helter-skelter all over the room.

"Can't we go on with the game?" said the would-be young merchant after a brief pause. Nothing hindering, she soon won the game, and a second game, and a third, and a fourth, till she had not only got back all that her stupid husband had lost, but the grand house, and servants, and wicked woman also.

Putting all her easily gotten treasure into large boxes, she then sent to the prison and released all the prisoners. Her husband came with others to thank her, but did not recognise his benefactress. She, however, specially noticed him, and asked if he would like to be her *sardár*.[6] Being thoroughly helpless, he agreed; and presently, having changed his ragged prison-garments for some suitable raiment that the young would-be merchant had sent for him, he appeared to arrange for her departure. His old ragged garments were placed in a little box by themselves. All the keys of the various boxes were entrusted to the

[6] Head-man.

sardár, but the key of the box wherein these ragged clothes were packed was kept by the would-be young merchant. Everything ready, they left, taking the wicked gambling woman with them.

On arriving near her own country the would-be young merchant said to her *sardár*, "I am going on a private business in this direction. But do not bother about me. Go straight to the city and take these things with you, and keep them carefully in your house till I come. I know your father, and can trust you. If I should not come to you within twenty full days, then these things will be yours."

By a circuitous path she went to her home. Her *sardár* also, with the wicked gambling woman and all the servants, and all the baggage except the box containing the ragged garments, went straight to his home. On reaching her home she told her father of her great success, and begged him to keep the matter quiet. In a few days she visited her father-in-law. As soon as her husband saw her he said—

"Do you remember how many times I have to beat you?" and saying this, he pretended to take off one of his shoes.

"Oh, fie! fie!" said his parents, "would you spoil this grand home-coming by such mean and cruel acts?"

And said his wife, "Now I see. I thought that you would certainly have learnt wisdom; but you have not. You are the same stupid that you always were. Look here. Bring that box to me—the little box that I have had in my own keeping all the way—bring it to me. Whose are these dirty garments? Yours or another's? Look on these and remember how the jailers treated you—how severely they beat you, what little and what bad food they gave you, and what bad names they threw at you! Ah! you tremble, and well may you tremble. Listen! I am the wealthy merchant's son who delivered you. The letter addressed to your father was brought to me. I read of your distress, and at once set out, and disguised as a young merchant, introduced myself to the woman who fooled you. I played with the woman, and won back everything that you had lost, and the woman's house and property besides. There is the woman. Go and ask her if she recognises me."

"Yes, yes," said the gambling woman.

The merchant's son said nothing; he was confounded. The merchant's wife looked on her daughter-in-law and blessed her. The merchant himself was too angry and disappointed with his stupid son to say or do anything. At last he said, turning to his wife, "Now do you believe that your son is a fool? Let all these goods and jewels be retained by his wife. She is too good for him."

PRIDE ABASED.[1]

In times long past there lived a certain king, who was so occupied with and so proud of his own thoughts and words and actions, that his name became a proverb in the land. "As selfish as our king," "As proud as our king," the people used to say. As will be supposed, the courtiers and *wazírs* of this king were thoroughly tired of hearing him, and of having to add fuel to the fire by assent and flattery.

"Ah! where is there such another country as this—such soil, so well irrigated and so fertile?" he would ask.

"Nowhere, O king!" the *wazírs* and courtiers would reply.

"Where are there such just and clever laws, and such a prosperous people?"

"Nowhere else, O king!"

"Where is there such a splendid palace as mine?"

"Nowhere anything to be compared with it, O king!"

"Ah! yes;" and then His Majesty would stroke his beard and draw a long breath, as though overburdened with a sense of his own greatness.

Nearly every audience of the king was disturbed by such performances as these. It was becoming very wearisome; and the more so as the king was a man of moderate attainments, and his country and people also were of an ordinary character. At length some of the *wazírs* determined to answer him truthfully the next time he put such questions to them. They had not long to wait for an opportunity.

"Think you," said His Majesty, "that there is another

[1] Narrator's name, Makund Báyú, who resides at Suthú, Srínagar.

king greater than I, or another kingdom more powerful and glorious than mine?"

"Yes, O king, there are," they replied.

On hearing this unusual answer His Majesty got very angry. "Where is this king? Tell me quickly," he said, "that I may take my army and go to fight with him."

"Be not hasty, O king," they replied. "Consider, we pray you, before you act, lest you be defeated and your country ruined."

But the king became more angry than before. He ordered his whole army to be assembled, and as soon as they were ready he rode forth at their head, and sent messengers in every direction to challenge the people to fight.

For a considerable time he would seem to have inspired all countries and all peoples with awe, because nobody accepted the challenge, there being no pretext for such slaughter as there would be in a big battle, unless it was to satisfy this selfish and proud king. But at last another king appeared with his army, and defeated the selfish and proud king, and took away all his kingdom and all his glory and all his power.

Here was an end to his pride. Crushed in spirit, he disguised himself and escaped with his queen and two sons to some place by the side of the sea, where he found a ship ready to sail. He asked the captain to take him and his little family on board, and land them at the place whither he was sailing. The captain agreed; but when he got a glimpse of the beautiful queen he changed his mind, and determined to fulfil only a part of the agreement, and to take the woman alone. "What a beautiful mistress she would make!" he thought; "and what a lot of money I could get if I wished to sell her!" So when the moment for starting arrived the queen first embarked; and then, just as the king and his two sons were about to follow, some strong, rough men, who had been suborned by the captain, prevented them and held them tight, till the ship was well out to sea.

Loudly wept the queen when she saw that her husband and two boys were being left behind. She smote her forehead, tore her clothes, and threw herself upon the deck in great distress, and finally swooned away. It was a long swoon, and although the captain used several kinds of restoratives, yet for more than an hour she remained as one dead. At last she revived. The captain was very attentive. He arranged a nice bed for her, brought her the best of food, and spoke very kindly; but it was all to no purpose, for the queen refused to look at him or speak to him. This continued for several days, till the captain despaired of ever getting her love, and therefore determined to sell her.

Now there was in the same ship a great merchant, who, seeing the queen's exceeding beauty, and hearing her refuse the captain's suit day after day, thought that perhaps he might buy her, and win over her affection. Accordingly he offered the captain a large sum of money for the woman, and she was handed over to him. Most earnestly and perseveringly the merchant tried to please her and make her love him, and eventually he so far succeeded, that when he told her that he had bought her for a large sum of money, and therefore she ought to consent to marry him, she said, "Although the bargain between you and the captain is void, because the captain had no right to dispose of me, I not being his, yet I like you, and will marry you, if you will agree to wait for two years, and if during this period I do not meet my husband and sons again." The merchant complied, and looked forward in blest anticipation to the completion of the period of probation.

As soon as the vessel was out of sight the hired men released the king and his two boys. It was useless to seek revenge, even if His Majesty had any desire for it; and so he turned his back on the sea, and walked fast and far with the two boys, who wept and lamented as they ran along by his side, till he reached a river, somewhat shallow but flowing swiftly.

The king wished to cross this river, but there was not any boat or bridge, and so he was obliged to wade it. Finding his way very carefully, he got across safely with one of his sons, and was returning to fetch the other, when the force of the current overcame him, and he was drawn down beneath the waters and drowned.[2]

When the two boys perceived that their father had perished they wept bitterly. Their separation, too, was a further cause for grief. There they stood, the one on this side of the river and the other on that side of it, with no means of reaching one another. They shouted to each other, and ran about hither and thither in their grief, till they had almost wearied themselves to sleep, when a fisherman came by in his boat. Seeing the great distress of the boys, he took them both into it, and asked them who they were, and who were their parents. And they told him all that happened.

When he had heard their story he said, "You have not a father or mother, and I have not a child. Evidently God has sent you to me. Will you be my own children, and learn to fish, and live in my house?" Of course, the poor boys were only too glad to find a friend and shelter. "Come," said the fisherman kindly, leading them out of the boat to a house close by, "I will look after you." The boys followed most happily, and went into the fisherman's house; and when they saw his wife they were still better pleased, for she was very kind to them, and treated them like her own real sons.

The two boys got on splendidly in their new home. They went to school, and in a very short time learnt all that the master could teach them. They then began to help their adopted father, and in a little while became most diligent and expert young fishermen.

Thus time was passing with them, when it happened that a great fish threw itself on to the bank of the river,

[2] Compare the legend of Sanvar and Nír, *Legends of the Panjáb*, vol. iii. p. 97 ff.

and could not get back into the water. Everybody in the village went to see the immense fish, and nearly everybody cut off a slice of it and took it home. Some few people also went from the neighbouring villages, and amongst them was a maker of earthenware. His wife had heard of the great fish, and urged him to go and get some of it. Accordingly he went, although the hour was late. On arrival he found nobody there, as all the people had satisfied themselves and returned. The potter took an axe with him, thinking that the bones would be so thick as to require its aid before they could be broken. When he struck the first blow a voice came out of the fish, as of some one in pain. The potter was very much surprised. "Perhaps," thought he, "the fish is possessed by a *bhút*. I'll try again;" whereupon he again struck. Again a voice came forth from the fish, saying, "Woe is me! Woe is me!" On hearing this the potter thought, "Well, this is not a *bhút* evidently, but the voice of an ordinary man. I'll cut the flesh carefully. Maybe I shall find some poor distressed person." He began to cut away the flesh carefully, and presently came upon a man's foot; then the legs appeared; then the body and head, all entire.[3] "Praise, praise be to God!" he cried aloud, "the soul is in him yet." He carried the man to his house as fast as he could, and on arrival did everything in his power to recover him. A great fire was soon got ready, and tea and soup given. The joy of the potter and his wife was very great when they saw that the stranger was reviving.

For some months the stranger lived with these good people, and learnt how to make pots and pans and other articles, and thus helped them much. Now it happened just then that the king of that country died (for kings die as well as other people), and it was the custom of the people in that country to take for their sovereign whoso-

[3] Cf. *Indian Fairy Tales*, pp, 66, 75, 76; *Kings of Kashmírá*, p. 91; and tale of "The Three Caskets," in *Gesta Romanorum*; also *Wide-Awake Stories*, p. 411, where instances of "living in animals' bellies" are enumerated.

ever the late king's elephant and hawk might select. On the death of the king the elephant was driven all over the country, and the hawk was made to fly here, there, and everywhere in search of a successor; and it came to pass that before whomsoever the elephant bowed and on whosoever's hand the hawk alighted he was supposed to be the divinely chosen one. So the elephant and hawk went everywhere, and in the course of their wanderings came by the house of the potter and his wife who had so kindly sheltered the poor stranger that was found in the stomach of the fish. It chanced that as they passed the place the stranger was standing by the door—and behold! no sooner did the elephant and hawk see him than the one bowed down before him and the other perched on his hand.

"Let him be king, let him be king!" shouted the people who were in attendance on the elephant, as they prostrated themselves before the stranger and begged him to go before them to the palace.[4]

The ministers were glad when they heard the news, and most respectfully welcomed their new king. As soon as the rites and ceremonies necessary for the installation of a king had been fulfilled His Majesty entered on his duties. The first thing he did was to send for the potter and his wife and grant them some land and money. In this and other ways, such as just judgments, proper rules, and kindly notices of any and all who were clever and good, he won for himself the best opinions of every subject, and prospered exceedingly.

[4] Very rarely a hawk shares with the elephant the right of selection of a successor to the throne. Amongst most Eastern nations, when a king died the choice of his successor lay wholly with the elephant on which the deceased king was accustomed to ride. The animal was decked in all its splendid coverings, and led along the streets, or allowed to wander about the streets of the town; and before whomsoever the elephant knelt, that fortunate individual was chosen king. Cf. *Folk-Tales of Bengal*, p. 100; *Madanakamárájankadai* (*The Dravidian Nights*), pp. 126, 127; *The Orientalist*, p. 151; *The Indian Antiquary*, vol. iii. p. 11, vol. iv. p. 261, vol. vi. p. 333; M'Crindle's *India as Described by Megasthenes and Arrian*, pp. 118, 119; also *Wide-Awake Stories*, pp. 140, 327, to which especially refer. Other tales in this collection in which reference is made to this incident are, the "Two Brothers," "Metempsychosis," and "How the Princess Found her Husband."

Within a few months, however, his health gave way. Such strict attention to public affairs was too much for him, and therefore the court physicians advised him to seek relaxation in out-door exercise. So sometimes His Majesty went a-riding, sometimes a-shooting, and sometimes a-fishing. He got especially fond of the latter amusement. Knowing this, a fisherman came to him one day and said, "Be pleased, Your Majesty, to accept this fish which came into my hands this day." The king was delighted to see such a large fish, and inquired when and how it had been caught. The fisherman explained everything to the king, and manifested such knowledge of, and interest in, his calling, that His Majesty got to like the man, and ordered him to be ready at any time to go with him on fishing expeditions, that he (the king) might learn everything about the art, and be able to land big fish like the one just presented to him.

"Your Majesty is very good and gracious, and whatsoever Your Majesty commands is accepted of all men as right and proper and just; but be pleased to listen for a moment to your servant. In my house are two sons, who are stronger and cleverer than I am. If Your Majesty will order it, I will take care that they are always ready to attend on you."

The king agreed. Whenever he went a-fishing he always took these two boys with him. A familiarity sprang up between His Majesty and the boys in consequence. His Majesty got exceedingly attached to them: they were so sharp and clever and handsome and good, that he finally arranged that they should generally be with him, no matter what his occupation.

Just about this time the merchant who bought the wife of the poor king, who had been supposed to be drowned, visited that country for the purpose of trading. He succeeded in obtaining an interview with the king, and opened out all his precious stones and stuffs before him. The king was very much pleased to see these wonderful treasures, and asked many questions about them and about the countries whence they had been brought. The merchant told him everything, and begged permission to trade in that country, and sought protection from His Majesty. The king readily granted the merchant's request, and ordered that some soldiers were to be at once told off for this special duty, and so arranged that one of them should be on guard always in the courtyard of the merchant. He also sent the fisherman's two sons to sleep on the merchant's premises.

One night these two boys were not able to sleep for some reason or other, when the younger asked his brother to tell him a tale to enliven the occasion, as it was miserable lying down there with only the glimmering light of a little oil lamp. The elder brother said, "All right, I'll tell you one out of our own experience," and began:—

"Once upon a time there lived a very great, learned, and wealthy king, but he was very proud. This pride led the poor king to the direst ruin and grief. One day, while going about with his army challenging other kings to come and fight with him, one great and powerful king appeared and conquered him. The defeated king escaped with his wife and two sons to the sea, hoping to find some vessel wherein he and his family might embark, and get away to some foreign land, and there forget all their troubles. After walking several miles they reached the sea-shore, and found a vessel about to sail; but, alas! the captain of that vessel proved to be a very wicked man. He took the beautiful queen, and then, when the king and his two sons were going to embark, some men, hired by the captain, kept them back till the vessel had sailed out of sight. Oh! what a terrible time that was for the poor king! With what a sorrow-sick heart he turned away with his two sons! He walked many miles, not knowing whither he went, till he came to a swiftly flowing river. As there was no bridge or boat near he was obliged to wade across. He took one of his boys and got over safely, and then was returning for the other, when he stumbled over a stone, lost his footing, and was carried away by the fierce waters, and has not been heard of since.

"You can imagine the state of the two boys. It was night, and they had neither food nor bedding, nor did they know where to go, nor how to get to one another. At length a fisherman came along in his boat, and seeing these two boys crying, he took them into his boat, and afterwards to his house, and got very fond of them, and so did his wife, so that they both became like father and mother to them. A year or two ago all this happened, and the two boys are supposed by every one to be the fisherman's two real sons. O brother, we are these two boys! And there you have my story."

The story was so interesting and its finish so wonderful, that the younger brother was more awake than before. Its narration had also attracted the attention of another. The merchant's promised wife, who happened to be lying awake at the time, and whose room was separated from the shop by the thinnest of partitions only, overheard all that had been said. She thought within herself, "Surely these two boys must be my own sons!"

Presently she was sitting beside them, and began asking them all sorts of questions. Two years or more had made a great difference in both of the boys, but there were certain signs that a hundred years would never efface from a mother's memory. These, together with the answers which she had elicited from them, assured her that she had found her own sons again. The tears streamed down her face as she embraced them, and revealed to them that she was the queen, their mother, about whom they had just been speaking.

She told them all that happened to her since she had been parted from them; how the captain of the vessel, finding that he should never be able to get her to live with him, had sold her to the rich merchant; how this rich merchant had been very kind to her, and really loved her, and was a thoroughly good man, besides being clever and wealthy; and how she, thinking that she should never meet with her husband, their father, again, had promised to marry this merchant at the end of two years, only three days of which remained now. She said, too, that she did not like the merchant enough to become his wife, and so she wished to contrive some plan for getting rid of him.

"The plan is," she said, "for me to pretend to the merchant that you attempted to violate me. I will pretend to be very angry, and not give him any peace till he goes to the king and asks His Majesty to punish you. Then the king will send for you in great wrath, and will inquire about this matter. In reply you must say that it is all a mistake, for you quite regard me as your own mother, and in proof of this you will beg His Majesty to send and fetch me, that I may corroborate what you say. Then will I declare you to be my own dear sons, and beseech the king to allow me to go free of this merchant and live with you, where I may choose for the rest of my days."

The sons consented to her proposal, and the next night, when the merchant also was sleeping on the premises, the woman raised a great shout, so that everybody was awakened by the noise. The merchant asked what was the matter.

"The two boys who look after your shop have tried to violate me; so I shouted, in order that they might desist."

Hearing this, the merchant was much enraged. He immediately bound the two boys, and as soon as there was any chance of seeing the king, he had them taken before His Majesty, and explained the reason of their thus appearing before him.

"What have you to say in defence of yourselves?" inquired the king. "Because if this is true we shall at once order the execution of both of you. Is this the gratitude you manifest for all my kindness and condescension towards you? Say quickly what you may have to say."

"O king, our benefactor, we are not affrighted by your words and looks, for we are true servants. We have not betrayed Your Majesty's trust in us, but have always tried to fufil Your Majesty's wish to the utmost of our power. The charges brought against us by the merchant are not correct. We have not attempted to violate his wife; we have rather always regarded her as our own mother. May it please Your Majesty to send for the woman and inquire further into the matter."

The king assented, and the woman was brought. "Is this true," he said, "which the merchant, your affianced husband, witnesses against the two boys?"

"O king," she replied, "the boys whom you gave to help the merchant have most carefully tried to carry out your wishes. But the night before last I overheard their conversation. The elder was telling the younger brother a tale—made up out of his own experience, so he said. It was a tale of a conceited king who had been conquered by another mightier than he, and obliged to fly with his wife and two children to the sea. There, through the vile trickery of the captain of a vessel, the wife was stolen, and taken away to far distant regions, where she became engaged to a wealthy trader; while the exiled king and his two sons wandered in another direction, till they came to a river, where the king was drowned. The two boys were found by a fisherman, and brought up by him as his own sons.

"These two boys, O king, are before you, and I am their mother, who was taken away and sold as a wife to the trader, and who after two days must altogether live with him; for I promised that if within a certain space of time I should not meet with my dear husband and two sons again, then I would be his wife. But I beseech Your Majesty to relieve me of this man. I do not wish to marry again, now that I have my two sons. In order that I might get an audience of Your Majesty, this trick was arranged with the two boys."

By the time the woman had finished her story the king's face was suffused with tears, and he was trembling visibly. Presently, when he had slightly recovered, he left the throne, and walking towards the woman and the two boys, embraced them long and fervently. "You are my own dear wife and children," he cried; "God has sent you back to me. I, the king, your husband, your father, was not drowned as you supposed, but was swallowed by a big fish and nourished by it for some days, and then the monster threw itself upon the shore and I was extricated. A potter and his wife had pity on me, and taught me their trade, and I was just beginning to earn my living by making earthen vessels when the late king of this country died, and I was chosen king by the elephant and the falcon—I, who am now standing here."

Then His Majesty ordered the queen and her two sons to be taken to the palace, and he explained his conduct to the people assembled. The merchant was politely dismissed from the country. As soon as the two princes were old enough to govern the country the king committed to them the charge of all affairs, while he retired with his wife to some quiet place and spent the rest of his days in peace.[5]

[5] This story should be compared with its most interesting variant, "Placidus," a tale from the *Gesta Romanorum.*

Another variant is to be found in *Tibetan Tales,* the story of "Krisa Gautami," pp. 222, 223. A third variant is "Swet-Basanta" in *Folk-tales of Bengal,* pp. 93–107. Another is that of "Sarwar and Nír" in the *Legends of the Punjab,* vol. iii. p. 97 ff.

THE TWO BROTHERS.[1]

HAPPILY passed the days in the palace, for the king was intensely fond of his wife, who thoroughly reciprocated his affection; while their children, two fine handsome boys, were clever, good, and obedient, and thought nobody equal to their parents throughout the wide wide world. In such a household happiness was obliged to reign, till Yama sent his dogs to summon any of them to their doom.[2]

Every morning His Majesty was accustomed to sit with his wife for a while in one of the verandahs of the palace, during which quiet time together they were often interested in watching a pair of birds carrying food for their younglings. One day they noticed a strange female bird flying with the other towards the nest, and carrying some thorns in her bill. Curious to know what had happened, the king ordered one of the attendants to climb the tree and inquire; when it was discovered that the male bird had lost his consort, and therefore had taken unto himself another; and the new bird, not liking to have to work for a nest of younglings which she had not hatched, thought that she would fetch them some thorns to eat and get rid of them; which she did, and the little birds were choked and died. All of them were seen lying over the corpse of their mother.

1 Narrator's name, Shiva Rám of Bánah Mahal, Srínagar.

2 Yama is the regent of the realms of death. "He is still to some extent an object of terror. He is represented as having two insatiable dogs with four eyes and wide nostrils, which guard the road to his abode, and which the departed are advised to hurry past with all possible speed. These dogs are said to wander about among men as his messengers, no doubt for the purpose of summoning them to their master."—*Dr. Muir.*

When the king and queen heard this they were both very sad.

"Is this the way with us and with the birds?" asked the king.

"Yes," replied the queen. "But may it never be so in our case. Promise me, my beloved, that if I die first you will never marry again."

"Give me your hand, my darling," said the king. "I promise most faithfully never to take to myself another wife, whether you are alive or dead, lest the same misfortune should happen to our two sons that has come upon these poor young birds."

Then was the queen comforted, and loved the king more than ever before. Strange to say, not long after this little incident Her Majesty died. What a grief it was to the king! People thought for some time that he also would die, so much did he grieve over her death. At length, however, he rallied, and again occupied himself in the affairs of his country. When a convenient space of time had elapsed the *wazírs* and courtiers and other great men of the place commissioned some of their number to speak to the king about marrying again. As will be imagined, this proved a most difficult and disagreeable task. At first His Majesty would not see them; but they persisted in their request, till he promised to reconsider the matter, and at last consented. One of the chief *wazír's* daughters was proposed and accepted, and the marriage was celebrated.

Unhappy day! As was expected, the new queen soon became jealous of the two princes, and began to plot against them. They tried hard to please her by anticipating her wants and never crossing her wish in any matter, but all in vain. The queen hated them, and longed for the day when she could secure their ruin and banishment. She bided her time, till she saw that the king was exceedingly fond of her and would do anything for her, and then she began to malign the princes, saying how very disobedient and very abusive they were to her, and how she could not have endured their behaviour if the king had not been good and kind to her. The king was exceedingly angry when he heard this, and immediately gave orders for the princes to be secretly taken to a jungle and slain.

Never having been accustomed to question even their father's orders, the two young fellows went most gladly with the soldiers. They knew not of their father's cruel order, but thought that he wished them to ride and see the jungle. When, therefore, on reaching the place, the soldiers drew their swords and made as if to strike them, they were much surprised, and knew not what to do. "O Bhagawant, help us," they cried; and their cry was accepted. The swords of steel were changed into swords of wood,[3] and the stern hearts of the soldiers were filled with pity, so that they dared not slay them, but let them go free.

Full of thankfulness to the Deity for His mercy towards them, the princes rode off on their horses as fast as they could, and determined never to return to their own country. They rode on far and fast, till they came to a spring of water pure like crystal, by which they thought they would dine and rest. They arranged that both of them should not be asleep at the same time, lest a robber or a wild beast should come and destroy them and the horses. So the elder brother went to sleep first, and the younger brother watched. While he watched two birds named Sudabror and Budabror came and perched on a tree close by, and began talking with one another.

"See," said Sudabror, "there are two singing birds in that tree overhanging the spring. Do you know what kind of birds they are?"

"Yes," replied Budabror; "they are most wonderful birds. I have heard say that whosoever eats the flesh of one of them will become a king, and whosoever eats the

[1] Cf. story of "Háya Band and Zuhra Khotan" in this collection.

flesh of the other will become a *wazír*, and the wealthiest man in the world, for every morning he will find underneath him, in the place where he lay, seven jewels, whose value cannot be estimated.[4]

The younger prince was very much excited when he heards these words, and at once shot an arrow at these birds and killed them. He cooked both the birds, took one himself, and left the other for his brother, who ate it as soon as he awoke. The following morning they resumed their journey. On the way the younger brother suddenly remembered that his whip had been left behind. This whip he valued very highly, and therefore went back for it. He found it by the spring, and was going to dismount to pick it up, when a great dragon [5] came out of the water and bit his foot, so that he fell down senseless. In this state he continued for some hours.

Meanwhile his brother got very tired of waiting, and therefore went on, thinking his brother would overtake him before the evening. He reached a certain city, whereof the king had recently died, and the people were in a state of great excitement concerning his successor. It appears that they had a custom of sending round an elephant to select their kings for them. Whomsoever the elephant acknowledged they acknowledged, be he rich or poor, learned or ignorant, of their own country and speech, or of another. This elephant was circumambulating the

[4] The story of the mystic fowl will be familiar to readers of European folk-tales. Cf. *Wide-Awake Stories*, pp. 139, 326; *Madanakamárájankadai* (*Dravidian Nights*), p. 126; Grimm's *Household Stories*, pp. 193, 383; *Russian Popular Tales*, v. No. 53, viii. No. 26, and pp. 464–467; *Tibetan Tales*, p. 129; also the footnote, in which Professor Schiefner calls attention to several other variants—Gaal, *Märchen der Magyaren*, Wien, 1882, p. 196; *Der Vogel Goldschweif*, especially p. 213; Hahn, *Gr. und alb. Märchen*, Leipzig, 1864, i. 227; *Das goldene Huhn*; Haltrich, *Deutsche Volksmärchen* Berlin, 1856; "Der seltsame Vogel," Miklosich, *Ueber die Mundarten der Zigeuner*, iv. No. 6; *Die Diamentem legende Henne.* Cf. also story of "Saiyid and Said" in this collection. The "golden egg" in some of these stories is supposed to represent the sun," which may be looked upon as a gleaming egg laid every morning by the brooding Night" (*Vide* Gubernatis, *Zoological Mythology*, ii. p. 311). "But the king-making power attributed to the bird's eaten flesh remains a mystery."

[5] *Azdár* (Persian *izhdahá*, *izhdár*, or *izhdar*).

place when the eldest prince arrived, and on seeing him at once bowed down before him. Accordingly he was proclaimed king of the country and conducted to the palace.

The younger prince was restored to life in the following manner. Living near the spring was a *jogí*, who was accustomed to visit it once every six months for the purpose of getting a little water thence. The day the prince was bitten by the dragon happened to be the day of the good man's coming. When he reached the place and saw the lifeless body of the young man he was filled with pity. He knew that the dragon of the spring had done this; so he muttered an incantation, and the waters dried up and the monster appeared,

"Why have you emptied the spring?" said the dragon.

"Because you have slain this young man. Why did you this thing?" the *jogí* replied.

"O *jogí!*" said the dragon, "there were two birds that often visited this place, and filled the air with their songs. The prince killed them. Therefore did I bite him."

"You have done wickedly," said the *jogí*. "Listen. Extract the poison from the man's foot, so that he live again, or you shall die."

"Forgive me," said the dragon, "and I will obey you."

Thus the prince was restored to life. After thanking the *jogí* he departed. However, he unfortunately took the wrong road, and instead of following after his brother, arrived at a village that was the resort of a band of fierce robbers. By chance he called at the house of one of these robbers and asked for hospitality, which was readily granted. They gave him a most hearty welcome, and provided him with the best of cheer; but, alas! when he went to lie down at night the bedstead and he descended right through the flooring, down into a most loathsome dungeon. Poor fellow! he would have died there if the daughter of one of the robbers had not seen him and fallen in love with him. She thoroughly knew the ins and outs of the house, and guessing that the stranger had been precipitated into the grave, as they called it, she secretly visited him and carried him some food, in return for which the prince gave her seven jewels.[6] This she did every morning, and got seven jewels each time. During these visits the girl's love increased rapidly, and as she was very beautiful and very clever, the prince reciprocated her affection, and promised to marry her as soon as possible. At last they both got free from the place, and escaped as fast as the swift horse would carry them to the seaside, where they immediately embarked in a ship about to sail. Among other passengers in that ship was a merchant, who was so captivated with the girl's beauty that he desired to kill the prince and make her his wife. Accordingly one day, while he and the prince were playing *nard* in the prow of the vessel, the prince bent forward over the ship-side to spit, when the merchant gave him a push.[7] Fortunately his wife happened to be standing by one of the port-holes, and seeing her husband's body appearing, put out her hands and saved him. There was great sorrow among the crew and the passengers when the report was circulated that the prince had fallen overboard; for the prince had ordered his wife not to discover the matter till they reached their destination. The merchant professed to be more grieved than any one, except the beautiful wife. However, he soon recovered, and commenced paying attentions to her, and at length asked her to marry him. The girl put him off for six months, saying that if she did not hear anything about her husband during that time she would be his wife.[8]

In a few months the ship reached her destination, where the prince revealed himself, and charged the merchant with attempting to drown him; whereupon the man was

[6] Note the number seven. Cf. also tales, "Good King Hátam," "Seven-legged Beast," "Jogí's Daughter," "The Ogress-Queen," in this collection. *Vide* also *Wide-Awake Stories*, pp. 432, 433. Seven is a sacred number in Aryan faith (*Zoological Mythology*, vol. i. p. 6).

[7] Cf. a Manípurá tale in *Indian Antiquary*, vol. iv. p. 260.

[8] Cf. *Wide-Awake Stories*, p. 429, for enforced marriages postponed for a season.

put into prison to await his trial. By a remarkable coincidence they disembarked by the chief city of the country over which the eldest prince was reigning. This king was in great sorrow at the time, wondering what had become of his brother; so, to comfort himself, he had given orders to his chief *wazír* to tell him a tale every evening. He hoped, also, that in this way he should hear something of his brother, as the *wazír* often related stories founded on what he had seen and heard during the day. The day the ship arrived this *wazír's* daughter came down to the shore, and heard the strange story of the prince and his wife and the wicked merchant, which she repeated to her father in the evening. On the following evening the *wazír* related to the king what he had heard.

"Where is the prince and his wife?" inquired the king, much excited. "Send for them immediately. At last I have found my long-lost brother!"

We can imagine what a joyous meeting there was between the two brothers. They fell on each other's necks and wept.

The younger prince was appointed chief *wazír* of the country, and the wicked merchant was hanged.

In course of a few years some messengers from their father reached that country, and said that the old king was longing to see them, as he had discovered his wife's wickedness and had slain her. Accordingly the two brothers started without delay to see their father. They reached safely, and saw the old man, and were reconciled. Soon afterwards their father died, when the elder brother succeeded to the throne, and the younger went and governed the country that had belonged to the other prince. Both of them prospered exceedingly, and were famed for their skill and justice and kindness.[9] [10]

[9] In nearly every country, and at all times, there have been legends concerning the existence of a huge monster which went abroad devouring and devastating all before it. This monster, or dragon, as it is generally called, is supposed to be the symbolical representative of arrogant power and cruelty, whose sole object is to oppose order and peace. Although it

is possible, as Brand says, that the dragon is one of those shapes which fear has created to itself, nevertheless, from the generality of the legends concerning this winged saurian, it is possible that the existence of some species of the pterodactyl, in very remote times, may have originated the superstition. However this may have been, it is certain that this mythical animal, in all ages, has been regarded as a minister of evil, the destruction of which was considered one of the grandest objects of human energy. The task was usually allotted to gods and heroes. Apollo killed the Python, and Perseus slew the dragon, and saved Andromeda. Hercules is also represented as a dragon-slayer. In the *Nibelungen Lied* Siegfried is represented as killing a dragon. Cf. also the "Epic of Beowolf." Among the Scandinavians, Thor was described as a dragon-slayer. In the Middle Ages the dragon was regarded as the representative of sin. Saints and martyrs are frequently depicted as trampling the reptile under foot. It is also used with this signification in the figure of St. George and the Dragon. *Vide Beeton's Dictionary*, whence these notes have been quoted.

[10] Compare the Kashmírí variant in *Wide-Awake Stories*, p. 138; S. Indian variant in *Madanakamárájankadai* (*Dravidian Nights*), the sixth story; the Tibetan variant in *Tibetan Tales*, p. 279, which Professor Schiefner translated from the *Kah-gyur*, all the legends and fables of which are merely Tibetan versions of Sanskrit writings introduced into the country in the twelfth and thirteenth centuries; the Egyptian variant, "The Tale of Two Brothers;" the German variant, Grimm's *Household Stories*, p. 192; and the English variant, viz., the legend of "St. George and the Dragon," as recorded in the ballad given in *Percy's Reliques*.

THE BASE FRIEND.[1]

ONCE upon a time a very great and wealthy king determined to send his son out into the world as a merchant in order that he might get to know something of the people and country, and thus be more prepared to govern wisely, when the time should come for him to sit on the throne. So he gave him plenty of money and several bales of goods, and told him to go whithersoever he wished, to keep his eyes open, and to make as much money as possible.

As soon as convenient the prince started, attended by the *wazír's* son, his great friend, and a large retinue of servants and horses. After much wandering about they came to some place by the sea, where they found a ship ready to weigh anchor, and being of an adventu rous disposition they embarked, and started for some foreign country. All went well for a while, till they passed under a certain island and cast anchor. Here the prince got out and walked about alone, as the *wazír's* son, not wishing to go, had feigned sickness. Wicked fellow! he persuaded the prince to go on shore and take a long walk round the island, while he bribed the captain and the sailors of the vessel to start without him. He got them to take the ship back again by a circuitous course to the place that they had recently left, and there he disposed of all the merchandise, and afterwards returned to the king.

"You have come back quickly. Where is the prince?" said His Majesty.

"The prince is dead, Your Majesty. We were sailing

[1] Narrator's name, Paṇḍit Lál Chand of Khunamuh in the Vihí *pargana.*

happily along by a certain island, when a wind suddenly arose, and increased so, that the ship capsized, and all that were in it were thrown into the water. I tried to save the prince, but, alas! I could not. It was with the greatest difficulty that I myself escaped."

When the king heard these words he was intensely grieved. He wept for his son many days, during which he seemed like one mad, not caring for anyone or anything, only raving about his son.

Meanwhile affairs were prospering with the prince. As soon as he discovered the treachery of his friend he began to look about for quarters for the night. He arranged a little "shantee" for himself by the side of a clear crystal spring, and then lay down to sleep, hoping for better things on the morrow. While he was sleeping, at midnight, a heavenly woman came out of the spring, attended by several soldiers, and sat down to eat. When she had satisfied herself she went towards the prince, and waking him up, offered him some food, which the prince took, and for which he was very grateful, as he had not tasted anything since he had landed.

"But tell me, fair lady," said he, "whence you came and who you are."

"Sir," she replied, "I am a heavenly woman. Please tell me your history. I may be able to help you."

"Fair lady," said he, "I am a prince. I am travelling about at my father's request in search of experience and knowledge, in order that I may be better able to rule the country after him. I was sailing to some place with a large quantity of goods, when the vessel put in here for a few hours while I got out to see the island, and when I returned at the time advised by the captain of the ship I discovered that she had started without me. No doubt this was done at the instigation of my friend, the *wazír's* son, who was accompanying me on my travels."

"The villain!" exclaimed the heavenly woman. "He shall suffer for this baseness. Sleep on now, sir. In the morning I will cause you to reach your father's place, whither this man has probably returned. You can then denounce him face to face."

On saying this, she disappeared by way of the spring, and the soldiers after her. At dawn she came again, and rousing him, gave him several most valuable jewels to make up for his losses, and then told him to go. Accordingly the prince started, and attended by several soldiers, presently found himself walking up the path to his father's palace.

"Who can this be coming?" asked the king, as he watched the procession from his bedroom window. "Quick! run," said he to the sentry at the door, "and give the man this bunch of pearls. How know we that he is not some powerful enemy?"

"Go back and tell your king," said the prince to the soldier, "that I am a friend, and that I come to inquire concerning his son. Certain strange reports have reached my ears of late."

On hearing this the king bade him welcome to the palace, and received him most graciously. He told him with tearful eyes the sad news of the prince's shipwreck, and called the son of the *wazír* to corroborate what he said.

"O father," said the prince, unable to dissemble any longer, "wipe away those tears. Your son has returned to you. I am he. No wind beset our ship, no waves destroyed me; but I was basely left on a little barren uninhabited island to starve. That man" (pointing to the *wazír's* son) "bribed the captain and crew to sail without me, in order that he might sell the goods and get all the profit for himself."

"Base villain!" cried the king. "Order the executioners to rid us of the presence of such a man in our midst."

Great was the joy of the king when he saw his son again. Not long after this His Majesty died, and the prince, his son, reigned in his stead.

HÁYA BAND AND ZUHRA KHOTAN.

You must know that not to have a son is accounted a great sorrow and shame. Well, in days long gone by, a certain rich merchant of this country was in great distress because he had not a son. Who would continue his name? Who would carry on the business? To whom should he bequeath his immense wealth? These questions were constantly revolving in his mind, and the sorrowful answer came back from his despairing soul, "I have no son! I have no son!" He earnestly prayed at the stated times, and was very attentive to the appointed fasts and the giving of alms, but it seemed as if God's eye was not upon him for good, and His ears not open to his cries. But it only seemed so. God's thoughts are not to be compared with man's thoughts. It was the Divine intention to bless him with a son; so at the right time a little boy was born. The merchant named him Háya Band. When he was five years old his father sent him to school, and he prosecuted his studies up to the age of ten years.

One day, while the merchant was sitting by his shop-window, he saw two ragged little boys going by. He called them and inquired why they were so poor, and they told him that their father and mother and brother were dead, and they did not know of any relatives or friends to whom they could apply for help. Whereupon the merchant had pity on them, and took them into his home and educated them with his own boy, thinking they would be agreeable companions for him, and be able to do some odd jobs about the shop as well. However, the boys

[1] Narrator's name, Paṇḍit Shiva Rám of Bánah Mahal, Srínagar.

turned out badly, as we shall see. Instead of being grateful to their kind master and affectionate playmate, and helping them in every way, they eventually plotted against them and tried to bring them to shame. Every day they went regularly to school with the merchant's son; but while Háya Band worked diligently, and became very good and learned, they were idle and careless, and learnt nothing, except all manner of wickedness, that they picked up from other boys of the school of the same character. One morning, as they all three were going to school together, they chanced to talk about marriage. "Look here," said they to Háya Band, "we know that you are going to be married very shortly. Could not you arrange with your father to marry us also?"

"Why not?" replied Háya Band. "Nay, I will beg my father to marry you first, and me afterwards."

A little while after this the merchant sent a go-between to several houses to try and procure a girl of wealthy parents, of great beauty, educated, wise, and virtuous. The go-between quickly fulfilled his commission, and a marriage was arranged.

On the day appointed the merchant gave a great feast to his friends and distributed much alms among the poor, and then, dressing his son in king-like apparel, sent him to the house of the bride. The two wicked boys knew all about this, and went on before, and tried to estrange the minds of the father and mother of the bride by declaring that Háya Band was demented; whereupon they were both very angry, and would have broken off the engagement, but what could they do? It was too late. The bridegroom was already on the way to the house. Then the wretched boys returned to meet Háya Band, and contrived somehow to get him to eat some drugged fruit, whereby he became very stupid. Afterwards they went as fast as they could to the merchant's house, and told him with tears in their eyes, as though they were awfully sorry at the discovery, that the woman to whom he had plighted his son was an ogress and devoured human beings. When he heard this the merchant was very angry, and would have broken off the match; but what could he do? The hour was approaching, and everybody was in expectation of the bridegroom.

On reaching the bride's house Háya Band was severely scrutinised by his intended father-in-law and mother-in-law, who, when they saw him in such a sleepy, stupid condition, felt certain that the words of their wicked informants were true, and refused to give their daughter to him. However, the wise and virtuous bride, whose name was Zuhra Khotan, suspected some trickery, and forced her parents to allow the marriage. She was certain that Háya Band's father was too good and honest a man to deceive. Accordingly the hymeneal rites were performed. Towards evening Háya Band began to recover from the effects of the drug. He soon came to his senses and recognised his wife, and was delighted with her.

In a few days they started together for his house, according to custom. As the way was rather long, they arranged to do it in two marches. They halted at a house in one of the villages about half-way, and determined to spend the night there. When retiring to rest, Zuhra Khotan suddenly discovered that she had not brought any present for her mother-in-law. Alas! what could she do? It would be such a disgrace to go to her husband's house empty-handed. The poor girl was in great distress. However, kind sleep at last closed her eyes. While she slept she dreamed a dream, in which she saw a man coming to her and saying, "O virtuous woman, be not afraid, but go to the river, and you will find a corpse floating on the water, on whose arm is a most valuable bracelet. Call the corpse towards you—it will obey—and take off the bracelet and carry it to your mother-in-law." This wonderful dream woke the woman. She immediately arose and walked to the river-side, where she saw a corpse floating at a little distance. She called it to her, and taking off the beautiful bracelet which was on its arm, returned to the cottage. All would have gone on well now had it not been for the two wicked boys. They were hankering about the place, and had seen everything. This was just what they wanted. They had only to sprinkle some sheep's blood along the path to the river and on the river-bank, and then run with all haste to the merchant, their master, and tell him to come and see his daughter-in-law's last exploit, to confirm their terrible lie to him about her. This they did, and the merchant came and saw the blood-marks, and wept like a man about to die. In the morning he went to his son and told him what he had seen and heard, but his son would not believe it, and got very angry. Presently, however, the *dáí* affirmed that her mistress went out of the cottage about midnight for a little while, but for what purpose she did not know. Háya Band was then very much surprised, and felt obliged to credit the wicked story, and kept away from his wife. It was a very sad wedding party that arrived at the merchant's house that afternoon. Zuhra Khotan was at once placed in a separate room, and nobody went near her except the *dáí*. One day her mother-in-law essayed to look at her through an open door, and nearly fainted from fright. A long time thus passed, during which Háya Band worked in his father's business together with his two wicked companions, whom he treated as friends, and the more so, imagining them to have told him the truth about his wife, and thus saved him from a most horrible death.

One day the merchant suggested that his son and the two young men (for they were getting quite young men by this time) should go on a little trading expedition. He did this, because he saw that Háya Band was grieving about his wife, and therefore wished to divert his thoughts. The three youths started, and went several miles, when Háya Band suddenly remembered that he had left his account-books behind, and rode back for them, promising to meet his companions at the end of the march in the evening. Now these account-books were in Zuhra Khotan's room. Why they had been placed there we do not know. So when Háya Band returned he immediately rushed up to that room to fetch them. Of course he saw his wife. Beautiful she looked in her sorrow, and so good and pure and loving! Háya Band could not resist. He drew her to him in fond embrace and kissed her. He stayed with her for a month or so, and then left secretly, to see what had become of his companions and the goods. He found them at the end of the first march, where he had promised to meet them. They had not stirred from the place, nor tried to dispose of the merchandise, but had spent their time in drinking and gambling and other suchlike occupations. Háya Band was very angry when he heard this, and sharply reproving them, went on alone; while these two wicked fellows returned. Enraged beyond measure, they resolved to wreak vengeance on Háya Band. They disguised themselves as *faqírs,* and learnt a few of the tricks of these people, and then went to the merchant's house and cried, "Oh, sir, be warned in time! There is an ogress in your house, who has lain with man and has conceived. For God's sake, for your own sake, turn her out of the place, lest she bring destruction on you and on those around you." On saying this they went away.

We can imagine that such words, coming from the lips of such people, would make a great impression on the merchant and his wife. They could not rest or do anything till they had ascertained the truth. They searched the premises, and had every woman examined, but found nothing as the *faqírs* had said. They then emboldened themselves to inquire of Zuhra Khotan, and found that she was *enciente.* In vain she protested that she was not an ogress, but a virtuous woman. The merchant sent to the *díwán* and got a writ for her execution. She was taken to a jungle, where her head was to be cut off. On reaching the jungle she prayed the executioners to have mercy on her. "O men," she cried, "ye will not be so cruel and unjust as to slay an innocent woman. I have done nothing worthy of death, nor can anything be proved against me. Wherefore do ye slay me?"

"We have received our orders," they replied.

Then the woman prostrated herself on the ground and prayed, "O God, have mercy on me. Thou knowest that I have not sinned. Intervene for me and deliver me."

On this one of the soldiers went forward and raised his sword to slay her, when behold! it was turned into wood. Then another soldier attempted to raise his sword, but he could not, for his hands were fastened in some invisible way behind him. Afterwards a third man went forward to do the deed, and he fell down senseless. Thus God heard the woman's prayer, and defeated the counsels of the wicked.

When the soldiers saw what had happened they believed that God was against the deed. "O woman," they said, "we will not slay you; but tell us, we beseech you, how we can save ourselves, for when the *díwán* and the merchant find that we have not fulfilled their orders they will be angry with us and punish us. Our orders were to slay you and carry back your head."

"Fear not," said Zuhra Khotan, gathering some earth and making clay of it. "I will form a head out of this." Thus saying, she shaped a head out of the clay like unto her own head, and entreated God to change it into flesh and blood. God heard this prayer also. The clay head was at once changed into a human head, and dripped with blood. "Take this," she said, "and give it to the merchant." And the soldiers took it and went.

When the merchant saw the gory head he was very glad. He hung it up outside his garden.

Zuhra Khotan lived in the jungle for some time, and ate such fruit and vegetables as she could find there. Afterwards, when she wished to leave that place, she told one of the trees to look for Háya Band and inform him whither she had gone. She went to another country, and lodged with a poor old widow whom she met there. By day she was going out to gather sticks and other such things as she could sell, and by night she slept in the old woman's house. By-and-by she gave birth to a fine little boy.

Now it chanced that at that time the queen also was expecting her confinement. She was praying and hoping that it would be a son, as the king had threatened to take away her life if a boy should not be born. The poor woman was very anxious. She sent for the royal midwives, and inquired whether she was going to have a son or not. They all replied in the negative, and advised her to get a newly-born male child, and put away the little girl, that they felt sure was about to be born. The queen accepted their advice, and sent messengers in all directions to search out such a child for her. One of these messengers happened to call at the house of the old widow, and seeing the little baby there, begged her to sell him to the queen. Being a very greedy, covetous old creature, she consented, and gave the child to the man, who quickly carried it to the queen. In due time the child's birth was proclaimed, and there was great rejoicing in the city.

As soon as the messenger had left, the old widow collected a few big stones, one of which she put in the place where the baby used to sleep, and the others she put in a cupboard. When Zuhra Khotan returned she pretended that a heavenly woman had visited the place and changed the child for a stone, as they had done to several of her children—witness the stones in the cupboard. This heavenly woman visited the place once a year, she added. Poor Zuhra Khotan! how she wept for the loss of her baby! Deprived of her husband, and now deprived of her child, she earnestly wished to die. This world was too wicked, too troublesome, for her. What had she to live for? It was a mournful existence for her—day after day collecting fruit and wood and such things as she could live by, and night after night returning to the wretched old widow and comfortless home.

Meanwhile her son (the prince) grew up to be a big, clever, and pious youth. In his peregrinations he often passed the widow's house. One day he caught sight of Zuhra Khotan as she was returning from her day's wanderings, and was so struck with her beauty that he ascertained where she resided; and when he got back to the palace he went to the king and entreated him to arrange for his marriage with her.[2] The king promised to think over the matter, and summoned Zuhra Khotan to the palace. He also was struck with her beauty and modest manner. He told her of the prince's ardent affection for her, and asked whether she would be his wife; to which she replied that she was a wife already, and knew not that her husband was dead; but she promised that if she heard nothing about him for the next six months she would marry the prince. The king complied with her request, and so the matter ended for a while.

. . . .

All through that year and several years afterwards Háya Band was travelling about the world, visiting different countries for purposes of trade. At last, about this time, he returned to his house a very wealthy man. He thought to find his wife, and to hear that she had been proved harmless and received into the family. We can imagine, therefore, his intense grief when he heard what had been done to her. He asked his parents which way the executioners had taken his wife, aud where they had carried out the cruel order, and when they told him he packed up some things and started off on the same road. By the goodness of God he reached this jungle, and passed by the tree that Zuhra Khotan had asked to inform him of her whereabouts. "Your wife is not dead," said the tree. "The head which was carried back to your father

[2] Cf. whole story of "Swot-Basanta" in *Folk-Tales of Bengal.*

was not your wife's head. Your wife is alive. Go on without delay till you reach a certain country, where you will find her whom you seek. Go, and God watch over you."

After some days journeying the young merchant reached that country; and one morning, while he was walking about the *bázár* of the chief city, he chanced to see some women carrying things to the old widow's house.

"For whom are these things?" asked he. "Where are you going?"

"There is a woman here called Zuhra Khotan, who is about to be married to the prince, and since she is very poor the king is sending her some clothes and jewels for the wedding. She came here several years ago from some other country."

On hearing these words Háya Band gave the old widow his signet ring, and begged her to show it to Zuhra Khotan. He would accompany her as far as the door, and there wait. The woman did so, and Zuhra Khotan at once recognised it, and went out and embraced her long-lost husband. Information of his coming was at once sent to the palace. The king was very disappointed; but the prince was exasperated. In a fit of desperation he ran off at once to Zuhra Khotan's lodgings and tried to prevail on her to go with him, when lo! he was somehow recognised and declared to be her son. Everything was fully proved. The queen confessed everything, and the old widow confessed everything, and the messenger who took the child away confessed everything; but besides these witnesses the strongest evidence was the great likeness of the child to both his father and mother.

The king was exceedingly enraged when he heard of this, and at once banished the queen, and had the old widow put to death.

Háya Band and his wife and son returned to their own country, where they lived happily together ever afterwards.[3]

[3] Cf. *Wide-Awake Stories*, p. 396, note (*d*).

THE CLEVER JACKAL.[1]

It was ploughing-time. A farmer started early for his fields, bidding his wife follow him soon with a pot of food. When the rice was ready the woman carried some to her husband, and put it down in the field at a little distance from him, saying, "Here is your food. I cannot stay now." In a little while, when the farmer went to look for his food, he found the pot empty. He was very angry at this, and when he got home in the evening sharply reproved his wife for playing tricks with him. She, of course, thought he was telling a lie, and felt very much aggrieved.

On the following morning, before going out, he repeated his request that she would bring him some food, and not allow him to starve like a dog. That day she carried a double quantity of rice to him in a large earthen pot, and put it down in the field again, saying, "Look now, here is your dinner. Don't say I did not bring it. I cannot stay, as there is nobody left to look after the house." Thus saying, she went.

In a little while a jackal came—the same as came on the previous day and ate up the man's food—and put its head into the pot. So eager was the beast to get at the rice, that it forced its head into the narrow neck of the pot, and could not take it out again. It was in a dreadful state. It ran about shaking its head and beating the pot against the ground to try and break it.

At last the farmer saw what was the matter, and came

[1] Narrator's name, Paṇḍit Wasah Kol of Kahipúra in the Krúhĕn *pargana*.

running up with a knife, and exclaiming, "You thief! You stole my dinner, did you?"

"Oh, let me go!" cried the jackal. "Get me out of this pot and I will give you anything you may wish for."

"Very well," said the farmer, and at once smashed the pot and extricated the animal.

"Thank you," said the jackal. "You shall not regret to-day's adventure." On this the beast wished the man "Good-day," and started for a king's palace some miles distant.

"O king," it said on entering the royal chamber, "give me permission and I will arrange for your daughter's marriage. Be not angry with me. I should not have presumed to speak to Your Majesty on this matter if I had not lately seen one who is worthy in every way of the hand of the princess."

"You can bring the man here," replied the king, "and I will see him."

Then the jackal immediately started back for the farmer's house, and entering, asked him to prepare himself quickly for a visit to the king of the neighbouring country, who was desirous of seeing him with a view of making him his son-in-law. At first the farmer demurred, on account of his ignorance and poverty. How would he know what to say to a king? how would he know how to behave in the company of so high a personage? and whence could he obtain suitable clothes for the visit? But eventually the jackal prevailed on him to accept the king's invitation, and promised to help him in every possible way. So the jackal and the farmer started. When they arrived at the king's palace the jackal went in search of His Majesty, while the farmer squatted on the floor of the entrance-hall by the palace, where the shoes were kept, and waited.

"I have brought the man of whom I spoke to Your Majesty the other day," said the jackal, going up to the king. "He has come in ordinary clothes and without any retinue or show, as he thought Your Majesty would be inconvenienced by having to arrange accommodation for so many people. Your Majesty must not be offended in this thing, but the rather should see in it a proof of the man's good sense."

"Most certainly," said the king, rising up; "lead me to him."

"There he is," said the jackal.

"What!" that man squatting by the shoes?" exclaimed His Majesty. "Friend, why do you sit in such a place?" he asked the farmer.

"It is a nice clean place, Your Majesty, and good enough for a poor man like me," replied the farmer.

"Observe the humility of the man," interposed the jackal.

"You will stay in the palace this evening," said the king. "There are a few matters concerning which I wish to converse with you. To-morrow, if convenient, I shall go and see your abode."

That evening the king, the farmer, and the jackal talked much together. As will be supposed, the farmer constantly betrayed his humble position, but the clever jackal contrived to arrange matters so that the king on the whole was rather favourable to the match.

But what about the morrow? The jackal had been revolving the matter over in its mind during the night. As soon as the king and the farmer started it asked for permission to go on ahead. It ran as fast as it could to the farmer's house and set it on fire, and when they drew near, went forth to meet them, crying, "O king, come not any farther, I beseech you. The man's house and property are destroyed. Some enemy's hand must have done this. Both of you turn back, I pray you."

So the poor simple king turned back. In due time he married his daughter to the ignorant farmer.[2]

[2] *Folk-Tales of Bengal*, pp. 226–236; Chilian story, "Don Juan Bolondron," in *Folk-Lore Journal*, vol. iii. p. 299; also Mongolian tale in same journal, vol. iv. p. 32.

A STUPID BOY.[1]

A POOR widow's misery was increased by the knowledge that her son, her only son, around whom she had built up many many hopes, was a half-wit. One day she sent him to the *bázár* with some cloth, and told him to sell it for four rupees. The boy went, and sat down in the most public thoroughfare of the city.

"How much do you want for that piece of cloth?" asked a man.

"Four rupees," replied the boy.

"All right; I'll give you six rupees for it. It is worth it. Here, take the money."

"No, no," said the boy; "its price is four rupees."

"You scamp!" exclaimed the man angrily, and went on. He thought the boy was joking with him.

On reaching home in the evening he informed his mother of this incident, and she was grieved that he had not taken the money.

Another day she sent him to the *bázár*, and advised him to *salám* everybody, saying that nothing was ever lost by politeness, but, on the contrary, everything was sometimes gained by it. The stupid boy sallied forth, and began making *saláms* to everybody and everything he met—a sweeper, a horse, some little children, a house. A number of asses, too, passed by with loads on their backs, and he said "*Salám*" to them also.

"Hey! you fool! what are you doing?" said the donkey-driver in charge. "Don't you know that we say

[1] Narrator's name, a Panditání, collected for me by Paṇḍit Ánand Kol of Zainah Kadal, Srínagar.

'*Fri fri?*' "[2] whereupon the boy commenced saying "*Fri fri*" to every person and thing. He passed a man who had just spread a snare for a bird that he very much wished to catch, when "*Fri fri*" shouted the boy, and most effectually frightened away the bird.

"You blackguard! what are you doing?" said the man. "You should say '*Lag lag*,' in a very soft tone."

Then the boy began to say "*Lag lag*." He was wandering about crying "*Lag lag*," when he came across some thieves coming out of a garden, where they had just been stealing the fruit.

"What do you mean?" said they. "Be quiet, you fool, or say something else. Go and shout, 'Let go one and take the other.'"

So the boy did, and while he was shouting these words a funeral *cortége* passed by.

"Be quiet," said some of the mourners. "Have you so little respect for the dead? Get along home."

At length, disappointed and disheartened, not knowing what to do or what to say, the half-wit returned to his mother and told her everything.

[2] *Fri fri* is an exclamation used for urging on donkeys.

FOUR PRINCES TURNED INTO STONES.[1]

In olden times there lived a king that had four sons, whom he ordered to patrol the country in turn by day and by night. One morning the eldest prince in the course of his wanderings came across a *jogí*, who was sitting by a pond, near which four horses were grazing. Seeing that the horses were of a better and different breed to any that his father possessed, the prince went up to the *jogí*, and said, "O *jogí*, who are you? Whence have you come? What do you want here?"

"I want you," replied the *jogí*.

"Me!" exclaimed the prince. "I am the eldest son of the king of this country, and my father has ordered me to look after this place, and to see that nobody wants for anything. Tell me if you are in need."

"O prince," replied the *jogí*, "I want nothing except you. But if you need anything, then tell me, and I will procure it for you."

"O *jogí*, I wish to ride one of your beautiful horses," said the prince.

"Very well," said the *jogí*. "Take it, but be careful to return it this evening, when I shall see you, and hope to hear some of your experience during the day."

So the prince took the horse and rode off. As soon as he had mounted, the animal ran away as fast at it could to a jungle, and there stopped by a little vegetable garden, which was so fenced round on every side that nobody could enter it. After riding a little farther into the jungle

[1] Narrator's name, Makund Báyú, Suthú, Srínagar, who heard it from a Musalmán.

the prince turned to go back. On the way he saw that all the sticks of the fence had changed into sickles[2] and were cutting the vegetables. He was astonished to see this, but could not tell the reason of it. On reaching the *jogí's* place in the evening the good man asked him if he had had a pleasant ride and what he had seen.

"I have seen," he replied, "a garden fenced in on all sides with an impenetrable fence; and I have seen the sticks of this same fence changed into sickles and cutting the vegetables."

"Well, what does it mean?" asked the *jogí*.

"I don't know," the prince replied.

"Don't know!" repeated the *jogí*, "and you commissioned by your father to supervise affairs! Be turned into a stone." And it was so. That very moment the prince became a pillar of stone.[3]

[2] The word here was *drot*, a small sickle with teeth, used by gardeners and grasscutters.

[3] Concerning metamorphoses of human beings into stones, cf. *Old Deccan Days*, pp. 10, 55, 75; *Indian Fairy Tales*, p. 140; *Madanakamárájankadai*, p. 149; and *Vana-parva*, the third book of the *Mahábhárata*, where Damayantí is said to have cursed a hunter, who was at once changed into a stone; a Greek story, "Das schloss des Helios" (Schmidt's *Griechische Maerchen*, Sagen and Volkslieder, p. 106); the tale of the "Two Brothers," in Grimm's *Household Stories*, p. 204; *Indian Antiquary*, vol. xix. pt. cxcvii. p. 191; *R.A.S. Journal*, vol. xix, p. 398; also "Tale of Four Princes" and "The Wicked Queens," in this collection.

In the *Rishináma* it is said that one spring She*kh* Núru'ddín, accompanied by some of his disciples, visited the Pír Pantsál. He had reached a place at the foot of the mountain called Zezah Nár, now called Lál Ghulám, where a black *dev* was in the habit of seizing passers by and eating them. The *dev's* name was Dahkádú. In consequence of this the She*kh's* disciples turned to him in great distress and besought him to deliver them. The She*kh* heard their petition, and taking hold of one of the ears of the *dev*, threw him over the mountain. As soon as the body touched the ground on the other side it was metamorphosed into a stone, which may be seen there, in the form of a man, to the present day. If any person should doubt this thing, that it was or is not within the experience of God's saints, let him read the following:—

"*Auliyá rá hast qudrat az Iláh*
Tíri jastah báz gardánad zi ráh."

Several of these stones, called in Káshmírí *dumats*, are to be seen about the valley. People think them to be as old as the Pándavas, and believe they are the petrified bodies of wicked men, whom some good folk in olden times cursed because they were troubled by them. Near Hari Parbat, a hill in Srínagar, are five or six of these stones, which people declare were formerly *chatáí-farosh* (sellers of matting), whom Lakshmí, the goddess, cursed because they would not sell some matting cheap. There is one, also, at Zĕwan, in the Wular *pargana*—the petrified body of a *gúr* (a milkman); and there is another in the *dal* (lake) near Srínagar; while near Shupiyon there are a lot of them in a ring, that are said to be the metamorphoses of a wedding party. In Kashmír, at any rate, this

The next morning the second son, while looking for his brother, passed by the *jogí's* place, and seeing the horses, he stopped and inquired who the *jogí* was, and whence he came.

"I am travelling in this country for a while," the *jogí* replied. "These four horses are mine. Would you like to ride one of them? Yesterday the king's eldest son came to me and asked permission to take one of the horses. I caused him to be turned into stone, because he could not explain something that he saw during his ride."

"Indeed!" the second prince exclaimed; "and what did he see?"

Then the *jogí* told him, and promised that if he could explain why the sticks of the fence were changed into sickles that cut the vegetables, he would restore his brother to life and former self."

"You ask a hard thing," said the prince. "How can I explain what I have never seen? But if I may use one of your beautiful horses, I will go and examine this thing, and give you an answer."

Accordingly he mounted one of the horses and rode away. On reaching the jungle he saw a newly-born calf suckling its mother. He tarried a long time looking at this strange sight, and then returned to the *jogí*.

"Well, what have you seen?" the holy man inquired.

"O *jogí*," the prince answered, "I have seen a calf giving milk to its mother."

"Do you know what this means?" asked the *jogí*.

"No," said the prince.

"What! you don't know?"

The prince did not reply a second time; consequently the *jogí* cursed him, and he became a pillar of stone.

On the following morning the third prince came by

idea of metamorphosis into stone would appear to be a popular attempt to account for the existence of remarkable and unexplained monolithes. Perhaps some of our numerous metamorphosis folk-tales are to be explained as folk attempts at explaining the existence of monolithes in other parts of the world.

the place where the *jogí* was staying, and attracted by the horses, went up to the *jogí* and asked him who he was and how he had obtained such beautiful animals. Evading these questions, the good man begged him to sit down; and when, in course of conversation, he got to know that this young man also was a son of the king of that country, and was searching for his two brothers, he informed him what had happened to these princes. "But," he added, "they shall be restored to their former selves, if you can tell me why the sticks of the fence were changed into sickles and why the calf gave suck to the cow."

"Thank you," replied the prince. "If you will lend me one of your horses I will go and see these strange things."

"Certainly," said the *jogí*. "Take one of the horses and go and see; but mind and come back by the evening."

So the prince rode off, and as he entered the jungle he saw a man carrying a load of wood on his back, who, not content with what he had already gathered, still went on picking up whatever lay in his path.

"What does this mean?" thought the prince. "What shall I say to the *jogí* when he questions me?"

Alas! alas! this prince too was unable to explain the strange sight, and therefore was turned into a pillar of stone.

The next morning the last and youngest brother appeared and saluted the *jogí*. "O *jogí*," he said, "have you seen my three brothers?"

"Yes," he replied. "They are all there—look," and so saying, he pointed to the three pillars of stone. "I metamorphosed them because they could not explain a few things that they saw in yonder jungle. But I will restore them to their former selves if you can tell me the meaning of these things." Hereupon he related what the princes had seen.

"I will try," said the prince, "if you will please allow me to use one of your horses. I should like to ride to the jungle and see for myself."

Permission having been given, the prince started. On reaching the jungle he noticed a pond, from which water was flowing and filling other ponds. Presently the big pond was empty, having exhausted itself over these other ponds. When he returned in the evening he told the *jogí* what he had seen, and confessed his inability to explain its meaning. Consequently he too was metamorphosed into a pillar of stone.

When the king of the country found that not one of his sons had been heard of for several days he suspected that some harm had happened to them, and went in search of them. In the course of his wanderings he passed by the *jogí*. "*Jogí*," said he, "have you seen or heard anything of my four sons?"

The *jogí* pointed to the four pillars of stone.

"What!" exclaimed the king. "You do not mean to say that they have been changed into stones?"

"There they are," replied the *jogí*. "I metamorphosed them because they could not tell me the meaning of some sights that they saw in the jungle. However, they shall be restored if you can explain those things for them. You can have one of my horses if you like to go to the jungle."

"No, thank you," said the king. "But if you will tell me what my sons' difficulties were, I will try to unravel them."

Then the *jogí* told him, "The eldest prince saw a garden of vegetables fenced all round so that no man could enter it; and the sticks of the fence thereof became sickles, and cut the vegetables."

Then the king replied, "This is a picture of the man in whose care some money has been placed, and when the owner of the money asks for it, the man hides or spends the money, so that the owner cannot get at it.'

Directly the king uttered these words the eldest prince appeared, standing before him, and alive and well.

"The second prince saw a calf giving milk to a cow," said the *jogí*.

"Strange that he was not reminded of a woman who lives on her daughter's hire," said the king; and on saying this the second prince stood up before him.

"The third prince saw a man with a load of wood on his back, and as the man walked he picked up other sticks and added them to the load," said the *jogí*.

"One thinks of those people who are never satisfied with their wealth, but are always adding every cowrie they can get," said the king; and no sooner had the king spoken these words than the third prince was restored, and stood before him.

"Your youngest son saw a pond that had emptied itself to supply six other ponds," said the *jogí*.

"Just like the world," said the king. "One man may spend and be spent for the sake of others, and what return does he get?"

As soon as he said this the youngest prince stood before him.

Glad and happy, the king and his four sons then returned to the palace. Soon after this His Majesty gave up the government of the country to his sons, and devoted himself entirely to the religious life.

THE BRAVE PRINCESS.[1]

THERE were two great and wealthy kings. The one had a very handsome son, and the other had a most beautiful daughter. Both these, the prince and princess, were of a marriageable age; and so the two kings were sending and inquiring everywhere for suitable partners. As luck would have it, one day the messengers of these two kings met, and in course of conversation each told the other the purport of his errand. They were very much surprised and rejoiced when they found that their errand was the same, that the two kings were of a fairly equal position in the world, and that the prince and princess were in every way a good match.[2]

When the kings heard of the success of their messengers they immediately communicated with one another. A match was arranged; the day was fixed; and the bridegroom went to the house of the father of the bride. After the usual preliminaries the wedding took place, and everything passed off splendidly.

But now a cloud came over the scene. How short-lived is joy! No sooner does a man snatch at it than it disappears and the hand closes on a shadow. Alas! alas! while the prince was returning with his bride he halted in a certain garden that happened to be the favourite resort of a company of fairies. These creatures came to the place at night, and when they saw the prince they were so fascinated with him that they determined to make him

[1] Narrator's name, Makund Báyû, Suthû, Srínagar.

[2] Cf. tale of "Prince who Became a Ram," and "How the Princess Found her Husband," in this collection.

their own, and therefore charmed him into a death-like sleep. In vain the princess and others tried to rouse him on the following morning. They thought he was dead, and wept and mourned for him exceedingly, as for one whose spirit had departed, and with whom they should not converse any more. It was a terrible time. Meanwhile Sudabror and Budabror[3] came and perched on a tree close to the little company of mourners, and commenced talking together. Sudabror said, "This prince should not be buried."

"Why?" said Budabror.

"Because he is not dead," replied Sudabror. "In a few days perhaps he will revive."

These words fell like nectar in the ears of the princess, who at once gave orders to leave the corpse as and where it was, and promised to tell them afterwards why she had thus ordered. Accordingly the prince was left in the garden, and the people went away to their homes—the sad bride and her retinue one way, and the people belonging to the prince another way. Great was the grief of the king and queen when they heard the cruel fate of their son-in-law. The poor princess wept day and night, and would not be comforted. Every minute she was looking for the return of her husband; but he did not come. At length she could not bear her grief any longer, and therefore craved permission from her father to leave the palace for a while and to wander about the country whithersoever she wished. The king did not like to grant her request, but eventually he was moved to do so at the advice of his ministers, who thought that unless the princess had her wish she would become insane. The princess wandered here and there on the highway bemoaning her sad lot. "Have you seen the prince? Have you seen the prince?" she inquired from every passer-by. Thus many days were spent, and nobody could tell her anything of the object of her anxious search. At last an

[3] These birds appear in the story of the "Two Brothers."

old man approached. "Have you seen the prince?" she asked.

"I have passed through a garden," replied the old man, "and in this garden I saw a handsome youth sleeping on the ground. Wondering why he had selected such a spot for a rest, I stopped, and behold! within a few minutes I saw some fairy-like women come and place a wand under his head, and he sat up and talked with them, and then they took the wand and placed it under his feet, and the youth fell back into sleep again. This I saw, and I wondered what this strange sight might be."

"Very curious!" exclaimed the princess. "Can you direct me to the garden where this youth lies sleeping?"

"Yes," replied the old man, who at once led her towards the ill-fated spot.

On their arrival they found the body of the prince lying on the ground, apparently lifeless. Quickly seizing the wand that was placed under his feet, the princess removed it and put it under his head, when, as the old man had said, the prince awoke and sat up.[4]

"Who are you?" he said to the princess.

"I am your wife," she answered. "Do you not know me?"

"How did you get here?" he said.

"By the help of yonder old man," she replied, pointing to her guide, who had tarried at a little distance from fear. "Get up and come—escape with me from this terrible place."

"Alas! I cannot," he said, "for the fairies will soon discover my absence, and come after me and kill me. Oh! if you love me, place the wand under my feet, and go."

"Never," she said.

"Then hide yourself quickly in the hollow of that tree, for you are not safe here now. The fairies may return at any moment."

[4] Cf. *Folk-Tales of Bengal*, p. 81; *Indian Antiquary*, vol. i. pp. 115–219; and the same journal, vol. xvi. pp. 190–211. In English fairy tales a "sleep-thorn" or other somniferous piece of wood is generally employed.

The princess did so, and as soon as she had got within her hiding-place the fairies came.

"Ah! what do I smell?" said one.

"Some human being has been here," said another.

On this two or three of them went to try and discover the stranger who had dared to invade their retreat, but they were unsuccessful. They then woke the prince and asked him if he knew of any human being that had ventured near. Of course he told them, "No."

"But we are certain there is somebody here near," they said, "for the smell of a human being fills the air. Anyhow, we will leave here to-morrow for another place."

So the next morning the fairies explored the garden, which was of immense size, and found another retreat for themselves, where they thought they would be free from the intrusion of any human being; and while they were away the prince called the princess, and said, "What will you do now, my wife? They will take me away to another place, where you will not be able to come, and I shall never see you again. Ah me! ah me!"

"Not so," replied the brave princess. "See, I will gather some flowers. Strew these," she continued, giving him a little bouquet of a certain kind of flower. "I shall then be able to track you."

The prince took the flowers and hid them in his clothes, and the princess ran away to the hollow in the tree.

In a little while the fairies appeared in sight, and beckoned to the prince to come after them. As the prince went he now and again dropped a flower. The following day the princess carefully followed the track until she reached a very large and grand building, which looked like a palace. This was the abode of a *dev* who instructed the fairies in all manner of magic. Nothing daunted, the princess entered the building, and not finding anybody inside, she sat down on one of the low seats and rested herself.

Within an hour the *dev* arrived. Seeing the princess, he thought she was his daughter, whom some other *dev* had recently taken away by force. "My darling daughter," he exclaimed, rushing up to her, "how did you get back? How did you escape from that wretch?"

The princess quickly perceived the circumstances of the case, and replied, "Yes, I contrived to get out of his clutches while he was asleep."

"My darling! my darling!" he exclaimed.

For some time the princess lived in the *dev's* house, and was recognised by him and all the fairies as his daughter. She had full power to do what she liked and to go where she liked; and at her earnest request the *dev* taught her many of his tricks: how to make a man dead and then alive again, how to find anything that had been hidden, and several others. One day, by virtue of her extraordinary powers, the princess noticed her husband concealed in an ornament that was hanging from the ear of one of the fairies. This earring she pretended to like very much, and asked the fairy to give it to her. The fairy refused; but at last, fearing to offend her teacher's daughter, she gave the earring to her, on the condition that it should be returned on the morrow. The princess promised. As soon as the fairy was out of sight the princess extricated her husband.

"O beloved, do you know me?" she asked, when the prince looked round on her and on everything with great surprise. "Do you not know me? I am your wife. For your sake I have left my father's house; for your sake I have dared to visit this garden and to follow you even to this *dev's* abode; for your sake I have endured his kisses and caresses. Oh! do you not know me?"

Then the prince, having recovered his senses, recognised her, and wept for joy.

"Come, come now," she said, "I will tell you what we must do. The *dev* and all the people thoroughly believe that I am his daughter, who was carried away forcibly by another. I shall take you to him, and profess that while I was escaping from the *dev* I met you, and overcome by your beauty, I married you. I shall also inform him of your royal station, and entreat him to sanction the marriage. He will be very glad when he hears this. Do not be afraid. Come and see."

The princess was not disappointed. The *dev* was exceedingly happy to hear of his daughter's good fortune, and made a great feast in her honour, to which he invited all the members of the fairy community.

For some weeks the prince and princess stayed with the *dev*, and then the prince quite naturally expressed a great wish to visit his home, and the princess wanted to go with him. Much as the *dev* wished to keep them both with him, he did not think it reasonable to refuse his permission, and so loaded them with presents and bade them return to him as soon as possible. Amongst other things he gave them a *pīṭh*, which, on any person sitting in it and wishing, would go to the place wished for. This was the very thing for the prince and princess, who at once packed their treasures in it, and then, saying farewell to their (beloved ?) *bhút*, and to all the fairies who had assembled to witness their departure, they sat in the *pīṭh* and began to float away in the air in the direction of the palace of the father of the princess. This was soon reached.

There was much joy in the palace and in the city that day and for long afterwards because the king's daughter had returned, and the prince, her handsome husband, was not dead, but was alive and well, and was with her.

THE THREE PRINCES.[1]

ONCE upon a time there lived a king, who was celebrated for his learning, power, and prowess. This king had three sons, who were all in every way worthy of such a father; for they were brave, and clever, and handsome, and wise, and good.

One day the king, wishing to arrange for a successor to his throne, summoned the *wazírs*, and bade them help him in the matter. "Take the princes," he said, "and thoroughly examine them, and the one whom you approve I will appoint to sit on the throne after me."

In the course of a few days the *wazírs* waited on His Majesty with their answer. The chief *wazír* was spokesman, and said—

"Concerning the appointment of a successor let the king not be angry, and we will speak. Our counsel is to send the princes out into the world and bid them to trade, and it shall be that whoever among them amasses the greatest fortune shall be king."

Upon this all the *wazírs* bowed their heads in token of their unanimous approval of the plan.

"Be it so," said the king, and immediately told his pleasure to the princes.

When everything was ready the three princes started. They all travelled together to the sea, and there took ship for some foreign country. As soon as they reached their destination they parted. One went in this direction, another in that, and the third in another; but before they

[1] Narrator's name, Makund Báyú of Suthú, Srínagar.

separated they each bound themselves to return by a certain time to the spot whence they had parted.

The two elder brothers went and traded with their money, and gained immense wealth, but the youngest brother wandered along the sea-coast, encamping here and there as it pleased him.

While he was meditating what he should do with his money, a *gosáín* came and stayed with him for three days. The holy man was so pleased with the respect and attention shown to him, that he determined to reward the prince.

"I am very grateful for your piety and goodness," he said. "Tell me your name, whence you came, and whither you are going."

The prince explained everything to him.

"I understand," said the *gosáín*. "You must stay here. Do not go any farther, but remain here till your brothers return. Send your servants into the city to buy as much corn as possible, and when they bring it throw some of it into the sea every day till it is all gone. Then wait, and you shall reap an abundant harvest." Saying this, the holy man blessed him and departed.

The prince acted according to the advice of the *gosáín*. He bought an immense quantity of corn, and had it piled up near his encampment. Every day for about six months he threw a certain measure of it into the sea, till the whole was spent. "Now," thought he, "I shall have my reward."

He waited in great expectation for several days, but nothing appeared. "The *gosáín* has deceived me," he said to himself. "I am a ruined man! Why was I so foolish as to listen to his wicked advice? What will my father and my brothers say to me when they hear that I have thrown all my money into the sea? How they will laugh at me! I shall never be able to show my face to them again! Ah me! Ah me! I will now go to another country. The day after to-morrow I will leave this cursed place."

But these words were hastily spoken. When all was ready, and the prince and his retinue were about to start, something happened. The corn that the prince had thrown into the river had been eaten by a big fish,[2] and as the news of the prince's liberality spread far and wide in the waters, shoals upon shoals of fish came together to the place. The king of the fish[3] also came with them. At last the supply was suddenly stopped.

"Why is this?" the king-fish asked. "We have been receiving corn for the last six months, and now for several days we have had nothing. Has the prince been rewarded for his kindness to us?"

"No!" said the whole company. "We have not received any order to that effect."

"Then hear the order," said the king-fish. "Go immediately and recompense the prince. Each one of you take a ruby and give it to him."

Away went all the company of fishes and deposited each one a ruby on the shore near to the place[4] where the prince was standing and looking mournfully across the sea. Attracted by the great noise in the water, the prince turned towards them, and saw the long row of rubies on the sand. "Wicked man that I am!" he exclaimed. "Why am I thus rewarded? My little faith does not deserve this." Saying this, he at once gave an order to have all the preparations for departure stopped.

"I shall remain here," said he, "till my brothers return. Pitch the tents again."

While the encampment was once more being got ready he and his head-man were occupied in collecting the long row of precious rubies which the fishes had brought.

"Be careful," he said to the man, "that nothing of this matter reaches the ears of the people of the city or any other person whom we may meet. Let no mention of it

[2] Kashmírí, *matsh* (Sanskrit, *matsya*), a fish; the fish *avatára* of Vishnu.

[3] In *Indian Fairy Tales*, p. 67, the alligator appears as king of the fishes; in *Tibetan Tales*, p. 291, the Leviathan.

[4] Cf. Chap. xvi. of *Hikáyátu's Sálihín*; *Indian Fairy Tales*, p. 66; *Folk-Tales of Bengal*, p. 221.

be made to my brothers either. I charge you; see to it that you fulfil your trust. You and the rest of my retinue shall not go unrewarded if you obey me."

The man promised, and every day after this, as long as the prince was in that place, the fishes were daily fed with abundance of corn.

Now, in order that his valuable treasures might not be discovered, the prince had them placed in cakes of dung, which were dried in the sun.[5] After a while the day arrived for him to leave, so that he might reach the place where he was to meet his brothers by the appointed time. He was so punctual, that he arrived there a day or two earlier than the other two princes.

"Well, what luck?" they said to each other when they all met.

Said the eldest prince, "I have been trading as a cloth merchant, and have gained such-and-such wealth," mentioning an enormous sum of money.

"Well done!" exclaimed the other two brothers.

Said the second prince, "I have been trading as a *baniyá*, and have amassed such-and-such money," also mentioning an enormous amount.

"Well done!" exclaimed the other two brothers.

Then spoke the youngest prince. "You see, O brothers, my fortune," and he pointed towards several loads of dung-cakes.

"Hie, hie!" cried the other two princes. "What made our brother choose such a disgusting and unprofitable business?"

As soon as possible a ship was hired, and the three princes, with their attendants, set sail for their own country. Now, it happened that a most foolish arrangement had been made about wood for the voyage. Before they had got half-way they had run short of that

[5] Kashmírí *Lubar* or *Drambar* (if a big one). Those used by potters are called *Munar* or *Kond*, which generally have a little hole in the middle. Poor people and others burn ordure for cooking and for heating their little braziers, as any one will soon discover who comes into close contact with them (in the winter) or visits their houses at cooking-time.

indispensable article, and therefore the two elder princes and the captain of the ship came to the youngest prince and begged him to allow them to use some piles of his dung-cakes, promising to pay him as soon as they landed.

The youngest prince consented, and the next morning gave them sufficient for the rest of the voyage, after having taken out the ruby that was in each of the cakes. Thus in due time the ship arrived at her destination, and the royal passengers disembarked. They immediately started for their father's palace, and the day after their return the king summoned the whole populace to a grand meeting to witness the appointment of his successor to the throne.

Accordingly there was an immense gathering. The king, attended by all his court, sat in state, and the people crowded round on all sides. Then the princes were summoned before His Majesty and the people to show their wealth and tell their experience. First came the eldest prince, who in a loud voice declared all that he had done and what fortune had attended him. Afterwards came the second prince, and did likewise. And when the people heard their words they cried, "Let him be king! Let him be king!" But when the youngest prince appeared and showed his piles of dung-cakes the king and all the people laughed at him, and told him to go.

"Be not hasty, O my father," he said, and then he turned and frowned on the people. "You laugh," he said to them all; "but presently you will repent of your laughter. See, in each of these dung-cakes there is a ruby whose price is beyond value;" and he broke open one of the cakes and let fall a ruby. "Look here! Look here! Look here! Look here!" he shouted several times, and each time broke one of the dung-cakes and let fall a ruby![6] Then all the people wondered!

"I have never seen such rubies before," said the king. "Truly their value cannot be estimated. This my

[6] Sometimes valuables (taken on a journey) are placed in bread or in fruit. Cf. other tales in this collection; also introduction to *Baital Pachísí*.

youngest son has got more wealth than the other two princes and I and all the people put together. He shall be king."

"Yes, yes, let him be king!" was the reply of the whole assembly; and after this they were dismissed to their homes.

Not long afterwards the old king died and was cremated, and the younger prince reigned in his stead, while the other two princes were appointed to the two chief positions under him.[7] [8]

[7] Why are Kashmíris so fond of "ship" stories? (1.) Perhaps the extensive communication carried on by boat in the Valley is responsible for much of the idea. (2.) Undoubtedly, too, the Sindibád tales have somewhat influenced the people, who are constantly reading and repeating them. Very few Kashmíris have seen the sea or a ship, but they often inquire about the *boḍ samundar* (great sea) and the *baḍi johaz* (the great ships), that sail upon it. The Tibetans, too, have sea stories.

[8] Folk-tales often make the younger or youngest son the most fortunate, —perhaps as a recompense for his position in the family, which is one of inferiority, and sometimes of poverty. Cf. *Folk-Lore Journal*, vol. iv. p. 73.

THE DILIGENT KING.[1]

Often it happens that wicked men pursue their evil course and prosper, while the righteous are hindered in their doings.

Once upon a time there lived a very kind and just king, whose great desire was, that his people should prosper in every way. One day he suddenly discovered that the inhabitants of his country were getting less and less. How to account for it he did not know. The laws were just and good; the taxes were very light; and the crops generally very prosperous. Why, therefore, this sudden depopulation?

In order to inquire the cause the king disguised himself as a *faqír* and went about the country. In this way he learned that a great *jinn* was constantly visiting the different towns and villages, and making depredations wherever he went. In the course of his peregrinations the king came across this monster, though he recognised him not, because he appeared to him as an ordinary man. His Majesty had reached a barren, desolate spot some distance from the city, when he saw a man kneeling on the ground with his eyes shut and his fingers in his ears, and beating the earth with his head.

"O man," said the king, "what are you doing? Are you mad?"

"No, no," replied he. "I have come here to meditate. My eyes I keep shut, that I may not look upon anything which the eyes ought not to see; my ears do I close, that I may not hear anything wrong; and with my head do I beat the ground, that all insects may be

[1] Narrator's name, Paṇḍit Chandra Kol of Srínagar.

frightened away, lest I tread on one, and so be guilty of slaying life."

"O holy man," said the king, "where do you live?"

"Yonder," replied he. "Come, return with me and stay the night, if you have nothing better to do. I perceive that you too are a man whose thoughts are not altogether occupied with the things of this world."

The king accepted, and so they both went to the holy man's house, on arriving at which he ordered his wife to get some warm water and wash their guest's feet, while he went outside for a minute or so. Filled with pity for the stranger, the woman, while bathing his feet, told him that her husband was a *kímyágar*,[2] and would slay him, as he had done hundreds of people lately. She advised him to take three *kulichas*, and to go immediately. Her husband would be back presently, and on his return would ask for him, and not finding him, would set a hunting dog after him. But he was not to be afraid, she continued, because if he threw down one of the *kulichas* the dog would eat it and return. The *kímyágar* would then send another dog, when he was to throw down another *kulicha*. Afterwards a third dog would overtake him, when he was to throw down the third *kulicha*. By that time he would have reached the city, whither the dogs would not follow him.

The king thanked the woman and departed. He ran as fast as he could. A dog soon came after him, and then another, and another—great ferocious brutes, that would have torn him to pieces if he had not diverted their attention with the *kulichas*. When he reached the city he went to his palace, and resuming his royal garments, without delay summoned a company of soldiers, and ordered them to go and slay the *kímyágar* and bring his wife to him. So the *kímyágar* died, and his wife was appointed to the charge of the king's *zanána*. Henceforth there was peace and prosperity in the country.

[2] An alchemist, a deceiver.

THE IVORY CITY AND ITS FAIRY PRINCESS.[1]

ONE day a young prince was out practising archery with the son of his father's chief *wazír*, when one of the arrows accidentally struck the wife of a merchant, who was walking about in an upper room of a house close by. The prince aimed at a bird that was perched on the window-sill of that room, and had not the slightest idea that anybody was at hand, or he would not have shot in that direction. Consequently, not knowing what had happened, he and the *wazír's* son walked away, the *wazír's* son chaffing him because he had missed the bird.

Presently the merchant went to ask his wife about something, and found her lying, to all appearance, dead in the middle of the room, and an arrow fixed in the ground within half a yard of her head. Supposing that she was dead, he rushed to the window and shrieked, "Thieves! Thieves! They have killed my wife." The neighbours quickly gathered, and the servants came running upstairs to see what was the matter. It happened that the woman had fainted, and that there was only a very slight wound in her breast where the arrow had grazed.

As soon as the woman recovered her senses she told them that two young men had passed by the place with their bows and arrows, and that one of them had most deliberately aimed at her as she stood by the window.

On hearing this the merchant went to the king, and told him what had taken place. His Majesty was much enraged at such audacious wickedness, and swore that

[1] Narrator's name, Shiva Báyú of Renawárí, Srínagar.

most terrible punishment should be visited on the offender if he could be discovered. He ordered the merchant to go back and ascertain whether his wife could recognise the young men if she saw them again.

"Oh yes," replied the woman, "I should know them again among all the people in the city."

"Then," said the king, when the merchant brought back this reply, "to-morrow I will cause all the male inhabitants of this city to pass before your house, and your wife will stand at the window and watch for the man who did this wanton deed."

A royal proclamation was issued to this effect. So the next day all the men and boys of the city, from the age of tens years upwards, assembled and marched by the house of the merchant. By chance (for they both had been excused from obeying this order) the king's son and the *wazír's* son were also in the company, and passed by in the crowd. They came to see the *tamáshá*.

As soon as these two appeared in front of the merchant's window they were recognised by the merchant's wife, and at once reported to the king.

"My own son and the son of my chief *wazír!*" exclaimed the king, who had been present from the commencement. "What examples for the people! Let them both be executed."

"Not so, Your Majesty," said the *wazír*, "I beseech you. Let the facts of the case be thoroughly investigated. How is it?" he continued, turning to the two young men. "Why have you done this cruel thing?"

"I shot an arrow at a bird that was sitting on the sill of an open window in yonder house, and missed," answered the prince. "I suppose the arrow struck the merchant's wife. Had I known that she or anybody had been near I should not have shot in that direction."

"We will speak of this later on," said the king, on hearing this answer. "Dismiss the people. Their presence is no longer needed."

In the evening His Majesty and the *wazír* had a long and earnest talk about their two sons. The king wished both of them to be executed; but the *wazír* thought that the prince only should be punished, and he suggested that, since the king's anger was such that he could never look on his son's face again, the prince should be banished from the country. This finally was agreed to.

Accordingly, on the following morning a little company of soldiers escorted the prince out of the city. When they reached the last custom-house the *wazír's* son overtook them. He had come with all haste, bringing with him four bags of *muhrs* on four horses. "I am come," he said, throwing his arms round the prince's neck, "because I cannot let you go alone. We have lived together, we will be exiled together, and we will die together. Turn me not back, if you love me."

"Consider," the prince answered, "what you are doing. All kinds of trial may be before me. Why should you leave your home and country to be with me?"

"Because I love you," he said, "and shall never be happy without you."

So the two friends walked along hand in hand as fast as they could to get out of the country, and behind them marched the soldiers and the horses with their valuable burdens. On reaching a certain place on the borders of the king's dominions the prince gave the soldiers some gold, and ordered them to return. The soldiers took the money and left; they did not, however, go very far, but hid themselves behind rocks and stones, and waited till they were quite sure that the prince did not intend to come back.

On and on the exiles walked, till they arrived at a certain village, where they determined to spend the night under one of the big trees of the place. The prince made preparations for a fire, and arranged the few articles of bedding that they had with them, while the *wazír's* son went to the *baniyá* and the baker and the butcher to get something for their dinner. For some reason he was delayed; perhaps the *tsuṭ* was not quite ready, or the *baniyá* had not got all the spices prepared. After waiting half an hour the prince became impatient, and rose up and walked about.

He saw a pretty, clear little brook running along not far from their resting-place, and hearing that its source was not far distant, he started off to find it. The source was a beautiful lake, which at that time was covered with the magnificent lotus flower and other water plants. The prince sat down on the bank, and being thirsty, took up some of the water in his hand. Fortunately he looked into his hand before drinking, and there, to his great astonishment, he saw reflected whole and clear the image of a beautiful fairy. He looked round, hoping to see the reality; but seeing no person, he drank the water, and put out his hand to take some more. Again he saw the reflection in the water which was in his palm. He looked around as before, and this time discovered a fairy sitting by the bank on the opposite side of the lake. On seeing her he fell down insensible.

When the *wazír's* son returned, and found the fire lighted, the horses securely fastened, and the bags of *muhrs* lying altogether in a heap, but no prince, he did not know what to think. He waited a little while, and then shouted; but not getting any reply, he got up and went to the brook. There he came across the footmarks of his friend. Seeing these, he went back at once for the money and the horses, and bringing them with him, he tracked the prince to the lake, where he found him lying to all appearance dead.

"Alas! alas!" he cried, and, lifting up the prince, he poured some water over his head and face. "Alas! my brother, what is this? Oh! do not die and leave me thus. Speak, speak! O God, I cannot bear this!"

In a few minutes the prince, revived by the water, opened his eyes, and looked about wildly.

"Thank God!" exclaimed the *wazír's* son. "But what is the matter, brother?"

"Go away," replied the prince. "I don't want to say anything to you, or to see you. Go away."

"Come, come; let us leave this place. Look, I have brought some food for you, and the horses, and everything. Let us eat and depart."

"Go alone," replied the prince.

"Never," said the *wazír's* son. "What has happened to suddenly estrange you from me? A little while ago we were brethren, but now you detest the sight of me."

"I have looked upon a fairy," the prince said. "But a moment I saw her face; for when she noticed that I was looking at her she covered her face with lotus petals. Oh, how beautiful she was! And while I gazed she took out of her bosom an ivory box, and held it up to me. Then I fainted. Oh! if you can get me that fairy for my wife, I will go anywhere with you."

"O brother," said the *wazír's* son, "you have indeed seen a fairy. She is a fairy of the fairies. This is none other than Gul'izar of Shahr-i-'Áj.[2] I know this from the hints that she gave you. From her covering her face with lotus petals I learn her name, and from her showing you the ivory box I learn where she lives. Be patient, and rest assured that I will arrange your marriage with her."

When the prince heard these encouraging words he felt much comforted, rose up, and ate, and then went away gladly with his friend.

On the way they met two men. These two men belonged to a family of robbers. There were eleven of them altogether. One, an elderly sister, stayed at home and cooked the food, and the other ten—all brothers—went out, two and two, and walked about the four different ways that ran through that part of the country, robbing those travellers who could not resist them, and inviting

[2] *Gul'izar* or *Gul'uzár* (Persian), rosy-cheeked; *Shahr-i-'Áj*, the city of ivory.

others, who were too powerful for two of them to manage, to come and rest at their house, where the whole family attacked them and stole their goods. These thieves lived in a kind of tower, which had several strong-rooms in it, and under which was a great pit, wherein they threw the corpses of the poor unfortunates who chanced to fall into their power.

The two men came forward, and politely accosting them, begged them to come and stay at their house for the night. "It is late," they said, "and there is not another village within several miles."

"Shall we accept this good man's invitation, brother?" asked the prince.

The *wazír's* son frowned slightly in token of disapproval; but the prince was tired, and thinking that it was only a whim of his friend's, he said to the men, "Very well. It is very kind of you to ask us."

So they all four went to the robbers' tower.

Seated in a room, with the door fastened on the outside, the two travellers bemoaned their fate.

"It is no good groaning," said the *wazír's* son. "I will climb to the window, and see whether there are any means of escape. Yes! yes!" he whispered, when he had reached the window-hole. "Below there is a ditch surrounded by a high wall. I will jump down and reconnoitre. You stay here, and wait till I return."

Presently he came back and told the prince that he had seen a most ugly woman, whom he supposed was the robbers' housekeeper. His plan was to explain everything to this wretched creature, and then get her to release them on the promise of her marriage with the prince. He would bring her back with him to their room. She would certainly demand this promise as payment for their escape. At first the prince was to pretend to demur, but afterwards he was to comply. The prince consented.

When the *wazír's* son came up to the woman she wept.

"Why do you weep?" he asked.

"Because of the short time you have to live," she replied.

"Weep not," he said, "but come and be married to the prince. Come now and ask his consent to this plan."

They went, and on reaching the room the *wazír's* son besought the prince to promise to marry the woman; but he refused, saying that he would sooner rot in the tower than give his hand to such as she was; whereupon the *wazír's* son fell at his feet and besought him more earnestly, till the prince yielded.

Glad and happy, the woman then led the way out of the enclosure by a secret door.

"But where are the horses and the goods?" the *wazír's* son inquired.

"You cannot bring them," the woman said. "To go out by any other way would be to thrust oneself into the grave."

"All right, then; they also shall go out by this door. I have a charm, whereby I can make them thin or fat." So the *wazír's* son fetched the horses without any person knowing it, and repeating the charm, he made them pass through the narrow doorway like pieces of cloth, and when they were all outside restored them to their former condition. He at once mounted his horse and laid hold of the halter of one of the other horses, and then beckoning to the prince to do likewise, he rode off. The prince saw his opportunity, and in a moment was riding after him, having hold of the other horse.

"Stop, stop!" shrieked the woman, "Leave me not. My brothers will discover my act and kill me."

"Run along, then," the *wazír's* son shouted. "Look, we are not riding so very fast."

The woman ran as fast as she could, and managed to keep within a fair distance of the riders. When the *wazír's* son perceived that they were out of range of danger he dismounted, and seizing the breathless woman, he tied her to a tree and whipped her. "Now," said he, "you ugly creature, if your brothers find you, you can say that we are *devs*, and thus escaped."

On, on they rode, until they reached a village, where they stayed the night. The following morning they were off again, and asked for Shahr-i-'Áj from every passer-by. At length they came to this famous city, and put up at a little hut that belonged to an old woman, from whom they feared no harm, and with whom, therefore, they could abide in peace and comfort. At first the old woman did not like the idea of these travellers staying in her house, but the sight of a *muhr*, which the prince dropped in the bottom of a cup in which she had given him water, and a present of another *muhr* from the *wazír's* son, quickly made her change her mind. She agreed to let them stay there for a few days.

As soon as her work was over the old woman came and sat down with her lodgers. The *wazír's* son pretended to be utterly ignorant of the place and people. "Has this city a name?" he asked the old woman.

"Of course it has, you stupid. Every little village, much more a city, and such a city as this, has a name."

"What is the name of this city?"

"Shahr-i-'Áj. Don't you know that? I thought the name was known all over the world."

On the mention of the name Shahr-i-'Áj the prince gave a deep sigh. The *wazír's* son looked as much as to say, "Keep quiet, or you'll discover the secret."

"Is there a king of this country?" continued the *wazír's* son.

"Of course there is, and a queen, and a princess."

"What are their names?"

"The name of the princess is Gul'izar, and the name of the queen"——

The *wazír's* son interrupted the old woman by turning to look at the prince, who was staring like a madman. "Yes," he said to him afterwards, "we are in the right country. We shall see the beautiful princess."

One morning the two travellers noticed the old woman's most careful toilette: how careful she was in the arrangement of her hair and the set of her *kasábah* and *puts.*

"Who is coming?" said the *wazír's* son.

"Nobody," the old woman replied.

"Then where are you going?"

"I am going to see my daughter, who is a servant of the princess Gul'izar. I see her and the princess every day. I should have gone yesterday, if you had not been here and monopolised all my time."

"Ah-h-h! Be careful not to say anything about us in the hearing of the princess." The *wazír's* son asked her not to speak about them at the palace, hoping that, because she had been told not to do so, she would mention their arrival, and thus the princess would be informed of their coming.

On seeing her mother the girl pretended to be very angry. "Why have you not been for two days?" she asked.

"Because, my dear," the old woman answered, "two young travellers, a prince and the son of some great *wazír*, have taken up their abode in my hut, and demand so much of my attention. It is nothing but cooking and cleaning, and cleaning and cooking, all day long. I can't understand the men," she added; "one of them especially appears very stupid. He asked me the name of this country and the name of the king. Now where can these men have come from, that they do not know these things? However, they are very great and very rich. They each give me a *muhr* every morning and every evening."

After this the old woman went and repeated almost the same words to the princess; on the hearing of which the princess beat her severely, and threatened her with a severer punishment if she ever again spoke of strange men before her.

In the evening, when the old woman had returned to her hut, she told the *wazír's* son how sorry she was that she could not help breaking her promise, and how the princess had struck her because she mentioned their coming and all about them.

"Alas! alas!" said the prince, who had eagerly listened to every word. "What, then, will be her anger at the sight of a man?"

"Anger?" said the *wazír's* son, with an astonished air. "She would be exceedingly glad to see one man. I know this. In this treatment of the old woman I see her request that you will go and see her during the coming dark fortnight."

"God be praised!" the prince exclaimed.

The next time the old woman went to the palace Gul'izar called one of her servants and ordered her to rush into the room while she was conversing with the old woman; and if the old woman asked what was the matter, she was to say that the king's elephants had gone mad, and were rushing about the city and *bázár* in every direction, and destroying everything in their way.

The servant obeyed, and the old woman, fearing lest the elephants should go and push down her hut and kill the prince and his friend, begged the princess to let her depart. Now Gul'izar had obtained a kind of charmed swing, that landed whoever sat on it at the place whither they wished to be. "Get the swing," she said to one of the servants standing by. When it was brought she bade the old woman step into it and desire to be at home.

The old woman did so, and was at once carried through the air quickly and safely to her hut, where she found her two lodgers safe and sound. "Oh!" she cried, "I thought that both of you would be killed by this time. The royal elephants have got loose and are running about wildly. When I heard this I was anxious about you. So the princess gave me this charmed swing to return in. But come, let us get outside before the elephants arrive and batter down the place."

"Don't believe this," said the *wazír's* son. "It is a mere hoax. They have been playing tricks with you."

"You will soon have your heart's desire," he whispered aside to the prince. "These things are signs."

Two days of the dark fortnight had elapsed, when the prince and the *wazír's* son seated themselves in the swing, and wished themselves within the grounds of the palace. In a moment they were there, and there too was the object of their search standing by one of the palace gates, and longing to see the prince quite as much as he was longing to see her.

Oh, what a happy meeting it was!

"At last," said Gul'izar, "I have seen my beloved, my husband."

"A thousand thanks to God for bringing me to you," said the prince.

Other appointments were arranged of course, and then the prince and Gul'izar kissed one another and parted, the one for the hut and the other for the palace, both of them feeling happier than they had ever been before.

Henceforth the prince visited Gul'izar every day and returned to the hut every night. One morning Gul'izar begged him to stay with her always, as she liked not his going away at night. She was constantly afraid of some evil happening to him—perhaps robbers would slay him, or sickness attack him, and then she would be deprived of him. She could not live without seeing him. The prince showed her that there was no real cause for fear, and said that he felt he ought to return to his friend at night, because he had left his home and country and risked his life for him, and, moreover, if it had not been for his friend's help he would never have met with her.

Gul'izar for the time assented, but she determined in her heart to get rid of the *wazír's* son as soon as possible. A few days after this conversation she ordered one of her maids to make a *piláv.* She gave special directions that a certain poison was to be mixed into it while cooking, and as soon as it was ready the cover was to be placed on the saucepan, so that the poisonous steam might not escape.

When the *piláv* was ready she sent it at once by the hand of a servant to the *wazír's* son with this message:—"Gul'izar, the princess, sends you an offering in the name of her dead uncle."

On receiving the present the *wazír's* son thought that the prince had spoken gratefully of him to the princess, and therefore she had thus remembered him. Accordingly he sent back his *salám* and expressions of thankfulness.

When it was dinner-time he took the saucepan of *piláv*, and went out to eat it by the stream. Taking off the lid, he threw it aside on the grass and then washed his hands. During the minute or so that he was performing these ablutions, the green grass under the cover of the saucepan turned quite yellow. He was astonished, and suspecting that there was poison in the *piláv*, he took a little and threw it to some crows that were hopping about. The moment the crows ate what was thrown to them they fell down dead.[3]

"God be praised," exclaimed the *wazír's* son, "who has preserved me from death at this time!"

On the return of the prince that evening the *wazír's* son was very reticent and depressed. The prince noticed this change in him, and asked what was the reason. "Is it because I am away so much at the palace?" The *wazír's* son saw that the prince had nothing to do with the sending of the *piláv*, and therefore told him everything.

"Look here," he said, "in this handkerchief is some *piláv* that the princess sent me this morning in the name of her deceased uncle. It is saturated with poison. Thank God, I discovered it in time!"

"O brother! who can have done this thing? Who is there that entertains enmity against you?"

"The princess, Gul'izar. Listen. The next time you go to see her, I entreat you to take some snow with you; and just before seeing the princess put a little of it into

[3] Cf. *Folk-Tales of Bengal*, pp. 90, 157; *Indian Fairy Tales*, 212; the first story in *Baital Pachísí*; also tale "*Lach* of Rupees for a Bit of Advice" in this collection.

both your eyes. It will provoke tears, and Gul'izar will ask you why you are crying. Tell her that you weep for the loss of your friend, who died suddenly this morning. Look! take, too, this wine and this shovel, and when you have feigned intense grief at the death of your friend, bid the princess to drink a little of the wine. It is strong, and will immediately send her into a deep sleep. Then, while she is asleep, heat the shovel and mark her back with it.[4] Remember to bring back the shovel again, and also to take her pearl necklace. This done, return. Now fear not to execute these instructions, because on the fulfilment of them depends your fortune and happiness. I will arrange that your marriage with the princess shall be accepted by the king, her father, and all the court."

The prince promised that he would do everything as the *wazír's* son had advised him; and he kept his promise.

The following night, on the return of the prince from his visit to Gul'izar, he and the *wazír's* son, taking the horses and bags of *muhrs*, went to a graveyard about a mile or so distant. It was arranged that the *wazír's* son should act the part of a *faqír*, and the prince the part of the *faqír's* disciple and servant.

In the morning, when Gul'izar had returned to her senses, she felt a smarting pain in her back, and noticed that her pearl necklace was gone. She went at once and informed the king of the loss of her necklace, but said nothing to him about the pain in her back.

The king was very angry when he heard of the theft, and caused proclamation concerning it to be made throughout all the city and surrounding country.

"It is well," said the *wazír's* son, when he heard of this proclamation. "Fear not, my brother, but go and take this necklace, and try to sell it in the *bázár*."

The prince took it to a goldsmith and asked him to buy it.

"How much do you want for it?" asked the man.

[4] Cf. *Indian Fairy Tales*, p. 134.

"Fifty thousand rupees," the prince replied.

"All right," said the man "wait here while I go and fetch the money."

The prince waited and waited, till at last the goldsmith returned, and with him the *kotwál,* who at once took the prince into custody on the charge of stealing the princess's necklace.

"How did you get the necklace?" the *kotwál* asked.

"A *faqír*, whose servant I am, gave it to me to sell in the *bázár*," the prince replied. "Permit me, and I will show you where he is."

The prince directed the *kotwál* and the policemen to the place where he had left the *wazír's* son, and there they found the *faqír* with his eyes shut and engaged in prayer. Presently, when he had finished his devotions, the *kotwál* asked him to explain how he had obtained possession of the princess's necklace.

"Call the king hither," he replied, "and then I will tell His Majesty face to face."

On this some men went to the king and told him what the *faqír* had said. His Majesty came, and seeing the *faqír* so solemn and earnest in his devotions, he was afraid to rouse his anger, lest peradventure God's displeasure should descend on him, and so he placed his hands together in the attitude of a supplicant, and asked, "How did you get my daughter's necklace?"

"Last night," replied the *faqír*, "we were sitting here by this tomb worshipping God, when a woman, dressed as a princess, came and exhumed a body that had been buried a few days ago, and ate it. On seeing this I was filled with anger, and beat her back with that shovel, which was lying on the fire at the time. While running away from me her necklace got loose and dropped. You wonder at these words, but they are not difficult to prove. Examine your daughter, and you will find the marks of the burn on her back. Go, and if it is as I say, send the princess to me, and I will punish her."

The king went back to the palace, and at once ordered the princess's back to be examined.

"It is so," said the maid-servant; "the burn is there."

"Then let the girl be slain immediately," the king shouted.

"No, no, Your Majesty," they replied. "Let us send her to the *faqír* who discovered this thing, that he may do whatever he wishes with her."

The king agreed, and so the princess was taken to the graveyard.

"Let her be shut up in a cage, and be kept near the grave whence she took out the corpse," said the *faqír*.

This was done, and in a little while the *faqír* and his disciple and the princess were left alone in the graveyard. Night had not long cast its dark mantle over the scene when the *faqír* and his disciple threw off their disguise, and taking their horses and luggage, appeared before the cage. They released the princess, rubbed some ointment over the scars on her back, and then sat her upon one of their horses, behind the prince. Away they rode fast and far, and by the morning were able to rest and talk over their plans in safety. The *wazír's* son showed the princess some of the poisoned *piláv* that she had sent him, and asked whether she had repented of her ingratitude. The princess wept, and acknowledged that he was her greatest helper and friend.

A letter was sent to the chief *wazír* telling him of all that had happened to our heroes since they had left their country. When the *wazír* read the letter he went and informed the king. The king caused a reply to be sent to the two exiles, in which he ordered them not to return, but to send a letter to Gul'izar's father, and inform him of everything. Accordingly they did this; the prince wrote the letter at the *wazír's* son's dictation.

On reading the letter Gul'izar's father was much enraged with his *wazírs* and other officials for not discovering the presence in his country of these illustrious visitors, as he was especially anxious to ingratiate himself in the favour of the prince and the *wazír's* son. He ordered the execution of some of the *wazírs* on a certain date.

"Come," he wrote back to the *wazír's* son, "and stay at the palace. And if the prince desires it, I will arrange for his marriage with Gul'izar as soon as possible."

The prince and the *wazír's* son most gladly accepted the invitation, and received a right noble welcome from the king. The marriage soon took place, and then after a few weeks the king gave them presents of horses and elephants, and jewels and rich cloths, and bade them start for their own land; for he was sure that the king would now receive them. The night before they left the *wazírs* and others whom the king intended to have executed as soon as his visitors had left came and besought the *wazír's* son to plead for them, and promised that they each would give him a daughter in marriage. He complied, and succeeded in obtaining their pardon.

Then the prince, with his beautiful bride, Gul'izar, and the *wazír's* son, with his numerous beautiful wives, the daughters of the *wazírs*, attended by a troop of soldiers, and a large number of camels and horses bearing very much treasure, left for their own land. In the midst of the way they passed the tower of the robbers, and with the help of the soldiers they razed it to the ground, slew all its inmates, and seized the treasures which they had been amassing there for several years.

At length they reached their own country, and when the king saw his son's beautiful wife and his magnificent retinue he was at once reconciled, and ordered him to enter the city and take up his abode there.

Henceforth all was sunshine on the path of the prince. He became a great favourite, and in due time succeeded to the throne, and ruled the country for many many years in peace and happiness.[5]

[5] Compare the first tale of *Baital Pachísí; Indian Fairy Tales*, pp. 207–215; also whole of the introduction to *Madanakamárájankadai* (*Dravidian Nights*).

A STRANGE REQUEST.[1]

One day a king was shooting in a jungle, when he came across a *faqír*.

"*Salám!*" said he. "Can I do anything for you?"

"No, thank you," replied the *faqír*. "Can I do anything for you?"

"Yes," said the king. "I want a wife exactly like myself in appearance and height."

"Alas!" said the *faqír*, "you have asked a hard thing; nevertheless I can do it for you. But be warned; the woman will prove unfaithful."

"Never mind," said His Majesty. "If you can grant me this request, please do so."

On this the *faqír* arose, and flourishing an axe, clave the king's head in two, and then buried the body.

"O God," cried he, "hear my prayer, and cause the king to appear again and a woman exactly like him in height and appearance."

The prayer was heard. The king rose again, and after him a woman like him.

In a little while His Majesty had a special palace built for his new wife in the jungle, and went to live with her there as often as he could. But, alas! the woman proved faithless, as the *faqír* had said. One day, when the king was absent, she noticed one of the *wazírs* passing by. He was a young and handsome fellow, and the woman immediately fell in love with him. She beckoned to him to come to her, and he went. In this way they often met, and became very much attached to one another. One

[1] Narrator's name, Paṇḍit Ánand Kol of Zainah Kadal, Srínagar.

morning they were nearly discovered. The king happened to reach the place when everybody thought he was far away. Therefore they decided to arrange so as to preclude every possibility of discovery. Their plan was to contract with a potter called Kiṭal to dig a subterranean passage from the city to the palace, in order that the *wazír* might come and go just as he liked. This was done privately, and for a time all went well. At length, however, their wickedness was found out.

The *wazír* prepared a great feast, and invited the king to grace the company with his presence. The king accepted, and went. The woman also was present, but in disguise. However, His Majesty recognised her.

"Is it a dream?" thought he. "No, it is she. I will make a little mark on her clothes, whereby I shall be able to tell on my return whether I am deceived or not."

So presently he just touched the corner of her wrap with a little turmeric, and then passed on as if nothing had happened. On reaching his palace at night he found the woman there waiting for him, and the stain was on her wrap. "Adulteress!" he cried, and drew his sword; and with one stroke he severed her head from her body.

On the following morning he resigned his throne and became a *faqír*.

THE UNJUST KING AND WICKED GOLD-SMITH.[1]

ONCE upon a time a king was walking in his garden, when a stag broke through the fence and began to run about and trample down the flowers. On seeing this the king was exceedingly angry, and ordered his servants to surround the place and catch the animal. He himself also rode after it, with a drawn sword in his hand. Suddenly the stag escaped from the garden. Off it went, as only stags can go, and the king riding close after it. His Majesty followed it for several miles, right up to the border of his territory, but did not overtake it. Not wishing to go farther, he stopped there, and being very hot and thirsty, dismounted and stripped himself for a bathe. While he was bathing some wicked person stole his horse and clothes. Here was a strange position for a king to be in! "What shall I do?" thought His Majesty. "How can I return to my palace naked? I cannot do it. I should be a laughing-stock to my people for many a day." Accordingly His Majesty determined to wander about the neighbouring king's country. In the course of his wanderings he picked up a pearl necklace of great value. "Thank God, thank God!" he exclaimed. "I shall be able to get some clothes and a horse with this. I will go into the city and try to sell it." So he walked on and on till he reached the chief city of that king, and at once sought out the head goldsmith there.

"Sir," said he, "will you buy a pearl necklace? I have a very valuable one to dispose of. I found it one morning as I was crossing a stream."

[1] Narrator's name, Shiva Báyú, Renawárí, Srínagar.

"Show it to me," replied the goldsmith. "You thief!" he continued when he saw the necklace. "How did you steal this? I made two necklaces like this for the king, and could not discover what had become of one of them. You impudent thief! Come with me to the king."

Thus saying, he called a policeman, and bade him bring the fellow after him to the king. His Majesty heard the goldsmith's petition, and commanded the man's feet to be amputated.

When the queen of that country, who was as humane and just as her husband was cruel and unjust, heard of the stern order of her husband she remonstrated with him. "How could you give such a terrible order," she said, "when there seemed to be so little evidence to support the case? And those goldsmiths are generally such wicked men. You know how they lie and deceive to make money. Truly, I would as soon have believed the poor man's words as the words of that goldsmith."

"Hold your tongue," said the king. "What business have you to interfere with my affairs?"

"I shall not be quiet," said the queen. "Lately I have been much grieved by your sternness in the *darbár*. Your counsellors are displeased with you, and your people are ready to rebel. If you continue in this course you will bring your country to ruin."

The king was very angry with the woman, and told her to leave the room. On the following morning he ordered her to be sent out of the country with the man whose feet had been cut off.[2] The queen minded not this thing. On the contrary, she was very glad to be released from such a husband. She went to the footless man and informed him of the king's order, and then put him into a long basket and carried him on her back to some place without the city, where she tended him, like a wife, till

[2] Favourite form of punishment. Cf. several tales quoted in *Folk-Lore Journal*, vol. iv. 308-349; story of "Nuru'ddín 'Alí and Badru'ddín Hasan" in *Arabian Nights*; *Proben der Volkslitteratur der türkoschen Stamme Süd-Siberiens*, vol. iii. pp. 347-354; also tale of "Karm yá Dharm" in this collection.

his wounds were healed. She soon got very fond of him, and as he reciprocated her affections, she became his real wife, and a little son was born to them. For a living she used to cut wood and go and sell it in the city. One day, while she was away in the city, her husband fell asleep, and the little boy, who had been left in his care, taking advantage of the occasion, crawled to the brink of a well that was near and tumbled in. When the man awoke and saw not the child his grief knew no bounds. He was like a wild fellow. "Some beast has devoured my child," he cried. "What shall I do?"

In the evening his wife returned. She too was grieved beyond expression; but being a brave and sensible woman, she controlled herself, and tried to comfort her husband by saying, "This is written in our lot."

At night the king could not sleep for thinking of, and wishing for, his little boy. And happily for him that he could not sleep, because about the end of the second watch two birds called Sudabror and Budabror came and perched on a tree close by their open door, and began talking together about them.

"What a world of trouble is this!" remarked Sudabror to his friend. "Listen to what has happened to this man. He has been obliged to leave his country; he has lived like a beggar in another country, where he was most unjustly punished; and now he is bemoaning the loss of his beautiful infant son. The boy was drowned in that well yesterday afternoon."

"What trouble for these poor creatures!" said Budabror. "Can nothing be done for them?"

"Oh yes," replied Sudabror. "If the king would jump into this well he could easily rescue the boy, and would regain his feet too."

The king heard all that the birds had said, and was very much surprised and glad. As soon as the day dawned he told his wife what had happened, and asked her advice.

"Obey the birds, of course," she said, "and jump into the well."

The man did so, and thus saved his child and regained his feet.

Some time after this the king met his chief *wazîr*, who had been wandering about everywhere inquiring after his master ever since His Majesty had left. From him the king learnt that all the people were longing for his return. Accordingly he went back, accompanied by his wife and child, and sat on the throne again, and governed the country as before.

The first thing he did after his return was to send his army to fight with the king who had so ill-treated him. His army was victorious, and the other king, very much ashamed of himself, was obliged to come and beg for mercy. He said that he had thus acted because of the wicked goldsmith, whom he would immediately cause to be executed. So the king pardoned him and let him go. Henceforth all was peace and joy. His Majesty lived very happily with the other king's banished wife, had many children, and finally died at a good old age, much to the grief of all his people.

THE PHILOSOPHER'S STONE.[1]

In olden times there lived a king, who one day went to the Phák *pargana* to hunt. He was near the village of Dachhigám, when he saw a stag, to which he gave chase, and followed it for several miles, till it disappeared into some woods and was lost. His Majesty was very angry and disappointed at this bad luck.

As he was returning to his camp he heard a cry, as of some person weeping, behind the hedge on the roadside. He looked to see who it was and found a most beautiful woman about seventeen years of age, and was fascinated with the sight.

"Who are you? What are you doing here?" he asked most tenderly.

"Oh, sir," she replied, I am the daughter of one of the kings of China.[2] My father was taken prisoner in battle,

[1] Narrator's name, Makund Báyú Suthú, Srínagar, who heard it from a Pandit living at Nágám.

[2] (*a.*) Tradition says that Kashmír was once a tributary of China; and because there was not much money in the valley and cattle was difficult of transport, men and women were sent yearly as tribute to that country. When Zainu'lábadín obtained possession of Kashmír he declined to pay the tribute, whereupon the Sháh-i-Chín sent a *parwána*, censuring him, and threatening him that if he did not quickly comply with the custom of his predecessors in the valley he would make war on him, and ruin him and every one and everything belonging to him.

Now Zainu'lábadín had heard of the Chinese, of their vast numbers, and power, and cleverness, and therefore was somewhat frightened by these stern words. He took counsel with his ministers and friends as to what he should do, but they could not help him. He then sought advice from *faqírs*. At that time there lived in Kashmír a very famous *faqír* by the name of Bahádín, who begged the king not to be distressed, and promised to arrange the matter for him. This *faqír*, by virtue of his sanctity, flew over to China in the twinkling of an eye, and brought back the Sháh-i-Chín lying on his bed to his own humble abode. In the morning, when the Sháh awoke and found himself in a meagre hut, he was very much surprised.

"Oh, holy man," said he to the *faqír*, "I perceive that you have done this thing. Tell me, I pray you, why you have brought me here."

"I have transported you hither," replied Bahádín, "in order that you might meet face to face with Zainu-'lábadín, and promise him that you and I, fearing to become the slave of my father's enemies, fled. I first came to some place, where I attempted to drown myself in a well, but the villagers were apprised of my state, and came and saved me. Afterwards I came here. You have heard my story; now please tell me yours."

"Fair maiden," he replied, "I am the king of this country, and am now out on a hunting excursion. Lucky day that brought me in your path."

On this the girl wept.

"Why do you weep, pretty maiden?" continued the king.

"O king, I weep for my father, for my mother, and for my country. I weep for myself. What shall I do here? Friendless and homeless, how can I live?" she replied.

"Weep no more," said he. "Henceforth I will look after you. Come to my palace and spend your days."

"That gladly will I do," said the girl. "Nay, ask me to be your wife. I can refuse you nothing."

"My beloved, my darling," said the king, "come with me."

Accordingly a marriage was arranged, and the king

will abolish this wicked custom. Give it up, and God will bless you, and the people of this country will thank you."

The Sháh-i-Chín was pricked to the heart by these words, and cutting his finger, so that the blood oozed out, he called for a pen and some paper, and at once wrote an order declaring Kashmír an independent state. Then Bahádin presented him with some peaches, apricots, walnuts, and other fruits, and caused him to arrive at his country again. When the Sháh related to his people what had happened to him and what he had seen, his people would not believe him; but afterwards, when he showed them the different fruits that the *faqír* had given him, they were convinced, and applauded his deed.

(*b.*) Nasím *Khán*, who accompanied Mr. Vigne to Iskárdo, tells many stories of the Chinese and their doings in Tibet and surrounding countries. Cf. Vigne's *Travels in Kashmír*, &c., vol. ii. pp. 199–202.

Several allusions to China occur also in Kashmírí songs, &c. For example: *Rang i roi Machín*, "The bloom on your cheeks is that of China;" *Kus Mani chhuh ámut chánih bumbah rang karanah?* "What Mani has been and painted your eyebrows?" This is, of course, the celebrated Persian painter, who went in disguise to China, whom Vigne makes out to have been the preacher of the Manichæan heresy, "for he travelled," says Mirkhoud, "through Kashmír into India, and thence proceeded to Turkestan, Kathai, and China."

(*c.*) It should also be noticed that it is a common way of explaining the origin of unknown girls in Musalmán tales, to call them women of China, handmaidens of the Emperor in China. Cf., *en passant*, the story of "Aladdin, or the Wonderful Lamp" in *Arabian Nights*.

became more and more fond of his wife from China. He built a beautiful five-storeyed building for her on the banks of the Dal,[3] close to Ishibar,[4] and spent as much time as he possibly could with her, to the entire exclusion of his other wives. Little did he know then what a terrible creature she was on whom he was lavishing his affection; and little did he know the awful disease that living with her had brought on him. By-and-by, however, he began to feel great pains in his stomach, and sent for the *hakims*, some of whom advised him this and some that; but none of them could cure him. At last a *jogí*, who was in the habit of flying over to this country every day to get some water from the Dud Gangá[5] and some earth from Harí Parbat[6] for his master and teacher, noticed the grand building that the king had constructed, and wishing to rest, went and entered it; and putting the sacred water in one corner of the room, and the sacred earth in another corner, and a box of precious ointment under his pillow, he stretched himself on the king's bed, and was soon asleep. Meanwhile His Majesty arrived, and was much surprised to find the *jogí* sleeping on his bed. He noticed the little ointment-box under the pillow, and the sacred water and earth, and wondered what they meant. Curious to see what the *jogí* would do when he awoke, he sat down and waited. The *jogí* did not keep him very long. How astonished he was to see the king, and how terrified when he could not find the little box of ointment and the sacred water and earth! The king had taken them. "Do not be afraid, O *jogí*," said he. "I have got all your things safely. Tell me how and why you came here, and you shall have them again." Then the *jogí* told him everything, and received back the things, and bowing to the king, left the palace. He flew back as

[3] The city lake close to Srínagar.

[4] A village on the eastern side of the lake. It contains a very sacred spring.

[5] A sacred stream crossed on the way to Rámú.

[6] A hill in Srínagar on which stands the fort protecting the city. In the month of March there is a Hindú festival in honour of Shárika held on this hill.

fast as possible to his master, who asked him the reason of his delay, whereupon the *jogí* related to him how he had been discovered sleeping in the king's bed, and how His Majesty had spoken to him.

"A good man!" exclaimed the teacher when he heard these words. "I am thankful that he gave you back the sacred ointment and the other things. Come, lead me to him."

Accordingly they both flew to this country by the aid of the ointment, and went before the king.

"O king," said the *jogí*, "my master and teacher has come to see you, and to thank you for returning those things to me."

Then said the *rishi*, "Yes, to thank you I have come, O king. Be pleased to ask anything at my hands and it shall be done for you."

"O holy man," replied the king, prostrating himself before him, "I have been caught with a disease in my stomach which all the skill and learning of the *hakíms* have as yet failed to alleviate. If you can cure me of this disease I shall be eternally grateful to you."

"Let me examine your body," said the *rishi*, looking earnestly at him. "Have you recently married a wife?"

"Yes," replied the king, and related to him the circumstances of meeting with his new wife and everything about her.

"I suspected this," said the *rishi*. "O king, you are really very ill. Forty days more without relief would have killed you. But now you are safe. I can cure you. Do what I tell you, and fear not. Order your cook to put extra salt into your wife's dinner this evening, and see that there is not any water in the room where she will sleep.[7] You yourself keep awake all the night and watch, and tell me in the morning whatever happens. Be not afraid. No harm shall come to you."

His Majesty implicitly followed the *rishi's* directions.

[7] Cf. *Folk-Lore Journal*, vol. iv. p. 24.

As was expected, the woman got very thirsty in the night, and rose up to drink some water; but not finding any water in the room, she first looked to see if her husband was asleep, and then assumed the shape of a snake and went out. She went to the lake to drink. When she had done this she returned, and changing herself back to a woman, lay down to sleep again. The king saw all this, and in the morning informed the *rishi*. When the *rishi* heard everything he said, "O king, this is not a woman, but a *vihá*. Listen. If for the space of one hundred years the sight of no human eye falls on a snake a crest forms on its head, and it becomes a *sháhmár;* if for another hundred years it comes not into the sight of a man, it is changed into an *ajdar;* and if for three hundred years it has never been looked on by a human being it becomes a *vihá*. A *vihá* can stretch itself to any length, possesses enormous power, and can change its appearance at will; it is very fond of assuming the form of a woman, in order that it may live with men.[8] Such is your wife, O king."

"Horrors!" exclaimed the king. "Would that I had known this before. But is there no way of escape from this wretched creature?"

"Yes, certainly," replied the *rishi;* "but you must be patient. Go regularly to your wife, and act towards her just the same as you have always done. Otherwise she will suspect you, and will destroy you. One breath of hers would blast the whole country. Meanwhile build a house of *lachh*,[9] and cover the *lachh* with a white washing, so that it may not appear. The house should contain four rooms —a sitting-room, dining-room, bedroom, and bathroom, and in one corner of the dining-room there should be a big strong oven with a cover. When everything is quite ready pretend that you are ill, and get the *hakím* to prescribe forty days' solitary confinement in the house of *lachh*, and to strictly order nobody but the woman to visit you."

[8] Cf. *Indian Antiquary*, vol. xi. pp. 230–235.

[9] A resinous substance, the basis of varnishes and lacquers.

All of which was done, and the woman was very glad to have the king all to herself, and to do everything for him in his sickness. This went on for a few days, when the *rishi* got to speak to the king. He advised him to heat the great oven in the dining-room, and to order the woman to make a special kind of bread for him. Then while she was busy looking to see how the bread was progressing, he was to pitch her into the furnace, and shut it up as soon as possible, lest by any means she should escape and destroy the whole country. This also was done, and to increase the force of the heat, the house too was ignited.[10]

"You have done well," said the *rishi*, when he heard what the king had done. "Now go to your palace, and wait there for two days, and on the third day come to me, and I will show you a wonderful sight."

On the third day His Majesty, accompanied by the *rishi*, went to the place where the fire was, and found nothing but ashes.

"Look carefully," said the *rishi*, "and you will find a pebble amongst them."

"Yes," replied the king after a few minutes' search; "here it is."

"It is well," said the *rishi*. "Which will you have, the pebble or the ashes?"

"The pebble," answered the king.

"Very well," said the *rishi*. "Then I will take the ashes." Whereupon he carefully collected the ashes into his wrap and disappeared with his disciple, and the king went to his palace.

From that hour His Majesty was cured of his disease. The pebble that he had chosen turned out to be the *sangí-páras*,[11] the stone which, on touching any metal, immediately converted it into gold. But what particular virtue

[10] Miyán Singh, Sikh governor of the Valley in Ranjít Singh's time, is said to have baked alive his favourite wife because she was accused of intrigue.

[11] The classical *Sparsha-mani*.

there was in the ashes he never knew, as he never saw the *rishi* or the *jogi* again.[12]

A VARIANT.[1]

'ALÍ MARDÁN *KHÁN*,[2] a former king of Kashmír, was one day hunting in the jungle near Shálimár,[3] when two old men came up to him and said, "O king, be pleased to hear us. We beseech you to proceed no farther, lest you be swallowed by a fierce *ajdar* that frequents this place."

"Nonsense," said the king.

"Nay, O king, but we have seen the monster," said they. "It goes down to the lake every evening to drink water, and comes by way of this jungle. Be warned, we pray you, and return."

"Very well," said the king, and turning his horse rode back to the palace. On arrival he sent for his *wazírs* to tell them what he had heard, and to ask their advice as to what steps he should take for the destruction of the monster. They advised him to order several sheepskins filled with lime to be thrown along the way by which the *ajdar* came down to the lake, and also to have two pits dug and filled with oil near to the place where the monster was wont to drink. Their idea was, that the *ajdar* would suppose the sheepskins of lime to be real sheep and would swallow them, and consequently get very thirsty; and then, thinking the oil-pits to be filled with water, would quench its thirst from them. A burning heat inside would of course ensue, and the *ajdar*

[12] Compare variants *Wide-Awake Stories*, pp. 189–195, 330–332; tale of "Lower than the Beasts," in *Gesta Romanorum; Kashmírí Proverbs and Sayings*, pp. 184–186; and *Indian Notes and Queries*, vol. iv. p. 153.

[1] Narrator's name, Paṇḍit Ánand Kol of Srínagar.

[2] Although the people invariably speak of him as a king, yet 'Alí Mardán *Khán* was only governor of Kashmír in the Emperor Sháh Jahán's days (cir. 1650). He was a Persian noble, and the same as acted as governor of Zandahár for some time.

[3] The name of the famous royal gardens by the Tayába hill, on the shores of the City lake.

would die. The king approved of the idea, and therefore it was carried into execution, and the *ajdar* was slain.

'Alí Mardán *Kh*án went to see the carcass, and ordered the soldiers to fire on it. He also, with the help of the two old men, discovered its cave and entered it. Within the place was a closed door, which he opened. This door led into a room, where he found a peculiar little box; and inside this little box there was a pebble. This pebble chanced to be the veritable *sangí-páras* by the touch of which everything is immediately changed into gold.

ANOTHER STORY.[1]

Once upon a time a man set out to climb the Ta*kh*t-i-Sulaimán.[2] Feeling very thirsty on the way up, the day being rather hot, he took a pear out of his pocket and began to peel it. While doing so the knife slipped and cut his hand. The man cleaned off some of the blood with the knife, and then rubbed the knife against a stone and put it back in his pocket. On reaching the top of the hill he sat down, and feeling rather hungry, took out another pear, and was going to skin it, when he noticed that the blade of his knife had been turned into gold. How could this have happened? Undoubtedly on the way up the hill he had rubbed it against the *sangí-páras*. He retraced his steps with all speed, but, alas! he could not find the stone again, so, for all we know, it probably remains somewhere about the Ta*kh*t to this day.

[1] Narrator's name, Lál Chand of Khunamuh, in the Wular *pargana*.

[2] A hill near Srínagar, about 1000 feet above the level of the Valley. It is called by the Pandits Sir-i-Shur, or Shiva's Head, or Shankaráchárya, after the great Hindu ascetic of that name.

HOW THE WICKED SONS WERE DUPED.[1]

A VERY wealthy old man, imagining that he was on the point of death, sent for his sons and divided his property among them. However, he did not die for several years afterwards; and miserable years many of them were. Besides the weariness of old age, the old fellow had to bear with much abuse and cruelty from his sons. Wretched, selfish ingrates! Previously they vied with one another in trying to please their father, hoping thus to receive more money, but now they had received their patrimony, they cared not how soon he left them—nay, the sooner the better, because he was only a needless trouble and expense. This, as we may suppose, was a great grief to the old man.

One day he met a friend and related to him all his troubles. The friend sympathised very much with him, and promised to think over the matter, and call in a little while and tell him what to do. He did so; in a few days he visited the old man and put down four bags full of stones and gravel before him.

"Look here, friend," said he. "Your sons will get to know of my coming here to-day, and will inquire about it. You must pretend that I came to discharge a long-standing debt with you, and that you are several thousands of rupees richer than you thought you were. Keep these bags in your own hands, and on no account let your sons get to them as long as you are alive. You will soon find them change their conduct towards you. *Salám*. I will come again soon to see how you were getting on."

When the young men got to hear of this further in-

[1] Narrator's name, Shiva Báyú, Renawárí, Srínagar.

crease of wealth they began to be more attentive and pleasing to their father than ever before. And thus they continued to the day of the old man's demise, when the bags were greedily opened, and found to contain only stones and gravel !

A STUPID HUSBAND AND HIS CLEVER WIFE.[1]

A MERCHANT when dying called his beloved and only son to his bedside and said, "Dear son, I am about to depart, and shall not return. You will be left alone in the world. I charge you to remember five pieces of advice which I now give you. Walk not in the sunshine from your house to the shop. Let *piláv* be your daily food. Take unto yourself a fresh wife every week. On wishing to drink wine go to the vat and drink it. If you want to gamble, then gamble with experienced gamblers."

Having spoken these words the merchant groaned and gave up the ghost.

Now the son, although good and obedient in all things, was also a very stupid fellow. He did not in the least comprehend his father's real meaning. He thought that these words were to be understood literally, and therefore immediately set about erecting a covered way from his house to the place of business. It cost him a large sum of money, and seemed most needless and ridiculous. Some of his friends suspected that he was mad, and others that he was proud. However, he minded not their remarks and coldness, but finished the building, and every day walked beneath it in the shade to and fro from his house to the shop.

He also ordered the cook to prepare *piláv* for him every day, and ate nothing else, as his father had directed him.

In the matter of getting a fresh wife every week he

[1] Narrator's name, Paṇḍit Makund Báyú, Suthú, Srínagar.

experienced very great difficulty. Some of the wives, by reason of their ugliness, or bad tempers, or slovenly manners, or unfaithfulness and other wickednesses, deserved to be turned off. But there were others who were beautiful, and good, and kind, and loving, and clean, and tidy, and these the young merchant found it extremely hard to get rid of. He had to provoke them to anger or to indifference before he could invent an excuse for sending them away. Many many poor women were thus ruined by him.

At last an exceedingly clever woman heard of the deceased merchant's advice, and having perceived the true meaning, she determined to try and arrange for her marriage with the young merchant. Being both beautiful and clever, she soon succeeded. The young merchant could not detect any fault in her or her work, though he was constantly on the watch for anything wrong. She did everything strictly according to his wishes, and was exceedingly careful about her speech, and dress, and manner, and work. Six days thus passed. On the seventh and last day of the week, his last opportunity, the young merchant ordered her to have some fish *pildv* ready for his evening meal, intending to grumble with it, and to pretend that he wanted a different kind of fish to that prepared. His wife promised that it should be ready for him as soon as he returned.

Soon after he left she went to the *bázár* and purchased two or three kinds of fish. At the proper time she prepared them in different ways, some with spices, and some without spices, some with sugar, some with salt, and so on. On the young merchant's return the dinner was waiting.

"Is dinner ready?" he shouted.

"Yes," replied the wife, and immediately put a dish of steaming sweet *pildv* in front of him.

"Oh!" he said, looking up in a rage, "I want a salt *pildv*."

"Very well," she replied. "I thought perhaps you would, and so got that also ready. Here it is," and she set a big dish of steaming salt *piláv* before him.

"Yes, yes," said he, still in a rage apparently, "but not this kind of fish. It is all bone."

"Very well," she replied; "then have this kind."

"But I don't mean this kind," he shouted; and he looked as if he would like to throw the contents of the dish at her head. "I would sooner eat dung than this."

"Then have it," she replied, "by all means."

Saying this, she kicked aside a small basket and discovered to his astonished gaze the dung of some animal that had been prowling about the place while she was preparing the dinner, but which she had not had time to remove, and therefore had thrown a basket over it, lest her husband should notice it and be offended.

Thoroughly defeated, the young merchant then said no more. After eating a little from two or three of the dishes he went to bed. During the night his wife made him promise to visit her father's house on the morrow, and to spend the day there.

In the morning the young merchant and his wife went together to the house of the latter. On arrival the wife told her parents all that had happened to her and all her secrets, and begged them not to cook anything special on account of their visit, but to prepare simply some *phuhurih*,[2] and give it to her when she should ask for it. They said that they would do so.

When they had been there some hours she took her husband into a little room, and asked him to wait there for the dinner, which would be ready presently. The young merchant waited a long time, until at last he got so hungry that he went and called his wife and entreated her to bring something to eat.

"Yes," she said, "in a few minutes. We are waiting for other guests, who ought to have been here a long time

[2] The plural of *phuhur*, burnt rice or bread.

ago. As soon as they arrive the food will be served up."

"But I am too hungry to wait," said the young merchant. "Give me something to eat at once. I do not wish to eat with these people, if your parents will excuse me."

"Very well," she replied; "but there is nothing but *phuhurih*. If you like to have that, I will go and bring it."

"All right," he said. "Bring it."

So she went and fetched some *phuhurih*, and he ate it gladly. When he had finished the plateful he said, "The taste of this *phuhurih* is better than *piláv* to me at this time."

Deeming it a good opportunity, she said, "Oh, why, then, do you always eat *piláv* in your house?"

"Because my father ordered me to do this, just before he died," he replied.

"Nonsense," said she, "you have mistaken his meaning."

"No, I have not," he said. "He advised me on several other points also." He then told her all that his father had said to him.

"Well!" she exclaimed. "On this account you built the covered way from the house to the shop, you eat *piláv* every day, and marry a wife every week! Are you really so stupid as to suppose for one moment that your wise and kind father wished you thus to understand him? Why, such a course of life will very soon bring you to ruin, besides making your life miserable and your name a reproach in the land! Listen! When your father advised you to go and come from your shop in the shade he meant that you should attend to your business, rising up early and retiring late, if you wished to prosper and to become great. When he told you to eat *piláv* every day, he meant that you should be economical in the way of food, and eat only to satisfy hunger. When he said,

'Marry a new wife every week,' he meant that you should not be too much with your wife. When the wife is away you want her. If you saw your wife only once a week you would return to her as to a new wife and enjoy her society more."

"Alas! alas!" he cried, "what have I been doing? How foolishly have I acted! O my dear father, that I should have thus misunderstood you! My dear wife, you have spoken wisely. Henceforth I will endeavour to atone for my stupidity. But you have not explained the rest of my father's words, that I may know what else to do."

"I will tell you," she replied. "But let us first go and bid my parents good-bye. I will explain the meaning to you on the way home."

As they were walking back she turned aside to a gambling-den, and showed her husband the wretchedness and villainy depicted on the countenances of nearly every one of the company.

"Look," she said, "at their terrible condition and be warned. Your father evidently wished you to see such a sight, that you might shun the path that leads to this state."

Then she took him to a large wine-shop that was near their house, and pointing to the immense vats of wine, told him to climb one of them and drink to his heart's content. He went up the ladder and looked over into the vat, but the stench was so great that he did not wish to remain there a moment, much less to drink.

"I will not drink any of the wine to-day," he said on reaching the bottom of the ladder.

"This is precisely the conclusion your father wished to arrive at," she said; "and therefore he told you to go and drink the wine from the vat whenever you wished to drink it."

"I see, I see," he replied. "Let us go home."

THE PRAYERFUL FAQÍR.[1]

Once upon a time there lived a poor man with his two children, a son and a daughter. He was so reduced in circumstances that he had not food or clothing for them, and was obliged to beg alms from house to house in almost a nude condition. One day, in the course of their peregrinations in quest of food, they met with a very holy, continent, and virtuous *faqír*, concerning whom it was reported that he never failed to obtain direct answers to his prayers. On seeing this holy man they made their *salâms*, and begged him to pray for the relief of their poverty. The *faqír* directed them to a certain place, saying that if they would enter that place one by one and heartily offer up their prayers it should be granted them. "But be very careful," he added, "and only ask for one thing." Then the *faqír* departed.

The daughter was the first of the trio to enter. She lifted up her voice and prayed for beauty, and her request was vouchsafed. She came forth to her father and brother a blushing, beautiful girl, with whom the king, who at that moment happened to be passing by, was thoroughly fascinated. His Majesty stopped, at once offered marriage, and was accepted. The quickly-found lovers rode off together.

But the father did not quite agree to this sudden separation from his daughter, and, besides this, he was exasperated by her remaining so long within the praying-place. Accordingly, full of angry thoughts, he entered this place, and asked most earnestly that the Mighty One would afflict his disobedient, faithless daughter with a

[1] Narrator's name, Paṇḍit Kailás Kol, Tuṅkipúr, Srínagar.

sore.[2] This prayer also was accepted, and the king noticing the sore upon his fair lady's neck, became disgusted with her and cast her off on the way.

At last the boy went within the place appointed and prayed thus:—"O Merciful One, grant me two things. I wish to be a king, and I wish to be wealthy."

This prayer, however, being contrary to the directions of the *faqír*, was refused.

Then the wretched beggar with his recreant daughter and foolish son went on their way in the same state as they came, hungry and *páṅsa*less.

[2] Cf. *Folk-Tales of Bengal*, pp. 113, 114.

UNITY IS STRENGTH.[1]

A TERRIBLE famine,[2] like a great ogre, stalked through the land of Kashmír, committing the most fearful depredation on every side. There was much distress and lamentation in many families whose dear ones had been slain or wounded by his cruel hand.

At such a time a company of four brothers determined to fly from the country. On a certain day, having packed up whatever was necessary for the way, they started on their journey. They had proceeded some distance, when they came to a spring, whose crystal waters invited them to stop and rest a while. The place was abundantly shaded by a large tree, in the long spreading branches of which a little bird was singing most merrily and sweetly. It was a lovely spot wherein to rest. Conversation as to their future prospects was indulged in freely, and various plans were suggested and talked over, till all were fast asleep. About midnight they were suddenly aroused by the shrill, insinuating cries of the little bird. The elder brother, in his rage, ordered one of the party to catch the bird, a second to take out his knife and kill it, and the third to get some wood ready for a fire whereby to cook it. All immediately bestirred themselves, rose up, and went quickly to fulfil their elder brother's commands.

Now this bird was an intelligent creature, and therefore had perfectly comprehended all that had been said. So, while the three brothers were going about to fulfil their

[1] Narrator's name, Rahmán, a carpenter liviog in Srínagar.

[2] Notwithstanding the usual fertility of the soil famines occur occasionally, and the consequences to the inhabitants, chiefly from the badness of the roads and the difficulty of transport, are sometimes very terrible, especially as they are usually followed by an outbreak of cholera or some other epidemic.

several tasks, it said to the eldest of the party, "Why do you wish to catch me? Why do you send for a knife and wood?"

The young man replied, "It is my intention to kill you, and afterwards to roast and eat you."

In a voice tremulous with terror the poor bird entreated for its life. "Spare, oh! spare me, and I will show you a treasury of wealth."

"Very well," said the man. "I will spare you if you will fulfil your promise."

"Then my life is spared," said the bird. "Dig, dig around the trunk of the tree, and you will find treasure untold."

The four brothers did so, and found as the bird had said.

"What reason have we now for continuing the journey? We have," said they, "enough and to spare. Let us go back to our country."

Four other brothers, of another family who were living in the neighbourhood of the grand building wherein the four wealthy brothers had taken up their abode, chanced to hear of the extraordinary manner in which they had met with their wealth, and they too, being driven to great straits by the famine, determined to visit the spring, the scene of the late find, and try their luck. They went; they saw the spring; they rested under the shadow of the big tree; they heard the pretty warblings of the bird; and sweated with curiosity and expectation. At length the eldest brother ordered his brethren to do as the eldest brother of the other party had ordered his brothers; but they would not obey him.

One said, "I cannot go."

Another replied, "Wherefore should I bring a knife?"

And the third pleaded, "I am too tired to fetch any wood. Go and get it yourself."

When the little bird saw the unwillingness and disobedience it said to the eldest brother, "Go back. Your errand is in vain. You will never obtain anything till you have first obtained command over your brethren. The men who preceded you were successful because they were united. They had but one will, one mind, one eye, one ear, one body."

THE PÍR OF PHATTAPÚR.[1]

A PÍR[2] once visited a certain village of which he was the spiritual guide to see his disciples. On his arrival they all gathered round to welcome him, and all promised to send him food. However, when evening had come, each one, hoping that some others would look after the *pír*, did not bother. The consequence was the *pír* got nothing, and was obliged to fast. For his own credit's sake he could not go out and beg. During the night a great wind sprang up and constantly burst open the door of the mosque where he was staying. Each time he thought that somebody had come, and rose up to receive them; but, alas! it was only the wind. On the following morning his disciples gathered round him and asked whether he had been comfortable, when he reproached them for their negligence; whereupon the people began to abuse one another for not bringing some food for the *pír*. "*Chánih pírah korih nikáh! Chánih pírah korih húni niwán! Chánih pírah korih rani!*"[3] said they, which words mean, "May your *pír's* daughter be married! May your *pír's* daughter be carried off by a dog! May your *pír's* daughter (have lots of) husbands!" Of course all the abuse fell on the head of the *pír*, who was so disgusted with them that he took up his wrap and went.

[1] Narrator's name, Lál Singh of Khádanyár, near Báramula. Phattapúr is a village in the Bángil *pargana*.

[2] These *pírs* (spiritual guides!) are a wretched lot of fellows—ignorant, negligent, sensual, selfish. They are supported by the inhabitants of their different villages, and are thought to be possessed of sanctity and of special powers of pleading before God. This conviction, of course, has to be supported, encouraged, and connived at; otherwise the poor ignorant, superstitious villagers would withdraw their support.

[3] This is one of the worst forms of Kashmírí abuse.

THE SAGACIOUS GOVERNOR.

I.[1]

ONE day the governor was sitting in *darbár*, when a crow came flying into the hall and made a great noise. The servants in attendance turned it out two or three times, but it persisted in flying in and making a great "caw, caw," as before.

"Evidently the bird has a petition," said the governor. "Inquire what is the matter."

Accordingly a soldier was sent on this errand, and as he left the hall the bird came and flew along before him. It led the way to the Guri Daur,[2] where a woodcutter was lopping a poplar, upon a branch of which the crow had built its nest. "Caw, caw, caw!" said the bird most lustily when it arrived at the tree, and then flew up to its nest. The soldier at once saw what was the matter, and ordering the woodcutter to stop his work, returned and told the governor.

II.[3]

ANOTHER day, when the governor was present in *darbár*, two men came and presented their petitions. They both claimed a certain foal. It was a very curious case. According to the country, they, being townsmen, had sent their ponies (mares) to the hills to

[1] Narrator's name, Mihtar Sher Singh, Officiating Governor, Srínagar.

[2] The native racecourse near Sher Garhi, Srínagar.

[3] Narrator's name, Mihtar Sher Singh, Officiating Governor, Srínagar.

graze. Both of the mares were with young, and while they were in the shepherd's charge gave birth to two foals, one of which was stillborn and the other lived. However, the living colt sucked milk from both. The shepherd was not present at the time of its birth, and therefore when he came and saw this he could not tell to which mare the colt belonged. Of course, when the season was over and the owners came for their ponies, both of them claimed the colt; and as neither of them seemed inclined to give way to the other, they went to the court about it.

After a little deliberation the governor ordered the men to take both the ponies and the colt down to the water, and to put the colt into a boat and paddle out into the middle of the river. "The mother of the colt," said he, "will swim after it; but the other pony will remain on the bank." Thus was the case decided.

III.[4]

A MAN refused to support his mother, who was a widow and had no other son. So the poor old woman, not knowing what else to do, went to the governor, and falling on her knees, before him, begged him to help her. "O my lord," she cried, "I am a widow, and have only one son, who declines to give me a little food and clothing, or even a corner in his house to lie down in. What shall I do? I cannot work. My eyes are failing and my strength is gone. Your honour is famous for wisdom and understanding. Please advise me."

On hearing her complaint the governor summoned the son of the old widow, and sharply upbraided him for not supporting her, to whom he was indebted beyond repayment.

"I do not owe her anything," replied the young man. "She never lent me a *páṅsa.* On the contrary, she owes

[4] Narrator's name, Paṇḍit Lál Chand, of Khunamuh, in the Vihí *pargana.*

me very much. I have entirely supported her for the last three years. But now I cannot provide for her any longer. I have a wife and family of my own to feed and clothe and care for."

"For shame!" said the governor. "Is it necessary that I should tell you how much you owe your mother?—yea, even your life and health and strength? Who carried you about every moment for nine long weary months? Who suckled you for twice that time? Who taught you to walk? Who taught you to talk? Who fed you with food convenient for you? Who saved you from many a fall, from many a burn, and from many a scald? Who pounded the rice and prepared your food for several years, till you were able to marry and get a wife to do these things for you?"

"These are things that every mother has to do and likes to do," said the young man. "She would not wish to live if she could not perform them."

"True to a certain point, but"—— Here the governor stopped, and turning to one of the *wazírs* in attendance, ordered him to see that this young unthankful fellow pounded four *sers* of rice[5] with a skin of water fastened round his stomach, and to beat him if he did not accomplish the task well and quickly.

The man soon got tired. The perspiration ran down over his face and neck. At last he could not lift the pestle any more; and the rice was not half pounded. Thwack, thwack, thwack, came down the whip on his bare shoulders, but it was no good, he could not pound another grain. He was then carried before the governor in a dead-alive condition.

"I need not say anything more to you," said the governor to him. "You have learnt something of what your mother endured for you. Go and repay the debt with kind words and kind deeds."

[5] It is the wife's business to pound the rice for her household.

IV.[6]

A MUSALMÁN owed some rupees to a Paṇḍit, but refused to pay him. At length the case was carried before the governor, who heard what they had to say, and then put both the men into separate rooms. In a little while he ordered the Paṇḍit to appear, and asked him whether his claim was a true one. The Paṇḍit replied in the affirmative.

"Then take this knife and go and cut off the man's nose for his dishonesty," said the governor.

But the Paṇḍit begged to be excused, saying that he did not care so much for the money that he would cut off a man's nose for it.

Then the governor ordered him to return to his place, and, as soon as he was out of hearing, sent for the Musalmán, and asked him if he owed the Paṇḍit anything. The man replied in the negative.

"Then take this knife and go and cut off the Paṇḍit's ear for his false accusation," said the governor.

The wicked Musalmán took the knife, and left with the intention of doing so.

But the governor called him back. "I see," said he; "you must pay the sum demanded by the Paṇḍit, and a fine besides. Tell me no more lies. The man who would not scruple to deprive a fellow-creature of an ear for a trifle is not the man to be trusted."

[6] Narrator's name, Mihtar Sher Singh, Officiating Governor, Srínagar.

THEIR ONLY RUBY.[1]

ONCE upon a time there lived a king who was obliged to banish his son on account of the young man's extravagance and wickedness. The prince left the country, attended by three friends, who would not be separated from him. He took with him a bag of rubies for the expenses of the way. Unfortunately, however, this bag was stolen one night while he and his companions were asleep, so that only one ruby was left to them which one of the party happened to have with him. On reaching the city the four friends visited the *bázár* and tried to sell it, and while they were arguing with a merchant concerning its price the king of that country passed by.

"What have you there?" asked His Majesty.

"A ruby that we wish to sell, but we cannot find any person rich enough to buy it, O king," replied the prince.

"Show it to me," said the king.

When His Majesty saw the beautiful stone he was desirous of having it, and therefore pretended that it was his, and that the young man must have stolen it from his treasury. "This is mine," he exclaimed. "I recognise it. You must have stolen it." And then, turning to the officer in command of the detachment of soldiers who were with him, he ordered the men to be seized and put in ward till further inquiries had been made.

The prince and his companions were much astonished at this behaviour. "Hear our story, O king," they said, "and you will change your opinion concerning us. We are not thieves, but honest men. One of us is the son of a king, as great in honour and power and wealth as Your

[1] Narrator's name, Paṇḍit Ánand Rám, Renawárí, Srínagar.

Majesty. Banished from his country, he has wandered hither; and the rest of us are his friends, who have elected to follow him. Between us all we have only this one ruby. Take not from us, we beseech Your Majesty, our only means of subsistence."

Touched with pity for them, the king promised that the ruby should be returned to them if they could point out the box it was in. His Majesty had five boxes prepared, and put a ruby in each. In one of the boxes, of course, he put the ruby belonging to the prince's friend.

When the time of ordeal arrived, the prince and his companions prayed earnestly to be guided to the right box, and immediately they had prayed the box that contained their ruby flew open of its own accord. Surprised and pleased at this wonderful thing, the king not only gave them their own ruby, but four other rubies too, and invited them to stay at his palace. Here the prince behaved himself so well and became so popular, that the king gave him his daughter in marriage and appointed him his heir, while the prince's companions were honoured with high offices under him.

THE JACKAL-KING.[1]

Once upon a time the jackals assembled together to elect a king for themselves. The lions had a king, the tigers had a king, the leopards had a king, the wolves had a king, the dogs and other animals had their kings; so they thought that they too ought to appoint one, who should be their chief, who should guide them in counsel and lead them forth to war.

"Elect your king," cried the old jackal, anxious to begin the meeting.

Whereupon all the jackals shouted, "You are our king! You are our king! You are our senior in age and superior in experience. Who is there so fit as yourself to rule over us?"

And the old jackal consented, and by way of distinction allowed his fur to be dyed blue, and an old broken winnowing fan to be fastened round his neck.

One day the king was walking about his dominions attended by a large number of his jackal subjects, when a tiger suddenly appeared and made a rush at them. The whole company fled and forgot their old king. His Majesty tried to escape into a narrow cave, but, alas! his head stuck in the hole, by reason of the winnowing fan that was around his neck. Seeing their leader thus, the tiger came and seized him, and carried him away to his lair, where it fastened him by a rope so that he could not run away. In a short while, however, the jackal-king did escape and get back to his subjects, who again wished him to be their king and to reign over them. But the jackal

[1] Narrator's name, Makund Báyú, Suthú, Srínagar.

had had enough of it, and therefore replied, " No, thank you. I am quite satisfied. Once being a king is quite sufficient for a man's lifetime." [2]

[2] Cf. *Játaka Book*, vol. ii. (No. 241) p. 293; *Tibetan Tales*, pp. lxv.–356; *Pancha-tantra*, i. 10, and Benfey's remarks thereon, pp. 224, 225; *Hitopadesha*, iii. 7; A. Weber, *Indische Studien*, iii. pp. 349–366; also *Dictionary of Kashmírí Proverbs and Sayings*, pp. 192, 193.

THE BLACK AND WHITE BEARDS.[1]

Two men, though differing much in age, had formed a very thick friendship with one another. They were constantly in each other's society, and had not a secret between them. The elder of the two possessed a fine beard, as black as charcoal, but the younger man's beard was quite grey.

"Why has your beard not turned grey before now? You are nearly twice my age," said the younger to the other one day as they were out for a walk.

"The secret is this, my friend," replied the other. "My house is a paradise, and my wife a pleasant plant therein, whose branches are constantly bearing fruit,—comfort and joy, and the perfumes of whose blossoms fill the house with an odour of sanctity and love. In such a dwelling man does not quickly become old. Come and see my abode."

The young friend most readily complied. To tell the truth, he was somewhat suspicious of the old man's story; his own experience was so diametrically opposed to it. Other conversation beguiled the rest of the way to the house. On their arrival the black beard produced a handkerchief full of sand, and giving it to his wife, ordered her to make bread of it, while he and his companion took a stroll outside. The good wife tried to blind her mind to the fact of the impossibility of the thing. Her duty was to endeavour to carry out her lord's behests. "Perhaps it may be," she said to herself, and set to work cheerily.

The stroll being over, the two friends re-entered the

[1] Narrator's name, Pandit Wasah Kol of Kahípúrah, in the Kruhĕn *pargana*.

house, and the old man inquired for the bread that he ordered.

"Sir," said the woman, "I tried my best, but all to no purpose. Please do not be angry. I could not do more than I have already done."

The old man then beckoned his friend to come aside, and said to him, "Notice how meek my wife is."

"Yes, indeed!" replied he.

"But I will show you still more of her meekness and patience," said the husband; and then turning towards his wife, ordered her to go to the top storey of the house and bring down some of the water-melons that were there. The woman went, but only found one water-melon, which she brought and placed before her husband. She thought that he had probably told a falsehood,—he knew there was only one water-melon in the place, but had spoken as if there were many, in order that he might appear great before his guest.

"Go up," said he, "and bring down a larger one."

The woman took the melon away, and brought it back again.

"There is another better than this in the loft. Go up and bring it," said he.

The woman went, and returned again with the same melon. This order was repeated ten times in various ways, and ten times the good dame climbed the stairs. Afterwards the old man nodded to his friend to come upstairs with him, and showed him what his wife had done. Poor woman! she was quite fatigued by her exertions, and sat down at the bottom of the ladder almost ready to faint.

"Have I not a good wife?" asked the proud husband.

"You have," replied his friend. "I see the secret of your black beard—the dye of home-joy, home-peace, and home-contentment, a wonderful triple mixture, warranted to keep a man young for ever. Now come and see my *zanána*."

"All right," said the other.

So away they went to the young grey-headed man's house. When they entered the place a woman came forward with angry countenance and shrieked out, "Where have you been? Where have you been wasting your time, while I toil here in this dingy hole?"

Her husband was too frightened to say anything. Presently, however, when there was a lull in the storm, he asked in a kind manner for some food for himself and guest. The woman sulkily placed before them some scraps, which were left over from her and the children's meal—cold, grizzly scraps, fit only for the grovelling pariahs that infested the neighbourhood. But the poor man wanted some meat, and told her so. Now the woman had been conjuring up all manner of grievances against her husband, until a sea of anguish tossed and raged within her breast. She could not restrain any longer; so, taking up a big earthenware pot, wherein some rice was being prepared, she took deliberate aim at her husband's head; and as if this was not enough, she angrily demanded the price of the broken pot that lay in shreds around his feet. Poor fellow! he was glad to make his exit. On getting outside he said to his friend, "My house is as a bad smell to me. I loathe the place. This is the cause of my broken spirit and scraggy, prematurely grey beard."[2]

[2] Cf. *Dictionary of Kashmírí Proverbs and Sayings*, pp. 39, 40.

THE STORY OF A WEAVER.[1]

Once upon a time there lived a weaver who made a beautiful piece of cloth every year and presented it to the king, who was so pleased with it that he always gave him two thousand rupees in return.

This weaver was a most ambitious man. Although the king and the court praised his workmanship, yet was he not satisfied, but strove each year to weave such a piece of cloth as both in texture and beauty should excel the cloth of the previous year.

One day a thief got to know all about the weaver's affairs, and determined to possess himself of the next piece of cloth, and go to the king and get more praise than he. "The first night after he has finished it I will enter the house and steal it," he said within himself.

This weaver was a religious man also. The neighbours constantly heard him ejaculating this prayer, "O God, keep my tongue from evil words." The thief too heard him, but he was too wicked a fellow to care much about anything. These words, however, had a great effect over him, as we shall see.

At length the piece of cloth was ready, and as there was plenty of time, it being only the second watch of the day when it was finished, the weaver washed and put on his best clothes, and took it to the king.

"What a take-in!" exclaimed the thief, when he met the weaver going with the cloth to the palace. "The man might have waited a little after finishing it."

When His Majesty saw the cloth he was more pleased

[1] A Musalmán story, collected for me by Paṇḍit Bálak Tok of Fateh Kadal, Srínagar.

with it than with any other of former years, and gave the weaver four thousand rupees. "Such workmanship demands our fullest encouragement," he said to his *wazírs* and others around. "But tell me how we can best use this beautiful cloth."

One *wazír* replied, "Your Majesty should make a tablecloth of it, so that it may always be before you."

Another *wazír* replied, "Have a turban made from it. Such cloth is worthy to cover the head of a king."

Another said, "Your Majesty should have the saddle of your favourite horse covered with it."

But the king did not agree to any of these suggestions. At last he turned to the weaver, and asked him what he should do with the cloth. "God has given you understanding to make it. Perhaps you can also tell me what use to make of it," he said.

"O king, reserve it for your funeral. Let it cover your corpse when they carry you to the grave," replied the weaver.

On hearing these words the king became very angry. He thought that the man was wishing for his death. "Keep it for my own funeral pall!" he repeated. "The man is evidently plotting my death. Take the fellow and behead him."

"O king, O king, stay the sentence, I beseech you. Give thy servant permission, and I will speak," shouted the thief, who was present, and had seen and heard everything.

"Let the man come forward," the king said.

"O king," pleaded the thief, "I pray you have mercy on this weaver. Every hour he prays to God to preserve his tongue from evil words, and now by chance he has been stricken by his own tongue."

"Very well," said His Majesty, "I will forgive him; but let him be more careful in future, and never speak to a king of death."

THE ROBBERS ROBBED.[1]

In olden times there lived a great and wealthy king, whose greatness and wealth were the envy of the world. Many kings had assayed to fight with him and had been defeated, till at last he began to think that he was unconquerable, and became careless and indifferent as to the state of his army. Meanwhile another powerful king had been carefully training his forces. He saw the condition of affairs, and determined to do battle with this king. The two armies met on a large plain, and fought bravely for several days. For some time the battle seemed to be equal, but at last the great and wealthy king was slain and his forces scattered. The strange king then entered the city and reigned in his stead. His first act was to banish the late king's wife and her two sons. They were sent out of the country without the least means of subsistence, so that the queen was obliged to pound rice for a *ser* of rice a day, while the two boys got what they could by begging.

One day the woman advised one of her sons to go to the jungle and cut some bundles of wood for sale. The eldest went; and while he was engaged in cutting wood he saw at a little distance a small caravan of loaded camels and mules attended by several men, who evidently were robbers. The boy was frightened, because he thought they would kill him if they knew he was there. So he climbed up into a tree to hide himself. The caravan halted by a small hut in a part of the jungle near to this tree. He saw the men unload their beasts and place all the bundles inside the hut, the door of which opened and shut by itself at the mention of a certain charm that he

[1] Narrator's name, Shiva Báyú, Renawárí, Srínagar.

heard quite plainly. He saw all this, and remembered the words of the charm, and determined to enter the hut himself as soon as the robbers departed.

Accordingly on the morrow, when the robbers were well out of sight and hearing, he came down from the tree, went to the hut, and uttered the words of the charm that he had heard. The door immediately opened to him, and he entered. He found immense piles of valuable treasure in the place—gold and silver, and precious stones, and sundry articles of curious workmanship were stored up there in abundance. He arranged as much of the treasure as he could place on a camel that he found grazing near, and then, repeating the charm, shut the door and went home. His mother was delighted to see the result of her son's day's work.

The following morning the younger prince thought that he also would visit this jungle and try his luck. So he quickly learnt the words of the charm and started. He arrived at the jungle, and climbed the same tree near the hut, and waited there patiently for the robbers' coming. Just before dark they appeared, bringing with them several loads of treasure. On reaching the hut they entered by means of the charm, as before. Great was their surprise and anger when they found that some person had been to the place and taken some of the things. They uttered such terrible oaths, and vowed such fearful vengeance on the offender, that the prince up in the tree trembled exceedingly, and began to repent his adventure.

In the morning the robbers again left; and as soon as they were well out of the way the boy descended the tree and went and repeated the charm whereby the door of the hut was opened. The door obeyed, and he entered. But, alas! the door closed as soon as he was inside, and would not open again, although the boy shouted till he was hoarse, and begged and prayed that he might be set free. Evidently the poor boy had omitted or added something to the words of the charm, and thus brought this misfortune on himself. Terrible must have been his feelings as he counted the hours to the robbers' return, and tried to imagine what they would do to him, when they saw him there! It was vain to hope for escape. He was shut up in a prison of his own making, and must bear the consequences.

Before nightfall sounds of approaching footsteps were heard, and presently the door opened and the robbers came in. A savage gleam of delight passed over their countenances as they saw the youngster crouching away in a corner and weeping. "Oh! oh!" they exclaimed. "This is the thief that dares to intrude into our quarters, is it? We'll cut him into pieces and strew them about the place, that others may fear to follow in his steps." This they really did, for they were bloodthirsty and had no feeling, and then went to sleep. The next day they started off on their marauding expeditions as usual, as if nothing had happened.

While they were absent the eldest prince arrived to see what had become of his brother, and to help him in carrying away the spoil. His grief was inexpressible when he saw the pieces of flesh strewn about the place. "They shall rue this," he exclaimed, and caused the door of the hut to be opened by means of the charm and entered. He collected the most valuable articles that he could lay hands on and put them into a sack. Afterwards he emptied the contents of another sack on the ground outside the hut, and placed the pieces of his brother's corpse in it. And then, having repeated the charm and shut the door, he took up the two sacks, threw them over his shoulder, and walked home. On reaching home he had the pieces sewed up in a cloth and buried.

When the robbers returned that evening and discovered what had happened they were very angry. They resolved to find the thief, and took an oath to rob no more until they had accomplished their desire. They went to the city, and lodged in different parts of the *bázár*, in order that they might ascertain if any one was living there who had suddenly become rich. One of the robbers happened to meet with the tailor who had made the grave-clothes for the young prince who had been so foully slaughtered, and heard from him that the mother and brother of the boy seemed to have got a lot of money lately, but how he could not say. Some people said that they were members of some royal family, but he did not know. Accordingly the robber went and found out the house where the queen and prince were living. He marked it, so that he might know it again, and then hastened to inform the rest of the band. However, the prince had fortunately noticed the mark, and guessing what it meant, went and marked several of the adjoining houses in the same way. He thus thoroughly nonplussed the robbers.

"This plan will not do," they said. "One of us had better get to know through the tailor where these people live, and then go to the house and cultivate their friendship. An opportunity for despatching the prince would soon be afforded."

This was agreed to unanimously, and the leader of the robber band was voted to the work. He soon made friends with the young prince and his mother, and was received into the house at all times as a welcome guest. One day, however, the woman observed a dagger hidden beneath his coat, and from this and one or two other things that she afterwards noticed, decided in her mind that the man was no friend, but an enemy and a robber. She wished to be rid of him. Consequently one evening she suggested to her son and his friend that she should dance before them, and they agreed. In her hand she had a sword, which she waved about most gracefully. Now she approached the robber, and now she receded slowly and smoothly, aud accommodated her gestures to a song, till at length she saw her opportunity, and running against the robber, struck off his head.

"What have you done, mother?" exclaimed the prince, who was horror-struck.

"I have simply changed places with our friend," she replied. "Instead of him murdering you, I have murdered him. Look! Behold the dagger with which he would have slain you."

"O mother," said the prince, "how shall I ever be able to repay you for your watchfulness over me. I did not notice anything wrong about the man. I never saw his dagger before. This must be one of the robbers, come to wreak vengeance on me for taking some of their treasure."

When the robber band knew of the death of their leader they divided the spoil and retired to their different villages.

The young prince married, and became a banker and prospered exceedingly.[2]

[2] Cf. story of "Ali Baba and the Forty Thieves" in *Arabian Nights*; and its European variant, "Simeli Mountain," in Grimm's *Kinder und Hausmärchen*.

THE YOUNG GAMBLING MERCHANT.[1]

HIS CONVERSION AND AFTER-ADVENTURES.

In times gone by there lived a very great and wealthy merchant. Some affirm that he was a Kashmírí, and resided in Srínagar; others say, "No, he came from far;" while others again refuse to believe that there is anything Kashmírí about the story. But, however this may be, we will hear the tale and judge for ourselves.

Well, this great and wealthy merchant had a most clever and learned son; but, alas! the son was a confirmed gambler. The merchant knew not what to do with him. Every scrap of money or valuable that came within his reach the son gambled away. He was shown the folly of the thing; he was warned that the family and business would be ruined if he continued in it; friends also spoke to him earnestly and affectionately; but all to no purpose, for the gambling propensities developed more and more every day.[2]

Perceiving this, the merchant was exceedingly sorrowful. Grief bent his back, stamped wrinkles on his brow, and caused his legs to tremble as he walked. This trouble was bringing him down to the grave. The thought of his speedy dissolution, when the immense fortune that he had amassed by dint of the greatest skill in trading and

[1] Narrator's name, Paṇḍit Makund Báyú, Suthú, Srínagar.

[2] Several tales in which gambling extraordinary and its attendant ruin crop up are to be met with in many Indian Folk-tales. The native certainly has a great taste for gambling, whether with cards, dice, chess, lotteries, or horse-racing, and in a few years will be as proficient as any other countryman in the world. The *Rajnít*, a Hindí work on the science of government, says:—"Cut off a gambler's nose and ears and remove him from the country in order that other men may not gamble. Although a gambler's wife and children may be in the house, do not consider them as being there, because it is not known when he may lose them."

most strict economy in general expenses would pass into the hands of such an unscrupulous gambler as his own son, weighed terribly on his mind, threatening its sanity. How could such a disaster be avoided? "It were better," he exclaimed one day in a paroxysm of grief, "to bury the treasures in the earth, than that he should have them and waste them in a day. I know what I will do. I will hide my money and valuables in the ground, and then, pretending that I am not so rich as people imagine, I will curtail expenses, and at my death I will appear to leave but little for those who come after me."

When he got opportunity he dug several holes in the ground-floor of some of the lower rooms of the house, and put his gold and treasures into them.[3] Then he carefully noticed the different places and made a list of them, which list he afterwards enclosed in a golden bracelet and gave to his son's wife, saying, "Take great care of this, for it will be as a charm to you; but if after my decease your husband should be reduced to very great straits, you can give it to him to sell."

Then the old merchant was comforted. He felt sure that his son would soon spend the little money and property that he would obtain at his death, and get to know the misery of poverty; and then his daughter-in-law would give him the golden bracelet, and tell him what his father had said. On opening the bracelet he would see the list of valuables, and taking them out of the ground, would find himself a rich man again, and then, perhaps, would give up gambling, and live quietly and happily the rest of his life.

In a little while the merchant died. Great was the grief in the city, and great was the grief in his family, for the old man was very much respected and beloved by

[3] Kashmíris, like all other Orientals, are very fond of hiding money and valuables in the ground. Pandits think that a snake watches over the treasure, and will not allow any but the rightful owner to touch thereof. Musalmáns believe that God looks after it, and will not permit it to pass into the hands of any except those in whose *qismat* the discovery of it has been written.

every one. His son faithfully performed all the necessary funeral rites and *sráddhas*.[4] For ten successive days after his father's death *pindas*[5] were offered, together with libations of water, &c., to the *preta*,[6] and then thrown into the river, and on the eleventh day a great *sráddha* was performed. On this occasion there was much feasting and feeing of the *bráhmans*, who had been invited to assist in the celebration; large sums of money were also distributed among the crowds of beggars of all classes who had flocked to the place in expectation of the same. For six months these *sráddhas* were regularly performed, and each time were marked by much feasting and *largesse;* and therefore we are not surprised to hear that at the conclusion of that period, when the young merchant began to examine his monetary position, he found that there was scarcely a cowrie remaining to him. What with paying his father's and his own debts, and what with the enormous expenses incurred by the funeral ceremonies and *sráddhas*, he really had nothing which he could call his own.[7]

In his distress he went to his mother, but he got very little sympathy from her. She only reproved him more than before for not listening to his father's advice.

"Oh that I had given up the wretched practice which has hastened my dear father's death, and brought the family and myself to ruin!" he exclaimed.

"It is of no use smiting the ground when the jackal has gone," said his mother. "Be up and doing, and by a life of industry and economy redeem your position."

"Yes," he replied, "I will renounce this gambling, and I will work hard and save money, and I will send you all that I may be able to put by. But meanwhile advise my

[4] Funeral obsequies, consisting in offering rice, fruit, &c., to the manes of ancestors.

[5] Balls made of flour or rice offered to the manes; they are afterwards thrown into the river or given to cows.

[6] The spirits of the dead.

[7] Incredible sums of money are often spent on these funeral ceremonies and *sráddhas*. Some Hindús spend more than they can afford, under the false idea that a debt is warranted by the great solemnity of the occasion, which is one of vast merit in popular estimation. Cf. the most interesting chapter on "Sickness, Death, and Shrad" in *Hindús as they are*.

wife to go to her father's house, where she will get the best of food and clothing and every care."

He then went to his wife and wished her farewell. On hearing the reason of his sudden departure she offered him the golden bracelet, and told him all that his father had wished about it. But he would not take it, because his father had given it to her, and because he feared that he should be tempted to speculate with it; "and besides this," he added, "it was given to you as a charm."

So the young merchant started in quest of a living; the wife was sent to her own home; and the mother stayed behind to look after the house and the few things that were left in it, and supported herself by spinning.

He wandered about for some time till he reached a certain city. Here he soon got employment under a great merchant of the place. At first he found it very difficult and trying work, because he had been brought up in rather a luxuriant way, and had not been accustomed to serve; but afterwards, when he had gained the confidence of his master, and had therefore been placed by him in a more responsible and affluent position, he got on very happily. He regularly laid aside the greater part of his earnings, intending to forward it to his mother in the best way he could.

One day it happened that his master told him of the approaching marriage of his son.

"I have arranged for his marriage," he said, "with the second daughter of a rich merchant who lives in the same city as you came from."

This rich merchant turned out to be none other than the servant's father-in-law, and the second daughter the servant's sister-in-law. However, he pretended to have no special interest in the matter beyond his master's pleasure and his young master's prosperity and happiness, and quietly awaited the day.

In due time his master and young master and several other relations and friends started for the home of the bride, which they reached safely. He, the deceased merchant's son, also accompanied them. They found the house in a state of great confusion. Preparations were being concluded on a grand scale for the coming event, and servants were rushing about hither and thither inside the house, while outside crowds of all kinds of people were waiting in great hope of a *tamáshá* and *bakhshish;* for the house was rich and had a great name in the country.

During the evening dinner was served, and when the company sat down to the feast, the servant, who was the son of the deceased merchant, also sat down, but he kept on his working clothes and sat down as last of all, and in the lowest place. He did so from a feeling of pride; he would not court recognition from his rich relations, much as he would have liked to have seen his dear wife again.

Nevertheless he saw his wife, for she had the superintendence of the dinner arrangements. At her order the servants divided the food and distributed it among the numerous guests. When all except him had been served, the deceased merchant's son found that every bit of meat had been eaten, and that only vegetables and rice remained. However, he said nothing, though his heart was inexpressibly sad. There was a dinner worthy of a king, and his own beautiful wife having the arrangement of it; but nothing of it was for him, though others, many of whom were very wicked men and of comparatively small position, had their fill. He might have been under the ground—thus was he ignored and forgotten. Well might he take his brass vessel of rice and vegetables, and leaving the banquet-room, go downstairs and out into the courtyard, and there, placing his dinner on a window-sill, lie down and weep.

In an hour or so the guests began to depart, but the poor man still lay there weeping. At last, when about two hours of the night had passed, his wife came into the courtyard, and after seeing that food was given to numerous beggars and others assembled, she beckoned to one man and told him to wait by the door, as she had a little work for him to do. Then she re-entered the house, and presently brought out a lighted lamp,[8] and a large brass tray piled up with sweetmeats and other delicacies. Giving the tray to the man, she bade him to follow her. The man placed the sweetmeats on his shoulder and did as he was ordered. The deceased merchant's son, who had seen and heard everything, also went after them, but unawares.

On the way the man stumbled and fell down, and the trayful of sweetmeats also fell down and was broken, and its contents spilt. The woman was very angry at this, and sharply reproving the man for his carelessness, ordered him to go back with her quickly to the house, and get another trayful. They both went and got some more; and the deceased merchant's son waited quietly till they came again. Meanwhile he worked himself into a great state of excitement, wondering at his wife's strange behaviour, and who was the person so dear to her that she denied herself rest and sleep, ventured her reputation, and risked her father's anger for him, and did not mind returning to the house for another trayful of sweetmeats in order that this person might not be disappointed.

Very soon they again arrived at the place, the woman (his wife) in front carrying a lighted lamp, and the man with the tray of sweetmeats walking after. They passed the deceased merchant's son, who followed at a convenient distance. Presently they reached the house of another great merchant. Here the woman took the tray, and ordering the man to go, knocked at the door.

Now it happened that this merchant was exceedingly enraged about something just then, and did not want to be interfered with by any person; and so, when he heard the woman's knock on the door, he rushed forward and struck her with a stick, besides abusing her fearfully for coming and disturbing him at that inopportune hour.

From the stroke of the stick the woman's gold bracelet

[8] *Dazawun shama*, a lighted *díwá*.

was broken—the bracelet which her father-in-law had given her before his death.

"Be not so angry, my dearest," she said. "It is not my fault that I have arrived so late. My sister's wedding was celebrated to-day, and then as we were coming along a knave of a fellow whom I asked to bring you some sweetmeats stumbled and dropped them, and we had to return and get a fresh supply."

The merchant was silent, and so the woman, who as yet stood in the doorway from fear, picked up the golden pieces of her bracelet and went inside.

Her husband, the deceased merchant's son, crawled up stealthily to the door and sat there. He saw the merchant and the woman sitting together and eating the sweetmeats, and when they had eaten as much as they wished, he heard the merchant ask her to show him the broken bracelet, saying that perhaps he could get it mended. The woman gave him the gold pieces, on examining which he found the late merchant's list, and pulling this out, he read it, and looked very much surprised. Noticing the expression of surprise on his face, the woman asked him what was the matter.

The merchant said, "Your husband was a very unfortunate man. Gambling! Gambling! How foolish! Clever idea of the old merchant!"

"How do you know? What idea?" inquired the woman.

"Why, this paper tells me so," replied the merchant. "Everything is written here. It appears that your father-in-law was a very wealthy man, as we all thought him to be, but were afterwards assured that he was not. He was afraid to reveal all his wealth to his son, your husband, lest the gambler should speculate with it and lose everything; and so he dissembled matters. He pretended that he was worth so much money only (mentioning a small amount), and hid the rest, the great bulk of his wealth. You will find the different hiding-places of this gold and treasure in the ground-floor of your husband's house.

See, here is a list of the different places and of what things are buried in each. Your father-in-law was a wise man. He thought, 'My son will certainly continue gambling till he is thoroughly ruined, and then maybe he will learn a lesson. This golden bracelet, I know, like all the other get-at-able valuables, will be turned into money, and then this hidden wealth will be discovered. Hearing that he has become rich again, he may be more careful in future. Oh that he may remember with what great trial and labour I have gained this wealth, and take care of it as though it were the result of his own economy and toil!'"

"Ah! now I see," said the woman, "why my father-in-law gave me the bracelet and charged me so strictly concerning it before he died. I was to give it to my husband only when he had reached a state of the direst distress."

Embracing the woman, the merchant asked her whether she loved her husband more than she loved him.

The woman replied, "I love you more, because my husband has troubled me very much, and has gone I know not whither. The gods only can tell whether I shall ever see him again."

"Then," said the merchant, "I know all about your father-in-law's house. I will go there and get the treasure, and afterwards, when it is all safely locked up here, I will tell you, and we will live together in ease and pleasure all our lives."

The woman agreed, and begged him to do all this quickly; "for," said she, "I long to be with you always."

The state of the wretched husband, who was sitting outside the half-open door, and had heard and seen everything, can be more easily imagined than described. With mingled feelings he walked back to his own house; he was grieved because of his wife's unfaithfulness, but he was rejoiced at the prospect of being a rich man once more. Thus sorrow and joy, joy and sorrow, fought against one another within his breast, so that he hardly knew what to do, to laugh or to cry. In an hour or so he reached his home, and saw his dear mother, and was welcomed by her as one alive from the dead.

After some conversation as to all that had happened to them both since they had been separated, the young merchant explained how it was that his father had died so comparatively poor.

"This wealth must be exhumed, dear mother," he added; "and since its whereabouts are known to others, and those others are no friends of ours, but confirmed enemies, it is necessary that we get spades and begin the work this very night."

Before midnight they had found all the treasure—gold, silver, and precious stones—a great heap, the value of which could not be reckoned; and long before the dawn of the next day they had re-buried the things in other holes, and filled up the old places with stones and rubbish. The next morning the late merchant's son was going about in genteel, respectable clothes as usual, and his mother was squatting by the door spinning as for her living. The young merchant at once gave up the other merchant's service and lived with his mother. In the course of a week the other merchant, who had discovered all about the deceased merchant's hidden wealth, disguised himself, and pretended that he had just arrived from some foreign country, and had brought some diamonds and other valuables as a present for His Highness the Rájá of that country.

Hearing this, the Rájá gave him an interview, and when he saw the presents, he was exceedingly pleased with the merchant, and said he should be glad to help him in any way. The merchant thanked him, and said that he should be grateful for a place to live in, where also he could keep his goods. The Rájá promised that he should reside in one of his own houses. But this the merchant did not wish; he wanted a house in the city, and told His Highness so, and begged that he would order some person to help him in the choice of a place. So the Rájá ordered his chief *wazír* to accompany the merchant to the city, and to give him whatever house he might select.

They had walked about together the greater part of the day, and had seen all kinds of houses, but not one of them had been approved of by the merchant; and so they were thinking of returning to the palace, when they came by the deceased merchant's house.

"This is a fine building," said the merchant, "and is in a good and busy part of the *bázár*. Whose is it?"

The *wazír* said, he thought the house had belonged to a certain deceased merchant, and was now inhabited by the widow, who would most likely be very glad to sell or rent it.

Accordingly they knocked at the door and asked who was there. The young merchant appeared and bade them to come in.

"My friend," said the *wazír*, "wishes to rent this house. How much money do you ask for it?"

The merchant's son replied, "Two thousand rupees a month."

"Very well," said the merchant; "agreed."

The *wazír*, however, had not been accustomed to see such a monstrous bargain concluded so easily, and therefore remonstrated. "No, no. Two thousand rupees! Tush! the fellow is mad. It is more than I would give for the place for a year. Take the house, and don't pay the man a cowrie for his impudence. I will see that you are not bothered by him."

But this mode of settling the matter, however much it might have recommended itself to the merchant on any other occasion, was not pleasing to him just then. "Two thousand rupees! What is that," he thought, "in comparison with the immense treasure concealed under the ground of the lower apartments of the house?"

And so it was arranged. The merchant paid down the

sum demanded, and the young merchant and his mother vacated the place and went elsewhere.

On the earliest opportunity the merchant dug up the earth in the several places enumerated in the list that was discovered inside the golden bracelet, but he found nothing except stones.

"What a misfortune is this!" he exclaimed. "Either the deceased merchant has written this list to deceive, or else some one got clue of this secret, and has been here before me. Cursed be this place! Cursed be all who have any connection with it! Cursed be they in their family, and cursed be they in their work! I am ruined! I am ruined!" So saying, he seized his shawl and shoes, and rushed like a madman to his own house, which, as we have seen, was a little distance outside the city.

As soon as it was known that the merchant had gone, the deceased merchant's son and mother came again and took up their abode in the house. Gradually the young merchant revealed his wealthy position, so that nobody's suspicions might be aroused, and in a little while he was accounted one of the chief traders of the country, and was respected quite as much as his father had ever been.

"The gods be praised that you have become great and wealthy in the land," said his mother to him one day. "Is it not meet that you should now send for your wife?"

"Speak not to me on this matter," he replied.

But his mother was resolute, and went to the wife's parents and got them to promise to try to persuade her son to send for his wife again. In a day or two they invited him to come and stay with them, and so pressed their invitation that eventually he went. Great preparations were made for the reception of such an illustrious member of the family as he had now become. The house was grandly furnished, the best of provisions were obtained, the father and mother were most attentive, while the wife was all smiles and affection, and could not look at him enough or do enough for him, for he had been absent such a long time, she said, and she thought that she should never see him again, and therefore she constantly wept.

At night, when the husband and wife were sleeping together in the same room, and when all was perfectly quiet, the young merchant started violently in his sleep and shrieked. "Oh!" he exclaimed, "is it true? Can it be true?" and then fell back on his bed again. Presently he recovered, and said, "I have dreamed; but oh! such a dream!"

His wife, of course, asked him what he had been dreaming about.

"I saw," he replied, "as though there was a great marriage in this house. Your sister was being married to the son of a merchant who had come from some distant country. I thought that I was one of the head servants of that merchant, and accompanied him and the bridegroom to the marriage. I sat down to dinner with the rest of the guests. You were superintending the distribution of the food, and so managed that every one should have meat and spices with their rice and vegetables except me, who appeared as the least of all in your sight. For very shame I smothered my feelings, and taking up my vessel of rice and vegetables, went out into the courtyard and sat down among the beggars and others assembled there. After a while you came and distributed some food to those beggars, and then, calling one of them, bade him to wait and help you to carry some sweetmeats to a certain person whom you wished to visit. I saw you come forth from the house with a lighted lamp and give a loaded tray to the man, and then start; and I followed you. In the midst of the way the man tripped, and dropped the tray, spilling its contents. And then I saw you go back and fetch another trayful of sweetmeats and start again. I watched you both till you reached the door of a certain merchant, when you took the sweetmeats, and, telling the beggar to go, knocked at the door. Evidently the merchant was in a great rage because you arrived so late; for I saw him strike you, and in the striking a golden bracelet that my dear father gave you was broken to pieces. All this I saw in my dream as plainly as I see you now; and therefore I started."

By the time he had got thus far in the narration of his dream the woman had borne as much as, or more than, she was able. The thought that she had been detected, and that her husband was relating no dream, but what was only too true, was more than she could bear; she there and then died from fear.

When the young merchant noticed that his wife did not move, but was as one petrified, staring at him with eyes ready to burst out of their sockets, he was afraid, and said, "I must have killed the woman!" There was no feeling of sorrow, for all love went on the remembrance of his wife's unfaithfulness. There was only a fear as to what his father and mother-in-law might say, and what unfavourable remarks his fellow-citizens might pass about him when the circumstances of the case were known.

"I must get the body away," he said to himself. So he put it in a big shawl, which he threw over his shoulder, and carried to the house of the merchant who had seduced the woman, and depositing it there on the doorstep, knocked at the door.

The merchant, thinking that it was the woman coming to him as usual, opened the door in a great rage, and commenced reproving her for staying so long with her husband. He did all this without noticing whether the woman was there or not. Presently, when nobody answered or came in, he got up again to see who was there. When he saw the dead body only he was very greatly astonished, and thought that the woman must have died since she knocked at the door. He took up the corpse, and wrapping it in a *thán*[9] of *puṭ*,[10] laid it in one of the large open cupboards in his shop.

[9] *Thán* (also Hindustání), a piece of cloth measuring about nine yards English.

[10] *Puṭ* (*paṭṭú* in the plains) is a coarse woollen cloth manufactured in Kashmír. Cf. Vigne's *Travels in Kashmír*, p. 127.

All this the young merchant saw from the outside of the window, and then returned.

It was quite late the next morning before the young merchant awoke, and even then he would not have got up if his father-in-law had not sent to inquire the reason of his not appearing at the morning meal.

"I was very tired," he said by way of excuse, "and could not sleep the first part of the night, owing to the strange behaviour of my wife, who got off the bed and went out, I know not where."

Hearing this, his mother-in-law, who was thoroughly aware of her daughter's intimacy with the other merchant, and had, in fact, somewhat encouraged it, thinking that the girl's husband was dead, made some apology for this strange behaviour. "Perhaps the girl is ill," she remarked, "and therefore went to sleep in another room. I will go and inquire."

While she was inquiring the young merchant asked his father-in-law to take him to his shop, as he wished to buy several things which he had not in stock in his own shop. The father-in-law agreed, and they started at once.

The young merchant saw all the goods, but did not find what he wanted. Then the father-in-law offered to take him to the house of another merchant, a great friend of his, who would most likely have the goods that he required. "It is a long way," he said, "but the road is pleasant, and the merchant is very clever and affable, and you ought to make his acquaintance." So they both wended their steps in the direction of the house of this very clever and affable merchant.

This personage chanced to be none other than the very man who had seduced the deceased merchant's son's wife. Strange coincidence brought about by Param-eshwar for the destruction of this wicked man! On their arrival the merchant welcomed them most heartily, and gladly showed them most of his goods and treasures. But there were some *thâns* of *puṭ* and pieces of *pashmína*,[11] silk, and other materials in a little inner room, which the young merchant happened to get a glimpse of, and wished very much to see.

"Those are ordinary goods," the merchant objected, "and like many others that you have seen, and therefore there is no need to fetch them."

However, the late merchant's son persisted, and even went forward in the direction of the room. Then the merchant, seeing that he could not possibly avoid showing the goods, and hoping that somehow the *thán* of *puṭ* in which the corpse was concealed would escape attention, had the cloths and other things brought out. Alas! among other rolls of cloth, the bulky piece of *puṭ* was opened, and the dead body discovered!

Imagine the condition of the three onlookers. The father of the woman so horrified that he fell down in a fit; the merchant, his friend, so trembled with fear as to the results of this discovery, that he had to support himself by leaning against the wall; while the young merchant rushed about the place apparently in the direst grief, shouting, "My wife is dead! My wife is dead!" and calling for the deputy-inspector to investigate the case and punish the murderer.

"Oh, keep quiet, keep quiet, my friend!" said the merchant. "You will bring the blood of this woman on my head by your shouting."

"Let me alone; I will explain everything to the police," said the young merchant, shaking off the hand, which had been placed tenderly on his shoulder.

"O friend, consider! What profit will there be to you from the death of another? The gods know that I am guiltless."

[11] *Pashmína* is a fine kind of woollen cloth manufactured in Kashmír. About 20,000 people are thought to be engaged in its manufacture. The finest goat's wool employed is brought from Túrfán, in Yárkand territory. This is called *Túrphání phamb;* all other qualities are generally called *Kashmírí phamb;* though these, as well as the former, are found only on the animals who roam the wind-swept steppes of Central Asia. Cf. also Vigne, *Travels in Kashmír*, pp. 124–134.

"Let me alone, I say," shouted the young merchant; "I will have justice. You shall receive the due reward of your cruel deed."

"O friend," said the merchant, "I beseech you to refrain. Ask of me what you will and you shall have it, but please keep quiet. One word outside, together with the fact that the body was found in my house, and wrapped up in a *thán* of my *puṭ*, would be sufficient proof against me. Take my wealth, my goods, my all, but save my family and my name."

By this time the father of the woman had come to his senses; and he, on being consulted, agreed to think that his daughter had died by the will of the gods, and that his friend the merchant was blameless, and to take his friend's money and goods as a bribe for thus thinking.

Then the merchant and his son-in-law returned. On the way back the latter begged to be allowed to go to his own house, and wished his father-in-law farewell.

His mother was surprised to see him again so quickly, and without his wife also. He told her that he intended to bring his wife after a while. He could not, however, keep the secret very long, for friends and neighbours continued to inquire the reason of his wife's deferred coming, till he was obliged to concoct some falsehood about her sudden death. Then he was urged to marry again, but he would not agree, saying that he had lost all confidence in women.

"But," said they, "all women are not alike. Some are good and some are bad. Some are as a spreading *buni*[12] tree, under whose shade one lies down in refreshment and peace, and others are like a bitch at the door, who is constantly biting one's heels going out and coming in."

[12] *Buni*, or, as I have also heard it, *Buiṅ*, (Persian, *chinár*), the *Platanus orientalis*, is a tree of great beauty in the valley. It has a very extensive geographical range from Kashmír westerly, and is admirably characterised by its derivative, πλατυς, ample, significant of its palmate leaves, its spreading branches, and shady foliage, the pale green colour of which last contrasts beautifully with the silver bark of its lofty stem. Cf. also Vigne, *Travels in Kashmír*, pp. 94–96.

Thus his friends urged him, till at last he said, "Well, perhaps it would be better for me to be married, but I must be allowed to make my own choice. The woman whose appearance, whose manner, and whose speech please me I will marry, and no other."

In a few days he commenced his search for a wife. He travelled towards the city where the merchant lived, whose servant he had been for some years, and whose son had married his sister-in-law. He reached the merchant's house, and after seeing that his charm was right he again applied for employment, and got the situation of cook.

Now this merchant had a very wise, beautiful, and chaste daughter. Her wisdom, beauty, and goodness were famous in the country. In order to prove whether she was as good as she was supposed to be, the young merchant had again taken service with her father.

One day the merchant expressed a wish to visit a certain *meld* that was being held at some place a great distance from his house. He wanted to take his wife and family as well, but did not know how to manage it. So he asked his wife, and she advised him to leave the beautiful and good daughter behind, saying that she would look after the house and goods; and besides, she ought not to go out in public now that she was grown up and of a marriageable age. She might remain certainly with the old *dái* and cook. The *dái* would carry the food to her room.

So they all went off to the *meld*, except the good and beautiful daughter, the *dái*, and the cook. The latter had express orders to take care of the house, and to be careful about the girl's food, and on no account to enter her room on peril of a heavy fine and dismissal.

The day after the merchant and his family left, the son of the chief *wazír* of the country chanced to pass by the merchant's house, and saw the beautiful girl standing by the door. He fainted at the sight of her beauty. As soon as he came to his senses he entered the house by the door at which he had seen the merchant's daughter, and meeting the cook, asked him to try and procure him an interview with her, promising to give him a magnificent present if he succeeded.

"It is in vain, your honour," replied the cook. "My master has strictly forbidden me even to take her meals to the room."

"But I entreat you to try and do this for me," urged the *wazír's* son.

"It cannot be," said the cook. "Only the *dái* goes to the room. You might, perhaps, go and speak to her."

"Call her at once," said the *wazír's* son. "Only let this meeting be accomplished, and both the *dái* and you shall be handsomely rewarded."

In a few minutes appeared the *dái*, who, on receiving a large present in money, immediately led the *wazír's* son to her young mistress's room. On entering the room the merchant's daughter asked him who he was and whence he had come,—two very important questions to have answered before she could tell how to receive him.

He answered, "Attracted by your beautiful face, I came to converse with you. I am the son of the *wazír*."

"Be it so," she said; "but know that before I will say another word with you you must give me a *lach* of rupees."

The *wazír's* son at once put his hand into his pocket, and taking out a note for that amount, placed it before her.

Then she said, "You have done bravely. Do you know at what great risk you seek this interview? Were your father to know of it he would be very angry, and should my father hear of your coming he would never forgive me;" and then turning to the *dái*, who was squatting by the door, she ordered her to go and fetch something to drink; and when this was brought she poured out two cups, one for herself and one for the son of the *wazír*;

but she most adroitly dropped some stupefying drug into the cup which she set before her visitor. Not knowing this, he took the cup and drank off its contents at one draught. After this but few words passed between them, for it was a most potent drug, and began to operate at once. Within a minute or two the son of the *wazír* was fast asleep. When she saw this the merchant's daughter bade the *dái* to carry the man to the stables. But the *dái* could not lift him of herself, and had to ask the cook to come and help her.

On recovering his senses the son of the *wazír* was astonished to find himself in a stable and surrounded by horses.

"Ah, the woman must have deceived me," he said to himself as he got up and walked out.

However, nothing daunted, he went again the following day and asked the *dái* to get him another interview, and again gave her a present of money. The young mistress sent out word not to let the son of the *wazír* enter the house unless he could pay another *lach* of rupees. He paid the money, and was again admitted. On seeing him the merchant's daughter ordered some food to be brought, in one plate of which she mixed a powerful drug. This plateful she placed before her guest, and he, suspecting nothing, ate it, and was soon overpowered with sleep as before, and fell on his side. Then the *dái* and the cook were summoned, and carried him for the second time to the stables, where they laid him on the grass among the horses.

When the son of the *wazír* recovered from the effects of the drug, and found that the merchant's daughter had again tricked him, he was very much ashamed and angry. Still he did not despair, but determined to go and see her again, and be more wary as to what he might eat and drink.

He went to the house again on the following morning, and as usual was asked for a *lach* of rupees, which he readily paid, and was therefore readily admitted. As on previous occasions, she returned his kind questions, and then ordered some food to be brought.

"Please, do not trouble yourself," he said; "I am not feeling hungry this morning. I am not well to-day. However, thinking you might urge your request for me to eat something, I have brought some special food which the *hakim* ordered for me."

"Then you have done wrongly," she replied. "How strange—a guest who brings his own food!"

"I beg you to pardon me," he said, "and if you are going to eat anything, to allow me to order my servant to warm that which I have brought."

"Go, *dái*," she said, "and carry out these wishes."

The *dái* went, and having received a hint from her mistress, threw some of the drug into the plate as she handed it to the servant of the *wazír's* son to warm. Directly the eatables were ready, the cook of the son of the *wazír* brought his master's plate, and the *dái* brought the merchant's daughter's plate. Assured that nothing could possibly be wrong this time, the son of the *wazír* ate moderately. He soon fell asleep again, when, for the third time, the *dái* and the cook were called to carry him to the stables.

Within an hour or so he came to himself, and when he found that he had been again duped, he exclaimed, "What a fool I have been! I have wasted three *lachs* of rupees over this woman. I will be wiser in the future." Saying this he got up and went home, and never went near the place again.

When the cook saw the chastity and cleverness of the girl he became very fond of her. "Many girls have I seen," he said to himself—"many chaste and clever and beautiful girls—but never one so chaste and clever and beautiful as this. She shall be my wife."

In a little while the merchant and his family returned, and then the cook asked to be paid his wages and let go, as he wished to see his mother and home again. The merchant agreed, though he was very sorry to part with such a good servant. So the cook went.

As soon as he reached home the young merchant's friends and relations assembled to hear and to ask questions, as it had been a very long time since he went away in search of a wife, and they were especially anxious to hear whether he had succeeded in finding one.

He told them that he had succeeded, and that she was the daughter of the merchant to whom he had hired himself as cook, and who lived in such-and-such a city. Then were they all very glad when they heard this, and heartily congratulated him, and begged him to arrange quickly for the wedding.

A go-between [13] was at once despatched to this merchant to treat with him for the marriage. Everything was concluded satisfactorily. In due time the wedding took place. A grander wedding there could not have been, for both families spared not any expense. A more suitable wedding, also, was impossible, because both the parties were rich and young and beautiful. Stories of the wealth and beauty of the bride and bridegroom were on the lips of every one, and great was the joy in that city on the wedding-day and for many days afterwards.

When the bride was carried to her husband's house, and they were alone together, she sat before him and began to examine him, to see whether he was such a wise and sharp man as she had heard and hoped.

But he said to her, "I am not the son of the *wazír*, that you can deceive me or rob me of *lachs* of rupees."

She was surprised to hear these words, and suspected that her husband was the man who had served her father in the position of cook, and therefore knew all her secrets.

[13] *Manzimyor*, masc., and *manzimyarĕni*, fem. (Persian *miyáṅ-jí*). Marriages in respectable families are generally effected in this way. Cf. *Hindús as they are*, p. 41. In Kashmír Musalmán male and female go-betweens frequently arrange matches for Hindús, but never a Hindú go-between for a Musalmán. Harah Lántsh, *i.e.*, Hara the Eunuch, is the favourite Hindú go-between in Srínagar.

She did not like this, and so got up and slept in a separate bed. Thus several days elapsed; they talked little with one another, and they slept in separate beds, till the bride was taken back to her father's house. Here she was left for several years, because the young merchant, her husband, never sent for her.

"Ah! so, so, is it?" said the forsaken wife, when she thought that her husband did not want her. "I will retaliate."

She bought a fine, sleek, beautiful horse and a beautiful saddle and bridle, which were covered with the richest cloth and studded with the most costly jewels. Then she asked her father to allow her to go on a short journey. Sanction having been obtained, she disguised herself as a merchant's son, and rode on the horse at the head of a little caravan bearing merchandise of different kinds. Thus she visited many countries, and after some time reached the country where her husband lived. Having ascertained this, she called on the Rájá, and presented him with many jewels and other valuables, and told him that she was the son of a merchant, and had come there to trade. The Rájá was much pleased with the supposed merchant's son, and with the rich presents that he had received, and gave orders that a special house should be set apart for him as long as he stayed in the city.

The supposed merchant's son got very popular on account of her good looks, fair manner, and wise counsels. Now and again she went to the *darbár* on special invitation, and sometimes she attended the Rájá when he went out riding. One day His Highness asked her to sell him the horse that she was riding.

"Your Highness shall have it," she said, "if you will pay me four *lachs* of rupees."

"Four *lachs!*" said the king. "Well, never mind. I do not need the horse so much as to pay that price for it."

The supposed merchant also made friends with her own husband, who was thoroughly ignorant of her real character, although he had constantly seen her at *darbár*, and had often heard her speak. He got especially fond of his friend, and when the supposed merchant's son intimated her intention of departing for her own country he was very sad.

"I too am sad at having to go and leave you," said the supposed merchant; "but let us not increase each other's grief. Tell me what I can give you in token of our friendship."

"One thing of yours I have always coveted since I first saw it," said the son of the deceased merchant, "and that is your beautiful horse."

"I am sorry," replied the supposed merchant, "that I cannot part with it under four *lachs* of rupees. Give me so much money and you shall have the horse."

"What do you mean?" asked the deceased merchant's son. "Are you joking? Speak plainly, please, for I really want the horse."

"Well," said the supposed merchant, "I will let you have the beast for three *lachs* of rupees."

"Jest not, please," said the other, "but tell me its real value, and I will pay you at once."

"Give me two *lachs* only, and the horse is yours."

"No, no, you are still trifling with me."

"I'll take one *lach*, then, because you are my very dear friend."

"It is not thus one treats a friend, to try and steal his money from him under pretence of giving him a bargain."

"Very well, very well, I will not sell the horse to you, for I love you, and wish you to have the animal. Take it, and let me have two kisses in exchange."

"Done," said the deceased merchant's son, for he thought that there was no harm in that, if nobody saw it. "All right, but please do not tell any person."

Then the supposed merchant seized his friend's head between both palms, and gave him such kisses that they left a wound behind. Afterwards she handed over the horse and took her departure.

After a while the citizens of the place began to ask the late merchant's son why he did not send for his wife. "Is she dead, or have you deserted her?" they said.

"Oh no, no, no," he replied; "I intend going to fetch her as soon as I can conveniently do so."

So one morning he set out, mounted on the horse which he had obtained at the price of two kisses, and went in the direction of his father-in-law's house. He was received with great affection and respect. He remained in the place for a month or more. The whole of this time, although he was such a great and wealthy man, he groomed his horse. He regularly rubbed him down, gave him water and grass, and did all else that was required. Noticing this, his wife asked him why he did not order one of the grooms to do this work, as it was really hard work, besides being most unbecoming one of his position. He said that the horse was of great value. It cost about four *lachs* of rupees, and he was afraid lest from carelessness on the part of the servant anything should happen to it.

"What! do you think me stupid?" exclaimed the wife. "Four *lachs* of rupees! How can a horse be worth so much? One could buy a whole stud of the best-bred horses for that sum of money. Somebody has surely been gulling you."

"Well," said the young merchant, very much annoyed at his wife's words, "you can believe me or not believe me, just as you like. I tell you that I paid four *lachs* of rupees for the animal."

"I must disbelieve you, then," she replied, "because I have very good authority for thinking differently. Did not you get the horse for two kisses, the imprints of which even now you bear on your cheek?"

When the young merchant heard these words he hung down his head in shame.

"You spoke to me so confidently one day about your cleverness and wisdom," she remarked, "that I thought I would play you a trick and show you that you were not so wise and sharp as you esteemed yourself."

"It is right," he said; "you have taught me a lesson. You are the master, I am the pupil. Forgive my conceit, love me again thoroughly, and come back with me to my house."

She consented; and on the following day they both set out for the young merchant's country, which they reached safely, and where they lived together many years in great peace, happiness, and prosperity.

THE DAY-THIEF AND THE NIGHT-THIEF.[1]

ONCE upon a time there was a woman who had two husbands, one of whom lived with her by day, and the other at night. Both of these men were thieves. One was named Duhuli-*Ts*úr, because he prosecuted his nefarious calling by day, and the other was named Rátuli-*Ts*úr,[2] because he used to steal at night. Neither of these men knew that their wife had another husband, as the day-thief always left the house before daybreak, and did not return till after dark, while the night-thief always left the house just before dark, and did not return till after daybreak. One day, however, they happened to meet, and learnt all about one another. They were very much surprised when they discovered that they were living in the same house and having the same woman as wife. At first they did not believe one another, but when they went home and inquired from the woman whose wife she was, the matter seemed clear enough. She was the wife of both of them. Now this arrangement, however satisfactory it might have worked as long as they were ignorant of it, could not continue.

"We cannot both be your husband," they said to the woman. "Therefore say you whom you prefer of us two; and the other will depart and find other lodgings."

The woman replied, "Him will I choose who will bring me the most valuable spoil two days hence."

"Very well," said the thieves.

At early dawn the next morning the day-thief arose

[1] Narrator's name, Lál Chand, Khunamuh, Wular *pargana*.

[2] These names mean the Day-thief and the Night-thief.

and put on rich apparel, and calling the night-thief, asked him to attend him as his servant. The man agreed, and they both went forth. The day-thief walked in a most dignified manner to the shop of a very wealthy jeweller, and after greeting him said, "The king has commissioned me to buy some valuable jewels."

"Certainly, certainly," said the jewel merchant. "It is very kind of you to remember me. Be pleased, I pray you, to take a little refreshment." Whereupon he led the thieves into an anteroom and placed several dishes of delicious food before them. By the time the meal was finished the jeweller had caused many cases of the most valuable jewellery to be arranged for their inspection.

"Ah, yes!" exclaimed the thief. "It will not take very long to select the jewels. What an excellent display! I will take these diamonds, please—these pearls—and some gold rings—and these few things, perhaps," he said, pointing to a little pile of precious stones of sorts.

"You will not mind His Majesty seeing them first. My servant will take them to the palace, while I sit here." And then, without waiting for an answer, he turned to the night-thief and ordered him to go to His Majesty quickly and show him the things, and to bring from the royal treasury the price of the articles which the king would select. "Do not tarry," he added, as the man was leaving the room. "I shall remain here till you return."

The night-thief went off at once, and carried the jewellery straight to his wife.

Meanwhile the day-thief had a little nap and drank some tea; then in an hour or so he rose up and yawned and inquired for the *zarúrí jagah.*[3] The merchant showed him the place, and left him there. This was just what the day-thief expected. He knew there was another door, that led out into the street from that place, by the which he accordingly made his exit, and was soon sitting down with the night-thief and his wife and laughing over his successes.

[3] Necessary-house.

The jeweller became demented as soon as he discovered that he had been duped.

In the evening the night-thief roused himself, and called to the day-thief to accompany him. "I helped you this morning," he said. "You come and help me to-night."

The man agreed, and so they both went forth together. They walked to the palace, where the night-thief climbed up to the window of the king's bedroom and went inside. There he saw a maid sitting at the king's feet.

"Speak a word and you die," he said, motioning to her to get away and allow him to sit in her place.

Presently the king woke up, and asked the maid (as he thought) at his feet to tell him a story; whereupon the night-thief told him the story of the two thieves, Duhuli-*Tsúr* and Rátuli-*Tsúr*. Before he had concluded the king was fast asleep again. Then the night-thief whispered to the maid to show him where the king kept his jewels. Afraid for her life, the girl told him that His Majesty kept all his special jewels inside a big golden fish that was inside the pillow whereon his head was resting. The night-thief then tickled the king, and made him turn over on to his side, so that he could easily abstract the fish; the which having done successfully, he again warned the girl to keep quiet, and left the bed-chamber by the same way as he had entered it, and went home.

When the woman saw the spoil that her husbands had brought home, she declared that they were equal, and therefore they must try again. Accordingly they both started off together on the following morning to try their luck. They came across an immense caravan bringing in much treasure from a distant country. They contrived to seize some of the precious loads without being noticed. In one of these loads was a quantity of beautiful shoes worked in pure gold. The day-thief noticed this, and a happy thought struck him. He would try to steal from the other thief. So, jumping on to the pony that was carrying the load of shoes worked in gold, he dashed off after the caravan on the pretence of wishing to get some more spoil. He soon turned off, however, on to a little path which led to the road home. When he had reached that road, and had ascertained that the night-thief had not come up, he dropped one of the beautiful shoes, and went on a little way and dropped another, and then hid himself and the pony behind a hedge.

The night-thief could not understand why his companion was so long absent. He waited for him until he was tired, and then started home. "Wretched fellow!" he thought to himself, "he was not content with having stolen as many loads as myself, and now he has gone and been captured. I hope he will not say anything about me." Thus musing, he came across a beautiful shoe on the road, and picked it up; but only finding one, he threw it away again. A little farther on he saw its fellow. "What a pity!" he exclaimed. "I wish I had kept the other shoe. However, there is plenty of time. I will fasten the pony to this tree and run back for it. It cannot be far. It will not take me long." And so he did.

Meanwhile the day-thief took his pony also, and whipping it on before him, rode quickly home. "Look, look," said he to his wife, "I have brought two pony-loads of treasure for you, while the night-thief is coming along behind with two little shoes only. Now listen to me. I do not wish to speak to him this evening, and therefore I will pretend to be dead. When he arrives, tell him with tearful eyes that I died suddenly.

The night-thief reached home very late that evening, as he had to walk the whole way. He appeared very angry, and at once asked after the day-thief.

"He is dead," said the woman.

"Dead!" he repeated. "Never! I'll soon wake him up. Where is his corpse?"

The woman pointed to a bundle in a corner of the room in reply.

"Let us see if it will move," he said, walking over it, and then emptying the contents of a crock of boiling water over its feet. However, the day-thief did not move or make the slightest noise.

"Yes, he is dead," said the night-thief. "Poor fellow! I will go out and bury him."

Accordingly he carried him out by the wayside for burial. Before doing so, however, he climbed a tree close by the open grave, and waited to see whether it really was not a sham.

While he was sitting up in the tree a company of thieves carrying much treasure approached the place.

"See, see!" exclaimed one of them, "this is a holy spot, for the dead has risen out of the grave."

"How foolishly you speak!" said another. "Look here! I will punish the fellow for his impudence in trying to frighten benighted wayfarers like ourselves." So saying, he took up a stone and threw it at the man's mouth and smashed some of his teeth.

This was too much for the day-thief. He could not refrain from shouting, "Oh, oh!" and then the night-thief, seeing his opportunity, shrieked out, "Go away, you blackguards. Who are you, disturbing the bodies of the dead?" On this all the thieves, dropping their loads, took to their heels and soon disappeared. The day-thief then got up and helped the night-thief to collect the things and went home.

The following morning the king discovered that his private jewels had been stolen. He also heard of the jewel merchant's robbery. Thinking that such dastard acts necessitated strong measures, he issued an order for the seizure and execution of all the thieves in the city. The day-thief and the night-thief, however, were not taken with the others, because they had never been convicted of any offence, and were generally supposed to be honest and respectable citizens.

His Majesty, however, repented of this stern order; so as the hour appointed for the execution of the thieves drew near, he issued a proclamation that if the thieves would confess their wickedness they should receive full pardon. Whereupon the day-thief and the night-thief went and prostrated themselves before the king and explained how they had done these things. His Majesty was very much surprised and pleased when he heard of their daring and cunning, and gave them many and great presents. But the woman he commanded to be executed, "because," said he, "the men would never have ventured on these works if she had not instigated them."

The day-thief and the night-thief then restored all that they had stolen from the king and the jeweller, and spent the remainder of their days as good and honest men.[4]

[4] Cf. "Adventures of Two Thieves and of their Sons," in *Folk-Tales of Bengal*; also John M. Morton's Farce called "Box and Cox."

THE CUNNING GOLDSMITH.[1]

A GOLDSMITH used to visit the small towns and villages in the Valley, taking with him a box of brass bracelets washed in gold, which he pretended were golden bracelets, and charged for accordingly. In this way he deceived many ignorant folk. One day, however, he was detected. A shrewd farmer's wife, not liking the man's manner, wished to have the gold tested. She took it to one of her friends and found that, excepting a thin wash of gold on the outside, the whole thing was brass. She was very much enraged at this, and determined to retaliate. So she begged her husband to nearly fill a *nut*[2] with earth, and to pour over the earth about a pound of *gyav*, and then to carry the *nut* with its contents to the goldsmith and get him to buy it as so much *gyav*. As was fully expected, since a small price only was asked for it, the goldsmith bought the *gyav*. The next day he discovered the fraud, and instead of being angry, he was so pleased with the idea that he sent for the farmer and asked him if he wanted employment, because, if he did, he would be very glad to give him something to do. The farmer agreed, and with the help of his clever wife was able to aid and abet the goldsmith in his wickednesses most effectually.

Some time after this a great and wealthy merchant died in the city. When he had been buried three or four days, the goldsmith said to his servant the farmer, "Look here, I think we can make something out of this

[1] Narrator's name, Qádir, Amírá Kadal, Srínagar.

[2] *Nut* is an earthenware vessel called *ghará* in the plains.

man even now. You go and lie down in his grave, and I will call on the deceased merchant's family and explain how that the good man had died in my debt to the extent of 10,000 rupees. In case they deny this debt, and most likely they will deny it, I shall ask them to come and speak to the corpse on the subject. If they come, I want you to tell them with sepulchral voice that this is a true debt."

"All right," said the farmer, who at once went to the grave and was interred.

The goldsmith went to the house of the late rich merchant, and presented his claim on the estate. The late merchant's relations were much surprised. They replied that they had had many long and special conversations with the late merchant about his accounts, and had also thoroughly investigated the books, but nothing had they heard or seen concerning this debt. "How was the debt incurred? Did the deceased borrow the money, or was it for goods purchased? What was the arrangement about payment?" To all these and other similar questions the goldsmith gave plausible answers, and then, finding that they were still unconvinced, he asked them all to attend at the grave at a certain time on the following morning, when he would prove incontestably the truth of his claim.

Accordingly the next morning all the family were assembled round the grave praying, and the goldsmith among them, when lo! there came forth from the grave a groan, and another groan, and lastly the voice of a man was faintly heard saying, "O help me! I am in great distress. Allah has consigned me to hell, because I owe 10,000 rupees to the goldsmith, and have died without paying it. Of your charity pay this money for me and relieve me of this agony."

On hearing this the relations and friends of the late merchant turned to the goldsmith, and begged his pardon, and asked him to accompany them back to the house, where they would pay him the sum stated.

Thus the goldsmith got the money; but he did not remember the farmer in the grave. For two whole days the man waited in that wretched hole till he could bear it no longer, and therefore pushed aside the earth above him and got out. He went straight to the house of the goldsmith. As soon as the latter saw him he said to his wife, "Listen! I will lie down here and pretend to be dead. You go to the door and meet that fellow, and ask him with loud and angry voice what he has done to me."

When the farmer came up to the door and saw the body of the goldsmith stretched out on the floor and the angry countenance of the goldsmith's wife he rushed away, fearing lest suspicion of murder should be cast on him and he be executed. "Everybody knows that I am his servant," he cried, "and will suppose that I have murdered him because of this money which has just come into his possession." So the farmer and his wife escaped as fast as they could out of the country, and have never been heard of since.

HOW THE PRINCESS FOUND HER HUSBAND.[1]

ONCE upon a time a king wished to marry his son, and therefore sent his chief *wazír* to seek out a suitable match for him. The *wazír* departed, and in the course of his wanderings came across the chief *wazír* of another king, who was travelling about in search of a suitable match for his royal master's beautiful daughter.

"Well met!" they exclaimed when they heard from one another the like purport of their errands. "Our kings are equal in wealth and power and might, and the prince and princess seem in every way worthy of each other. Let us return to our countries and endeavour to arrange a match."

This was not a very difficult matter, for both kings readily accepted their proposals. The wedding-day was appointed. But, alas! before the time arrived the prince's father died, and in consequence of this the other king broke off the contract, and sought another prince as husband for his daughter. The wedding-day was fixed, and at the appointed time the prince who had been accepted for the bride came, attended by a magnificent retinue, riding through the country of the prince whose father had just died, because that was the only way. Accordingly the latter prince heard all about him and where he was going, and he made friendship with him, and got an invitation to the wedding. So, mounted on a beautiful swift horse, with a servant on another horse behind him, he went to see the *tamáshá*. On arrival he was appointed to one of the places of honour and sat down to the feast. But he did not eat anything; his heart was too saddened

[1] Narrator's name, Paṇḍit Chandra Kol of Srínagar.

by his father's death and by the other king's consequent rejection of him. According to custom, the bride was present at this great banquet, and noticed the prince's sorrowful demeanour and want of appetite. She pitied him, and sent her maid to inquire why he did not eat and enjoy himself like the rest of the guests; to which the prince replied that the feast was forbidden to him. The princess then went herself and asked what was the matter with him, as she could not bear to see him looking so sorrowful at such a time.

"O princess," he replied, "you are my lawful wife, but your father is going to give you to another. Has my father's death impoverished me? Has it rendered me unholy? Why, therefore, has he done this thing?"

"I know not," said the maiden; "but I will marry you. If you have a swift horse bid me meet you at a certain hour of the night, and I will go with you whithersoever you wish."

The hour arranged was midnight, when the prince and princess, mounted on the swift horse, and an attendant on a horse after them, left the place as quietly as possible. They had ridden several miles, when the princess suddenly remembered some jewels that she very much wished to have, and quite intended to bring with her.

"Never mind," said the prince when he saw how intent she was on having them; "tell me where they are, and I will go and fetch them. They will not suspect anything if they see me, and I can easily bribe the servants. Let me go. You stay here with the servant. It will be all right. Go to sleep. I shall be back soon."

So the princess told him where the jewels were, and he went back and succeeded in getting them without being discovered. But sorrow! a hundred sorrows! he did not find the princess when he came again to the place where he had left her. A robber had visited the spot, and finding the princess and the servant asleep, had carried off the princess on one of the horses.

In the morning, when the king discovered his daughter's absence, he was very much perplexed. He did not know what to do. "Perhaps," thought he, "she has eloped with some one, or perhaps she has been carried off by some foul robber." However, he hoped for the best, and married his second daughter to the prince in her stead.

It being dark, the princess did not notice the robber, and therefore spoke to him as though he were the prince. "How quickly you have ridden!" she said. "Have you succeeded in getting the jewels?"

"Yes," replied the robber; "but do not let us talk just now."

The man did not care to expose himself just then, as he was afraid the princess would shriek and wake the servant. Therefore he replied thus. He made the horse go as fast as it could, till he arrived at the edge of the forest, when he turned off to a little isolated village, where the princess wished to rest.

"Go," she said, "and get some food. Fasten the horse to the tree and go."

So the robber went, thinking the woman would never ride off alone, but he was mistaken. The princess had been accustomed to ride ever since she was a little girl, and was not afraid to mount the most restive steed. She therefore got upon the horse as soon as the robber was out of sight and rode off. She rode for several miles, till she came to a goldsmith's house, where she stopped and asked for a drink of water. Fascinated with her beauty, the goldsmith desired to marry her, and told her so; and she agreed on the condition that he gave her there and then a pair of gold earrings worth one hundred rupees. At that time the goldsmith happened to be making several gold ornaments for the queen, and so had the very thing she wanted. He thought he would give them to the woman and get her to marry him, and take them away from her again afterwards.

The wedding was arranged for the following day, and

then the princess rode away. She went as fast as the horse could carry her for several miles, and then stopped at a hut belonging to a poor old man and his wife, to whom she gave the gold earrings and all her valuable jewels, and asked for some food and a lodging. She stayed the night with them, and on the following morning disguised herself as a man and left.

She rode on the horse to a certain city, where it happened that the king had recently died and left nobody to sit on the throne after him. Accordingly the *wazírs* and others had determined to send an elephant to choose his successor. Before whomsoever the beast bowed down he was to be king. Strange to relate, the elephant happened to meet the princess as she approached the city, and bowed down before her; and so she was proclaimed king.

Meanwhile the prince's servant, who had been left with the princess, had awoke, and finding himself alone, without horse or mistress, had turned his back on the world and become a *jogí*. The prince, too, when he returned with the jewels, and found neither the princess nor the servant, thought that the servant had run away with her, and became a *jogí*. The thief, also, on finding how he had been duped by the princess, determined to give up his wicked profession and become a *jogí*. The goldsmith, also, sought refuge in the religious life, as he was afraid that the king would kill him, when he heard what had become of the queen's earrings. Thus they all became *jogís*, and wandered about sad and miserable, bemoaning their lot.

The princess reigned prosperously. Nobody had a shadow of a suspicion that she was a woman, so perfectly did she maintain her disguise. Again and again was she urged to take unto herself a wife, but she always contrived to excuse herself. But she was not happy. She longed to see the prince and to speak to him. One morning she summoned a celebrated artist, and attiring herself as a woman, ordered him to paint her likeness, and to make it appear as if she had been stabbed and was dying. This, of course, was all private. Nobody but the painter knew, and he had been bribed to say nothing about it. When the picture was ready, she had it hung on a wall in one of the public thoroughfares of the city, and ordered a detective to take particular notice of everybody that made any remark about it, and bring him before her.

One day the thief passed by that way, and seeing the picture, exclaimed, "Oh! this is the picture of that woman. How did you get away? How came you to be killed?" Whereupon the detective seized him, and took him before the king, who commanded him to be thrown into prison.

At another time the servant passed by, and looking at the picture, said, "Ah! the prince took you away and left me to die in the jungle. How did you die?" on saying which he was at once marched off to the king, who appointed him to the command of all the troops.

Afterwards the goldsmith passed by and saw the picture. "Oh!" said he, "you are the woman that deceived me. I am glad you are dead;" when he, too, was taken before the king, who commanded him to be put into prison.

Then came by that way the old man and woman who had been so kind to her, and when they saw the picture they recognised her, and wept, whereupon they were carried before the king, who gave orders for them to live in the palace and have everything they wished.

And last of all the prince arrived, and seeing the picture, fainted. By the time he recovered his senses he found himself in the presence of the king, who inquired after his welfare and bade him stay at the palace. In a little while, much to the astonishment of many people, she made him her chief *wazír*. Thus affairs continued for some time, till the princess (the king) could not bear it any longer, and therefore discovered herself to him. The gladness of the prince was beyond expression when he knew who the king really was. At a convenient time the princess revealed everything to the people, and advised them to transfer the kingship to her husband, to which the people agreed.

Henceforth all was joy and prosperity to the prince (now king) and his wife. They had many children, lived to a good old age, and at last died respected and regretted by all the people.

THE CLEVER PARROT.[1]

A *FAQÍR* had a very clever, talkative parrot, of which he was very fond, and which he very much valued.

One day, when not feeling very well, he said to the bird, "You do not tell me any news. You never tell me anything."

The parrot replied, "Very well, I will do so. Hitherto I have feared to do so, lest you should sometimes hear things that you might not care to hear."

The *faqír* said, "Never mind. Tell me everything.

The following morning, previous to setting out for a certain village that he had to visit, the *faqír* ordered his wife to cook a fowl, and to eat half of it herself and keep the other half warm for him. But the woman ate the whole fowl. She was so hungry, and the meat tasted so savoury that she could not resist. And when the *faqír* returned in the evening and asked for his fowl, she told him that the cat had eaten it.

"Well, well, it cannot be helped," he said. "Get me something else, for I am very hungry. I have had nothing to eat since I left the house this morning."

While the woman was preparing the food the *faqír* turned towards the parrot and asked, "Well, my pretty bird, what news to-day?"

"Your wife has told you a lie," replied the bird. "She ate the fowl. I saw her eat the whole of it."[2]

Of course the woman altogether denied the truth of the bird's statement; and the *faqír*, in order to keep the

[1] Narrator's name, Qádir, Amírá, Kadal, Srínagar.

[2] Cf. *Tibetan Tales*, pp. 172, 173; and "Story of the Husband and the Parrot" in the *Arabian Nights*.

peace, pretended to believe her. However, after this little episode the woman never felt happy with such a bird about the house. Not that she was a flirt, or an adulteress, or a thief, but she could not do any little thing out of the ordinary way without its being noticed by the bird and being duly reported to the *faqír;* and so at last she went to her husband and said, "We had better be separated. The parrot seems everything to you now. You believe its word in preference to mine. You like to talk with it more than you do with me. I cannot bear this any longer. Either send me or the parrot away; for we three cannot stay peaceably under one roof."

Now the *faqír* loved his wife very much, and when he heard these words he felt exceedingly grieved, and promised to sell the parrot.

As he rode along the road on the following morning, carrying with him the parrot, the bird said, "Hear me, O my master. Do not sell me to any person who will not pay you the sum which I will mention."

"All right; I understand," replied the *faqír.*

He rode as far as the sea-shore, which was a long way from his house, and there determined to spend the night.

"I am very tired," he said to the parrot about midnight, "but I cannot sleep. I am afraid that you and the mare will take advantage of me and escape."

"Never," said the parrot. "Do you think us so disloyal? Trust us. Let the mare roam about at her pleasure, and open the cage and set me free. I will not leave you, but will fly to yonder tree and keep watch over the mare and yourself during the night."

Believing that the bird was sincere, the *faqír* consented to its request, and lay down to sleep. The parrot kept careful watch. During the night it saw an animal something like a horse [3] come out of the water and jump on to the mare, and then return to the water.

The *faqír* rose very early, and calling the bird, put it

[3] The word here used was *Zalgur*, meaning literally a river-horse.

back again in the cage. The parrot did not inform him of the strange thing that it had witnessed during the night. The *faqír* rode along by the sea-shore till he arrived at a great and prosperous city, where he met the *kotwál.*

"*Salám,*" said the *kotwál;* "do you wish to sell your bird?"

"Yes," replied the *faqír.*

"But you could not buy me," said the parrot.

"What a wonderful bird!" exclaimed the *kotwál.* "I must go and inform the *wazír* of your arrival, because he has been wishing for a long time to get such a bird. Come along quickly with me, before the *wazír* goes to *darbár.*"

So they walked together, and soon reached the *wazír's* house.

"Thank you very much," said the *wazír* when he had heard of the trouble that the *kotwál* had taken; "but I cannot think of buying the bird for myself till I know whether His Majesty the king wants it or not. I heard the other day that he was inquiring after such a bird."

Accordingly they all three went to the palace.

"What is the price of the bird?" inquired the king, when he was informed of their errand.

"Ten thousand rupees," answered the parrot.

The king was so pleased with the bird's clear and ready reply, that he instantly paid the money.[4] On receiving so large a sum of money the *faqír* was very glad. Before he left, the parrot, thinking it a good opportunity, made the *faqír* promise in the presence of the king that he would give His Majesty the next issue of his mare.

Henceforth the parrot lived in grand style. It was placed in a beautiful silver cage, and had silver vessels for its food and water. The cage, too, was hung up in the king's *zanána.* The bird became a general favourite, and

[4] Cf. *Tibetan Tales*, p. 173; *Old Deccan Days*, p. 107; *Folk-Tales of Bengal*, pp. 209, 210; and story of "Gullálá Sháh" in this collection.

was talked to, and played with, and petted by the king's wives constantly. In this way time passed very pleasantly, and nothing was left to be desired, till one day the king's wives came up to the cage and asked the parrot to give them its opinion of their looks. Nothing suspecting, thinking that it was done in fun, the bird replied that they were all very pretty except one, mentioning the name of the woman who was especially beloved by the king. Her face, he said, was like the face of a sow.[5] On hearing this the woman fell down in a swoon.

"Send for the king," she cried as soon as she recovered possession of her senses.

Accordingly His Majesty was called.

"I am very ill," the woman said to him. "Give me the flesh of this parrot, or I shall die."

The king was very sorry when he heard these words; but he loved the queen, and therefore ordered the parrot to be killed.

"O king," cried the poor bird, "spare me, I pray you, for six days. For six days let me wander whither I will. Afterwards I promise you most faithfully that I will return and submit to whatever Your Majesty may think right to do with me."

"It is granted," replied the king. "Mind you return after six days."

So the parrot was set free, and at once flew away. It had not flown very far before it met with twelve thousand parrots, that were all flying together in a certain direction.

"Stay, stay!" shrieked the king's parrot. "Whither are you going?"

"O friend," said they, "we are flying to an island where a princess feeds us with pearls and candy. Come with us and share our joy."

The parrot consented, and joined the company. They soon reached the island, and were treated as the birds had said. When the feast was over and the other birds were

[5] Cf. *Folk-Tales of Bengal*, p. 223.

going away the king's parrot feigned sickness and lay stretched out on the ground.

"What is the matter with you, pretty parrot?" asked the princess coming up to the bird. "What is the matter? Are you ill? Come along with me. I will look after you. You shall soon be all right again." Whereupon the princess took it to the palace, and made a little nest for it, and attended to it herself. She gave the bird many pearls and much candy; but the parrot pretended to care for none of these things.

"O princess," it said, "you are kind and good. You give us pearls and candy. But my master, the great king, whose dominions extend on all sides from north to south and east to west, and whose is this island also, although you know it not,—he scatters pearls and candy before fowls. Oh that you knew him! Would that you were married to such a king, for he is worthy of you and you are worthy of him, O princess!"

Excited by the words of the parrot, the princess went to the king her father, and entreated him to allow her to go on a visit to this king, and to marry him if it could be so arranged.

"I cannot allow you to venture on this errand," replied the king; "but I will write a letter to this king and send it by the parrot. I will ask the great king to come himself on a certain day for the marriage. If all that the bird says is true, the king will not fail to come. Fear not; I will arrange for your marriage."

The princess agreed, and the bird was immediately despatched to his master with the letter of asking.

Just before the close of the fifth day the parrot flew in before the king and dropped the letter.

"You have arrived in good time," said His Majesty.

"O king," cried the bird, "I beseech you not to slay me. I have not wronged you or any of your royal household. The women of your *zanána* asked me to say what I thought of them, and I answered them. I spoke no untruth, O king. You surely will not kill me to satisfy a mere whim of one of Your Majesty's wives. She will not die even though I live. Her life does not depend on my death. But even if it were so, O king, I could procure for you another and far more beautiful wife in her stead. Behold, here is a letter which I have brought from the father of one of the most lovely princesses in the world, asking for your acceptance of the hand of his daughter in marriage."

Then said the king, "You speak fairly, and you have always acted honestly. I will not slay you. I will agree to your petition and marry this princess. But how can I reach the island where these people live?"

"Be not anxious, O king," answered the parrot. "I have not advised you thoughtlessly. If Your Majesty will order the *faqír* to send you the foal that he promised you, the journey can easily be accomplished."

"Very well," said the king, and immediately gave orders for the foal to be brought.

Not knowing the valuable character of the animal, the *faqír* sent it without the slightest hesitation. He was rich,—what did he want of it? And it was but a small return, he thought, to make to one who had treated him so generously.

Accordingly the king mounted the foal, and attended by the parrot, started for the island. When His Majesty arrived at the sea-shore and looked upon the mighty waters his heart failed him, and he was about to turn back.

"How can we cross the great water?" he inquired.

"Without any difficulty," replied the parrot. "The foal that Your Majesty is riding is no ordinary beast. Thus mounted Your Majesty can cross to any place. Fear not; but direct the foal into the water. It can go as easily in the water as it can on land."

Reassured by the parrot's reply, the king did so, and quickly reached the island.[6]

[6] Cf. *Folk-Tales of Bengal*, pp. 214–249.

The king of the island gave him a most enthusiastic reception, and the princess was glad beyond description.

On seeing her the king loved her, and asked that the wedding might be arranged as quickly as possible. All being of one mind, the ceremony was soon performed. Everything was concluded most successfully; and then the great king and his lovely bride departed.

They both rode on the foal, and the parrot flew before to guide them. He did not return the same way as he came, but by another way, in the midst of which there was a certain uninhabited island.

"I wish to rest here," said His Majesty. "I am feeling very tired."

"Please do not," said the bird, "for there is great danger here.'

"Never mind," said the king; "I cannot go any farther without a rest. After a little sleep we will resume the journey."

So the king and his wife landed on the island and went to sleep; and the parrot perched on a branch of a tree close by and watched. Within an hour a ship sailed up to the island, and the captain, who was a great merchant, noticing two people sleeping there, got out to see who they were. Struck by the beauty of the queen, he took her into his ship. He took the foal, also; but the king he left to sleep on. All this the parrot saw; but it was afraid to give any alarm, lest the merchant should shoot at it and kill it. So the ship, with the queen and the foal, sailed away, and then the parrot roused the king.

"Oh my parrot," exclaimed the king, "would that I had listened to your advice and not halted here! What shall I do? There is no food to be had here. There is no animal here to carry me through the waters. What shall I do? Advise me, help me, if you can."

The bird replied, "O king, there is only one thing left to you. Cut down this tree and throw it into the sea, and then throw yourself into the sea, and let the tree bear you whithersoever God will. Besides this I know not what you can do."

So the king cut down the tree and did as the bird had advised. By the mercy of God a great eagle, that was flying over the water at the time, noticed the tree, and swooped down and carried it off and the king with it. The eagle carried the tree to a certain jungle, and there let it fall. Thus was the king saved.[7]

"Stay here now," said the faithful parrot, who had seen all that had transpired. "Do not stir from this place. I will go and search for the queen and the foal, and will come again to you."

The king promised.

After much wandering the parrot discovered the beautiful queen. She had been taken by the merchant to his own house, and was there living with him as his *saís.* When she saw the parrot she cried for joy.

"Where have you been? Where is my husband? Is he alive? Tell me quickly," she said.

The parrot told her everything.

"Go back at once," she said, "and inform him of my circumstances. Take these jewels and give them to him. He may require them to buy food. Tell him to come here quickly, and to get himself employed as *saís* to this merchant, and then we shall be able to arrange to escape together on the foal. Once on that foal nobody will be able to overtake us by land or sea."

The parrot flew off as soon as possible, and informed the king of his wife's state, and advised him to start at once and release her. The king agreed, and in a few days reached the merchant's house.

How joyful was the meeting between him and his wife! They had despaired of ever meeting one another again, but God had mercy on them and brought them together again.

[7] Cf. *Old Deccan Days*, pp. 14, 132. Sindibad also escapes by holding on to a big bird. Cf. *Arabian Nights*, First and Second Voyages; also story of "Saiyid and Said," p. 91, in this collection.

On the evening of the day that he arrived the king and his beautiful bride rode out of that city on the wonderful foal, and the parrot flew before to show them the way. They soon reached the king's country, and were welcomed by the people with much music and singing.

Afterwards the king lived in happiness to the end of his days. The parrot was appointed chief *wazír*, and helped not a little to preserve the kingdom in that state of prosperity and honour for which it had so long been famous.[8]

[8] Cf., *en passant*, *Old Deccan Days*, pp. 126-153

THE MALECONTENT CURED.[1]

One day a dissatisfied fellow was sitting under a walnut-tree, and a great gourd[2] was growing close by.

"O God," said the malecontent, "how foolish Thou art to give such small nuts to this big tree, while yonder plant is overborne by its immense fruit! Now, if pumpkins were growing on this tree and nuts on the gourd I should have admired Thy wisdom."

On this a walnut fell down on the man's turban and somewhat startled him.

"O God," he continued, "Thou art right after all. If the pumpkin had fallen on me from such a height I should surely have been killed. Great is Thy wisdom, and power, and goodness."[3]

[1] Narrator, a zamíndár at Bijbihára.

[2] *Al* (*cucurbita maxima*), the red gourd or pumpkin.

[3] A German friend tells me that this tale is current in his country also.

THE STUPID PEASANT.[1]

I.

One morning a peasant started off for his work with ten *chapátís*, his day's allowance, tied up in his loin-cloth. He had not proceeded very far from the house when he felt very hungry, and therefore sat down to eat. One, two, three, four *chapátís* disappeared, but he was not satisfied. Four, five, six, seven, eight *chapátís* were eaten; still he was hungry. However, he rose up and walked on.

"What shall I do?" he thought. "I ought not to eat all these *chapátís* before commencing my work. If I do, what will there be left for the rest of the day? And yet my stomach is not full."

Such reasonings, however, proved in vain. Hunger got the better of the argument, and the peasant sat down again and finished off the other two *chapátís*, and then felt happy.

"Alas!" said he, "what a fool I was not to have eaten these last two *chapátís* first of all! There would then have been eight in my loin-cloth for the rest of the day. Now I shall perish from hunger."

The foolish fellow thought that the first eight *chapátís* had not in the least helped to satisfy his hunger.

II.[2]

Ten peasants were standing on the side of the road weeping.[3] They thought that one of their number had

[1] Narrator's name, Paṇḍit Ánand Kol, Zaina Kadal, Srínagar.

[2] Narrator's name, Paṇḍit Ánand Kol.

[3] "The broad Herculean build and manly features of the Kashmírían peasant, contrasted with his whining and timid disposition, if considered

been lost on the way, as each man had counted the company, and found them nine only.

"Ho, you! what is the matter?" asked a townsman passing by.

"Oh, sir," said the peasants, "we were ten men when we left the village, but now we are only nine."

The townsman saw at a glance what fools they were; each of them had omitted to count himself in the number. He therefore told them to take off their *ṭopís*[4] and place them on the ground. This they did, and counted ten of them, whereupon they supposed they were all there, and were comforted. But they could not tell how it was.

III.[5]

A PEASANT went to a *baniyá* to buy a *páṅsa*-worth of black pepper. The *baniyá* gave him about a handful. Thinking this was merely a bit to taste, the peasant threw it into his capacious mouth, and then opening his *vĕtharan*,[6] said, "Rather bitter; but never mind. Weigh me a *páṅsa*-worth quickly."

IV.[7]

A PEASANT was constantly praying to God to give him a horse. One day, while out walking, he cried aloud, "O God, grant me a horse!" when a Paṭhán appeared riding on a mare, that gave birth to a foal just as it reached him. As the foal could not immediately follow its mother, the tyrannical paṭhán forced the peasant to carry it along after him to his house. When he arrived at the place he was so tired with his load that he changed his mind, and cried,

apart from the effects of a long-continued subjection to tyranny and despotism, may, perhaps, form a subject for physiological speculation" (Vigne).

[4] *Ṭopi* or *kalahposh*, a skull-cap. This is often all the covering the poor Musalmáns have for their heads. In the case of those who are better off it forms the foundation and support for the ample folds of the voluminous turban.

[5] Narrator's name, Paṇdit Ánand Kol, Zaina Kadal, Srínagar.

[6] *Vĕtharan*, a sack made of grass, and generally used by the poor cultivators of the soil in the Valley.

[7] Narrator's name, Paṇdit Lál Chand of Khunamuh, in the Vihí *pargana*.

"O God, I thank Thee for answering my prayer by giving me this foal, but pardon me if I return it. I do not want a horse now." Thus saying, he threw down the beast on the ground and departed.

V.[8]

It was in the month of October, when a man from the villages came to the city to sell his cotton. It was his first visit. As he walked through the *bázár* he noticed the goldsmiths constantly putting gold ornaments into the fire, and then selling them directly afterwards. Thought he, "There must be some trick in this. I will do the same. Why should I wander all over the place to sell my cotton when I can thus command purchasers?" So he went to a blacksmith's shop and threw his basket of cotton into the furnace, and then waited. Of course the cotton was destroyed.[9]

VI.[10]

There is a saying in Srínagar-City, "Rupees come to rupees,"[11] which is equivalent to the English, "Money makes money."

Once upon a time a stupid peasant heard this saying, and understanding it literally, went to a money-changer's shop, where he saw two or three piles of silver and copper, and put a rupee in one of the chinks of the wall, saying, "Come, come, rupees, to my rupee." In his excitement the foolish man put the rupee in so far that it tumbled down inside the shop, and was counted among the money-changer's money, whereupon he wept and went home.

[8] Narrator's name, Paṇḍit Lál Chand of Khunamuh.

[9] Customers nearly always oblige the goldsmith to test the metal in the fire and on the touchstone. There is a Kashmírí proverb, "Gold is known on the stone, whether it is alloyed or pure."

[10] Narrator's name, Ahmad Jú, a huckster of Srínagar.

[11] *Rupeyih nish chhĕh rupe wátán.* There is a parallel saying, *Páṅsa nishih chhuh páṅsa pphaṭán*, "*Páṅsa* bursts forth from *páṅsas*."

Some time afterwards he met the person who had quoted the saying to him, and told him how he had proved the falsity of it.

"Not at all," said the man. "I spoke correctly. Your rupee went to the money-changer's rupees. They, being the more, had the greater power."

KARM YÁ DHARM.[1]

A CERTAIN bráhman was very much distressed at not having a son. Day and night he cried unto Parameshwar, gave much alms to the priests, and richly endowed many temples, in the hope that his desire would be granted. At length a son was born in his house. There was much rejoicing, and many and liberal were the gifts that were lavished upon the priests.

At the age of twelve years the boy was sent to school, soon after which the bráhman died. And then the boy fell sick, and was nigh unto death for many a day. It was a terrible time for the poor wife and mother. She had just lost her husband, and now her son was about to go. "O Bhagawant, have mercy and save, have mercy and save!" she cried continually. Her prayer was heard. A *jogí* visited her house, and promised her that if she attended to his instructions the boy should live.

"Get me some fish, and cook it as soon as possible," he said.

When the fish were ready she set them before her visitor.

"It is well," he said. He divided the fish into three portions. One portion he himself ate, another portion he gave to the bráhmaní, and the third portion he sent to the sick boy, after uttering some words of incantation over it. On eating the fish the boy was cured.

When she saw her boy's recovery the woman's gratitude was indescribable. She fell on the ground at the *jogí's* feet and entreated him never to leave them. "Oh, stay with us," she pleaded. "It is little that we have. But it may be that Parameshwar, through you, will bless us and increase our store."

[1] Narrator's name, Shiva Báyú, Renawárí, Srínagar.

The *jogí* replied, "Fear not! Your future will be chequered, but prosperous. Fear not!"

A few days afterwards the *jogí* put some collyrium over the eyes of the boy, and the boy got wings and could fly about like a bird. Then the *jogí* ordered him to go to the royal treasury, fly in through the window, and get as much money as he could lay hands on. The boy obeyed, and brought back as much money as would enable them to live in peace and plenty to the end of their days.

When the king's officers discovered the robbery they were much troubled. They went to the king in great distress and informed him of all that had happened. They tried every way to find out the thief, but failed. Then the *jogí* went to the palace, and seeing the king's anger, promised to discover the thief to him.

"Let the king order a great smoky fire to be raised in such-and-such a place" (naming a spot near the bráhmaní's house).

The king immediately gave the strange order, and it was done.

Attracted by the blaze and smoke, the boy went out of the house and stood by the fire. But the smoke was too much for him. He was very soon obliged to withdraw to a distance, rubbing his eyes like the rest of the bystanders. Alas! that he did do so, for on rubbing his eyes he rubbed off the collyrium, and on rubbing off the collyrium he lost his wings, and thus was discovered.[2]

"There is the thief! There is the thief!" shouted the *jogí* to the king, who was also present. "Take him."

The boy and his mother were turned out of their house, and obliged to beg from door to door for their daily bread, till one day a *baniyá* had pity on them and took the lad into his employ. The lad was still working in the *baniyá's* shop, when one evening the king of that country sent for his two beautiful daughters and asked them which was the greater, *Karm* or *Dharm*. The younger daughter,

[2] Cf. note on "Invisibility" in *Wide-Awake Stories*, p. 423.

who answered first, said "*Karm*," but the elder said "*Dharm*."[3] When he heard their answers the king was so angry with his younger daughter that he gave her in marriage to the young thief, the servant of the *baniyá*.

"You have answered," he said. "See now the proof of your words."

It was a sad experience for the young princess to have to sit and spin all day and to live on the coarse and meagre meals that her and her poor husband's united labour brought to them. However, she had unwavering faith in her convictions, and was fully persuaded that there was a glad day coming. She prayed continually and waited patiently; but it was a hard struggle for her.

At last her faith and patience were rewarded. In that country there was a tank which was such, that whoever went near it became blind. One day the *baniyá*, for some trifling matter, got angry with the bráhman lad, and sent him to this tank to get some water. The lad went, not knowing the deadly property of the water; and it came to pass that when he reached the side of the tank a voice came out therefrom, saying unto him—

"Oh, my son, I am beaten with pity for you. Why have you come here? Do you not know that whoever takes of this water will become blind?"[4]

"I know it not," replied the lad. "My master bade me come here and fetch some water."

"Cruel man! He has some spite against you. However, I will not harm you. Fill your pot and take it to your master. But mind you take also a little sand from yonder spot, and tie it up in a corner of your wrap, and be careful not to unfasten the knot until you reach home." On saying this the voice stopped.

As soon as he reached the shop the lad gave the water

[3] *Karm* (or *Karma*), fate. *Dharm* (or *Dharma*), duty—especially that enjoined by the *Vedas*.

[4] There is a spring sacred to the goddess Kálí, in the middle of Srínagar-City, by Sháh Hamadán's *ziárat*. A big stone covers it. It is said that whoever lifts this stone and looks into the spring will be blinded.

to his master, who made him a little present in money. This was quite an unusual thing, but the *baniyá* thought that the fellow would soon lose his sight and want the money.

At night the lad went to his home. "Look here," he said to his wife, "look, the *baniyá* has actually given me a present. I cannot understand it. But I have such a strange thing to tell you. When I reached the tank in such-and-such a place," describing where he had been, "to get water for the *baniyá* this morning, I heard a voice that told me to take some of the sand on the side of the water, and to tie it up in my wrap, and not to unfasten it till I reached here. See, do you unfasten it."

The woman did so, and lo! the sand was changed into the most valuable precious stones.

"*Karm* is greater! *Karm* is greater! *Karm* is greater!" cried she. "I have not trusted in vain."

Henceforth the bráhman and his wife were very rich. At a convenient time the *baniyá's* service was given up. The bráhman discovered his wealth gradually, lest suspicion should be aroused; and then, when he had obtained an influential position in the country, he gave a great feast. The king, also, was invited to come and grace the feast with his royal presence, and he complied. It was a most splendid entertainment. The rarest things were provided; the most delicious perfumes filled the air; the sweetest music and singing sounded on all sides. Everything was done to minister to the pleasure and comfort of the guests, and the king was exceedingly pleased with all the arrangements.

At the feast His Majesty was waited on principally by his own daughter; but he knew not that she was his daughter, for she had much altered since her marriage; and besides this, she appeared before her father in a different dress each time that she brought anything to him.

At last, when the king was about to depart, she went up to him and informed him that she was his younger daughter, whom he had married to the poor *baniyá's* boy.

"Tell me now, O father," she said, "is not *Karm* greater than *Dharm?* Behold my husband's house, my husband's wealth. There is not one in all the country so wealthy and so great as he, save yourself, O king."

Then was the king convinced of his wrong-thinking and wrong-doing; and embracing his daughter, he promised to give the kingdom to her husband, for thus *Karm*[5] had determined.[6]

[5] The common Hindú notion is, that Brahma descends from his high abode and notes upon the forehead of each Hindú babe born into this world everything that is destined for it. "No one escapes the decree of Brahma." "The writing of Brahma will not fail in the least," says the Tamil proverb. "However wisely man may contrive for his good, it is in the power of Fate to turn it to evil. If there be a spark of fire, and man wishes to put it out, and if Fate would have it otherwise, the man mistakes the pot of melted *gyav* for water, and pours in on the fire," says the *Rájá Tarangini*. But the popular idea concerning fatalism among Hindús must not be confounded with Necessitarianism in philosophy or Predestinarianism in theology. Cf. an article on "Fate in Bengali Folk-Tales" in *Christian College Magazine*, vol. iv. pp. 409-419.

[6] Cf. a paper on "The Outcast Child" in *Folk-Lore Journal*, vol. iv. pp. 308–349.

FOUR WICKED SONS AND THEIR LUCK.[1]

A CERTAIN king had four sons, all of whom were addicted to intoxicating habits. One was fond of wine, another of *charas*,[2] another of opium, and another of *bhang*.[3] A more wretched, dissolute quartette of fellows could hardly be found throughout the wide wide world.[4]

One day a *wazír*, who was the king's special friend and counsellor, informed His Majesty of the wicked doings of the princes, and entreated him, for the sake of his country and people and house, to put a check on them. The king was very angry when he heard of his sons' wickednesses, and ordered them to be immediately banished from the country. He would adopt one from another family rather than allow any such wicked fellows to sit on the throne after him.

Vowing vengeance on this *wazír*, the four princes packed up a few necessaries and left the place. Within a few weeks they found themselves in another country, where they sought an interview with the king to ask him for some employment. But the king of that country was too well acquainted with their vices to entrust any work to them, and therefore dismissed them with orders to quit his country as soon as possible.

In a little while they reached another country. Night came on as they neared the chief city of that country, so they fixed their quarters under a big tree, and laid down just as they were to eat and sleep.

1 Narrator's name, Qádir, a barber living at Amírá Kadal, Srínagar.

2 *Charas*, the exudation of the flowers of hemp collected with the dew and prepared for use as an intoxicating drug.

3 Or *bháng*, hemp (*Cannibus Sativus*) of which an intoxicating potion is made.

4 Cf. tale xxi. of *Baital Pachísí*.

That very night a great merchant of the city had died, and his friends were going about in search of some person to watch by the corpse till the time of burial. Strange to relate, they could not find any person who was willing to do this thing. At last it struck one of the party that, perhaps, a beggar or stranger might be found just outside the city who would be glad to do this act of kiudness for the sake of a few rupees; so he went to the outskirts of the place, and there came across the four princes sleeping on the ground.

"Ho, ho!" said he, waking them. "Would one of you mind watching by a corpse this night? A good present will be given."

"Yes," said the princes. "We will help you; but we require four thousand rupees for the business."

"Very well," said the man. "Come along with me."

On arriving at the deceased merchant's house the four men were shown the room where the dead body was lain. They decided to watch in turn. For the first watch of the night one of the princes sat up, while the others slept. When one hour or so of his watch had elapsed, the dead man sat up and began to speak.

"Will you play a game of *nard* with me?" he said.

"Yes, certainly," replied the prince. "But what is the stake?"

"You pay me two thousand rupees if you lose," said the corpse.

"But that is all one-sided," said the prince. "What will you pay me if you lose?"

"Oh, never mind that," said the deceased merchant. "There is plenty of treasure hidden in such-and-such a place in this house. If you wish, you can go and take as much as you can carry."

"All right," said the prince, and the play commenced. The prince beat the deceased merchant twice, and would have won another game if his watch had not been up.

As soon as he turned to wake up one of his brothers the corpse reclined and was quiet again.

"Get up," said the prince to his brother. "It is your turn to watch now. But do be careful, for the corpse is possessed."

The second prince had not been long watching before he wished to smoke. But the fire was outside, and how could he leave the corpse for a moment with safety? Four thousand rupees depended on their careful watching that night.

"I know what to do," said the prince to himself. "I will fasten the corpse to my back with my waistband."

While he was out lighting his *chillam* he saw what he thought was another little fire a few yards distant, but it turned out to be a one-eyed devil[5] looking at him with his single eye as if he would like to slay him.

"Who are you?" asked the prince. "What do you want here? Be off or I will kill you and tie you up to my back like I have just done to this person," pointing to the corpse on his back.

The one-eyed *jinn* was frightened at these words, and begged the prince to have mercy on him, promising that he would give him any thin he asked for.

"I do not require anything," said the prince; "but you can go, if you will, and divert the course of the river, so that it may flow by the way of the king's palace."

"Certainly," said the *jinn*, and went at once and did so.

The second watch of the night was over; so the prince replaced the corpse on the bed, and woke up one of his brothers to fulfil his time, and after admonishing him to be very careful, as the corpse was possessed, went to sleep.

Within an hour or so the third prince heard the sound of an ogress's voice, like the voice of an old woman weeping. He fastened the corpse to his back and went out to

[5] One-eyed is a certain sign of an evil disposition. Cf. proverbs about the one-eyed man in *Dictionary of Kashmírí Proverbs and Sayings*, pp. 95, 96; also *Wide-Awake Stories*, p. 426. For one-eyed demon cf. *Wide-Awake Stories*, p. 295; and *Fairy Tales from Brentano*, p. 118.

see what was the matter. He discovered an old woman standing outside the house, and supposing her to be an ogress, he drew his knife and struck at her. The old woman noticed the action, and turned to escape, when her leg was cut off. The rest of the old woman disappeared.

"Very strange!" exclaimed the prince, taking up the woman's shoe and putting it inside his coat. "How could she have got off with only one leg?"

He then went inside and waited to the end of his watch, when he roused the other prince to come and take his place, warning him to be very careful, as the corpse was possessed.

This prince was sitting by the dead body, when suddenly he saw a *jinn* pass by the door carrying the lovely daughter of the king. He quickly fastened the corpse to his back and followed the *jinn*. He saw the monster carry the princess to a place about a mile distant. There he put her down, and telling her not to go away, went off himself at a great pace to the woods. He went to get some fire wherewith to cook the princess. The prince conjectured this, and therefore ran up to her and asked her to change clothes with him, and to go immediately with the corpse to the late merchant's house and watch by it in his place. "I shall remain here," he said. "Do not fear for me. I shall be all right."

In a very short time the devil returned with some fire and a great pan of oil. A big fire was soon prepared, and the pan of oil put over it. When the oil began to bubble the *jinn* told the princess (as he thought) to walk around it, but the prince begged to be excused, as he did not understand. The *jinn* said it was not very difficult, and walked round a few times to show what he meant. Evidently the monster intended to push his victim into the pan of oil during one of these circumambulations, but the prince guessed his intention, and gave the *jinn* a shove instead. Oh what a wail there was when the *jinn's* head disappeared beneath the boiling oil! It seemed as if the very earth must split open.' Then the prince returned to the deceased merchant's house, and giving back her clothes to the princess, bade her return to the palace. Everything was just finished in time to allow the prince to resume his position beside the corpse when his watch was ended.

It was now morning, and the friends and relations of the late merchant came and handed over to the watchers the four thousand rupees which they had promised. But the princes would not accept the money. They demanded twice the amount, and threatened to petition the king if it was not given. They would not, however, explain the reason of their demand. Of course the late merchant's people would not assent. Accordingly the four princes went and told their case to the king. "O king," said they, "we have been wronged. Eight thousand rupees are due to us from these people, and they consent to pay us half only. Be pleased to do justice in this matter." Whereupon His Majesty summoned all the relations and friends of the deceased merchant to appear before him. The case excited great curiosity in the city; so the hall of audience was crowded.

"What is the truth of the matter?" the king asked. "These men declare that you owe them eight thousand rupees, and wish to pay them four thousand rupees only."

"These men speak not the truth, O king," they replied. "We agreed to pay them four thousand rupees only for watching by the dead body of our relation. Of this arrangement we have many witnesses. You know us, O king! We are not dishonest; nor are we so poor that we need to defraud any man of his right."

"Do you hear what they say?" said His Majesty to the four princes.

"Yes, O king," they replied; "but these men know not what has transpired since this arrangement was made. Listen, O king, and judge the right. During the night one of us played *nard* with the late merchant and won four thousand rupees, which the deceased promised should be paid out of some treasure that he had kept hidden in such-and-such a place in his house."

"You have heard," said the king, turning to the late merchant's relations. "Is this true?"

"No, O king," they replied; "we do not know of any hidden treasure."

Then the king ordered some soldiers to be sent to search the house, and one of the princes—the prince who kept the first watch—to accompany them. Every room in the late merchant's house was well searched, till at last an immense amount of treasure was discovered hidden under the ground of one of the bedrooms. When the prince and the soldiers returned and showed the treasure the king was much surprised, and ordered the eight thousand rupees to be paid.

Then the prince who kept the second watch went forward and prostrated himself before the king. He informed His Majesty how he had frightened the *jinn*, and prevailed on him to cause the river to flow by the way of the palace. The king was very glad at this, and ordered a suitable reward to be given to the prince.

On this the prince who had kept the third watch asked permission to speak, and related how he had fought with an ogress and cut off her leg. He then presented the king with the ogress's shoe, with which His Majesty was so pleased that he gave orders for a large reward to be given to this prince also.

Lastly, the prince who had stayed by the corpse during the last watch of the night went forward and explained how he had saved the princess from the clutches of a most terrible *jinn*, and killed the monster in a pan of oil wherein he intended to boil his victim. When the king heard this he was astonished beyond measure, and sent for his daughter to inquire whether it was true or not. On discovering that the prince had spoken the truth he at once rose up and embraced him, and then handed the princess to him, saying, "Take her. She is your wife. Many have sought her hand in marriage, and I have refused them; but now she is yours. Surely I shall never find another so worthy of her as he who has preserved her from such a terrible death." Whereupon all the people shouted, "Blessings on the king! Blessings on the princess! Blessings on her husband! May they all live long and prosper exceedingly!"

That day and for many days afterwards there was great rejoicing in the city, such as had been never before or will be ever again.

The four princes stayed in that country for many years, and were very much prospered. The prince who had saved the princess was the acknowledged heir to the throne, while his three brothers were appointed to the three principal positions under him. However, they were not thoroughly happy. They wished to see their own country again. The king knew their wishes, and had hitherto refused them, fearing lest they should depart and never return. At length, however, moved by their earnest and persistent entreaties, he was obliged to sanction their going, and gave them money and troops for the journey.

On reaching their own country the four princes fought with their father's troops and defeated them. When the king, their father, heard that his own sons fought against him, he went forth to meet them, and falling down on the ground before them, begged them to stay the battle. He told them that he had banished them at the advice of his favourite *wazír*. Then was the old king reconciled to his sons, and there was great joy in the city.

On the following day the *wazír* was executed.

Henceforth everything went on prosperously. Two of the princes returned to the other country to help in affairs there, while the two other princes abode with their father and helped him.

SHARAF THE THIEF.[1]

A LITTLE before Ranjít Singh's time (born A.D. 1780) theft and robbery were so very common, and were practised with such proficiency in the "Happy Valley," that good and honest folk were put to their wits' end to know how to retain what they, by their industry and economy, had gathered together.

One of the most celebrated of the thieves and robbers in those days was Sharaf *Tsúr*.[2] So cunning, so daring, and so successful was he, that his name was seldom mentioned without trembling, whilst his character was supposed to be almost supernatural. Whether or not it was that the common people thought that he possessed the evil eye, or else some sort of mesmeric influence, they left him alone to prosecute his plans without let or hindrance. One or two of the more determined dispositions are quoted as having brought the thief before the courts, but as nothing could be thoroughly proved, nothing could be really done, and so those bereaved of their property had to submit, their only consolation being in the thought that this was their *qismat* or lot.

Sharaf *Tsúr* was the son of Kabír Ghaní, who was a very great and wealthy shawl merchant, and lived near the Zaina Kadal, the fourth of the seven bridges spanning that part of the river Jhelam which flows through the city of Srínagar, and forming the principal means of intercommunication between the two sides of the city. Supposing that he would inherit his father's wealth,

[1] Narrator's name, Lál Chand, Renawárí, Srínagar, and others.

[2] *Tsúr* is the Kashmírí word for thief. This man is known in the Punjab under the name of Ashraf Chor.

Sharaf made no effort to learn his father's business or to provide himself with any other means of livelihood. Consequently he developed into a lazy, listless, and profligate fellow, apparently having as the only objects in life eating, drinking, and spending money. One is not surprised to find, therefore, that on his father's death he at once appropriated all his goods and money, and had soon squandered everything in magnificent feasts, expensive *náches*, and bad society. What was he to do now? He could neither beg nor dig, so he determined to cultivate the craft of thieving.

A few native friends have given me the following stories still extant concerning this man, and as they form part and parcel of the folk-lore of the country, being quoted concerning others besides the hero of this chapter, I have included them in this volume:—

I.

One day Sharaf visited a certain garden disguised in a dress of great pomp and style. Some children of very respectable parents were playing there in the shade of the beautiful trees. Sharaf noticed that several of the youngsters were wearing nice new shoes, and, going near, told them to sit down. According to custom, the boys took off their shoes before doing so, but the thief bade them not to act thus on this occasion, as Sharaf *Ts*úr might be near, and would certainly take them. The boys laughed at the idea. "Take them!" they said. "What would you have us to think? Are we fools or blind? These shoes are placed close by our side. How could they possibly be removed without our noticing it?" The disguised thief, now finding his opportunity, replied, "Wait a moment. I will show you how." Sharaf then went away a little distance to well scan the neighbourhood, and seeing that there was nobody to mind at hand, he returned, took up all the shoes in a cloth, and again went away. A second time, however, he did not return, although the little company of boys shouted for him on all sides, and waited anxiously for his appearance. They had a suspicion that the man was Sharaf *Ts*úr, and the matter was blazed abroad over the city, but nothing could be discovered.

II.

Batmálun is the name of a big village situated close to the city of Srínagar. *Bata*,[3] in Kashmírí, means food, cooked rice, &c., and *málun* is probably derived from the word *mál*, which means desire for food. Hence, perhaps, the meaning of Batmálun is *faqír*, *i.e.*, one who kept under his body, and was always more or less in want of food. At any rate, there is a famous mosque in this place, sacred to the memory of a celebrated *faqír*, from whom both the village and the mosque derive their name. The holy man's grave is to be seen close by the mosque. Sharaf entered, and assuming the guise of an *imám*, began to cry the *báng*.[4] Many peasants, on hearing this, went and entered the mosque, and at a given signal arranged themselves for prayer. Before commencing their devotions, Sharaf advised them to collect their *tsádars*[5] (*i.e.*, sheets or woollen shawls, which they wear very much like English ladies wore 'clouds' when they were in vogue), and place them before them in a heap; "because," said he, "Sharaf *Ts*úr, I know, is wandering about near this building, and is not at all particular whether he thieves in a mosque, or in the *bázár*, or upon the highway." And they did so.

Now every one who has watched a company of Musalmáns praying knows with what regularity they go through their genuflexions, according as the *imám* proceeds with the prayers. During one of the long prostrations Sharaf, the pseudo-*imám*, hastily got up, and quietly seizing the bundle of woollen cloths, left the service by a little side-

[3] *Bhatá* in the plains.

[4] The Muhammadan call to prayer.

[5] *Chádar* or *chadar* in Hindustání, and *chádir* in Persian.

door in the building. All this time, about the space of a minute, the congregation were waiting and wondering what the *imám* was doing. Perhaps they thought that he was a little faint. However, at last one worshipper lifted his head, and on discovering that both their priest and wraps had disappeared, shouted to his fellow-dupes, "Sorrow, a hundred sorrows, O brethren! Sharaf *Ts*úr has met with us. We have been led in prayer by an unbelieving rogue!"

III.

On another occasion it is reported that a weaver was coming from a certain village, and bringing with him some linen cloth to sell in Srínagar. Sharaf chanced to be passing that way, and saluting the man, asked him for how much he would dispose of his burden. The weaver answered, "Three rupees." After a little flattery and quibbling Sharaf again asked him once and for all to state the proper price. The man then, calling upon the name of God and His Prophet, said that the cloth cost him only eight *ánás* less than he asked. "Was this too much profit for all his labour?" Sharaf, however, appeared not to believe him even then, but gathering some dust together and smoothing it a little into shape, ordered the man to consider it as the very tomb of Muhammad, and to swear again accordingly, putting his hands in orthodox fashion upon the little heap.[5] The good weaver, in all confidence, did so; but Sharaf had kept some dust in his hand, and whilst the man was bending in all reverence over the supposed grave, took a good aim at his eyes, and picking up the bundle of cloth, ran away. It is not necessary to add that the poor weaver was so blinded and surprised

[5] It is a common ordeal amongst ignorant people to stick a twig into the ground and suppose it to be the staff of Pír-i-Dastagír, the famous saint of Baghdád, who flourished A.D. 1078–1166, and is better known as 'Abdu'l-Qádir Jílání; or to take a hair and imagine it to be one from the Prophet's own beard, and cause the friends with whom they are bargaining or bantering to swear by it. It is astonishing the influence this exercises over the people.

that he was unable to see or to do anything except to roll about in agony lamenting his sad lot.

IV.

One day Sharaf sat by a tomb and pretended that he was reading the *fátiha*, or first chapter of the *Qurán*. Meanwhile a man passed by, whom Sharaf called to come near to him. The man obeyed, and asked what he desired. Sharaf replied, "May God bless you! Please bring me some bread. I will give you the money. I want the bread for distribution among the poor in the name of my deceased father." The man, considering this to be a real work for God, gladly consented, and started to fetch the bread. When he had gone a little distance Sharaf again called to him, saying, "Come here. Perhaps you will not return. Please to leave your wrap here with me until you come again with the bread." As there was nothing suspicious about this arrangement, the man unfastened his cloth and deposited it by the side of the supposed devout man. Alas! no sooner had he got out of sight than Sharaf, taking the linen cloth, departed in another direction. It was rather a good bargain—a big strong cloth for a few *páṅsas!*

V.

A horse-dealer once unluckily happened to cross the path of Sharaf. He was mounted upon a sleek, swift horse. Sharaf in his heart admired the animal, and wished to have it. "How much do you want for the horse?" he asked. "One hundred rupees," was the reply. "Very well," said Sharaf. "I will try him, to see if he has any vice or not. Let me get up." No sooner was Sharaf upon the horse than he dug his heels into the beast's sides, and was soon out of sight, far far beyond the poor duped horse-dealer's shouts and cries.[6]

[6] This very trick was played upon an official at Firozpúr in 1880, the horse being eventually recovered by the police at Jammú.

VI.

A *paṇḍit*[7] walking on the river-side happened to be wearing a new well-made *tsádar*. Sharaf, seeing this, jumped into an empty boat which was fastened by a string to a post fixed in the bank, and pretending that he was a boatman somewhat unwell, asked the *paṇḍit* to come and help him, in return for the short cut and ride in the boat. The *paṇḍit* readily consented.

It was some time before they arrived at their destination, and already darkness had set in; so the boatman, assuming an expression of great gratitude, said to the *paṇḍit*, "It is already late, and your home, you say, is yet distant; will you not take dinner here at my expense, and sleep in the boat, and then in the freshness of the morning go to your house? Take this rupee, friend, which I willingly offer you, and go and buy food." The *paṇḍit* took the money, and was going to purchase some dinner with it, when Sharaf called him, saying, "Come here. You must be tired. I am quite recovered now, and can arrange for your dinner. Sit here in the boat whilst I go and hire a servant to cook your dinner. And you had better give me your blanket, so that the cook may bring the dinner in it." The *paṇḍit*, nothing suspecting and nothing loth, gave up his blanket, and patiently waited in the boat for some time; but at last, cold for the want of his blanket, and hungry for want of his dinner, he got low-spirited, and after a little time longer wept aloud, exclaiming, "I must have met with Sharaf *Tsúr*."

[7] The term *paṇḍit* in Kashmír does not necessarily mean a learned man. All Kashmírí Hindús, on the assumption that they all belong to the Bráhman caste, are called *paṇḍits*.

Mr. Growse, in his book, *Mathurá, a District Memoir*, makes the following remark:—In the genuine Veda there was no mention of caste whatever, nor was it possible that there should be, on the hypothesis, that the institution of caste was the simple result of residence in a conquered country. This is confirmed by observing that in Kashmír, which was one of the original homes of the Aryan race, and also for many years secured by its position from foreign aggression, there is to the present no distinction of caste, but all Hindús are Bráhmans.

Thus, too, the remarkable lines from the *Mahá-Bhárata*:—There is no distinction of castes; the whole of the world is Brahmanical as originally created by Brahmá. It was only in consequence of men's actions that it has come into a state of caste divisions.

VII.

The next is the story of another weaver, who also, like the weaver before mentioned, was on his way to Srínagar to try and sell his cloth. We have noticed that Sharaf had a special liking for cloth. Accordingly, like the cunning fellow he was, he ran forward a little way, and then lay down upon the path puffing and groaning, apparently in great pain. Some men who were travelling in that direction collected round him and expressed their sympathy. The weaver too came up and looked on.

Sharaf gradually became better. He opened his eyes and seemingly for the first time noticing the weaver's bundle, he begged him in the name of God to lend it to him, so that he might bind his loins therewith.[8] The weaver had compassion upon the man and lent him the cloth. The effect of the bandage was marvellous. Only a few minutes after he had tied it Sharaf said that he was better, and begged the lookers-on to go, that he might have more air. They all left except the weaver, to whom Sharaf spoke in a most earnest tone—"God bless you for all your kindness! Please do one thing more for me. Bring me some water from the well of yonder mosque, that I may quench my thirst. This pain has dried up my very soul." The man went for the water, doubting nothing, and meanwhile Sharaf went also, so that when the poor weaver returned he was nowhere to be seen.

VIII.

The natives are accustomed to keep their money and little valuables either tied up in the waist-cloth or fastened in a knot at the end of the *tsádar*, or else secreted within the turbans. The *pír* of whom we are now going to write

[8] Natives are in the habit of binding their heads or arms or feet or legs just above the spot where the pain is, as a good strong binder has the effect of checking the blood, and so lessening the pain. All nations seem to have discovered this way of obtaining relief. We English used tight bandages very much in cases of operation before the discovery of chloroform.

followed the latter plan. He had bought a piece of gold from a certain goldsmith, and was on his way home, tired and weary because of his hot and long journey.

Sharaf got to know that this *pír* was carrying a piece of gold in his turban, and racked his brains to find means of depriving the good man of it. He walked fast, and when he had got well ahead he sat down by the wayside and began to weep.[9] When the *pír* had reached the spot he requested him to sit down and rest and take some refreshment, which he offered him in the name of his father. The *pír* was very glad to do so, and was very soon enjoying the meal and the exceedingly pleasant conversation of his chance host.

Whether it was from eating some drugged bread or because of his long and trying walk we do not know, but it is certain that presently he began to feel drowsy, and yielding to Sharaf's advice, soon lay down and slept. Sharaf took off his turban for him, and in various other ways soothed the *pír* until he was fast asleep. Now was the opportunity for Sharaf. He took up the turban, and with a look of contempt for his sleeping guest, walked off quietly to some secret place, and there lay down himself to sleep, exceedingly pleased with the day's business. The piece of gold was worth at least one hundred rupees.

IX.

Another of Sharaf's dupes was a poor fellow who was wont to go every day to the celebrated mosque of Baháu'd-dín, and there to pray for treasure. Like many others, he supposed that the great God, through Shekh Baháu'd-dín's intercessions, would grant him the desire of his heart, and so he went time after time praying with all sincerity, "O Baháu'd-dín, give me some treasure, give me some treasure." One day Sharaf was walking past the mosque, and over-

[9] He sat down by the side of a grave. Musalmáns prefer to bury their dead as close to the public way as possible, in order that the devout passers-by may offer up a prayer for them.

heard the man at his devotions. He thought that he might not only deceive him, but probably also make some profit out of him.

Accordingly early on the following morning he went to this mosque, and secreted himself in a very dark corner. He waited till the man came as usual, and when he uttered his request for treasure Sharaf, from out of the darkness, replied, "O holy man, you have certainly been most assiduous in your devotions, and have been most persistent in your request. Now understand that I am well pleased with you, and am quite ready, yea willing, to comply with your wishes." The man, thinking this to be none other than Baháu'd-dín himself, again pleaded, and now with bolder voice, his request. Sharaf told him to come at an appointed time with the tools and implements necessary for unearthing the treasure. He was to bring one hundred rupees also, and two *tsádars* for taking home the treasure, and to be very careful not to broach the matter to any one. The man returned to his house with great joy, and could not sleep for the thought of the great treasure which would be discovered to him on the morrow. He was a very poor man, and not having one hundred rupees at hand, was obliged to sell his property to get the money.

On the morrow, at the dead of night, he was at the place of meeting, tools on his shoulder and money in his blanket, while another blanket was thrown over his other shoulder. Sharaf came forth to greet him. After the usual salutation he led the way into a little jungle whither man seldom wandered, and showed the treasure-seeker the place where he would find the answer to his prayers. He ordered him to dig two yards deep. The man soon accomplished half of his task, but the sweat-drops were upon his brow. Sharaf noticed them, and told the man to take off his clothes and lay them on one side, and then he would be able to work easily. The man did so, and in a short while had dug so deep that he could not be seen at a short distance from the hole, nor could he see anything outside.

Now his clothes had been laid well aside. Sharaf had seen to this arrangement. So when the man had almost dug the two yards and was at the pitch of excitement, expecting every moment that his spade would strike something hard, either gold or silver or some other precious thing, Sharaf carefully took up the clothes, blankets, and one hundred rupees, and was soon lost in the darkness and intricacies of the jungle.

It is said that the poor treasure-seeker worked on until he had only just sufficient strength to draw himself up to the top of the pit, and then, on seeing that his money, wraps, blankets, and saint were not there, he loosened his hold and fell back insensible into the pit.

X.

One day Sharaf met a poor peasant who was pushing along a sheep to the market. Sharaf inquired the price of the animal. The peasant replied, "Four rupees." After a little wrangling the price was finally fixed at three rupees, and Sharaf told the man to bring the sheep to his house, where he would give him the money. The man consented, glad to get rid of his burden so quickly. They had not proceeded far before Sharaf noticed an empty house, having a door in front and a door at the back. He told the man that this was his humble abode, and taking the sheep, swung it over his shoulders and walked inside. He then shut the front-door, and bade the man to wait whilst he went for the money. As will be imagined, while the peasant was most patiently and happily squatting outside the door, Sharaf had gone out by the back-door, and knowing every yard of the neighbourhood, and being swift of foot also, he soon managed to elude all possibility of being taken. After an hour or so another man, in order to cut his journey short, had entered the same dwelling by the back-door, and was coming out by the front-door, when the peasant seized him and demanded his sheep. The traveller was rather annoyed at this sudden and unwelcome interruption to his journey, and showed his displeasure in a rather practical way.

The poor peasant, when he had recovered from the beating which the traveller had given him, tried the neighbours' houses; but, alas! no sheep and no purchaser of the sheep, only blows and insults, until at length he was obliged to depart, a sadder but wiser man, back to his village.

XI.

The following story will show that Sharaf's heart was in his profession, and that he followed it not so much for the gain which it brought to him as for the sport which it afforded.

One day he noticed a very poorly dressed man pick up a dead dove which was lying on the road. He pitied the man's distressed look and state, and followed him, curious to see what he would do with the dead bird. As soon as the man had reached his house and had shut the door, Sharaf rushed up and bent down to see and listen. He saw the little hungry-looking children standing, or rather dancing, round their father, pulling at his ragged garments, and asking whether he had brought them anything to eat. The history of the family was a very sad one. They had once been in affluent circumstances, but a change in the government had not been in their favour, and they had succumbed to their lot.

The man told the little ones, "Yes, I have got a dead dove. Take it and roast it for dinner."

Sharaf *Tsúr* heard and saw everything, and his heart was moved with compassion for the poor people. He shouted to be allowed to come in, and on being permitted to do so, he gave the man five rupees, saying, "Procure ome food with this money, and throw the dead bird away.

I am Sharaf *Tsúr*. Up to this time I have stolen and robbed for my own aggrandisement, but henceforth I will rob and steal for the great God. I promise you that I will visit you again the day after to-morrow, and will hand over to you, for your own use, as many rupees as I may get by that time. Fear not, but hope with gladness. Your adversity shall be turned into prosperity."

The poor man thanked him, and falling upon his knees before him, said, "Your honour's pleasure. God bless you abundantly!"

On the following day Sharaf visited the mosque near this man's dwelling, and spent much time in earnest prayer. Prayer over, he sat to rest a while. Presently the *imám* came in. Sharaf at once commenced conversation with him, and spent the remainder of the day and part of the succeeding night with him in the mosque. Sharaf thought that he was never going to leave. At last, about one in the morning, the *imám* went to his home. No sooner had he departed than Sharaf, who had previously hired a swift and strong horse, started at post-haste for Sopúr.[10]

On arriving at Sopúr Sharaf made straight for the treasury, and thence stole many bags of rupees. He fastened these bags round his waist, and then again mounting his horse, returned to the place whence he had first started as quickly as he came. The bags of rupees he at once took to the poor man whom he had promised to help, and then went and lay down again in the mosque. He slept soundly the remaining half-hour of the night.

The next morning the treasurer discovered that a robbery had taken place. "Some bags have been taken," he said. A report was at once sent to the Viceroy at Srínagar, with a hint that it was Sharaf *Tsúr*'s work.

[10] Sopúr is a moderate-size town midway between Srínagar and Báramula, the town where visitors exchange mules and coolies for the boats on their way to the "Happy Valley."

The Viceroy instantly summoned Sharaf to appear before him. When he was brought he was at once ordered to speak the truth and deliver up the money.

Sharaf assumed a look of intense surprise, and did not appear in the least frightened. "When was the money stolen?" he asked. "Yesterday night," was the reply. Sharaf then quietly asked them to allow the *imám*, with whom he spent the greater part of yesterday and yesterday night, to be sent for. "Send for the *imám*, please, and inquire from him whether I was not with him at the time of the robbery. How could I be here and at Sopúr at one and the same time?"

The *imám* was brought, and testified to the truth of Sharaf's words, and so the thief and robber was set at liberty.

XII.

Another time Sharaf, arrayed in the dress of a great man, went to pay his respects to a very famous *pír*. He sat down in the presence of the holy man with an air of much dignity. The *pír* asked him whence he came and what he wanted. Sharaf, after a little hesitation, informed him that he was the son of a most respectable man, and knowing the *pír* to be a holy man and well instructed in the faith, desired to be taught by him. The *pír* was exceedingly pleased, and then and there began to teach him. For three days Sharaf stayed in the *pír's* quarters, and then, apparently overflowing with gratitude for the good professedly received, he told the holy man how happy he was, and how much he desired to make a feast for his benefactor. "Send for a skilful cook," said he, "and please order him to prepare various dishes. I will spend thirty rupees on a really good dinner, and make the cook a present besides."

The cook promised to do his very best, and asked for the loan of some of the *pír's* saucepans and rice-pots, which were at once handed over to him.

After some time had elapsed, and Sharaf knew that the feast must be ready, he asked permission from the *pír* to go and see to the arrangements. The cook's house was a little distance off. On arriving at the place Sharaf upbraided him because of the delay, and ordered that on account of this he should send the feast with him to the Zaina Kadal, where he called a boatman and had the things placed in a boat.. He himself then entered the boat, and sent away the coolies who had brought the dinner.

On the promise of a good dinner the boatman paddled right lustily, and they were soon beyond all hope of discovery. After a short time the *pír*, whose appetite had been somewhat increased by expectation and delay, went to the cook's shop, and was terribly astonished to find that his friend and pupil had taken the dinner and utensils, and left him to pay the expenses.

This *pír*, however, was an obstinate character. He made quite sure in his own mind that the deceiver was Sharaf *Tsúr*, and in revenge he determined to bring the matter before the Viceroy, at that time 'Átá Muhammad Khán,[11] and get the thief punished. The Viceroy listened with great interest to the *pír's* story, and at once issued a warrant for Sharaf's arrest. A day or two after this Sharaf was brought before the Viceroy, and charged with having stolen the saucepans, spoons, &c., of the *pír*, and in other ways deceived him. The *pír* eyed Sharaf with such a look that the thief at length pleaded guilty, and begged for pardon, promising to supply the Viceroy with enormous wealth if he would let him go free. 'Átá Muhammad Khán, however, was immovable. He would not listen to his pleadings for a moment, but gave strict orders that his right hand should be cut off, so that he might be hindered from carrying on his wicked profession in the future.

This was done; but it is said that Sharaf got an iron hand made, with sharp-pointed fingers, and that he would

[11] 'Átá Muhammad Khán was one of the fourteen Governors or Viceroys during the sixty-six years (1753-1819) the country remained a portion of the Durrání empire.

strike any one on the neck with this hand who would not consent to give up his money or valuables. He killed three or four people in this way.

There are many other stories extant in Srínagar and in the villages concerning the cruelty and cunning of this man too numerous to note here.

Some readers may wish to know something of Sharaf's latter days. A great *pír*, named Buzurg Sháh, sent for him one day, and advised him to desist from such works and give his mind a little to heavenly things. He promised that if he would do this he would allow him to reside in his house as a companion and help. Sharaf's heart was touched by the kind offer and manner of the *pír*, and being thoroughly weary of wrong-doing, he accepted the proposal.

He remained in Buzurg Sháh's house until his death, and proved himself in every way worthy of the confidence and esteem bestowed upon him by his benefactor.

It is not known when Sharaf *Ts*úr died or where he was buried.

A KING AND HIS TREACHEROUS WAZÍR.[1]

ONCE upon a time there lived a king who had a very wicked *wazír*. This *wazír* conceived the terrible desire of murdering the king and seizing the kingdom. Fortunately the king got to know of his great danger. One day, when he went to the stables to look at his horses, a favourite *zalgur* that was there wept exceedingly. Going near the animal, His Majesty inquired what was the matter; whereupon the *zalgur* told him of the *wazír's* treachery, and warned him to flee from the country as soon as possible on its back. The king did so, and was soon beyond all fear of pursuit. Being very tired, he went to a butcher of the place, which he had reached, and asked him for a night's lodging. The man agreed; so the king fastened the *zalgur* by a rope in the yard and went inside the house to sleep.

Alas! however, he had but escaped from one danger into another, from the hands of one villain into the hands of another villain. At midnight the butcher called to his wife and asked for a big strong knife, because he intended to kill the stranger and take his money and *zalgur*. The king, who was lodging in the next room, overheard their conversation, and, rising up, went to them and besought them not to do this wickedness, and he would give them all his money and the *zalgur*, and he himself would remain with them as a slave. The butcher, of course, consented.

One day the wicked man ordered the king to clean the paunch of a sheep. While the king was doing this the daughter of the king of that country, who chanced to

[1] Narrator's name, Paṇḍit Shiva Báyú, Renawárí, Srínagar.

be walking by the river at that time, noticed him, and perceiving that he was of a noble mien and countenance, was much surprised, and said in her heart, "This man must be of some royal family." Accordingly she beckoned to him to come forward, and asked him of his antecedents and how he had come thither. Seeing that she was kind and good, the king informed her everything of his sad experience; whereupon the princess was struck to the heart with love and pity, and determined to marry him. She took him to her father, the king, and repeated all that he had said, and entreated her father to allow her to marry him. The king agreed, for he too was moved by the sad tale, and noticed the superior manners and appearance of the man. As soon as possible the marriage was celebrated. Everything was done with great *éclat*, and everybody was pleased.

The day after the wedding the wicked butcher was beheaded, and the *zalgur* restored to the king. And within a few months His Majesty, having received some troops from his father-in-law, returned to his country and slew the treacherous *wazír* who had conspired against him. Henceforth all was peace and gladness. The king lived to a good old age, had several children, and prospered exceedingly.

THE SHIPWRECKED PRINCE.[1]

THERE was a very wise and clever king, who had four sons, and each of these sons was equally as wise and clever as his father.[2] One day the king, wishing to test the wisdom and talents of these sons, called them all to him, and among other questions asked them each one, singly and privately, by whose good fortune it was that he possessed such a large and powerful kingdom, and was enabled to govern it so wisely and so well. Said he, "Is it through my own good fortune, or your mother's, or yours, or your brothers'?" The eldest son replied, "It is by your own good fortune, O king, our father, that you have this kingdom and this power." Likewise replied the second and the third sons. But when the fourth and youngest son was thus inquired of, he answered that all this might and power and glory were obtained through his own good fortune and not another's.[3]

The king was as much enraged at the bold and decided reply of his youngest son as he had been pleased with the fawning, truckling answers of the other three sons. In a wrathful tone he said, "Was not I a wise and powerful king before thou wast conceived in the womb? This kingdom and power did not come with thy birth, O proud and stupid boy! Away! away!" and then calling the doorkeeper, he bade him remove the lad far from his presence.

1 Narrator's name, Makund Báyú, Suthú, Srínagar. He heard it from a Musalmán; hence the constant occurrence of the word "God" in the story.

2 Literally, "who were one cleverer than the other" (*Yim ási ak aki sindih khutah gátuli.*)

3 The story of "The Fan Prince in *Indian Fairy Tales* begins something like this; cf. p. 193; compare also, *en passant*, *Indian Antiquary*, vol. xvi. p. 322.

The boy, however, did not require any pressing to go. Being of a most determined and independent disposition, he hastened away, packed up a few necessaries, and left the palace. Soon afterwards, the king's anger having in the meantime softened, when it was known throughout the royal city that the youngest prince had really departed, messengers from the throne were despatched in all directions to find him and bring him back. He was overtaken on a certain way;—but it was in vain that the messengers recounted to him the king's anguish, and how His Majesty would load him with honours and presents if he would only return. The young prince persisted in going on.

Great was the sorrow in the court that day. A veil of mourning and lamentation shrouded the city and people. But none could tell the anguish of the exiled prince's wife, and none could comfort her. She tore her beautiful hair, she beat her milk-white breasts, she cast aside her jewels and ornaments, and was as one mad and about to die. Finally, she decided to follow her beloved, and resisting her mother-in-law's and other relations' entreaties, she dressed herself like a female *faqír* and went forth penniless and unattended in search of her husband.

It was not long before she succeeded in reaching him, for love had made her feet swift and her search keen. The prince was overjoyed at seeing her, and lavished upon her all the affection which she deserved. With her he felt rich and happy, and cared not to occupy himself again with the business and excitement of the court. "What is thy thought, O my beloved, the light of my eyes?" said he. "Shall we not abide here in the woods, and live upon what this bow and sling will bring us?"

She consented, and for some time the days and weeks passed pleasantly, until one day the bow and the sling lost their charm, and no prey came to hand. This state of affairs continued till at last, feeling very hungry, they were obliged to leave their jungle-home and beg by the wayside and in the far-scattered villages around. In the course of their wanderings they reached the sea. Great was their surprise on seeing the boundless expanse of waters; and as they watched the tide, now rushing forward and then receding, they thought that they were living waters, and that they were trying to swallow them up and all the country behind them. Nevertheless they did not dread the sea, but the rather wished to live upon it, and tried hard to get the sailors of some of the ships which now and again touched at the port of that place to let them sail with them. But the sailors always refused, because the prince and his wife were so poor and had nothing to give them. At length, however, one day a trader, kind and wealthy, heard of their desire, and perceiving that they were gentle-mannered people and of a good countenance, he had compassion upon them, and engaged for them a berth on board one of the vessels then about to start on some distant voyage. Before they left the trader inquired who they were and whence they came and what was their intention. "For surely," he said, "ye both are of a princely mien and countenance, and by some foul trickery have become thus poor and helpless."

"True, true!" replied the young prince, weeping; and he related to him all his history.

I am a prince, said he,
Of splendid destiny.
Through me alone the king doth rule and power obtain.

But on an evil day
Did my fond father say,
"Whose fortune is it—mine or thine—by which I rule?"

I told him, "Mine, O king."
Said he, "What—thine! What thing
Is this? Away, O proud and foolish child, far hence!"

And so my home I left,
Of father's love bereft,
And wandered far and lone unto the desert wilds.

Then came my wife to me,
And we lived happily,
Till bow and string refused me help to strike the prey.

Next hunger drove us forth
East, west, and south and north,
To seek for bread and shelter with a beggar's cry.

And last God brought us here
To give us such good cheer
As thy kind sympathy and help provideth us.

O friend, to thee long life
And happiness without strife,
And after death to dwell in richest joys above!

The trader was so much moved by the prince's touching tale that he could scarcely keep from weeping. "I know that what you have said is correct," he said, "because as soon as you left your father's kingdom my agent, who lives there, sent me word that a foreign force had entered the city, slain many of the inhabitants, and taken the king and his brothers, together with their wives and families, prisoners."

When the prince heard this, he wept bitterly, and mourned his poverty and helplessness to afford succour to his father and brethren and people, whom he so loved. It was useless for his wife and the trader to try and cheer him by saying how thankful he should be to have left the city before these sad events occurred. The prince was of far too noble a character to attend to such words; nay, he rather reproached himself the more, knowing that if he had but tarried at home these things would not have happened.

After a long time had elapsed they were sailing with a boisterous wind not far from the country where they hoped to disembark; but the wind became fiercer and the waves rolled mountains high, threatening every moment to overwhelm the ship. All hands were at work, and everything was done that could be done for the safety of the crew. For hours and hours they thus lingered between life and death, until at last one great wave, swifter and larger than the rest, broke upon the ship, so that it divided into two pieces, and everyone and everything were swept into the waters. Only two were saved, and these two were the prince and his wife, who had caught hold of a spar and a plank from the wreck, and were thus carried to the shore. The prince, however, was carried to one part of the country, whilst the princess floated to another part, perhaps, of another country far distant. The place where the princess landed was near a large garden, which had evidently been laid out with great care, but was flowerless and leafless. As soon, however, as the princess approached its walls the trees and shrubs began to freshen, and here and there a tiny bud appeared. Great was the surprise of the head-gardener when, on going his customary round of inspection the following morning, he noticed these things. He had come as usual to give orders concerning the withered trees, that they might be uprooted and taken away for fuel or other purposes; but lo! there was life in them; so he told the under-gardeners to go for that day, as there was no work for them. The gardener then hastened to inform his master, who was the king of that country, concerning the good news. The king was exceedingly glad to hear it, and thought that at last God would cause the trees to bring forth fruit and the flowers to blossom in the garden, over which he had expended so large a sum of money. Then the gardener returned once more to feast his eyes upon the new sight, and saw a woman squatting by the gate. He inquired who she was, whence she came, and what she had come for; but never a word escaped the princess's lips, and so he left her.

The place where the prince arrived turned out to be close to the walls of a large and magnificent city. In the course of his peregrinations through this city he came upon a most beautiful garden, one blaze of colours and redolent with perfumes. He looked within the entrance-gate, but dared not venture right in, as, seeing no person there, he thought that people were prohibited from entering, and therefore stopped. He was still there, looking at this wonderful sight, when the royal gardener came. Seeing a man at the gate gazing with such longing eyes upon the flowers, he suspected that he had trespassed inside the garden and stolen some of them, and for the moment he was filled with fear and trembling, not knowing what the king would do to him if such were the case. But when he discovered that no harm had been done, he felt rather pleased with the stranger, and perceiving that he was clever and gentle, he asked who he was and what business he had there.

"I am a beggar come from a far country," was the reply.

"Then follow me," said the gardener. "I will make some arrangement for your food and clothes."

Of course the beggar-prince was only too delighted, and followed the gardener to his house. There it was told how that he was a poor man wandering upon the face of the earth for a bit of bread; and food was set before him and clothes provided, and he was invited to draw near to the fire and warm his shivering limbs. During conversation the stranger-guest asked why the gardener had plucked the flowers. The gardener replied that it was the order of the king that fresh flowers should be provided every day for the pleasure of the royal household. Hence his extreme care over the garden that no flowers be stolen, lest there should not be sufficient daily for the palace.

"I wish," said the prince, "that you would allow me to arrange these flowers into bouquets. They would look so much more beautiful, and His Majesty the king would be so much better pleased with them."

The gardener consented, and presently there were several bouquets of flowers tastefully arranged, ready to be taken to the palace.

The king and all the royal family, when they saw the beautiful bouquets, were greatly pleased, and giving many presents to the gardener, ordered him thus to prepare the flowers every day.[4] The gardener made his obeisance and departed.

On reaching his house he told his wife of the pleasure of the king, and of the many presents which had been given to him; and then went and honestly told the prince that all this honour was through his skill, and that he must abide in their house and arrange the flowers every day, because if he now left them the king would not have his wish, and perhaps would imprison him (the gardener) or take away his life. The prince, thinking that nothing better would offer itself—at all events for a long time—readily complied. And so matters continued. Every day the king and the royal household were delighted with the most delicious bouquets of flowers, and every day the gardener returned with rich rewards.

Becoming more and more wealthy, and loving money the more as it increased to him, the gardener and his wife were sometimes filled with terrible fears lest their guest, the prince, should suddenly depart and leave them as they were before. Accordingly they hit upon a plan to marry him to their only daughter, that he might be certain not to leave them; for said they, "Though he came to us in great distress, yet how do we know that he is not some great man reduced by trickery and falsehood to this state? At all events he is wise and skilful, and of a noble countenance, and by his means we have attained to this great wealth."

And so it was arranged to ask the prince to marry the gardener's daughter. The prince at first demurred, but afterwards consented, on condition that he should be allowed to depart when and whither he wished. The gardener complied readily, making sure in his own mind that if the stranger were once settled and comfortable in his own house he would not care to leave it.[5]

[4] Cf. *Wide-Awake Stories*, pp. 150, 151; *Madanakamárájankadai* (*Dravidian Nights*), pp. 190, 191; *Indian Notes and Queries*, vol. iv. p. 49; Grimm's *Household Stories*, p. 407; *Old Deccan Days*, p. 11.

[5] Gardeners and their families occupy a prominent place in Euro-

The marriage took place, and much money was spent, and there were great rejoicings. All things went smoothly for a while, and everybody seemed as happy as could be, until one day the gardener could not go to the palace, and so was obliged to ask his son-in-law to go instead of him and take the bouquets of flowers. He did so; but on returning the king's daughter met him, and seeing that he was clever, gentle, and handsome, she at once fell in love with him, and ordered one of her female attendants to follow him and see where he lived. She saw him enter the gardener's house, and came and told her mistress so. On the following morning the princess sent to the gardener, telling him on no account to let this young man go, but to give him food and supply him with everything that he might require. The gardener was astonished at this strange order, and went immediately to tell his wife and son-in-law.

"What is it thou hast done," he said to the latter, "to provoke this request? Hast thou seen the princess, spoken to her, or looked upon her with eyes of love? Tell me the reason of this strange order."

The prince acknowledged that he had seen the king's daughter when returning from the palace, but added that he had scarcely noticed her, much less spoken to her. Great was the suspense until the reason was known.

Meanwhile the princess lost her appetite and became very pale and weak. When her mother noticed that she was getting thin and sickly, she begged her daughter to tell her if there was any pain or sorrow, and if so, to tell her, that it might be remedied. Or, perhaps, she wanted something; if so, let her make these wants known, and the king would satisfy them. Anything and everything rather than she should pine away like this and die.

"O mother, dear mother!" replied the princess, "it is not that I am in pain, or that any one has grieved me;

pean and Indian tales. While glancing rapidly through the first half of *Old Deccan Days* I found some nine or ten instances of this. Cf. *Indian Fairy Tales*, p. 277, n. 2.

but God has guided hither the man whom I love, and whom I wish to marry."

"Tell me," said the queen, "who he is and where he dwells, and I will inform the king, that a message may be sent for him."

"It is the young man," answered the princess, "who resides with our chief gardener; that wise and handsome man who brought the flowers here the other day for the gardener."

The queen was astounded at her daughter's request, and begged her to consider what she was asking for.

"A gardener's lackey!" said she. "With such would a princess fain unite herself? The idea is preposterous. Surely my daughter must be mad!"

"I am not mad, dear mother," answered the princess. "This man is not of mean birth, as you suppose. He is of a noble type of countenance and of gentle manners, which bespeak high blood and gentle training. Send and inquire, I pray you, and see if this is not so."

The queen promised to do so. When the king heard the reason of his daughter's indisposition he too was very much astonished, but thinking that there might be some truth in the princess's surmisings, he deferred speaking to her until he had sent and ascertained who and whence this young man was.

The gardener told the king's messengers all that he knew about his son-in-law:—

It was a beggar that I saw—
But now my handsome son-in-law—
A-gazing at the garden-gate
In wretched guise and piteous state.

I thought at first he'd been within
The closely guarded garden green;
But finding every flower entire,
I quickly stayed my ill-roused ire.

And tempted by his pleasant face,
I asked him did he want a place?
If so, then he could follow me
And kind of under-gardener be.

And he, consenting, came to us
And stayed, as you may well suppose;
For such a clever gardener he,
Without his aid I could not be.

The king's delight, those bouquets rare,
Did his own skilful hands prepare;
And then in sweet unselfish wise
He bade me gladden the royal eyes.

Thus through his skill we honours gained,
And countless riches we obtained,
Until we feared he would depart
And leave us ignorant of his art.

Hence was he married to our blood,
With gifts of coin and clothes and food:
We thought he then would surely rest,
Choosing such fortune as the best.

And now to you I've frankly shown
All that of this strange man is known:
Go tell the king, and beg that he
Will of his mercy pardon me.

But who he is, or whence he came,
Or even of the stranger's name,
I cannot tell; for never he
Hath told his fortune unto me.

On hearing this strange tale from the messenger the king, desiring to know more concerning this underling, summoned the head-gardener. With much fear and trembling the head-gardener entered the royal presence.

"Now tell me," said His Majesty, "who is this man? Whence came he? What is his business here? How didst thou find him? What does he in thy house? And tell me, too, of his behaviour and attainments. What is thy own opinion of this man?"

The gardener then told all he knew about his son-in-law—how he met with him, had pity upon him, and married him to his only daughter because he made bouquets which delighted the king; how wise and skilful he was in all manner of conversation and work, and how gentle, good, and kind he was. Not one thing did the head-gardener keep back of all that he knew about his son-in-law. Then the king dismissed him, bidding him not to fear, as no harm, but rather good, would happen to him as the result of these inquiries.

As soon as the head-gardener had departed the king sent a special servant to see really how this under-gardener behaved himself, and to bring him word again. He bade him be very careful in his observations, as it was his (the king's) intention, if possible, to marry this man to his own daughter. The servant left and thoroughly inquired into all matters.

"It was quite true," he said to the king, "what the gardener told you. But may it please Your Majesty to call for the man and see him."

The king was pleased to do so; and soon the under-gardener stood before him. A little conversation and observation served to convince the king that this man was no ordinary personage; and so he informed him of his daughter's wish, and added that he too was of similar mind.

"Will you agree, and become the king's son-in-law?"

"I will," he replied; "but only on the condition that you allow me to leave the country whenever I wish."

The king promised, and at once gave orders for a certain house adjoining the palace to be prepared for him, and for clothes and jewels and the richest food to be provided for him, so that in every way he might be as the king's son-in-law, and every cause for reproach removed. It was so; and soon all the people, even the *wazírs*, began to acknowledge him as one great and wise in the land, and the accepted son-in-law of their king.

In course of time the marriage took place. There

were great rejoicings, such as had never been known in the city before. The air was filled with gladness, and everybody was arrayed in his gayest and his best; the poor, also, were well clothed, well fed, and loaded with presents. The praises of the king and the queen and the bride and bridegroom were in the mouths of every one; and never did there appear such another glad and happy city.

And so matters continued. The king had no reason to regret the union, for his son-in-law increased in knowledge, wisdom, and popularity. He knew all languages, could solve the most difficult questions, and was most holy and good, giving alms to the people and attending to the cries of the sick and the distressed. Only one thing seemed against him, and that was his refusal to attend the *darbár*.

One day his wife asked him the reason of his not doing so. "It is not meet," she added, "that you, the king's son-in-law, should always be absent from the great assembly. You should certainly go sometimes, and manifest, at all events, a little interest in the government of the country whose king is your wife's father."

The prince—for he was now a recognised prince—then told her that he was a prince by birth, and that his father was ruler over a larger and more powerful country than that in which he was now living. He told her also how he had arrived in her father's country, and all that had happened to him, and added that his heart longed to visit once more his home and fatherland. However, he saw the wisdom of what she advised, and promised to attend the king's court henceforth. Accordingly the prince was present in the *darbár* on the following morning, arrayed in his best, and looking most noble and handsome. The king was exceedingly pleased to see his son-in-law, and gave him the seat of honour, and especially consulted him concerning the present pressing difficulties of the country. Thus matters continued. The prince went regularly to the court, and in all affairs behaved himself so wisely and so well, that the king loved him more than any of his other sons, and especially so when he heard from his daughter that her husband was a great prince in his own right, but that he had been obliged by unkindness to leave his country and beg for bread in a foreign land. The king's love and attention knew no bounds when he had ascertained for certain that his favourite son-in-law was of noble birth also. He told him all his private affairs and all the secret State difficulties; in all matters he sought his counsel, and at all times he wanted his society.

"Thou hast become an absolute necessity to me, O my son-in-law," he said to him one day. "Think not, I pray thee, of ever leaving me. Ask what thou wilt and thou shalt obtain it here."

Now, when the other sons-in-law and sons of the king perceived the great affection of His Majesty for the new prince, and how that he seemed to be unable to move or stir without him, they were filled with jealousy, and plotted together how they might estrange him from the royal favour. They did not know that he was a born prince, and therefore a skilful archer, but supposed that he was only the gardener's son, and consequently would be altogether ignorant of the use of the bow and the habits of wild animals; and so they suggested to the king that they should go on a shooting expedition, and that this prince should accompany them. The king consented, and expressed a wish to his favourite son-in-law that he also should go a-hunting. The prince said that he would obey his royal pleasure; but on leaving his father-in-law's presence he appeared to be going to his own house. This furnished rather a good joke to the other princes, who immediately sent each other word, saying, "There goes that gardener's son to his house. Of course *he* cannot shoot or ride. Aha! Aha! Whom have we for a relation and confidant of the king!" And so they mocked him, and afterwards went to the king and said, "He whom Your Majesty ordered to go with us, your favourite son-in-law, in whom you trust, must surely be of low degree, for he shirks this expedition; and rightly so, perhaps, knowing that he cannot well take part in it." Thus did they endeavour to turn the king's mind against his favourite son-in-law.

But besides the thought that their brother-in-law would not be successful in the sport, they had an idea also that he could not ride, and therefore had previously given full instructions to the grooms that if this prince went shooting with them he was to be mounted on a certain mad mare which was kept separate in the royal stables, and which no man had yet been able to ride. However, their envied brother-in-law was a magnificent horseman as well. In short, there was nothing he had not thoroughly mastered; and so, when he had gone home and acquainted his wife with his intentions, and fully armed himself, he went to the royal stables, and on asking for a horse, was told that the mad mare was the only beast available. All the other animals belonged to different members of the royal family, and would be presently required, as everybody was going with this expedition. However, the prince did not care what beast he rode so long as it was strong of limb and swift of foot, and so he mounted the mad mare without any hesitation. As will be imagined, the mare only became more mad at the presumption of the prince. Never had she been mounted before, and she cared not to carry any person now. So she plunged, and then rose up on her haunches, then backed, then shied, and finally, after other tricks, all of which were well known to the prince, she started off in the direction of the jungle at such a pace that her feet seemed scarcely to touch the ground. Firm as a rock the prince retained his seat, and quickly reached that part of the jungle whither the wild beasts were said to resort. A keen sportsman, he soon discovered their favourite haunts, and shot a jackal, a bear, and a leopard.

Not being able to take them away with him for want of help, he cut off the jackal's tail, the bear's nose, and the leopard's ear, and left the jungle.

Now, the other princes, thinking that the favourite prince had gone to his house, did not start so early, and when they did go they went by another road to the hunting-ground. On reaching it they discovered the corpses of the three animals which the other prince had killed and left, and having been unsuccessful in shooting any animal themselves, they gave orders that these three dead beasts should be taken to the king and presented as having been shot by them.[6]

On reaching home the favourite prince's wife asked him why he had returned so quickly. "Perhaps," she remarked, "you have not been shooting." But he drew from his pocket the tail of the jackal, the nose of the bear, and the ear of the leopard, and showed them to her, saying that he had left the bodies of these three animals in the jungle, as he had nobody to bring them away for him.

Late in the evening the rest of the royal party returned, carrying with them the corpses of the jackal, the bear, and the leopard. On the following morning, just before the business of the *darbár* commenced, the king inquired what sport they had on the previous day. The jealous princes quickly answered, "We shot a jackal, a bear, and a leopard, whose carcasses are outside in the yard, waiting Your Majesty's inspection. More than these we do not think are in the jungle just now."

But the king had observed that his favourite son-in-law had not spoken, and in consequence of his brothers maligning him the day before he was especially anxious to know whether he had been shooting or not; and if so what success he had. So he turned to him and said, "What news of thy sport?"

[6] Cf. story of "The Boy with a Moon and Star" in *Indian Fairy Tales*; *Indian Evangelical Review*, vol. xiii. p. 337; a Koi tale given in *Christian College Magazine*, vol. v. pp. 352, 353; "The Tale of Two Brothers" in Grimm; *Nineteenth Century*, Nov. 1879, p. 838.

"Oh," replied one of the other sons-in-law, "ask him not, O king; as, being unaccustomed to the sport, he went home. Increase not his shame by advertising the whole matter."

Now, the favourite son-in-law's dignity was offended and his anger justly aroused by these lying words. However, he waited until the others had said their say, and then, looking at them with scornful eye, he said, "I also went to the sport, O king, but alone; and three animals came to my hand, a jackal, a bear, and a leopard."

The other sons-in-law, when they heard this, were greatly surprised, and especially so, as the three carcasses which they had brought back with them and displayed before the king as the result of their shooting were of these three animals. What were they to do now? How could they convince the king of the truth of their words? Only by telling more lies, and therefore they waxed vehement, and swore that the prince had spoken falsely, because they had seen him enter his house directly after yesterday's court, and knew, from many and various proofs, that he had not stirred forth therefrom until this morning.

Calmly the prince waited again till they had finished their answer, when he begged His Majesty to allow him to send one of his servants to his house and bring thence a little parcel, the contents of which would prove the truth of his speech. As will be imagined, there was greater surprise than ever at these words. A little parcel to be brought forward as a witness to this matter! The king himself now began to doubt the sanity of his favourite son-in-law. "Much learning," thought he, "has turned his brain." However, beyond general conversation, every one forebore passing any remarks until the servant had returned, which he did presently, for the prince's house was very near the royal court. Within the little parcel were the tail of the jackal, the nose of the bear, and the ear of the leopard; and when the king opened these out to view the prince said, "Behold, O king, behold, my brethren, the tail of the jackal, the nose of the bear, and the ear of the leopard which I shot yesterday in the royal preserve, but the carcasses of which I left in the jungle, because I was alone and could not bring them for Your Majesty's and your honours' inspection. And see ye further that these things before you are none other than those belonging to the three carcasses which my brethren brought back with them yesterday evening, and which they are thought to have killed. You see it is not so, O king, but that out of the envy and malice of their hearts have they done this thing, that my name might be degraded, and that the king's favour might pass from me. If Your Majesty will but step forth into the courtyard and look at the three dead beasts lying there, Your Majesty will find that my testimony is true, and my brethren's false."

The king immediately rose and went into the courtyard as advised, and lo! the jackal was there, but wanting a tail; the bear was there, but without a nose; and the leopard was there, but having only one ear. Here, then, was undoubted proof of the veracity of the prince's words; and the king was so glad to find he had not reposed his confidence in vain, that he almost forgot to reprove the other princes and members of the *darbár* for their mean and false behaviour.

Henceforth the king's special affection was more than ever marked, and eventually it was settled that the favourite prince should succeed to the throne, while the other princes were promised only minor estates and offices. Not long after this final settlement of the succession the prince was filled with an intense longing to visit his father and country, and told the king so, promising that after he had fulfilled this wish he would return. The king was much grieved to hear this, and entreated the prince not to go, but to send messengers and inquire about his father and people and the affairs of the kingdom. The prince, however, so urged his request, that at length the royal consent was given. On reaching home he told his wife of the proposed journey, and bade her not to grieve or fear, as he should soon return; but she would not hear him or the entreaties of the king and queen—so great was her love.

"Whither you go I too will go," she cried; "I will never leave you. Come trial or pleasure, I will be with you. I live only because you live!"

And so it was arranged that this loving pair should both go.

Now, the prince's country was far distant, and could not be reached except by crossing the sea. However, the royal couple did not hesitate on this account, though the prince had once been nearly drowned and lost his first wife in the shipwreck, and the princess had a horror of the sea. Passages were quickly engaged in a vessel soon to sail for the desired country, and they embarked full of plans and expectations.

It is not necessary to give another account of a shipwreck; for, alas! the vessel had not proceeded far upon her journey when the cruel waves engulfed her, and the prince and princess and all the rest of the passengers and crew were precipitated into the waters. It was a terrible time, though nothing was seen and not a sound was heard, because of the darkness of the night and the roar of the waves. Each one seemed to die, singly and unmourned. Afterwards, however, it was discovered that two out of all those on board had been saved, and these two were the prince and his beautiful wife. As was the case with the prince and his first wife, so now: they had each clung to different pieces of wood, parts of the wreck, and had drifted to different and far-distant places.

The princess was carried by the waters to that place where her husband's first wife had been carried before her. She too entered the unfruitful and flowerless garden, and there sat down and wept bitterly. And lo!

as soon as she entered the garden the flower-buds grew larger and increased in number, and the trees began to shoot out their branches. When the head-gardener visited the garden on the following morning to make his usual inspection he was surprised to find so many more buds, and the trees too giving some promise of eventually bearing fruit and affording shade. He gave the under-gardeners a holiday for that day, and went at once to inform the king of this glad matter. The king was delighted with this further sign of God's blessing upon the garden, and richly rewarded the gardener. For very joy the gardener went back to the garden to assure himself that his eyes had not deceived him; and on reaching it he saw another woman sitting in the garden, and weeping and silent, in spite of kind and reiterated questionings. "This is strange," he thought within himself. "When the first woman came here the trees and the bushes budded; and now on the arrival of this second woman the buds become larger and many, and the trees give out branches and increase in height and thickness. Perhaps these women are very holy women, and therefore blessing rests upon the garden. On this account, also, they will not speak with me."[7] He visited the king a second time that day to tell him so. The king was pleased to hear this, and immediately ordered a holy person to go and commune with these women, if possible, and get to know all their circumstances. But this holy person could not make anything of them, and told the king that probably the gardener's surmisings were correct,

[7] Natives, but especially *faqírs*, of both sects and sexes, sometimes give themselves up to such absolute contemplation of the Deity that they will not hold converse with any person for weeks and months and years in succession; and some, when they do speak, will only speak with those whom they recognise as holy as themselves. There is a *panditání* at Báramula who constantly sits for days without uttering a syllable. There is a famous *faqír* residing at Lár who says nothing for weeks together. And at Srínagar, two years ago, there died a bráhman, named Íshar Sáhib, who is reported to have kept perfectly silent for over thirty years before his death. Chana Sáhib, living at Renawárí, Srínagar, and Rajab Sháh, who resides at Káriyár, an adjoining district, with many others, are also quoted as famous silent *faqírs*.

and therefore he advised that suitable food should be daily provided for them, lest God should be angry and cause the garden to wither as before. Accordingly food was sent every day from the palace, and in other ways special attention was manifested to these strange persons.

As has been mentioned, the prince, their husband, reached some other place, which chanced to be a great and magnificent city. While walking in the *bázár* of this city he observed a learned pandit reading aloud from the *Shástras* in the shop of a certain merchant, and many people were assembled there to listen to the sacred words and wise interpretation of the same. He too joined the company, and when the reading was over and people had dispersed he remained behind by the merchant's shop. On closing up the place for the night the merchant, seeing the stranger still there, spoke to him, and inquired who he was. He replied:—

A cruel fate forced me from home,
Far in a foreign land to roam;
There I became most wise and great,
And raised to second in the State.

In time my heart began to yearn
Unto my kindred to return;
To see again my home, and there
To tell them of my fortune fair.

I bade my wife behind to stay
With patient heart until the day
We met again, to part no more
Till one should enter at Death's door.

She hearkened not these words of mine,
But said, "O love, my fate is thine!
Whither thou goest there go I,
With thee I live, with thee I die."

Thus, though the king our absence wailed,
The mighty bond of love prevailed,
And kept us happy by the way,
In loving longing for the day,

When, all the weary journey o'er,
We'd see the dear old home once more,
The welcome bright of loved ones dear,
The smile of love and best of cheer.

The ways of God God only knows:
A mighty wind and waves arose,
And ship and all have passed away
Except this waif that pleads to-day.

And then he added in a most earnest tone:—

And must I plead, kind friend, in vain
For aid in this my life of pain?
Give me thy help, and thou shalt see
How helpful I shall prove to thee.

The merchant was much moved by this story, and gave him permission to sleep in the shop, saying that he would send him some food presently from his private house. Accordingly the prince arranged a little place in the shop for himself, and the merchant departed to his house and ordered his servants to prepare and take some food for the man at the shop. The next morning the prince was accepted as a servant by the merchant, and verified his promise by a most grateful and respectful demeanour and ready and efficient help. By-and-by the merchant discovered that his servant's services were indispensable, and told him so, adding that, such being the case, he had better make his abode there and marry into the family. Would he care to marry the merchant's daughter? The merchant for some time had had long and difficult conversations with his wife touching this subject; for, with a keen, business-like foresight, he had long seen the inevitable conclusion of matters. "In spite of his apparent destitution," said he, "I feel that the man's story is true, because he has such knowledge, understanding, and skill, and is of such gentle behaviour."

At length the wife agreed; hence the communication of the matter to the prince. But the latter did not at all consent. "It was not meet," he replied, "that such as the merchant's daughter should be allied to one of his present low estate, and who existed only through her father's kindness."

However, after much urging, he agreed, but only on the condition that the merchant would not hinder his leaving the country whenever he wished. The merchant was satisfied, feeling sure that if this man was once settled in a comfortable home with a beautiful wife, and with plenty of honour and money, he would not care to leave—not even for his father's house, and especially if a voyage intervened on the way thither. The marriage took place, and was celebrated with such great show that all the city was stirred at the sight. Fabulous sums were quoted as having been spent over it.

In a few years, in consequence of his son-in-law's great skill and wisdom, the merchant's business increased to such an extent, and he became so wealthy, that both his business and his wealth became a proverb in the country, and people said, "As rich and prosperous as So-and-so, the merchant."

But, alas! the merchant's son-in-law was not satisfied. He wished still to see his people and his fatherland, and told his father-in-law of this wish. The merchant was intensely grieved to hear it, and entreated him even with tears to relinquish his desire and stay with him. It was all in vain, however; his son-in-law would not listen. He then informed his wife of his intentions, and begged her to remain, promising to return soon; and then they would always live happily. His wife altogether refused, saying that she would never be parted from her husband. And so passages were engaged for both in a vessel about to leave for the prince's country, and they started. By God's will this vessel was also wrecked, and all the passengers and crew perished in the waters except the prince and his wife, who escaped, as the prince and his other wives had done, on pieces of the wreck. The wind and waves carried the prince in one direction and his wife in another direction.

Marvellous to relate, the woman was borne by a piece of timber to which she clung to the very spot where the other two wives of her husband had been carried, and were now sitting silent and sad, mourning their bereavement. The third wife, too, went within the garden enclosure and sat down by them; and lo! as soon as she entered the buds bloomed and the branches of the trees put forth their leaves, changing the whole appearance of the garden, so that it now was pleasant to the sight and to the smell and afforded a welcome shade. When the head-gardener visited the garden on the following morning he could scarcely believe his eyes. It seemed too good to be true, that God should thus bless this garden after such a long delay. Dismissing the under-gardeners and coolies, saying that they might leave for the rest of that day, he went at once to tell the king the good news. His Majesty was delighted, and again gave the head-gardener some valuable presents. As before, the head-gardener returned to look once more upon the beautiful sight, when, behold! he saw another woman sitting and weeping with the other two women. "Hence," thought he within himself, "the reason of this greater blessing. It is another of these holy women who has come, and whose goodness has attracted the especial notice of the Deity." So he went and informed the king; but the king ordered him not to trouble her with questions, but to give her food and raiment and all things necessary.

The prince, her husband, had landed on some island weird and uninhabited. After some rest and sleep he set forth to reconnoitre the place, and in a little while entered a large and intricate jungle, where he again rested, mourning and lamenting his lot. "For what reason," cried he, "does God thus thwart me? Why does He thus make my life miserable and my heart to long for death? Is it that I have sinned in marrying, or how?"

Now, in this jungle appeared not a living creature, neither man nor beast. After a while life became intolerable. The prince often laid himself down to die. At last one day, while wandering in the upper part of the jungle, he reached a cave, and by this cave he saw a woman sitting. This was passing strange. "Surely," thought he, "this can be no ordinary person, for such cannot exist here. This must be a goddess, or some especially holy woman."[8] He went still nearer, and when the woman saw him she began to weep; whereupon the prince asked her why she wept on seeing him. "I have come to comfort and not to trouble you," he added; "and great and many have been the trials and dangers through which I have passed before I reached hither."

On hearing this the woman brushed away her tears, and, smiling, called him to sit beside her, and gave him rich food to eat and pleasant drinks to assuage his thirst. And then she asked him how he had arrived there; for it was the chief residence of an ogre,[9] who ate men and women as easily as the prince was eating the dinner before him; hence the reason of his not meeting with any living creature, man or beast, before coming to the cave. Alas! alas! all had been slain and devoured by this ogre. "As for me," continued the woman, "I am the daughter of a king, and was brought hither by the ogre, who at first determined to eat me, but changed his mind when he saw that I should make a pleasant companion, and appointed me his mistress. It would have been better had he slain me. Now he is on some

[8] The words used here were *atsa-ratsh* and *shánts*. *Atsa-ratsh* is the Kashmírí for the Sanskrit *apsaras* (female divinities of surprising loveliness, who reside in Indra's heaven, &c.); it is also the ordinary pandits' word for a very lovely woman. *Shánts* means a very abstemious, honest, devout person.

[9] The narrator's word here was *rákhus* = the Sanskrit *rákshasa*. As far as he remembered, the Musalmán who told him the story mentioned the word *jinn*. Cf. notes to *Wide-Awake Stories: jinn*, p. 318, and *ogre*, p. 327.

marauding expedition, and doubtless will return at evening. Ah me! Ah me!" whereon she fell to weeping bitterly, and it was with great difficulty that the prince persuaded her to lift her lovely face and hope for the best.

"But tell me of yourself," she said. "Who are you? Whence came you? How came you hither? And tell me quickly, that I may know your state and hide you safely before the ogre's return; for did he but get a glimpse of you his appetite would be rekindled and he would devour you. Think not of escape by any other means. If you had the strength of many men, and could travel as a bird, yet you could not fly from this powerful monster, who passes over the way of a year in one day."

So the prince hastily recounted all that had happened to him:—

A cruel fate forced me from home,
Far in a foreign land to roam;
There I became most wise and great,
And raised to second in the State.

In time my heart began to yearn
Unto my kindred to return;
To see again my home, and there
To tell them of my fortune fair.

But God had other will than I:
Three times have I been like to die;
Three times I 'scaped to different soil,
Sick and alone to mourn and toil.

Yet God is gracious still to me,
That He hath brought me unto thee;
Here let me tarry thee beside,
Here let me evermore abide.

The woman consented, and immediately told him to follow her inside the cave, where she would hide him. She put him in a strong box that was kept in one of the innermost recesses of the cave, and locked it up, with a prayer that God would protect him.

Towards evening the ogre arrived, and being tired, he at once stretched out his massive limbs upon the ground, while the woman, with a large pointed piece of iron, picked his teeth, which were crammed full of bits of flesh and bone, shampooed [10] his arms and legs, and in other ways coaxed and wheedled him. As luck would have it, the ogre was in a good temper that night. "Thanks, a thousand thanks!" the woman said to herself, "the prince will escape for this night." But, alas! she had scarcely encouraged this hope before the ogre's keen sense of smell detected a man in the cave.' [11] He said:—

A man there is within this place,
Oh! let me quickly see his face.

To which the woman answered:—

In vain, my lord, these words to me;
For here a man could never be.

But the ogre was decided, and continued:—

Woman, my nose is never wrong;
So see that you delay not long.

Nothing daunted, however, the princess replied:—

What power have I to make a man?
Find such yourself here if you can.

And added:—

All the day long have I sat here,
And seen no living creature near.

These answers made the ogre very angry; so now, with a terrible and flushed countenance and awful rolling eyes, he looked at her, and said:—

---

[10] *Muth dyun*, to rub and percuss the whole surface of the body in order to mitigate pain or to restore tone and vigour. Coolies in Kashmír, after a long march, throw themselves upon the ground and get their fellows to trample, &c., upon them. (The word for rubbing, polishing, and thrashing or trampling corn by the feet of oxen is the same as in Persian, *málish.*)

[11] The words used were *insánah sunz mushk áyí tamis*, *i.e.*, the smell of a man came to him. For a survey of the incidents concerning ogres in Indian Folk-tales cf. *Wide-Awake Stories*, pp. 395-397.

A man there is within this place!
Unless I see him face to face,
Within two minutes more you die,
As surely, wretch, as now you lie!

Terrified by his frightful words and looks, the poor woman, pale and trembling, asked him whether he had not met with sufficient prey, and therefore wanted a man for eating; whereupon the ogre answered that he was not hungry, but he was certain that there was a man within the cave, and rest he could not until this man was discovered. Then the princess, pale and trembling, so that she could scarcely speak, told him that perhaps it was true; at all events, since the ogre was so decided, she would have a good search in every hole and corner.

Finally, after much rummaging and turning out, during which the ogre impatiently waited, now belching and then coughing, so that the very cave even seemed to shake with the noise, a man was pulled forth from a box at the end of the cave.

"Ha! ha! Yes, humph! I thought so," said the ogre, as the prince approached him.

The priuce was ordered to sit down and explain himself, which he did with such a fearless grace, that the ogre was quite pleased with him. Encouraged by the ogre's good temper, the princess confessed the whole truth of the matter—how that the prince had been shipwrecked and wandered thither, and how she had been moved with compassion and told him to reside in the cave; and then she begged the ogre to spare him and allow him to dwell there, as she felt so very sad and lonely at times; and, besides, the man was skilful and clever, and would serve the ogre faithfully and well. The ogre agreed, and said that neither of them need be afraid, as he should never be tempted to eat such a skeleton of a fellow as the prince seemed to be. Hearing this, the prince sat a little nearer the ogre, and joined the woman in rubbing and pressing the monster's hands and feet; and the ogre got more pleased with him. And so the prince lived in the cave, and became ever more and more fond of the princess, even as the princess became more and more fond of him; and the days passed very happily. Every morning the ogre went forth for his prey, and left the prince and princess alone; and every evening he returned, to be pampered and served by them.

Generally he brought back with him some rare fruit or precious jewel, or anything that the prince and princess asked of him or expressed a wish for. However, there was always a lingering fear lest in a moment of rage or indisposition the ogre should devour them, and so they were always thinking of some plan to rid themselves of him. They soon discovered that might would not overcome him, and that if they would take him they must trick him into telling them the secret of his life, —in what his great strength lay, and therefore they determined if possible to find out this thing. One evening, when they were cleaning the ogre's teeth and shampooing his limbs, the princess sat down beside him and suddenly began to weep.

"Why weep you, my darling?" said the ogre. "Tell me your distress, and I will relieve it to the utmost of my power." Saying this, he drew her to him in tender embrace.

"I cannot tell you all my thoughts," she replied, "but sometimes I fear lest you be slain, and we be left alone here in this solitary cave, without a comforter or friend; for then starve we must,—because who could bring us food? Moreover, you have been so good to us, filling our stores with the choicest provisions, and satisfying our every wish, that our hearts are one with thine. What could we do and how could we live if you were slain and lost to us?"

The ogre laughed heartily on hearing these words, and replied that he should never die. No power could oppose him; no years could age him; he should remain ever strong and ever young, for the thing wherein his life dwelt was most difficult to obtain, even if it should be known. This was just the reply that the woman wanted, and so, smiling most sweetly and affectionately, she praised God for this assurance of the ogre's safety, and then entreated him to inform her of this thing. The ogre, nothing suspecting, complied, and said that there was a stool[12] in the cave and a honeycomb upon the tree yonder. He mentioned the stool, because if anybody would sit upon it and say whither he or she wished to go it would at once transport them thither. He mentioned the honeycomb because if any person could climb the tree and catch the queen-bee within it, then he, the ogre, must die, for his life was in that bee. But the bees within that honeycomb were many and fierce, and it was only at the greatest risk that any person would dare to attempt this thing.[13] "So you see," added the ogre, "you weep without cause. I shall never die."

Then the woman smiled with joy, and told the ogre how thankful she was, and how henceforth she should abide in peace, happy by day and happier at night, when he returned; and how glad she was that he had told her of the stool and the honeycomb, for although there was not the slightest cause for fear concerning their safety, yet she should have pleasure in especially guarding them —remembering that his dear life was holden in them. After some further conversation they all arranged themselves for sleep.[14]

[12] *Pith* was the word used. Cf. *Indian Fairy Tales*, p. 156; *Madanakamárájankadai*, p. 29; the fifth story in *Baital Pachísí*; *Wide-Awake Stories*, p. 425; also tale of the "Ivory City and its Fairy Princess," "Brave Princess," and "Saiyid and Said," in this collection.

[13] This species of bee manifests such fury and determination on being annoyed as to make it a very formidable enemy. A large nest (honeycomb) was hanging from the roof of the Mission Hospital at Srínagar for a long time. No one would remove it. The natives everywhere are terribly afraid of them. Now and again cattle are stung to death by them. Wilson, in the *Abode of Snow*, p. 14, mentions the case of an Englishman who was so severely stung by these insects that he died from the effects. Many such cases have from time to time been reported.

[14] Cf. tale, "Prince Lionheart and his Three Friends," in *Wide-Awake Stories*, pp. 58–60; also tale of "True Friendship" in this collection; also "Life Index" in *Wide-Awake Stories*, pp. 404, 405.

On the following morning the ogre went out as usual. Before midday the prince and princess concluded their arrangements for bringing about his death. The prince was to do the deed. He clothed himself from head to foot most carefully. Every part was well covered except his eyes. For these a narrow horizontal aperture was cut in the cloth which was wrapped about his face. Thus prepared he sat on the stool, and soon was seen floating away in the direction of the tree. It was an exciting moment when he lifted the stick to strike the honeycomb. It seemed as if thousands of bees came out and attacked him; but he was thoroughly protected, and so cared only for his eyes. His purpose was to catch the queen-bee and to crush her, and thereby crush out the life of the ogre. He succeeded; and no sooner had he dropped the lifeless bee than the ogre fell down stone-dead upon the ground with such force that all the land around trembled with the shock. The prince then returned to the cave on the stool, and was welcomed by the princess with much rejoicing and congratulation. Still there was fear lest the shock which they felt should only have been an earthquake, and the ogre, having told them a lie, should return. But the evening arrived, and then the night; no ogre turned up; and so they felt sure that they were rid of their enemy; and gathering together the special treasures which were in the cave, they both sat together on the stool, and were quickly carried away miles distant to the spot where the ogre's carcass lay stiff and cold, stretched out to a tremendous length upon the ground. Reassured by this sight, the prince bade the stool to carry them to the place where his three wives were, living or dead. The stool obeyed, and they were quickly landed close by the king's garden. The prince at once rose from the stool, and, telling the princess that he would presently return, asked her to remain. He had not gone far before some poisonous insect alighted on him and stung him, so that he then and there got the disease of leprosy.[15] What was he to do now? For very shame he could not return to the stool. The princess waited until her patience was exhausted, and then speaking to the stool, she was borne within the garden, and descended right by the very place where the other three wives of the prince sat silent and sorrowful. She too did not say anything, but wept aloud. Directly she entered the garden the flowers bloomed magnificently and gave forth the most delicious perfumes, while the trees were so richly laden with fruit that they could scarcely hold up.

When the head-gardener came round as usual the next morning, lo! he saw such a sight as he had never expected. At last the flowers were in the fullest bloom, and the trees were covered with the most splendid fruit; and as he was leaving the garden to go and tell the king of this good news he beheld another woman sitting and weeping. He asked her who she was and whence she came, but never a word came forth from her mouth. So he said to the king, "Behold, O king, a fourth woman has entered the royal garden, and now it is perfect. Your Majesty will, perhaps, come and see this great sight."

The king was exceedingly glad, and rose up hastily to accompany the head-gardener to the garden. On reaching it he saw the four women, and questioned all of them, but not one of them answered a word. Then the king, after inspecting the garden, returned to the palace and informed the queen of these strange visitors, and begged her to go and see them on the morrow; perhaps they would converse with one of their own sex, with her the

[15] *Kyúm* was the word, but this is used generally for any and every insect and small reptile. I heard some time ago that natives, especially Hindús, believe that if the urine of a bat falls upon any person it at once gives leprosy. The word for leprosy in Kashmírí is *myund.* Strabo (*Geógraphika*, xv. 1, 37, cf. J. W. M'Crindle's *Megasthenés*, p. 56) tells us that there are in some parts of the country serpents two cubits long, which have membranous wings like bats. They fly about at night, when they let fall drops of urine or sweat, which blister the skin of persons not on their guard with putrid sores. Elian (*Hist. Anim.*, xvi. 41) gives a similar account.

queen. On the morrow the queen went and spoke kindly to each of the women, but not one of them replied. The only notice they appeared to take of Her Majesty's words was to weep the more. The queen was very disappointed, and knew not what to think of them. "Undoubtedly they were very holy women," she said, "or God would not have thus signally blessed their coming to the garden. Perhaps they had been betrayed by some foul monster or bereaved of one most dear. It could not be because of their sins that they thus wept. It might be, if the king sent a certain very holy man to them, that they, perceiving in him a kindred spirit, would hold conversation with him." The king agreed, and this very holy man was sent. But he returned also, and said that he could not get them to speak. Then the king issued a proclamation that great rewards and honours would be bestowed on the person who should succeed in making these women speak.

Now the prince, who was suffering terribly from leprosy, and loathsome to behold, heard of this royal proclamation, and inquired from a man who chanced to pass by that way, "Is this true?" Said he, "I will cause these women to converse with me." This matter was reported to the king, who at once, attended by a large number of courtiers and servants, came and wondered at the presumption of the wretched leprous man. However, as he did not know the mind of God, he told the man to go and speak with the women. The leprous man went and sat down before the first woman, and begged her to listen to his tale:—

"Once upon a time there was a certain great king who had four wise and clever sons. One day the king called these sons to him to ask them each separately by whose good fortune it was that he ruled and prospered. Three of the sons replied, 'By your own good fortune, of a surety, O king, do you reign over so vast a kingdom and prosper in your rule.' But the fourth and youngest son gave answer, 'By my good fortune, O king, and not another's.' Exceedingly angry with this answer, the king banished his youngest son, who, with his wife and a few necessaries, immediately left the palace. After some weeks' residence in the jungle and wandering by the wayside they arrived at the sea, and longing much to live upon the water, they told their affairs to a certain merchant, who had pity upon them and gave them free passage in one of his ships. Things went on most happily for a time, until one night the ship was wrecked and all were drowned except the prince and princess. These were saved by clinging to the spars and rafters of the ship, but were carried in different directions, the prince to one country and the princess to another."

For the first time for many years this woman was seen to lift up her head; and when the leprous man inquired what reward she would give him if he brought the prince her husband there, she readily replied, "Ask what you will and it shall be given you."

When the king and his company saw the woman speaking and looking quite happy he was much surprised. At the same time, also, through God's mercy, the pus, which was escaping from the man's leprous sores, stopped.

Then he went and sat down beside the second woman and asked her to listen to his tale:—

"In a certain country there lived a gardener—the royal gardener—in whose house a beggar prince from some distant country chanced to arrive. This prince became the gardener's servant; but making himself so thoroughly useful, and being of a noble and gentle mien, he soon became the gardener's son-in-law. One day the daughter of the king of that country saw the prince —though she knew not that he was a prince—and begged her mother to solicit the king to marry her to him. After full inquiries the king discovered that he was a great and clever man, and therefore assented to his daughter's request, and made great preparation for the wedding. The wedding took place, and there was great rejoicing, and the new prince prospered exceedingly and grew more and more popular both with the king and people. Only his brethren envied him. At last, tired of their envy and seized with an irrepressible longing to visit his home and country, he left with his wife in a ship then about to sail for the desired haven. Alas! the ship was wrecked, and only two persons were saved out of the whole ship's company—the prince and princess, who escaped on two pieces of board. One landed in one country and the other landed in another country."

For the first time for many years the second woman lifted her head, and when the man inquired what reward he should have if he could bring the prince before her she replied, "Ask what you will and I will give it to you."

When the king and his company saw the woman's happy face, and that her lips moved, they were much surprised. At the same time, also, the man's leprous sores closed up and looked as if they would soon heal.

Then the man went and sat by the third woman and begged her to hear his story:—

"In a far-distant city there resided a certain rich merchant, who had pity upon a poor traveller whom he had noticed standing one day by his shop, and made him his servant; but afterwards, finding that he was so wise and good, and that the business prospered by his means, he made him his son-in-law. In course of time the son-in-law wished to visit his home and country, and so left with his wife, promising to return soon. But, alas! alas! the vessel went down with all hands except the prince and his wife, who escaped upon planks and timber from the wreck, one reaching one country and the other arriving at another country."

When the woman heard these things she lifted her

head, and when she further heard that the prince was alive and near the place, she entreated the man to show him to her and she would give him a great reward.

When the king and his company saw the third woman's happy face and ready speech they exceedingly wondered. At the same time, also, the sores of the leprous man thoroughly dried up and were like to altogether disappear.

Then the man went and sat down beside the fourth woman and asked her to listen to his story:—

"In a certain jungle resided a great ogre who had captured a beautiful girl, a king's daughter, and kept her for his own service and amusement. By chance one day a man arrived at the entrance of the cave where this woman was sitting and lamenting her lot. He inquired why she wept, and she told him all that had happened to her. Both being clever and beautiful, they quickly entertained affection for one another, and by the evening, when the ogre usually returned from his excursions, finding that the man would not leave her, she concealed him in a box. However, the ogre discovered him, but did not eat him, seeing that he was pale and thin; he kept him there as a servant. By-and-by the princess discovered the secret of the ogre's life, and the prince accomplished his death; and then they both, the prince and the princess, sat on the ogre's enchanted stool, and were transported to within a short distance of this place. Then the prince left the princess and never returned, because a foul leprosy had attacked him and so changed his whole appearance, that when the princess came and looked upon him a few hours afterwards she did not recognise her husband, but turned aside within this garden and wept."

On hearing this story the woman stopped crying, looked up, and lo! she beheld her lost loved husband; for now every trace of leprosy had passed from him, and he was the same handsome, wise-looking, noble prince that he ever was.

After much embracing they then both went together to the third wife, the merchant's daughter, and the prince was also recognised and embraced by her; likewise, too, by the second and first wives. Oh what a time of rejoicing it was for the prince and all his wives, who had never expected to see one another again!

Now, when the king and his attendants saw this they were more surprised than before; for here was not only the man who had made them speak, but the evident husband of them all. He seemed also a man of great learning and of noble birth.

"Who art thou?" inquired the king, now drawing near. "Tell me thy history, and all that has happened to thee."

Then the prince recounted to him his whole life—how he had left his home, how he had married with these four women, and how they had all been brought together there.[16]

The king was intensely interested by the account, and invited the prince and his four wives to come and stay at the palace. Everything they wished for was provided for them, and the prince became so much in favour with the king that he was entreated to permanently take up his abode there and promised the kingdom after the king's death. To the great joy of the king the prince consented, and went daily to the *darbár*. Fresh plans were now attempted, new laws fixed, and other great improvements made, so that the kingdom became exceedingly great and prosperous. Wishing to be more thoroughly allied with one so great and good as this

[16] Notice that the marriage with the gardener's daughter is not recognised, nor is she sent for when the prince arrives in his own country. On being asked the reason, the narrator simply answered, "It was so, *sáhib.*" I see, however, that the same thing occurred in the story of "The Boy with the Moon and Star," given in *Indian Fairy Tales*, p. 135. Perhaps the other wives despised her because of her humble birth, and therefore she was deposed.

prince, the king sought to marry him with his only daughter. The queen, the prince, and all the court accepted the king's wish, and the marriage was eventually celebrated with great rejoicing. And thus affairs continued increasingly happy and increasingly prosperous.

The prince, however, was not satisfied. He desired to know of his country and his father's house. Accordingly messengers were sent to make inquiries, and after a long time they returned, saying that the king the prince's father's country had been conquered by strangers, and that the king and all the royal family had been taken prisoners.[17] When he heard this the prince's heart was filled with remorse for not having sent before to ask concerning them. He now determined to make war against these foreign conquerors, and for this purpose he sought help from his royal fathers-in-law. Money and troops were liberally granted him, and at length he started with the prayers and good wishes of every one in the kingdoms of all his fathers-in-law. It was a long and difficult journey, but the prince and his army safely reached their destination, and immediately commenced battle with the foreign king's army. They fought for days, and there was much bloodshed on both sides, but at last the prince got the victory. He at once released his father and brethren; but they did not recognise him until he told them that he was the fourth son and the banished prince. "The king, my father," said he, "banished me for saying that he held the kingdom by my good fortune. And was it not true, O king?" he added. "Directly I left the kingdom I heard that it was taken away from you, and that you were cast with your family into prison; and now as soon as I return unto you, behold you are free again, and the monarch of a large and powerful kingdom."

[17] It will be remembered that the prince had heard this account before he started on his first voyage. I noticed this to the narrator, and expressed my surprise that such a good and wise prince should have so long delayed avenging his father's and family's imprisonment and trials. "Perhaps the sea intervening prevented him," was the answer.

"True, O son!" replied the king feebly. "We wronged thee. 'Twas not the pride and haughtiness of thy heart, but of our hearts, and God has sorely punished us for it;" and then, locked in each other's embrace, they forgot all their past trials in present joys.

As the king was now very old and infirm it was arranged that the prince should henceforth occupy the throne, while minor estates and offices should be given to the other princes. All being in a good temper and most grateful to the prince for having delivered them, this was most readily agreed to. Accordingly the prince sent word to the different kings, his fathers-in-law, advising them not to expect him, but to send his wives, as he was now ruling over his own father's kingdom. Congratulations poured in from all sides; the wives safely arrived; and the prince, now a mighty king, and increasing in wisdom and power continually, passed the rest of his years in peace.[18]

[18] Cf. the interesting paper on "The Outcast Child" in *Folk-Lore Journal*, vol. iv. pp. 308–349.

GAGAR WOL AND HIS SERVANT RATUN.

I.[1]

GAGAR WOL was once going to a village, of which he was the *kárdár*,[2] attended by his servant Ratun. While on the march this foolish fellow suddenly remembered that it was pay-day, and running for his *qalamdán*[3] and paper, asked him to write an order for his wages. Of course he was told to wait till they had reached their destination and rested a little. They arrived at the village late in the evening, but although it was so late, Gagar Wol summoned the *muqaddam*,[4] *patwárí*,[5] and other officials and took their accounts. Meanwhile Ratun got very drowsy; he could hardly keep his eyes open; but as his duty was to remove his master's turban every night before he retired, he dared not go to sleep. At length he could bear it no longer, and therefore went right up to Gagar Wol while he was sitting in the midst of the village officials, and taking off his turban, hung it up on a peg. Instead of being angry with the man Gagar Wol only laughed, as indeed did all the company. It seemed so ridiculous for him, a great man, to be sitting there bareheaded and surrounded by people. When Ratun saw his master laugh he thought within himself,

[1] Narrator's name, Paṇḍit Ánand Kol of Srínagar.

[2] *Kárdár* is the overseer of a village, a Government officer, whose duty is to collect the Maháràjá's share of the grain.

[3] *Qalamdán* (generally pronounced *kalamdán* in Kashmír) is a small box containing inkstand, pens, paper-knife, &c., generally carried by the official, or his servant, everywhere he goes.

[4] *Muqaddam* (pronounced *mukaddam* in Kashmír) is the chief man of a village.

[5] *Patwárí* is an official belonging to a village whose business it is to keep an account of the various crops reared by the villagers.

"Ha! he is rested now. I will go and get my wages." Accordingly he returned with some paper and asked him to write an order for the amount.

II.[6]

One day Gagar Wol laughed aloud, as though he was specially glad about something.

"Why do you laugh?" asked Ratun.

"Because I have just made a hundred rupees by cutting the paper[7] of these village accounts," replied he, meaning that he had falsified the accounts to that amount.

"Ha, ha!" thought Ratun, "how easily earned! I will do the same on the first opportunity."

Accordingly, as soon as Gagar Wol went out for his constitutional, Ratun took the scissors and cut his master's account-book to pieces. Of course he did not get anything. He was very angry at this, and when his master returned he went up to him and said, "You are a liar. You said that you got a hundred rupees by cutting the account-books. Look, I have done the same, but cannot find a *páṅsa*." On saying this he threw down the pieces of the account-book that he had cut and left the room. When Gagar Wol saw what the foolish fellow had done he nearly went mad, because all his accounts, receipts, disbursements, everything were written in it.

III.[8]

One day Gagar Wol went to a graud feast, accompanied by his servant Ratun. During the feast a servant of one of the guests said to his master, in the hearing of everybody, "A bulbul has alighted on the stem of a flower;" by which he meant that a grain of rice had

[6] Narrator's name, Paṇḍit Lál Chand, Khunamuh.

[7] The word used here was *kághaz-buri*.

[8] Narrator's name, Paṇḍit Lál Chand, Khunamuh.

fallen on his master's beard. His master understood, and brushed it off. All the guests, of course, admired the servant's speech, and wished they had a servant like him. After the feast Gagar Wol went outside, and Ratun followed him.

"Look here, Ratun," said he, "mind you remember to say what that servant said when a grain of rice falls on my beard."

"All right," replied Ratun.

Not long afterwards Gagar Wol was invited to another feast, and took the ever-faithful Ratun with him. While eating he purposely let fall a grain of rice on his beard.

"Oh, sir," said Ratun, "that thing you spoke to me about outside So-and-so's house the other day is on your beard;" whereupon all the guests laughed aloud.

IV.[9]

ONE day Gagar Wol was very angry with his servant for boiling the rice so badly, and told him to inform him the next time the rice was ready for straining, so that he might show him how to do it properly. On the morrow Ratun kindled a fire as usual, and began to boil the rice and other things, while Gagar Wol went to the *kharman*[10] of the village to examine the stores. When the rice was ready for straining he went and called his master. He did not go right up to him, as any ordinary servant would have done, but stood with the lower part of his body behind a tree some way off and shook his head to Gagar Wol to come. But Gagar Wol did not notice him so far away, so the stupid servant waited there for more than three hours. At length Gagar Wol finished his work, and was returning to his lodgings, when he saw his servant sitting down by a tree and looking very miserable.

[9] Narrator's name, Paṇḍit Lál Chand, Khunamuh.

[10] *Kharman*, the Government granary in any place.

"Why are you sitting there?" he asked. "How is it you are not cooking my dinner?"

"O master," replied Ratun, "you ordered me to give you notice when the rice was ready for straining. Accordingly I came here, and have been nodding my head to you to ask you to come, until now it is ready to fall off. Alas! alas! by this time the rice will all be burnt as black as charcoal."

And sure enough it was so!

V.[11]

ONE day Gagar Wol visited a certain village, accompanied by his man Ratun. On arrival he called the chief man of the place and asked him to give him some *dál*[12] for his dinner. The farmer, anxious, like all other people, to ingratiate himself in the favour of the collector, gave the servant one *kharwár's*[13] weight.

What do you think the stupid Ratun did with it? He went and cooked every grain of it—a mighty feast indeed, thirty or more big earthen pots of steaming *dál!*

[11] Narrator's name, Prakásh Rám, Suthú, Srínagar.

[12] *Dál* is a kind of pulse.

[13] *Kharwár* is 192 lbs. Concerning any unnecessary extravagance Kashmíris generally quote this man. *Rutnun sas*, Ratun's *dál*, is a well-known saying in the Valley.

THE WICKED QUEENS.[1]

THERE was a king who had three wives, two of whom he loved more than the other, because they had borne him two daughters, but the third wife had not borne him anything. At length the third wife became pregnant, and the two other wives were in such great fear lest she should give birth to a son, that they plotted with the midwife to make-away-with the baby, if a boy should be born. The midwife was to change the child for a bird, or a stone, or the young of any animal.

A few days before her confinement the queen sent for the midwife and entreated her to say whether a male or a female child would be born. The woman replied that neither a male nor a female child would be born, but a certain kind of bird. She added that she could not tell how this would be, but she had a fairly sure presentiment that this would be the case. On hearing this the queen was very sad, and begged the midwife to keep the matter perfectly secret, that it might not reach the ears of the king. The woman promised, and advised her to say that the child was stillborn, if anybody should ask about it. Accordingly when the hour of her delivery drew near the queen gave orders that the midwife only should be present. As was expected, a son was born, but the midwife hid the child and showed the queen a young crow instead, saying, "See, my words are fulfilled. Do not be anxious about it. I will at once go and hide it. Nobody shall know of this."

1 Narrator's name, Makund Báyû, an old Musalmán shepherd at Suthú, Srínagar, who heard it from Krĕndih, near Bijbihára.

Thus saying, the wicked woman took up the child and the young crow and went and showed them to the two other wives of the king, who were very glad, and promised her a great reward.

These two wives quickly put the infant into a box and threw it into the river, hoping that the box would sink, and that there would be an end of the matter. But the box did not sink. By the kindness of Parameshwar it floated on the water and was picked up by an old gardener, who opened it and took out the child. Having no children of his own, he was delighted to find such a lovely boy, and gladly procured a woman to feed it and look after it for him.[2]

Another year passed by, and the third wife was soon expecting another confinement. Jealous and fearful lest this also should be a boy, the two other queens again arranged with the midwife to deceive the mother and steal the child. Again it happened that a boy was born; but the midwife declared that a young crow had been brought forth, and left the room at once to hide it, that it might not be known to the king and the rest of the royal household. She carried the child to the two wicked queens, who treated it the same way they did the first baby; but by the mercy of Parameshwar the box floated on the water to the same place as the other box, and was picked up by the same old gardener, who gladly adopted the child also.

Before another year had elapsed the third wife was again hoping for a child. But, alas! her hopes were only formed to be crushed. Encouraged by their former successes, the two other queens bribed the midwife to change the child; so that when the third wife gave birth to twins, a little boy and a little girl, the wretched woman declared that the queen had been delivered of a pair of

[2] Cf. *Indian Fairy Tales*, p. 121; *Old Deccan Days*, pp. 256, 302; *Story of Sassí wa Punnún*; sixty-fourth *Story of Dastán i Amír Hamza*; also tale of "The Jogi's Daughter" in this collection.

puppies,[3] and hastened out of the room as before on the pretence of burying them out of sight. These two infants also were treated in the same way as their predecessors, but by the mercy of Parameshwar they too reached the same kind shelter. No tongue could describe the intense grief of the queen when she found herself thus thrice disappointed. She did not care to see any person or to eat anything, but wished to die.

A few nights after this, when the two other queens were talking with the king, they told him about the strange creatures that had been born to him by his other wife. His Majesty was very much surprised and disgusted at their words, and sent immediately for the midwife to inquire whether they were true. The midwife affirmed that they were true, whereupon the king at once gave orders for the banishment of the poor queen as soon as she could be removed. However, she was not banished. The palace servants suspected that this was all owing to the trickery of the other queens, whom they knew to be jealous of their favourite mistress, and therefore they persuaded the king, for the sake of his own good reputation, not to send the woman out of the country, but to build for her a house in some distant garden, and to give her sufficient money for her maintenance. The king complied, and this was done.

The children were well looked after by the old gardener. They all grew up to be quite big, and were sent to school. The boys were also instructed in the business of gardening.

One day a wise old woman, who made it her business to collect all the gossip of the place, and to retail it out to anybody who would listen to her and give her money, visited the two wicked queens. Knowing her to be a wise woman, they asked her why they did not get any sons, and begged her to call a holy man who could help

[3] Cf. *Folk-Tales of Bengal*, p. 242; *Old Deccan Days*, p. 17; *Indian Fairy Tales*, p. 121; the tale of "Háya Band and Zuhra Khotan" in this collection; also *en passant* Sebillot's *Cartes Populaires*, vol. i. p. 124.

them to the fulfilment of their desire. The woman replied that it was vain for them to try to alter the will of the Deity. Whom He would He denied, and whom He would He blessed. And then she mentioned the case of the gardener who had become possessed of a little family of three boys and one girl that were brought to him in boxes on the river. When they heard these words the two queens were much astonished. They inquired what the gardener had done with them, whether he had educated them, and if they were living in his house. The old woman told them everything—how beautiful they all were, how clever, and how the three boys were working in the old man's garden, and how devoted they were to their sister. The two queens pretended to doubt the sincerity of the boys' devotion to the girl, and therefore begged the old wise woman to try their affection by persuading the girl to ask them for a beautiful bird that was to be had for the seeking. "It is a wonderful bird," they said, "and the girl will not fail to desire it, for the creature speaks like a human being, and sings as no other creature on earth can sing." They promised to give the woman a very handsome reward if she would do this thing for them. The old woman said that she would, and then left.

She soon became friendly with the girl and informed her of the wonderful bird, and the girl was so excited by her accounts of its doings that she had no peace day or night for wishing to possess it. The three brothers noticed their sister's unhappiness, and inquired the cause of it. They determined that one of them should go in search of the bird. The eldest brother set out first, because they could not all be spared at one time from the work of the garden. His way led through a jungle, where he met a *shikárí*, and asked him if he knew the whereabouts of the bird. The man told him that he did know, but warned him of the danger of the undertaking. "Many people," said he, "have essayed to go there, but have died on the road." The boy, however, was not to be daunted. He was determined to get the bird, and therefore again asked the way. So the *shikári* showed him, and he went on. He next reached a very large plain, where he did not come across a single human being except a *jogí*, to whom he revealed all his heart. The *jogí* ordered him not to attempt the journey; but the boy would not be dissuaded, and therefore entreated the holy man to show him the way and let him go. Then the *jogí* gave him a pebble and a little earthen pot, and told him to throw the pebble on before and to follow its leadings. The pebble, he said, would guide him to the bottom of a great mountain, where he would hear a great noise like the sound of thunder and of a mighty wind. He would probably hear his name called. But he was not to be afraid or to turn back on any account, otherwise he would be changed into a pillar of stone.[4] And when he reached the summit of the mountain he would see a lake of golden water, and on the bank of that lake he would see a tree, and on one of the branches of that tree he would see a cage hanging. In that cage was the bird. On arriving at the tree he must first lay hold of that branch, and then look around to see the way he had come. He was especially to remember this, as afterwards he would certainly forget the path. The bird would ask why he had ventured up there; he was to reply that he had come to take it away. Afterwards all would be safe. If he attended to all these directions he would experience no special difficulty, and would soon return with the bird.

The boy left, and for some distance everything went on well; but when he came to the mountain, and heard

[4] Cf. *Indian Fairy Tales*, pp. 138–152; *Indian Notes and Queries*, vol. iv. p. 186; *Indian Antiquary*, vol. xvi. p. 191; Schmidt's *Griechische Maerchen, Sagen und Volslieder*, p. 106; Tylor's *Primitive Culture*, pp. 147, 377; *Songs of the Russian People*, p. 99; *Tales and Traditions of the Eskimo*, pp. 46, 299. The danger of looking back when going on any especial errand like the above crops up in the tales and practices of many nations.

the loud shoutings and thunderings and the great wind, he turned back, and at once became a stone.

Some days after this the second brother thought that he would go and see what had become of him. He reached the jungle that his brother had passed through, and saw the *shikárí*. He then walked on to the great plain and met the *jogí*. Both of them earnestly advised him not to go. He was also informed of the death of his brother, undoubted proof of which was the return of the pot and the pebble to the *jogí*. When he heard this the boy asked the *jogí* if there was not a remedy for his brother, and the man replied that there was, but that only he who obtained the bird could perform it. "Then give me the pot and the pebble, and let me depart," said the boy. The *jogí* did, and the boy left. He went on all right for a time, like his brother, but when he reached the mountain and heard the awful noises he also turned back, and was changed into a big stone.

Some time afterwards the youngest brother determined to go in search of the missing ones. With a sorrowful but brave heart he bade farewell to his sister and adopted father and started. He came to the jungle and saw the *shikárí*, and then went on to the great plain and saw the *jogí*. He heard from them of the death of his two brothers, and was warned not to attempt the undertaking; but he would not desist. "Of what good, of what pleasure, is life to me without my brothers?" he said in reply to the *jogí's* earnest remonstrances. "Let me have the pot and the pebble, and I will go and try to get possession of the bird, by which the lives of my brothers can be restored and my sister be satisfied."

Accordingly the *jogí* gave him these things and allowed him to depart. The pot and the pebble did not return to the *jogí* this time, for the boy persevered and was not afraid, and did not look back till he reached the top of the mountain. There he saw a lake of golden water and a tree growing on its bank, and on one of the branches of the tree he saw the cage of the bird, whose sweet notes filled the air. On his catching hold of this branch of the tree all the shoutings and thunderings ceased. Not a sound was heard, save the voice of the bird asking him what he had come for and what he desired. The boy answered that he wanted nothing except the bird, and some of the golden water, and the branch of the tree on which the cage was hanging, and that his two brothers should be restored to life. The bird told him to cut that branch off the tree and to fill his pot with golden water. The bird also bade him to get another potful of the water. He would find a pot lying about somewhere. The boy did so, and then, taking the cage and the other things, began to descend. On the way down the bird asked him to sprinkle one potful of water over the big stones that were scattered over the place. The boy obeyed, and straightway all the stones were changed back into men. Kings and princes and many great, brave, and holy people were thus restored to life, and came and thanked the boy and offered themselves as his servants. His two brothers also were restored, and came forward to greet him.[5]

In the course of a day or two a great procession of people approached the *jogí*, with the three boys at their head. When he saw the boys the *jogí* knew that the youngest boy had been successful, and blessed him. A little farther on the *shikárí* came to meet them. They reached the gardener's house in safety, and were welcomed back by the old man and their sister as those who had returned from the dead. The great company of people who had been restored by the youngest brother followed them to the house and would not leave them.

"How can we entertain all these?" said the old gardener.

[5] Cf. *Old Deccan Days*, pp. 15, 62; *Indian Fairy Tales*, pp. 76, 77, 282; *Indian Antiquary*, vol. xvi. p. 191.

"Be not anxious," said the bird. "All things will be supplied."

The words of the bird proved true. Every day food was forthcoming. There was great abundance and great variety of everything, and all the guests were satisfied. As soon as possible the gardener and his three adopted sons had a magnificent house built for their numerous visitors. They also had a big place dug out for a pond, and poured the potful of golden water into it; and they planted the branch of the tree that the youngest brother had brought on the side of the pond, whereupon the hole was filled with golden water and the branch became a most beautiful tree. Prosperity waited on the old gardener and his family. Riches and honour abounded unto them. They possessed more wealth than they could possibly reckon, so that their names became famous throughout the whole world. The king himself visited them, and treated them in every way as his equals.

One day His Majesty asked them to tell him how they had brought the beautiful and clever bird to their house, and the youngest brother related everything. His Majesty also asked how they had become the possessors of so many grand attendants and such immense wealth.

Then the bird spoke, saying, "Hear, O king, and I will speak. These three youths and the beautiful girl whom you see before you are not the children of the gardener, as all people suppose, but are your own children."

"How so?" said the king, very much surprised. "What a chatterer the bird is!"

"O king," replied the bird, "be not angry and I will speak. I am not talking foolishly. These are none other than the four children of your youngest wife, whom you banished from the palace. She did not give birth to young crows and puppies, as your other wives wickedly represented to you. They lied to Your Majesty, lest you should prefer the other queen and despise them. With their own hands they shut up the babies in boxes and threw them into the river, thinking to drown them, but Parameshwar was pleased to save them by the hands of this gardener. Some years afterwards the wicked queens got to know of the existence of the children, and persuaded your daughter, the princess here, through an old wise woman, to wish for me, knowing that I was very difficult to obtain, and that many hundreds of people had lost their lives in trying to get me. They knew that the princes here would certainly try to fulfil their sister's wish, and hoped that they too would perish like the rest. The two elder princes were turned into stones, and would probably have always remained in that petrified state if the youngest prince had not succeeded in reaching me. O king, you have heard my words."

Then the bird ceased speaking, and there was dead silence in the place for the space of several minutes. At length the king spoke:—

"What have I done?" he cried. "Oh, my poor innocent, beloved wife! Why did I listen to the lying words of my other wives and banish you?"

Then the king wept most bitterly, and all the company present wept. As soon as His Majesty returned to the palace he dismissed the two wicked queens and recalled the banished one. The joy of the king and his favourite wife when they were restored to one another and knew themselves to be the parents of three such fine boys and such a beautiful princess cannot be described. Suffice it to say that they lived to a good old age, and were honoured and beloved by every one, and that after them the three princes ruled the kingdom.

A VARIANT.[1]

I WILL tell you a story of two princes. Once upon a time there lived a king who had three wives; but

[1] Narrator's name, Pandit Ánand Rám of Renawárí, Srínagar.

although he had so many wives, yet had he not a son. This was a great trouble to him, because he naturally wished that one of his own blood should rule the country after him. Moreover, he knew no suitable person whom he cared to appoint to this important work. At length, however, the difficulty and trouble seemed about to remove. His third wife became pregnant. Great was the joy of the king when he heard of this. He inquired regularly concerning the queen's state, and constantly repeated orders for every care and attention to be shown to her. As will be imagined, such intense solicitude on the king's part provoked the jealousy of the other queens. They liked not that His Majesty should be always thinking about her and never come near them, and they feared that this state of affairs would continue, and especially so if a son should be born. So they plotted to prevent this.

As soon as they saw their opportunity they called the royal midwife and bribed her to promise to substitute a pup for the child as soon as it should be born. She kept her promise, and the beautiful little boy that was born was carried away and dropped inside a carpenter's shop. When the king heard of this strange birth he was very grieved, and knew not what to do.

After a time the third queen again became pregnant. "Surely now I shall have the desire of my heart!" thought the king, and gave orders, as before, for the greatest care and attention to be taken of the queen. But the other wives' jealousy revived, so that they again arranged with the midwife to change the infant, which wickedness was accordingly done, and the child—a fine little boy—was taken away and dropped in the carpenter's shop like his brother. When the king heard of this second disappointment he lost all patience, and ordered the queen to be banished from the palace. The poor woman was turned off without a *páṅsa* and obliged to beg from house to house for a living.

Meanwhile her two bonnie sons were carefully and affectionately looked after by the kind carpenter, who used constantly to praise God for sending him such treasures.

Some years elapsed, when the boys were one day playing on the roadside near the palace with a wooden horse which their adopted father had made for them; and the king watched them.

"Would that I possessed two sons like these!" he exclaimed. "Come here, you youngsters," he said, calling them. "Would you like to live in the palace and be my servants?"

"No," replied they both unhesitatingly. "We are only the children of a poor carpenter, and are not worthy to engage in so high and important a service."

Thus saying, they turned and ran for a little distance, and then recommenced their play; the king still watching them wonderingly. Presently he saw one of the boys take a spoonful of rice and go to the horse's mouth and say, "Eat it, O wooden horse, eat it whether you will or not." Then he saw the other boy take a cupful of water and go to the animal's tail and say, "Drink, O wooden horse, drink whether you like it or not." The king saw and heard everything, and was astonished at their stupidity.

"Come here again, you youngsters. Come here, and tell me what you are doing," he said. "How can a wooden horse eat and drink? Don't you know better than that yet?"

"Yes," said the boys; and then remembering what they had heard about the strange births of the banished queen, they continued, "O king, how can a woman give birth to a pup?"

The absurdity of the thing suddenly struck the king, and he wondered how he came to believe such nonsense.[2]

[2] Cf. *Tibetan Tales*, p. 141; *Dictionary of Kashmírí Proverbs and Sayings*, pp. 31, 32; Grimm's tale of "The Peasant's Wise Daughter" (which is also one of the *Lithuanian Tales*, Scleicher, No. I.).

"Go away," he said to the boys, and entered the palace.

The following morning he had a special interview with his *wazírs*, and asked them their real opinion of the matter. They all replied that they had never credited the story, but that they had feared to say anything to the king about it. His Majesty then asked them what they thought was the truth of the case, when they told him that undoubtedly the other queens had been jealous of the king's increased attention to the third queen, and therefore had plotted against her; and they advised him to send for the midwife and command her on pain of death to confess what had been done with the children. This was done, and the two reputed sons of the carpenter were brought before him, and proved to be his own boys; whereupon the third queen was immediately recalled, and the two wicked queens sent away.

Henceforth all went happily. The king and his wife lived for many years, and the two princes grew up to be fine, clever, good, and handsome men, a joy to their parents, a credit to their country, and the praise of all.[3]

ANOTHER VARIANT.[1]

ONCE upon a time there lived a celebrated king who had four hundred wives, but no son. The king had a favourite parrot, of which he was exceedingly fond. He always used to send for it on returning from *darbár*, and always seemed unhappy if, for some reason or other, the bird was not near him.

One day one of the *wazírs* was standing by the cage, when he noticed that it was very dirty; so he called a

[3] Cf. "Boy with Moon in his Forehead" in *Folk-Tales of Bengal;* "Punchkin" and "Truth's Triumph" in *Old Deccan Days;* "Bel-Princess" in *Indian Fairy Tales;* seventh story of *Madanakamárájankadai;* also the Greek story, "Das Schloss des Helios," in *Griechische Maerchen.*

[1] Narrator's name, Paṇḍit Chadh Rám of Srínagar.

servant, and taking out the bird, gave him the cage to clean. Meanwhile he thought he would try the parrot's flying powers, and therefore tied a long piece of thread to its leg and let it go. The bird went to the full extent of the thread, and then finding itself hindered cut the thread with its beak and got free. Away it flew, and the *wazír* after it. The poor man determined to follow it and get it if possible, and if not, to go on to another country; for he dared not return to the king without the bird. The parrot led the way past several fields and over a broad river, and then perched on a big shrub that was growing by the water, and got caught by a woman, who carried it to her home. Fortunately the *wazir* saw this, and went after her and got the bird. How glad he was! Out of gratitude to the woman he offered to marry her to the king, and promised to pay all the expenses of the wedding. The woman accepted. Accordingly the *wazír* gave her thirty thousand rupees to prepare her house and clothes, &c., for the occasion, and bade her be in readiness within a few months, when she should hear from him. On reaching the palace the *wazír* informed the king what had happened, and spoke so enthusiastically about the woman's beauty and cleverness, that the king expressed a desire to marry her. The wedding was soon arranged. The king became very fond of his new wife. His affection for her increased when he discovered that she was *enciente.* "At last," thought he, "my desire for a child will be satisfied. May it be a son!" He gave especial instructions for every care and attention to be paid to her, and in other ways showed his great regard for her. . As will be imagined, this extreme anxiety on his part only stirred up the jealousy of the other wives, who determined, if possible, to disappoint him. Some time before the birth they called the midwife and bribed her with jewels and money to substitute a stone for the child as soon as it should be born. This was done, and the baby—a fine little boy—was put into a box and dropped into the river. When the king heard of the strange thing to which his wife had given birth his affection changed into the most intense hatred and disgust. He ordered the woman to be banished to the palace-stables, and to eat barley like the beasts.

On the following morning a very holy man, while performing his ablutions at the riverside, noticed the little box floating down the stream. Curious to know what it contained, he cried, "O box, if thou art of any service to me, come here; if not, go on thy way;" whereupon the box came towards him, and he picked it up and carried it home. On opening it he saw the pretty little child that had been born on the previous evening, and was very glad. He handed the baby over to the care of his wife, and was very thankful to see it thrive and get more and more beautiful.

One day, when the boy was nine years old, he went to play with some other boys in the palace-yard, where he was noticed by the king's wives, who thought how very much he was like His Majesty, and wondered whether he was his son, the child that had been thrown into the river. They called the midwife and pointed him out to her. The woman looked earnestly at the boy's head, and then replied in the affirmative. She recognised him by the peculiar dent at the back of his head, which she noticed at the time of his birth. When they heard this the king's wives were very much alarmed. They feared lest His Majesty should somehow get to know of the boy's existence and punish them for their wickedness. So they earnestly begged the midwife to try and do something to prevent such a disaster, and promised her all sorts of presents.

The woman first found out where the child lived, and then went to the house and introduced herself to his adopted father's wife as her sister-in-law. It was not a very difficult matter to ingratiate herself in this simple woman's favour. Other visits followed, and were so appreciated that at last she was invited to come and stay in the house for a time. While there she often spoke of the boy and praised his good qualities. "But there is one thing that he will not do, I feel certain," she said one day to the proud (adopted) mother. "He will not go to a certain country wherein is a beautiful garden, and in that garden, by the side of a well, a sandal-tree with branches of gold and flowers of pearls. If he will go there and get that tree, his character will be established and his fortune made."

When the boy returned from his play in the afternoon his adopted mother told him what she had heard, and how anxious she was for him to go. The boy agreed, and on the following morning set off on his perilous journey with a few *tsuchih*[2] tied up in his *kamarband*. He walked far and fast till he reached a spring, where he sat down and rested. In a little while a woman came up out of the spring and began to talk with him. She asked him where he was going, and the boy told her; whereupon she begged him not to attempt the thing, as the garden swarmed with *devs* and wild beasts. But the boy would not be dissuaded, and seemed so earnest about the matter, that the woman thought the best thing for her to do was to give him all the help in her power. "Listen," said she. "Since you have set your heart on this matter, it will be needful for you to know that there are two tigers standing by the entrance to the garden, whose hunger you must satisfy with the leg of a sheep; otherwise they will pounce on you and kill you. Do not be afraid of them, but throw a leg of a sheep down before them, and ask them to help you. They will admit you within the garden. You will find many *devs* there, but fear not. Address them as your uncles, say how glad you are to see them, and ask them to help you. They will guide you to the well, around which you will find

[2] Plural of *tsuṭ*, a loaf, bread.

many serpents of different kinds. Do not be afraid of them. Throw a few *tsuchih* and some *zámut dod*[3] on the ground for them, and they will not harm you. The sandal-tree grows by the well. You will not experience much difficulty in bringing it. Go, and prosper."

The boy's path seemed clear enough now. He tramped on with a very merry heart. As soon as he found that he was approaching the garden he provided himself with a leg of a sheep, some *tsuchih*, and some *zámut dod*. Everything that the woman at the spring told him came true. He reached the garden and met the tigers, whom he satisfied with the sheep's leg; he saw the *devs*, and introduced himself to them as their nephew; he saw the serpents, and fed them liberally with *tsuchih* and *zámut dod;* and then he uprooted the sandal-tree and returned. On coming out of the garden one of the tigers went up to him and insisted on his riding home on its back. It was a strange sight—a boy riding a tiger and flourishing a young sandal-tree over his shoulders. The report of his return soon spread through the city, and reached the ears of the king and his wives.

All the people marvelled. But the king's wives did more than marvel; they wept also for fear. They felt certain that His Majesty would soon discover the truth of the matter and punish them. In their distress they again sent for the midwife and entreated her to help them. Accordingly a week or so after his return this woman again visited the wife of the holy man and asked all about the boy's adventures.

"Here is the tree," said the proud adopted mother. "Is he not a brave boy?"

"Yes, certainly," replied the midwife; "but I am sorry that he has not brought the covering, which is kept in an emerald box by the well. You must have this. Without it the tree will perish during the winter. Let the boy go again and get it, and I will praise him."

[3] Curdled milk.

Anxious to please her, and to get all the glory she could for her adopted son, the woman spoke to him about it in the evening, and asked him to attempt a second visit. Nothing daunted, the boy readily complied. He rode on the tiger, which had not returned, and soon reached the spring where he had lain down to rest on his former visit. The woman appeared again and asked him where he was going. He told her; whereupon she again entreated him not to go, saying that this was a more difficult business than before. The box was placed on the edge of the well, wherein dwelt two *sháhmárs*, exceeding great and fierce. However, the boy would not be turned back. When the woman saw his determination, she advised him not to go near the well himself, but to ask one of the *devs* to fetch the box for him; and if he succeeded in obtaining the box he was to come back by the way of the spring and let her know; all which the boy did. He rode to the garden on the tiger, and got one of the *devs* to fetch the box for him, and then came and informed the woman of his success; whereupon she blessed him, and said she would accompany him to his home. What great excitement there was in the city when he returned triumphant a second time from the terrible garden! The king sent for him, and made him his chief *wazír*, and in other ways honoured him.

"Now," thought the king's wives, "we shall most certainly be discovered. What shall we do?"

What could they do, except wait in the most terrible suspense? Their opportunity for seizing him had gone by.

They had not long to wait. One day the *wazír*, advised by the woman of the spring, gave a great feast, and invited the king also. The king accepted the invitation and came. While they were eating, the woman of the spring started up and shouted to the company to keep silence. All eyes were directed towards her, when she said in clear, slow accents, "O king, behold your son, the son of the woman whom you have banished to your stables and made to eat barley, like the beasts of the field! The story of the stone was fabricated by your other wives, who were jealous of the poor woman's state and of your solicitude for her health and safety."

"Is it so?" said the king. "Is this true? Yea, mine own heart tells me that it is true! Banish all these cursed women, and call back the queen to me and to her child; for queen she shall be; none other will I henceforth look to. Behold, a true wife and a beautiful son are born to me in one day! I am happy!"

THE FOUR PRINCES.[1]

In days long since gone by there lived a king most clever, most holy, and most wise, who was indeed a pattern king. His mind was always occupied with plans for the improvement of his country and people; his *darbár* was open to all; his ear was ever ready to listen to the petition of the humblest subject; he afforded every facility for trade; he established hospitals for the sick, *saráe* for travellers, and large schools for those who wished to learn. These and many other such-like things he did. Nothing was left undone that ought to have been done, and nothing was done that ought not to have been done. Under such a wise, just, and beneficent ruler the people, of course, lived very happily. Few poor or unenlightened or wicked persons were to be found in the country.

But the great and good king had not a son. This was an intense sorrow to him, the one dark cloud that now and again overshadowed his otherwise happy and glorious life. Every day he prayed earnestly to Shiva to grant him an heir to sit upon the throne after him. Long and patiently he had waited for an answer, when one day Shiva visited him in the garb of a *jogí*,[2] and was so fascinated with his good and respectful manner that he said, "Ask anything of me, and you shall have it."

1 Narrator's name, Makund Báyú, of Suthú, Srínagar, who heard it from Pandit Mahtáb Jú of Habbah Kadal, Srínagar.

2 Shiva is the great representative *jogí* or *tapasví*; the ideal of what can be attained by the keeping of the body in subjection and by exclusive contemplation of divine things; hence he is the *mahájogí*, and in this character is depicted with ash-covered body, matted locks, and in a most emaciated condition. He sometimes appears to his devotees in the disguise of an ordinary *jogí* or *gosáín*. Cf. *Old Deccan Days*, p. 253; *Indian Fairy Tales*, p. 224; *Baital Pachísí*, pp. 99–101.

"I am in need of nothing," replied the king. "Parameshwar has given me wealth, honour, might, majesty, peace, contentment, everything—yes, everything except one thing, and that who will give me?"

"Are you afraid to ask me for this thing?" said the *jogí*. "Do you know what you are saying, O king?"

"True, true," answered His Majesty, "I speak as one who is (religiously) mad. O holy man, forgive me, and if you have any power with the Deity, I pray you invoke Him on my behalf."

"Be of good cheer," said the *jogí*; "you shall have many sons. Take these four fruits and give them to your wife to eat on Sunday next before sunrise; then shall she give birth to four sons,[3] who will be exceedingly clever and good."

The king took the four fruits and thanked the *jogí*, who then departed.

His Majesty at once went and informed the queen of his interview with the *jogí*. She, of course, was extremely glad to hear the good news. Anxiously they both waited for the following Sunday. On the sunrise of that day the queen ate the four fruits; and according to the word of the *jogí* she presently conceived, and at the appointed time bore four sons. Her sickness and travail, however, were too much for her. As soon as the fourth and last son was born she gave one long, piercing shriek, and gave up the ghost.

Poor woman, to have died just as her long-cherished hopes were being realised! Poor little, forlorn, helpless

[3] Among other extraordinary powers, *faqírs* seem to be able to grant sons to the barren. Some special fruit-eating is the general remedy. In Indian folk-tales some *faqírs* have recommended mangoes; one ordered *líchí* (*Scytalia litchi, Roxb.*), a fruit like a plum, to be eaten; another gives the queen an apple to eat; another a drug which is to be swallowed with juice of pomegranate flower; one old *faqír* gave the queen a barley-corn; another ordered a certain drug; and another sends some medicine to the barren queen. *Indian Antiquary*, vol. xv. p. 369; *Tibetan Tales*, p. 21; *Qissa Agar o Gul* in Urdú; also tale of "True Friendship" in this collection; cf. *Indian Fairy Tales*, pp. 91, 187; *Wide-Awake Stories*, pp. 47, 290; *Old Deccan Days*, p. 253; *Folk-Tales of Bengal*, pp. 1, 117; *Dravidian Nights*, pp. 55, 56.

ones, to be thus left on life's threshold! Poor king, to have his great desire for a son and heir fulfilled, but at the cost of losing his beloved and beautiful wife! Sorrow, like a great dark cloud, seemed to shroud the palace and city for many days, because the king was overwhelmed with grief and would not be comforted.

The four babes were handed over to the tender mercies of four nurses, and they grew up strong, healthy, clever, and beautiful boys. The king was exceedingly fond of them. He appointed the best masters for their instruction, and lavished the most rare and expensive gifts on them. Nothing was too good, nothing was too costly; the greatest trouble and attention were not too much for the king's four beautiful and clever boys.

Meanwhile His Majesty married again, and had other sons by his second wife. But it was a sad day when the king took to him this second wife; because she naturally became very jealous when she saw the first queen's sons growing up so beautiful and wise, for she thought within her heart that they would have the king's favour, and so interfere with her own sons' succession to the throne. Accordingly she determined to ruin their character in the estimation of her husband, or failing that, to somehow or other compass their death.

It has been said that the king was thoroughly engrossed in the desire to improve his country and people. To do this work properly he constantly felt his extraordinary position as a king a great hindrance. Though he very much depended on his ministers and subordinate officials, knowing that for the most part they were honest and just, yet he was convinced that he himself must go in and out among the people, see things with his own eyes, and hear what the people were saying with his own ears, if he would rightly understand their state; and, therefore, he frequently visited towns and villages in different disguises and under cover of the night. In this way he thoroughly ascertained the needs of his subjects, so that they wondered at his sagacity and skill.[4] This continued for some time, until early one morning, while returning from an excursion to a neighbouring village, it commenced to rain very hard. Not having expected this quick and heavy shower, His Majesty was quite unprepared for it; and so, what with the long ride and the mud, he arrived at the palace looking more like a porter than a king. The soldiers at the gate, even, almost allowed him to pass in without the customary royal salute.

The queen at once heard of the king's plight, and when, having changed his wet and muddy garments, he went to her room she met him with a frown.

"Wherefore this frown, my wife?" he said.

"I like not," she replied, "that you, my lord and king, should do these things. They do not become either your position or your age. Why don't you command your sons to do this work? They are grown up, and are good and wise enough to perform it. Command them to do this work, I pray you. Thus shall I be saved much anxiety concerning you, while the affairs of the kingdom will not suffer in the least."

"You have spoken wisely," answered the king. "It is better that I should resign these duties to younger hands—and who are more wise and diligent than my own sons? They too will be kings and rulers some day, and ought to learn experimentally now, while I am alive to direct and help them, what will be expected from them hereafter. I will immediately call them and explain my wishes."

Accordingly the four princes were at once summoned before the king; and when they appeared His Majesty

[4] Many native princes have disguised themselves and patrolled their cities at night. The present Mahárájá's late grandfather, the Mahárájá Guláb Singh, often did so. Cf. also *Folk-Tales of Bengal*, p. 147. Many a tale, also, of the adventures of the great Hárún Ar-Rashíd in disguise is current in the East. Vigne (*Travels in Kashmír*, vol. ii. p. 82) tells a story of Timur Lang one night wandering in disguise about his capital, Samarkand. Cf. also story of "The Diligent King" in this collection.

told them of his conversation with the queen, and that he had determined to hand over this itinerating work to them. "You are younger and stronger than I am," he added. "I trust you will endeavour to fulfil you duties to my satisfaction and to the people's profit."

The four princes expressed their pleasure at this manifestation of their father's confidence in them, and assured him that he should never find that his confidence had been misplaced. Directly that day changed into night they commenced their work of secret supervision. They each had a special round, and whatever was worth notice they reported to the king. Under such a strict and regular supervision it was no wonder that the kingdom continued increasingly happy and prosperous.

But seeds of mischief were being sown at the palace against these princes. The queen was getting more and more jealous of them as she saw her own sons growing into manhood. She plotted in every imaginable way against them. At first the king heeded not her lying insinuations and unkind wishes; but afterwards, overcome by her skill and charms—for the queen was both very clever and very beautiful—he began to speak harshly to the four princes, and now and again he looked with suspicion on them. The princes noticed that the face of their father was being changed towards them, and that there was a marked lack of the trust and affection that had hitherto encouraged them to prosecute unflaggingly their arduous labours.

This state of affairs went on for several months. At last, worn out by unpleasantries by day and watchings by night, the four princes met together to solemnly consider what they should do. They appointed their meeting at midnight, and in a most unfrequented part of the jungle. Each prince told his tale of sorrow, and each one, except the eldest, on the conclusion thereof added, "And now my counsel is, dear brethren, that we fly this part of the country and go whithersoever Parameshwar may lead us. What will be, will be."

"Not so," said the eldest prince. "Stay, my brethren. What foolishness is this that you entertain in your hearts? Not so, not so, I counsel you. You know not what you are proposing. Deprived of sleep, you have become deprived of your wits also. In a sane state of mind you would not speak thus. What! would the sons of the greatest and holiest king that ever sat on the *masnad* [5] disobey their father, and run away like mean, spiritless curs before his commands? No, never!—this is not your meaning. Listen, O my brethren. I warn you not to think any more about leaving your country. Get to your beds and rest. I will watch for this night. To-morrow night another of us will watch, and the next night another, and the night after that another. Thus shall we get more and abundant rest, and the work of supervision will be regularly carried on."

Saying this, the eldest prince wished them all good-night, and started to fulfil his watch. The other princes also left, and being thoroughly impressed by their eldest brother's advice, went home and soon forgot their sorrows in sleep. The next night the second prince went, while the first prince rested, and on the third night the third prince watched, and on the fourth night the youngest prince, while all the others took rest in sleep. This arrangement lasted for many months, and answered well. The princes bore their father's unkindness bravely, and in every way behaved as they should do. Their piety, goodness, and attention to public affairs won praises from everybody, except the king, and the queen who deluded him.

How true is the saying, "Real virtue never continues unrewarded by the gods!" One night, while the eldest prince was going his rounds of inspection, he reached a

[5] A large cushion of velvet, silk, and precious stones doing duty for a throne.

small hut wherein a certain bráhman resided with his wife. The prince noticed them through the open window; and as he watched the bráhman arose, opened the door, and came out. As usual the good man looked up at the heavens, and no sooner had he done so than he turned and rushed indoors again, exclaiming, "*Tráh, Tráh!*"[6]

"What is it?" his wife inquired somewhat timidly.

"Oh," said the bráhman, "I saw the star of our king obliterated by another star."

"What is the interpretation of this sign?" asked the wife.

"It means," the bráhman replied, "that our king will die in seven days from this time."

"Die!" said the bráhmaní, almost in tears. "How will His Majesty die? By sickness, or by the hand of an enemy?"

The bráhman replied, "On the seventh day hence, just after the first watch of the night, a deadly black snake will descend from the sky, and will enter the king's bedroom by the door thereof, that opens out into the courtyard which is on the east side of the palace. This snake will bite His Majesty's toe, so that he will die."

"But surely this must not be," said the bráhmaní. "The king can be delivered from this cruel death. Tell me how his deliverance may be accomplished. Of a truth it cannot be that a king so just and holy and clever as our king is should perish in this way."

"The gods prevent such a disaster!" said the bráhman. "Get me some *gyav* and a few pieces of wood, that I may make an offering to them. For it is written in the *shástras* that if a man, when he knows of any misfortune about to happen to the king, will offer at that time something in the fire to the gods, the king will be saved from the misfortune; otherwise the king will not be saved. Who knows but that our king may be

6 *Tráh, Tráh!* (also Sanskrit), an exclamation denoting "Mercy! pardon!"

spared to us?"[7] So saying, he took the sticks, kindled a fire, and cast the *gyav* into the fire; and then, after many prayers and invocations, rose and, turning to his wife, said, "His Majesty will be delivered if one of his relations will attend to these instructions. The man in whose heart is the wish to do this thing must dig pits in the courtyard that is on the east side of the palace; and some of the pits he must fill with water, and others he must fill with milk. He must also throw flowers into these pools, and on the intervening spaces right up to the door of the king's bedroom. This done, he must be present at the doorstep at the appointed time with a sword in his hand. The snake will surely come, and will swim across the water and the milk, and after passing through these elements and over the flowers, will be rendered comparatively harmless. On the arrival of the snake at the doorstep the man who has taken upon him to perform this work must strike at it with the sword and slay it. After killing the snake he must take some of its warm blood, and going into the king's room, smear it over His Majesty's toes. In this way the king will be preserved from evil; but, alas! who is there to perform these things?"

The prince, whom curiosity had drawn very near to the window of the bráhman's hut, heard everything that was said, and was very much surprised. In the morning he communicated the matter to his three brothers. Not a hint, however, reached the ears of the king. For six nights the four princes continued going their rounds as usual, but on the seventh night the eldest prince begged to be allowed to go out of his turn, because it was in his heart to save the king.

Accordingly he went and dug some pits in the court

[7] *Hom*, a kind of offering by fire, which can be made by bráhmans only. It is an offering for special occasions. The method for making it is as follows:—During the utterance of prayers and invocations, according to the object of the sacrifice, five kinds of wood, together with *darbá* grass, rice, and *gyav*, are kindled and burnt. The fire is kept burning only as long as the occasion for it lasts. The *hom* is a most efficacious offering, compelling the obedience of the gods and changing even Fate.

on the east side of the palace, filled some of these pits with milk and some with water, and threw flowers on every side and right up to the door of the king's bedroom. Then, when everything was ready, he took a naked sword in his hand, and standing on the doorstep, awaited the coming of the serpent. All this had been done after the king and queen had retired to rest.

The first watch of the night had scarcely passed, when the prince, thus standing on the alert, heard a sound as though something had fallen. Presently he noticed the faint movement of some animal through the pools of milk and water; then there was a rustling through the flowers which he had scattered about the palace; and then he descried what looked like the body of a serpent wriggling towards him. Now was the time! The prince tightened his hold on the sword, and as soon as the snake reached the doorstep he cut it in two. He quickly took some of the warm blood of the reptile, and having blindfolded himself, quietly opened the door of the bedroom and entered. He had covered his eyes, because he did not like to look on his father in his private room. Carefully he felt for the toes of their Majesties, and when he had hold, as he thought, of the toes of the king, he smeared some of them with the blood. But he could not see what he was doing, and stained some of the toes of the queen instead. This awoke Her Majesty, who was a very light sleeper; and when she noticed a man leaving the room she shrieked aloud and aroused the king.[8] Presently she noticed some blood on her toes, and imagining that a *rákshasa*[9] had visited them, she became almost frantic with fright. The king also woke just in time to see the figure of his eldest son pass out of the bedroom.

"Yes, yes," exclaimed His Majesty, "it is all true,

[8] Cf. *Folk-Tales of Bengal*, pp. 46, 147, 148.

[9] For other cases of human beings having been suspected of being *rákshasas* and *rákshasís* cf. *Wide-Awake Stories*, p. 396; also story of "Háya Band and Zuhra Khotan" in this collection.

even as you said. Now I am quite assured of the wickedness and deceit of my sons. To-morrow I will order the execution of all four of them. Such wretches must not be allowed to live."

Of course the queen improved the occasion. When she had sufficiently recovered from the shock she reiterated to the king all that she had seen and heard, with sundry additions. She also showed the king her blood-stained toes. These things, together with what His Majesty himself had witnessed, made him resolve on the speedy execution of his sons.

"Undoubtedly," he said, "when my sons found that by themselves they could not harm me during your life-time, they compacted a league with *rákshasas.* May the gods deliver us!"

The queen's joy was now almost complete. At last she thought she had gained the end of her desires! Bright pictures of the future passed before her mental vision. She saw her own sons, great, clever, and wise, ruling in the land, all people praising them and all countries doing them honour. Impatiently she waited for the day when the only obstacles to the accomplishment of this wish would be cleared away.

Very early next morning the king went to the council-chamber, summoned his friends and advisers, and ordered his four sons, now prisoners, to be brought before him. Deprived of their princely robes, their faces and hands soiled from contact with the damp, dirty walls of the dark vault wherein they had been imprisoned for the greater part of the night, they looked very wretched. Still they did not despair. Hope was written on each one of their foreheads.

Not a sound was heard when the four princes entered and walked up to the place appointed for them to wait and hear their sentence. After a few minutes' pause the king, trembling with anger, charged them with having done what was worthy of death, an act which the gods, and therefore he, could not pardon. He accordingly ordered their immediate execution.

On the conclusion of the sentence the executioners ran forward and laid hands on the prisoners. Then some of the ministers and others present took upon themselves to ask what the crime of the four princes might be. But the king would not listen. "Remove these men," he said. "I will explain their crime afterwards."

At this moment one of the four princes signed with his hand and prostrated himself before the throne, as if he wished to say something.

"Let him speak," said the king. "Maybe he wishes to relieve his heart of some foul secret. Let him speak. Let him speak."

The prince said, "O great and merciful king and father, hear me, I beseech you, before I die:—In past times there lived a merchant whose only son grew up to be exceedingly clever and wise in all manner of works, and was also very good. One day the merchant, wishing his son to have a large experience, bade him to make arrangements for going abroad, as it was his intention to send him to some foreign country with merchandise. Within a week the young merchant got ready and started. Many strange people he met with and many wonderful things he saw. I could occupy the attention of Your Majesty and of this assembly for several days in the narration of some of these, but one incident only I ask permission to mention.

"In the course of his journeyings the young merchant met with four men who were wildly disputing with one another over the possession of a poor dog that they were dragging about most unmercifully.

"'Why quarrel-ye thus one with another?' he asked.

"'We are brethren,' said one of the disputants, 'and our father has recently died. We have just been trying to arrange our several shares of the property, and all proceeded most amicably, till we had to decide about this dog. We each have a cow apiece, an equal share of the rice and other grain, an equal number of sheep and goats; but this dog we cannot divide so that each one of us may have an equal portion; and therefore the eldest brother says, 'It is mine,' and attempts to seize it; and I wish to have it, and so lay hands on it; and my other two brothers also think they have a right to it, and try to get it. You wonder, perhaps, that we care to wrangle over such a trifling matter; but this is not an ordinary dog. Each of us would gladly relinquish his right to it had we not learnt that this is no common animal. Our dear father, when on the point of death, bade us sell it for 20,000 rupees; but nobody will give us so much money for it. We took it to the *bázár*, and the people laughed at us for asking such a price. Some thought that we were mad, others thought that we were joking, and a few struck at us for our apparent folly.'

"'Strange story,' said the young merchant, 'very strange! Cannot you possibly sell the dog for a smaller sum?'

"'No,' replied the four brethren most decidedly. 'We could not disobey our deceased father, who charged us so strictly concerning this matter.'

"The young merchant believed them, and thinking that the dog must in some way or other be worth the money, he said, 'I will buy it.' Besides this, his father had warned him not to miss the first purchase or sale, even though it might be to his loss;[10] so he at once took the dog and paid the money. The rest of the way he was very much prospered, and in a few years he returned to his father and country a most wealthy and experienced man.

[10] Kashmírís have a saying, *Guḍanuk sodá gatshih nah ráwarun*, *i.e.*, "One must not lose the first trade." Traders in the Valley, like those of many European cities and all over India, are very superstitious about refusing handsel, or the first bargain or sale of the day. They will often lose rather than give up the first chance of trade.

"He had not been back from his travels very long before his father died. Owing to some mismanagement concerning the property the young merchant suddenly found himself without anything except the clothes in which he stood upright and the dog that cost him so great a sum of money. In the hour of his distress he visited another merchant who was a great friend of the family, and begged him to advance 15,000 rupees on the dog. This merchant readily complied. Taking the money, the young merchant went and traded, and gained for himself another little fortune.

"Meanwhile the other merchant became very fond of the dog. He used to take it about with him by day, and kept it fastened up to a peg in the middle of the court-yard at night. The dog, too, was very fond of his new master, and seemed never so happy as when he was with him.

"One night the animal's sagacity and faithfulness were put to the test. When everybody was asleep and every place was covered with a thick darkness some robbers arrived at the merchant's house. They came along very stealthily. However, the dog's quick ear detected their approach. It barked loudly to wake the household, but no one was aroused. It barked again and again, and yet more loudly, when it saw the robbers enter the house, and ran about most wildly to the full tether of its chain, longing to get free. At last, just as the robbers were departing with their ill-gotten treasure, the chain broke. The dog dashed forward, and would have jumped on them, but seeing that they had arms in their hands, he refrained. He reflected that it might be killed in the affray, and to what purpose? Better, it thought, to follow quietly on behind, to see whither the robbers conveyed its master's things.

"The robbers walked far and fast till they reached an out-of-the-way place in a little jungle, where they stopped, dug a large pit, and therein deposited their treasure, intending to come again and arrange for its distribution as soon as the excitement about the robbery had subsided. When they were quite out of the way, the dog went up to the place and scratched the earth round about, so that he might recognise the spot, and then returned to his master's house.

"On the following morning the merchant rose and found the front door of his house ajar, and all his cupboards and boxes open, and their contents rifled. 'Robbers must have been here,' he cried, and rushed hither and thither tearing his beard and smiting his breast. The neighbours, attracted by the noise, came round and wept also.

"'Alas! alas!' said one, 'would that we had taken more notice of the dog's barking!'

"'Surely it must have awakened you?' said another.

"'No, no,' replied the poor merchant.

"At mention of the dog the merchant took the animal and placed it before him, and like a madman fondled it and talked to it, saying, 'Oh that you could speak and tell me who has taken my goods!' whereupon the dog seized the merchant's right sleeve between its teeth and began to pull towards the door.

"'Perhaps,' remarked one of the neighbours, 'the dog knows where the treasure is concealed. I would advise you to follow its lead.'

"On, on the dog trotted for many a mile, till it came to the place in the jungle where the robbers had buried the goods. There it scratched away and threw up the ground most vigorously. The merchant also, and the few friends who had accompanied him, began to dig at the place. Presently they came on some of the stolen property; and then all of the things appeared! The merchant was overjoyed at the sight.

"As soon as he had got his goods back again in his house and had arranged them in more secure places he wrote to the young merchant the following letter:—

"'To the abode of wisdom and bravery and goodness, beloved of all men, *salám!* After an expression of my intense desire to see you, be it known to you that I am your obliged servant for ever. You let me have a dog some time ago. That dog has just saved me from ruin. I send a request that you will kindly sell it to me. You let me take it as a security for 30,000 rupees, of which amount 15,000 rupees were at once paid you; so I enclose a cheque for the same amount again, making altogether 30,000 rupees. If you will please grant this my request I shall always pray that blessings may wait on you from every side.'[11]

"Having sealed the letter, he placed it within the dog's mouth, and told him to go to his old master.

"When the young merchant saw the dog running towards him he thought that he had escaped, and that therefore his present master would soon follow and demand repayment of the money, which would not be at all convenient just then. So he determined to kill the dog; and then, if the merchant came and asked for his money, he would be able to say, 'Give me back my dog and I will return the money to you.' But grief, a thousand griefs! No sooner had he slain the dog, and taken him up to bury him in some secret place, than the letter fell out of the animal's mouth. The young merchant picked up the letter, and on reading it dropped down insensible."[12]

[11] Specimens of the mode of addressing letters to persons of different rank are given in Vigne's *Travels in Kashmír*, &c., vol. ii. pp. 137, 138.

[12] Evidently a popular story. Cf. story of "Faithful Weasel" in *Kalila u Dimna;* "The Marrí Baloches' Story" in *Punjab Notes and Queries*, vol. iii. pp. 94, 95; "Oudh Legend" in *Indian Notes and Queries*, vol. iv. pp. 46, 150; Sinhalese story in *Orientalist*, vol. i. p. 214; story in the *Hitopadesa* of "The Bráhman and the Weasel;" *Folk-Tales of Bengal*, p. 155; the Malays have a similar tale, cf. *Journal of the Straits Branch of the R.A.S.*, June 1881, p. 23; story of "The Ichneumon and Snake" in *Panchatantra;* the story is also current in Sindh, cf. *Sind Revisited* (Burton), vol. ii. pp. 89, 303; the same idea forms the basis for a *Katáchintámani* (Tamil) story, Book vi. No. 30, which has also been published in Canarese; also Breton story of "Redbeard" in Sebillot *Littérature orale de la Haute Bretagne*, p. 41 ff.

One of the most popular of English tales is the story of "The Faithful Greyhound" (No. I. of *Heritage's Translation of the Gesta Romanorum*), a counterpart of which story is to be

The prince told this sad story with great feeling, so that the king and all the assembly were much moved by its narration. Not the slightest sound was heard in the *darbár* when the prince, after pausing a few minutes, said, even more solemnly than before, "O king, you have commanded our speedy execution; but we are as innocent as that poor dog. May it not be that you will regret this hasty work, and, like the young merchant of whom I have spoken, repent when it is too late?"

"The order is irrevocable," whispered the king; "I cannot hear the man."

Then another of the princes prostrated himself before the throne, and begged that he too might be permitted to say something before he died.

"Say on," said the king, slightly waving his right hand.

The prince began:—

"O great and gracious king, there were in times long past a celebrated *shikárí*, who entirely supported himself by the several beasts and birds which he killed in the jungle. One day it happened that nothing came to his hand. He was in great distress about this, as there was no food in the house for the morrow. So he went on for three days wandering farther and farther into the jungle in the hope of getting something, till at last he came to a hut outside which some *shikárís* were sitting. They asked him who he was and whence he came; and

found in the Welsh translation of Prince Llewellyn, so familiar to tourists at Beth Gelert (cf. also the Hon. W. R. Spencer's ballad). Although the Welsh point to the ruins of a certain priory that Prince Llewellyn founded to mark his penitence for the hasty act, and to a stone as a mark of the place of the dog's grave, yet there appears no doubt that the story was borrowed directly from the *Hitopadesa* (quoted above) and its translations. This explains the likeness it bears to the stories of "The Bráhman and the Weasel," "The Widow and the Mongoose," &c. Professors *Benfey* and Rhys Davids trace the *Hitopadesa*, *Pancha-tantra*, and other Sanskrit works to a Buddhist source (*vide* Introduction to *Buddhist Birth Stories*; and *Chips from a German Workshop*, vol. ii. pp. 227–232). Cf. also Mr. Lewis's notes in *The Orientalist*, vol. ii. pp. 49, 50; and *Folk-Lore Journal*, vol. iv. pp. 189, 190.

This story seems to refer to that extensive series of tales in which the machinations of the wicked wife or mistress are counteracted by the stories of the king's advisers. See the Sindibád Cycle, *passim*.

when they heard that he was in search of food, and had not partaken of any for three days, they set some meat and bread before him, and promised to take him in a short while to a spot where *shikár* would certainly be found.

"After a good meal and a refreshing sleep he and one of the other *shikárís* went in a certain direction in the jungle and killed a *bárah-singá*,[13] some smaller animals, and a bird or two. These the other *shikárís* would not think of touching.

"'No, no,' they said, 'these are yours. Take them home quickly to your wife and children, who must be starving by this time. We would like to keep you with us longer if it were not for the thought that you must be anxious to return home at once. However, we hope to see you again.'

"'Thank you much for your goodness to me,' replied the *shikárí*. 'I shall undoubtedly come and see you often, and shall always be ready to help such friends as you have proved to be. Had it not been for your timely aid I and my house would have perished. Of course you will see me again.'

"On arriving at his house he found his wife and family almost dead from starvation. They had waited and waited for his return, until they had become quite ill from want of something to eat. So he quickly got a fire ready, cooked some venison, and made some broth.

"The next day they were well and happy again, and related to each other all their wretched experiences, and blessed the *shikárís* in the jungle, who had been so kind to them.

"In a few days the *shikárí* told his wife that he must visit his friends in the jungle, as he had promised that he would go and see them again soon. So he prepared

13 *Bárah-singá*, a twelve-timer (*Cervus elaphus*), more often called *hánglu* or *hangul*.

some presents and went. The other *shikáris* were very glad to see him, and treated him right hospitably. He stayed with them many days, during which he did much hunting, and arranged that the beautiful daughter of the chief of the party should be married to his son; for thus the two families would be bound together by other than ties of friendship.'

"In due time the wedding took place, and the bridegroom was invited to come and sleep in his father-in-law's house. He went, and in the middle of the night the happy pair were disturbed in their slumbers by a great howling of jackals. Now, it happened that the bride understood the speech of every bird and animal. Accordingly, as she lay awake listening, she heard the jackals saying to one another, 'A dead body is floating down this river, and round one of the arms of the corpse there is a bracelet of five precious stones. Where is that person who will go and drag the body to shore and take off the bracelet of precious stones, and thus do three good works, viz., cleanse the river of this pollution, save the five precious stones from being lost altogether in the bed of the river, aud provide us poor hungry beasts with a good meal?'

"When she heard this the bride rose from her bed and walked out towards the river.[14] Her husband also, moved by curiosity, went after her unawares. On reaching the brink of the water the woman leapt in and swam towards the floating corpse, which was just discoverable in the faint moonlight. She seized the body, and having pulled it to the bank, she took off the beautiful bracelet, that was tied round one of the arms, and then returned to the house.

"Her husband arrived first, as he had not waited while she untied the bracelet. 'What can she have gone to the river for and bathed at this time of the night?' he

[14] Concerning talking animals and understanding non-human language, cf. *Wide-Awake Stories*, pp. 412, 413.

thought. No sleep came to him because of this; but his wife slept soundly till the morning light.

"According to custom, the husband on rising went immediately to the river for a bathe. What was his horror and disgust to find in the very place where his wife had jumped in during the night the half-eaten body of a human being! He said within himself, 'My wife must be a *rákshasí*. She has devoured half of this body, and will certainly come to-night and devour the remainder. Thinking this, he feared to return to her, and so went by an unfrequented path back to his father and his father's house.

"'Father,' he said on arrival, 'why did you marry me to a *rákshasí*? I am sure that this woman is a *rákshasí*, because last night she feasted on a human body. In proof of this you can go and see the remains of the corpse lying on the river-side. What an unfortunate man I am!'

"When the *shikárí* heard these words, he thought that either his son was not speaking the truth or else he had gone mad; so he hastened to ascertain the real state of affairs. When he was yet some distance from their house, the father of the bride and several other members of the family came forward to greet him, and to inquire the reason of his son's strange and sudden departure.

"Thinking it wise to dissemble matters till the truth concerning the woman was fully known, the *shikárí* bade them not to be anxious about his son, as he was safe at home, having returned quickly in obedience to his directions. The boy was not grown up, he added, and therefore he had been ordered to return home quickly. He hoped they would forgive any apparent rudeness, and allow the bride to accompany him.

"The other *shikárís* were quite satisfied with these explanations, and agreed to let the bride go. After eating a little the *shikárí* (the father of the bridegroom) went back to his house with his daughter-in-law.

"He soon managed to walk behind her, for he was afraid to keep up with her, lest she should really be a *rákshasí* and eat him. They had proceeded some way in this fashion, when the girl, feeling tired and weary, sat down by a little pool of water under the shade of a large and beautiful tree. The *shikárí* also, encouraging himself in the thought that his son had probably only had a nightmare, sat down beside her, and taking out some provisions, with which the girl's father had supplied him, gave her some to eat.

"While they thus sat, enjoying the rest and the food and each other's conversation, a few crows gathered round and commenced cawing and making a great noise as they hopped and flew about from branch to branch and stone to stone, with eyes fixed on the scraps of the meat, ready to pounce down on the first opportunity and carry them off. One of them, an old crow, wished to be especially friendly. 'Who is that person,' he cawed, 'that can hear and understand my speech? Near the roots of this beautiful tree there lies a potful of precious stones, and under this pot are thousands and thousands of ants, that are destroying the very life of the tree. Oh! where is the person that will dig up this pot, and thus save the tree, and us who have built our nest in its branches, and besides this, enrich himself beyond thought and speech?' The girl heard these words, and laughed and wept alternately.

"On seeing this her father-in-law got very frightened. He thought that she laughed and wept because she was a *rákshasí*, and was then meditating making a meal of him. With a tremulous voice he asked her, 'Of what nature are you? If you are a *rákshasí* I beg of you to spare me.'

"The girl, exceedingly surprised at these strange words, answered, 'I am not of a bad or sanguinary nature. What have you observed in me or heard about me to prompt such a question?'

" 'How came that half-devoured corpse on the river-side the other morning?' he said. 'Why did you laugh and weep just now, and almost in the same breath?'

" 'What! shall I tell you?' she said. 'Are you really supposing me to be a *rákshasí* for these reasons? Is this the cause of my husband, your son's, sudden disappearance? Is it on this account that you have walked behind me almost all the way here? What folly! What wrong is this! Listen to the truth of the case. On the night of the day that your son visited my father's house the jackals prowled about the place and made such a noise that we both awoke. Their conversation was loud and long that night, and no wonder, for they had seen a corpse floating slowly down the river, and on one of the arms of the corpse, they said, a beautiful bracelet was fastened. Understanding their speech, I thought that I would go down and drag this corpse to land and get the bracelet. Look, here it is;' and she showed it to her father-in-law wrapped up in a dirty piece of cloth. 'The dead body I left on the river-bank. Perhaps the jackals came afterwards and devoured it. I did not, you may be sure. It was a half-eaten corpse that your son probably saw in the early morning, and as he had very likely noticed my going to the river in the middle of the night, he thought that I was a *rákshasí*, and therefore had devoured the body. And so he fled.'

"Saying this, she laughed heartily. The *shikárí* also could not help laughing.

" 'And then again,' she continued, 'just now a crow perched on yonder branch, and by cawing said that much treasure was concealed near the roots of this tree. Understanding the speech of birds also, I laughed and cried from joy at the thought that I should get further treasure, and thus be able to bring ease and pleasure to my husband and family. Wasn't that quite rational? Oh! please do not think me to be a *rákshasí*, or anything of that nature. I wish to be a faithful wife to your son, and to do good to all people.'

"The *shikárí* was very glad to hear this. He thoroughly believed his daughter-in-law's words.

"Presently they both dug together round the roots of the tree and found the treasure—some most valuable stones and riches. In the excitement of the moment the *shikárí* embraced the girl, and begged her to forgive both him and his son for their misapprehensions concerning her.

"Most happily they recommenced their journey. It was a most beautiful road. The trees made one long avenue, through which they walked in a most grateful shade the whole way; flowers of every form and beauty strewed the ground; and streams meandered in all directions, carrying with them life and strength and gladness.

"From one of these streams the *shikárí*, feeling thirsty, asked his daughter-in-law to bring him some water. She at once obeyed, and as she stooped down to take the water a frog croaked and said, 'In the name of mercy, will nobody listen? Within this stream a treasure lies concealed, and therefore the stream is filled with insects. Who will hear me and take out the treasure? Thus would the waters be healed and travellers who drink of it be benefited; the frogs would be able to enjoy themselves without hindrance from unpleasant pains in the stomach, which they are constantly experiencing from life in this water; while the finder of the treasure would be enriched beyond all want.'

"On hearing this the girl went at once and told her father-in-law, who immediately came to the stream and found the treasure. Having securely fastened it round their waists, they proceeded on their journey.[15] When

[15] Kashmíris have various devices for carrying their money or other little valuables. Sometimes they conceal it in their turbans, sometimes in their *kamarbands*, sometimes in their sleeve-cuffs, sometimes in their ears if the thing is small, and sometimes tie it up in a knot at the end of their wrap.

they arrived near the house the *shikárí* asked his daughter-in-law to go on ahead. She did so, and while she approached the entrance of the house her husband saw her; and observing that she was alone, he at once thought that she had killed his father and now she was coming to slay and eat him; therefore he armed himself with a sword, and when she came up, expecting to be welcomed by her husband and looking forward to showing him their great wealth, he struck off her head.

"In the course of an hour his father reached the house. 'O father,' said the son, 'God be praised that you have been preserved from the hands of this blood-stained woman! Be glad now. Henceforth we shall dwell in peace and safety. I have slain her. Behold, her life-blood stains the doorway!'

"When he saw the marks of blood about the place the *shikárí* fell down insensible. It was a long time before he again came to his senses. Great was his grief, but greater the grief of the hasty husband, when he heard the truth of the case."[16]

There was perfect silence during the narration of this story. With great power the moral seemed to be brought home to the heart of the king.

"O king, our father, the prince said in conclusion, "be not hasty, we beseech you, concerning this matter of our execution, lest you also come into similar grief."

His Majesty, however, hardened his heart and would not hear the thing.

Then another of the princes prostrated himself before the throne and begged to be permitted to speak. He said:—

"Many years ago there lived a king, whose favourite sport was falconry. One day this king visited a certain jungle for *shikár*, and reached a spot where he had never been before. He was so charmed with the place that he ordered his tents to be pitched there.

[16] For an interesting variant of this tale cf. *Folk-Tales of Bengal*, pp. 150, 153.

While this was being done His Majesty got very thirsty, and asked for some water. According to custom, a sword was in the right hand of the king, a hawk perched on the left, and the royal flag in front; and so it happened that when the king was about to drink the hawk flapped its wings and upset the cup. A servant went and brought some more water, but again the hawk caused it to be spilled. This time the king was angry, and spoke harshly to the bird. Again a servant went and got some water, but for the third time, when His Majesty took hold of the cup and lifted it to his mouth, the hawk fluttered about very much, upsetting the water and discomposing the king exceedingly. His Majesty was very angry, and raising his sword killed the bird.[17]

"On this one of the *wazírs* came up and suggested that there was some special reason for the hawk's persistent and apparent rudeness. Perhaps some evil was in the cup.

"The king then ordered that the stream, whence the servant had brought the water, should be thoroughly examined. For some distance nothing was discovered, till they came to another little stream running into it, whose waters were of a greenish hue. This tributary stream they also followed, and in a short while came on a large python,[18] out of whose mouth green slime—rank poison—trickled. Frightened at the sight of this terrible monster, the servants ran back to the camp as fast as they could.

"When His Majesty heard their account he beat his breast and tore his beard, saying, 'Oh, why was I so hasty? I have slain my preserver! My handsome, faithful falcon is no more! Oh that I had waited to inquire the reason of the bird's behaviour!'"[19]

"O king, our father," added the prince after a few

[17] Cf. *Legends of the Punjab*, vol. i. p. 467 ff.

[18] *Ajdar* (Persian *azhdar*), Sanskrit *ajagara*.

[19] Cf. variant of this story, *Folk-Tales of Bengal*, p. 154.

moments' pause, "we beseech you to inquire thoroughly before you deliver us over to death."

Then the king began to relent. He doubted the truth of the queen's story, though he did not know how else to account for the marks of blood on Her Majesty's toes and the presence of the eldest prince in their private room at that time. "Tell me," he said, turning to his eldest son and heir, who as yet had kept perfectly silent, "everything concerning last night; and if you can answer satisfactorily then you and your brethren shall go free."

The eldest prince, having prostrated himself before the throne, replied:—

"O king, our father, your goodness and kindness are well known to all men. We do not hesitate to answer you about this matter; for our consciences are clear, and we are assured that Your Majesty will receive us again into your confidence, when you have listened to our petition.

"While going my rounds one night I reached a hut where lived a bráhman and his wife. Attracted by the man's strange behaviour—for he came out of the hut, looked up at the heavens, and then went in again exclaiming, '*Tráh, Tráh!*'—I drew nearer to the place, and heard that Your Majesty's star had been destroyed by another star, and that this meant that Your Majesty would die on a certain night. From further conversation between the bráhman and his wife I learnt that a serpent would descend from the sky to kill Your Majesty, and would enter the palace by the door that opens into the court to the east. There was no hope of safety,' said the bráhman, 'unless one of Your Majesty's relations would dig pits in the palace-court, whence the snake would enter, and fill them with milk and water, and cover the pools thus made with flowers, so that the snake by passing through them might lose its poison; and further, the man who would do this thing must also slay the snake before it entered the palace, and smear some of its warm blood over Your Majesty's toes.

"Therefore, O king, our father, I took upon myself to do this. I was present at the door on the east of the palace at the appointed time. The pits were dug and everything arranged as the bráhman had ordered. The serpent came, and I duly slew it; and then, fearing to enter Your Majesty's private room with my eyes open, I blindfolded myself. Hence the mistake I made of putting the blood on the queen's toes instead of on Your Majesty's. No *rákshasa* entered Your Majesty's room.

"O king, our father, why do you suspect us? We are true sons. You have listened to the words of the queen, who wishes her own sons to have the throne and the great places in the kingdom, and so has maligned us. We have never deceived you, O king, or wished you harm."

The king hung down his head in sorrow and shame. In a few minutes he arose and dismissed the assembly, saying, "Ye have heard. I will go myself and ascertain the truth of these things."

Accompanied by his four eldest sons, the king went and saw the pits that had been dug and the blood-stained place where the dead body of the snake had been thrown. He then visited the bráhman's hut, and closely interrogated him concerning the eventful night. All was found to be perfectly correct.

There was great rejoicing in the city that night when the news was blazed abroad how near the four princes had been to death, and how they had been saved. It was soon arranged for these princes to govern the land. The eldest son became king, and the other sons were appointed *wazírs*. They lived together most amicably and prospered much. The poor bráhman and his wife were well provided for during the remainder of their lives. The plotting, malicious queen was divorced and exiled. The old king retired to a jungle, that he might entirely devote himself to meditation and prayer. In this jungle he obtained a very great reputation for sanctity, and at length died at a very great old age.[20]

[20] Cf. variant of this story, "Strike but Hear," *Folk-Tales of Bengal*, pp. 147–159.

THE JOGÍ'S DAUGHTER.[1]

It was a time of general distress. Among others who suffered was a certain bráhman. Not having been brought up to any trade, this poor bráhman was unable to do anything for a living, and no man gave unto him. He was in great straits. If it had not been for a scanty pittance of food, which was earned by his wife, who went every day to help in pounding the rice for a very rich family that lived in the neighbourhood, he and his family would have starved to death.

One day, when the bráhman was going to perform his regular *púјá*, his wife said to him, "Oh that you would do some *púјá*, some service, whereby the gods would favour us and grant us food and clothing!"

"I will," said the bráhman. "Make me some biscuits."[2]

The biscuits were got ready, and the bráhman took them and went. He took his idols also.

It was spring-time. The country all around was covered with blossom. The bráhman walked far and fast, till at last, feeling tired, he sat down to rest under an apple-tree that grew by the side of a pretty little purling brook. "Here," thought he, "I will worship and meditate." For several hours he tarried there wrapt in meditation. Then he arose, put back his idols into the bag, and commenced to return. On the way he noticed a column of smoke ascending slowly into the air. He drew near, and saw that it proceeded from a *jogí's* fire, and that the good man was squatting by it. Bowing reverently, he also squatted down beside him. The *jogí*

[1] Narrator's name, Makund Báyú, Suthú, Srínagar.
[2] The name of these biscuits is *yáj*.

opened his eyes and inquired what was his errand. The bráhman told him of his great distress, and how he had been wandering about that day doing special *pújá* in the hope that the gods would have pity on him and help him.

On hearing his sad tale the *jogí* said, "Go to my daughter, who is sitting over yonder. Perhaps she will help you."

The bráhman thought it was rather strange. Still, he went to the girl and repeated what he had said to her father. The girl was very much affected by his account of himself, and wept profusely. Tears streamed down her cheeks, and lo! every tear that touched the ground became a rich lustrous pearl. "Take them," she said; "they are yours." Then she laughed, and lo! from her mouth there came forth most magnificent flowers of gold. "Take them," she said again; "they are yours." Then she arose and walked slowly a few paces, and lo! each footprint that she made was covered with gold. "Collect the gold," she said; "it is yours. You will now have sufficient to provide yourself and family with food for many days. You can go."

Glad and happy, the bráhman went home. The gods had blessed him; his prayers had been heard at last. "Look," said he to his wife, "the gods have had pity on us. For several hours I worshipped and meditated, and was returning home, when I came across a *jogí* sitting by his fire."

"Tell me no more," she interrupted. "You are not speaking the truth. You must have got the wealth by theft. I shall not believe you till you have been to the king and told him everything. If His Majesty is satisfied with you I shall be satisfied also."

Seeing that she was determined, the bráhman took the pearls and gold to the king, and informed him how he had come by them. His Majesty was astonished. However, he believed the bráhman, and gave him a present of several bags of money.

When the bráhman's wife saw the king's present she was persuaded, and hesitated no longer to enjoy the wealth that her husband had so strangely and so opportunely obtained.

A short time after this interview the king sent for the bráhman and inquired further about the daughter of the *jogí*; and being much impressed with the bráhman's account of her, he begged him to go to the girl's father and solicit the hand of his daughter in marriage. "Such a wife," thought he, "would be of inestimable benefit to me and my kingdom."

"Be not angry, O king," replied the bráhman, "and I will speak. Suppose the *jogí* is angry with me and curses me?"

"I care not," said the king. "You must arrange some plan for getting the girl to be my wife."

There was some more conversation, and then the bráhman left.

He was in great anxiety. The wealth that had lately come into his hands seemed about to pass out of them as quickly as it had come into them. What was he to do? Go he must; but how to fulfil his errand he knew not. The next morning he started, and in much trembling approached the *jogí*, who was still seated in the same place where he had found him before. "Have pity on me," he cried, "and hear my petition. The king wishes your daughter in marriage, and will not rest till he hears of your consent to the union."

"Be not troubled," replied the *jogí*. "Go and tell His Majesty that his request is accepted, and bid him come on such-and-such a day with a company of people for the wedding. The people who attend him must all be over the age of seven years. Go, fear not. My word has been given."

Overwhelmed with joy, the bráhman hastened to the king and informed him of the success of the visit. The appointed day arrived. The king, with an immense retinue, came to the *jogí*, and was most graciously received. In due time the ceremony was celebrated.

Everything went off well, and everybody was much pleased. And then the king left.

On the way back the bride, being very thirsty, asked for some water; but the woman in whose charge she had been placed demurred.

"Why do you tarry?" said the bride.

"I dare not obey you," replied the woman, "for in this river there dwells a serpent that will not allow any one to drink of the water unless that person first gives it a pair of human eyes for the draught."

"Be it so, then," replied the bride. "Fetch a knife and take out my eyes, and bring me some water."

The cruel act was done; the water was brought; and the girl drank of it and was satisfied.

Now this woman, whose business it was to look after the bride, was a very wicked woman. She took advantage of the darkness of the hour—for it was night before the company had reached half-way—and changed the clothes of her mistress for the clothes of her own daughter. The two girls happened to be about the same age. She then placed the *jogí's* daughter in a box, which she put into the river, and afterwards she put her own daughter into the *dolí*.[3]

The wicked woman's daughter arrived at the royal palace, and, as soon as it was light the next morning, the impatient king visited her and asked her to cry and laugh and walk, so that he might get some pearls and gold. But the girl was only astonished, and said nothing. When he saw this the king sent for the bráhman and charged him with falsehood and deceit. The bráhman protested his innocence, and begged His Majesty to wait. "The girl, perhaps, is confused," he said, "with the sudden change in her position."

The *jogí's* daughter floated down the river in the box, and was found on the following morning by a washerman, who, seeing that she was blind, took her to his

[3] Cf. *Indian Fairy Tales*, pp. 3, 4, 143, 144, and *Old Deccan Days*, p. 224.

home, gave her food and clothing, and treated her in every way like his own child. The next day, as she walked about the washerman's little garden, it was noticed that her footprints were footprints of gold. Somebody told her of this, and she answered, "I know. Collect it and give it to the washerman." The following morning something caused her to laugh, when flowers of gold fell down from her mouth. This also was told her, when she answered, "I know. Take them to the king's wife. Perhaps she will be pleased with them, and will wish to buy them. If so, then tell her that the price is a pair of human eyes."

The washerman went to the palace with the golden flowers and showed them to the wife of the king. Her mother (the queen's maid) was present when he arrived. As was expected, the young queen was fascinated with the flowers, and asked the washerman to say how much he wanted for them. "Two human eyes," said he.

"Two human eyes?" repeated the queen. "How can I pay you in this way? Ask me for some money or for any special honour, and you shall have them. But how can I get for you two human eyes?"

"I will procure them for you," said the maid, who went into an adjoining room and returned with a little box, wherein were the two eyes of the *jogī's* daughter. The washerman took them, gave the queen the golden flowers, and then left.

"How glad I am you have succeeded!" exclaimed the *jogī's* daughter, when the washerman gave her the eyes. "These are none other than my own eyes. Put them back into their sockets and anoint them with this eye-salve."

The washerman did so, and the girl's sight was restored to her whole as before.

When the king went to see his wife that evening the cunning maid showed him the golden flowers, and pretended that they had been produced by the queen. The king was very glad at this, and lavished on his wife and her maid all sorts of presents. "Now," thought he, "I shall soon be the richest monarch in the world."

Weeks passed. Nothing more was produced by the wife of the king. But the *jogi's* daughter daily produced some pearls, or golden flowers, or gold, according as she wept, or laughed, or walked. In this way the washerman quickly became very rich. Various reports of his incredible wealth, and of the mysterious manner by which he had obtained it, spread everywhere. The king too got to know of it, and sending for the man, asked him how he had contrived to make so much money in so short a time. The washerman, who was very much frightened, informed His Majesty of the whole truth. "Your Majesty," he said, "the *jogi's* daughter, who is your rightful wife, has been cruelly deceived by the woman in attendance on the girl that now occupies the position of queen. On the way back from the wedding this woman prevailed on the *jogi's* daughter to take out her eyes; and then, when the girl was blind and knew not what was going on, she took off her garments and put them on her own daughter, the present queen. She then clothed the *jogi's* daughter in the garments of her own daughter, and shutting her up in a big box, set the box afloat in the river. The *doli*, with her daughter seated inside, reached the palace; the box, with the *jogi's* daughter, floated to my house. It was not long before I discovered the wonderful virtues of the *jogi's* daughter. Whenever she wept or laughed, or wherever she walked, a pile of pearls, or golden flowers, or gold was the result.[4] Once, at her request, I brought some of the golden flowers to the queen, and demanded two human eyes as the price. The queen's mother, this wicked woman, was present at the time. She handed to me the pair of eyes that belonged to the *jogi's* daughter. I took them and left. On my return home I gave the eyes to the girl, who at once replaced them in their sockets; and then, on

[4] Cf. *Wide-Awake Stories*, p 426, Class iv., note (*c*).

the application of a little eye-salve, was able to see with them as well as before."

"Go and fetch the *jogí's* daughter," said the king. "I have been deceived."

Presently the washerman appeared with the *jogí's* daughter. The king asked her to relate the whole matter; and when he heard again the same account as the washerman had given him he was convinced. He immediately gave orders for the execution of the wicked maid and her stupid daughter; but the washerman and the bráhman he promoted to great honour. Henceforth the *jogí's* daughter lived with him, and he became richer and richer, till he had so much wealth that he was obliged to leave off counting it.

GULLÁLÁ SHÁH.[1]

In a certain country there lived a fowler, who pursued his calling with far-famed success. An incredible number of birds were reported to have been snared or shot by him every day. Some of these he set by for his own use, and the rest he sold. However, being a spendthrift, he did not become rich, but rather grew poorer and poorer. As fast and as much as he earned, so fast and so much did he spend. Now this was all very well for a time, and for some years affairs proceeded comparatively happily; but by degrees it became manifest that the birds were getting fewer and more wary. Consequently there was an abatement in his success; and so the fowler looked sad and anxious, and wondered what he should do for a living.

While he was in this state Rájá Haṁs[2] summoned all the bird-world to a great assembly, and the few birds that remained in the fowler's country were also invited. The conference was an immense one, and all the arrangements were magnificent beyond description. Much business was done, and every bird expressed himself very pleased with all that he had seen and heard. At length, the conference being concluded, the birds were dismissed to their several countries; but the little company which attended from the fowler's country did not prepare to leave. Seeing this, Rájá Haṁs inquired the reason.

"O Rájá," replied the birds, "in our country there lives a fowler, whose aim is deadly and snares undis-

[1] Narrator's name, Shiva Báyú of Renawárí, Srínagar.

[2] A swan or goose, cf. *rájahaṁsa*, *s. v.* राज in Monier-Williams' *Sanskrit Dictionary*. A favourite bird in Indian tales.

coverable. Nearly all our brethren have been slain by him. In former days we were a great and mighty company, but now behold, O Rájá, the smallness of our numbers and our strength. We pray you to have mercy on us, and deliver us out of the hand of this cruel man."

Rájá Haṁs was exceedingly grieved when he heard their sorrows, and immediately sought to relieve them. He had two chief ministers, an owl and a parrot,[3] whom he loved very much, and to whose advice he always attended. Accordingly he now called them to him, and first addressing the owl, said—

"O Owl, I am ruler over all the birds, and ye are my ministers. A portion of my subjects are terribly troubled by a certain fowler, whose tricks and snares they are powerless to resist, and yet they do not wish to leave their country. You will make arrangements for the preservation of these my subjects."

The owl was astonished when he received this difficult command; but, remembering the parrot's superior knowledge and wisdom, he replied, "O Rájá, this your order cannot be executed by me, owing to my blindness by day. The parrot, however, with Your Highness's permission, will fulfil it."

Then Rájá Haṁs turned to the parrot and commanded him to perform the order which he had just given to the owl. The parrot at once agreed, made his obeisance, and departed. He went to the aggrieved birds, and bade them to be patient and to do nothing of their own counsel, but to be guided by him, and to believe that

[3] Both the owl and the parrot occupy a prominent position in Indian folk-lore. The former is generally regarded as most skilful in foretelling events, and on this account would prove a most useful bird if men could only easily understand its speech. The parrot is also quoted as a most accomplished soothsayer, as well as a cheerful companion and faithful friend. An educated man living at Awá, in the Etá district, told Mr. Crooke that he had acquired his knowledge of magic by spending a night naked and alone with an owl, who communicated all sorts of wisdom to him. Cf. also story of "Wise Hans" in Grimm's *Household Stories*. There are many interesting notes on these birds in *Indian Notes and Queries*.

the Bhagawant would interpose in their behalf. The birds with one accord consented.

When the fowler discovered that there was not a bird left in the country, he became more sorrowful than ever. His case appeared hopeless. How to provide for his wife and family he knew not, because he had never learnt any other trade and had never possessed a special friend. It was a sad sight to see his children gathering round him when he returned in the evening to ask him what sport he had had, for they were very hungry, and then to watch them one after the other going away again, on being told that nothing had come to his hand that day.

Thus affairs continued until the birds returned from the conference; when the fowler, having heard from one of his children that the birds had again appeared, went forth with net and bow to try and catch them. He spread his net in a most likely place, and looked so fierce and determined that the birds were more afraid than before, and went to the parrot, saying, "In such-and-such a place the fowler has spread his net. Tell us how we may escape, for we are certain that if this man fails to snare us in his net he will shoot us with his bow."

The parrot gave them permission to hide themselves in different places, and promised that he would make provision for their permanent safety. So away they all flew, and were soon out of sight. Then the parrot went and walked straight into the fowler's net and was snared; but no other bird was caught that day, and the fowler was almost frantic with despair. On reaching home his family rushed to him as usual, and inquired what luck he had had. "Nothing but this parrot came into my net to-day," he replied, "because of your bad fortune." [4]

Saying this, he took the bird out of his cloth and

[4] A large number of stories might be quoted in which the supposition that prosperity or adversity is sometimes dependent on the *qismat* of another is mentioned. Cf. story of "The Ship-wrecked Prince" in this collection.

made as though to kill it for food; but the parrot, guessing his intention, said, "Why are you going to slay me? Do you not know that my flesh is not fit for food? And even if you could eat me, what satisfaction for your hunger could you get out of such a morsel as I am? Would it not be a wiser plan to sell me to some dealer in the *bázár* and provide yourself with provisions for many days from the price that you would obtain for me?"

The fowler acknowledged the wisdom of what the bird advised, and therefore put it into a safe place for the night, intending to rise early on the following morning and go to the *bázár* with it.

As soon as the sun was up the next day the fowler was up too, and off to the *bázár*, proclaiming to the people that he had this parrot for sale. "Who'll buy? Who'll buy?" he cried; and many people stopped to look at the bird. They all seemed pleased with it, and many wished to have it, but on account of the small sums which they offered, the parrot refused to go with them.[5] Of course this behaviour made the fowler very angry. He had been walking about in the heat all the day, and was very tired and disappointed; and when he reached home, and saw again the hunger and distress of his family, he was exasperated beyond bounds. He swore that he would kill the parrot there and then. Poor bird! It thought that its doom was now most certainly sealed. However, it again begged the fowler to have patience with it. "You will perceive that I have not any personal interest in this delay," it added. "In refusing to be sold for such small sums as were offered for me to-day I have not been rude. Please, do not think me ungrateful for the preservation of my life. If you will wait till to-morrow, and then place me in a nice cage and cover the cage with a pretty cloth, and take me here and there about the palace-grounds, some

[5] Cf. *Old Deccan Days*, p. 107; also *Folk-Tales of Bengal*, pp. 209, 210.

great and rich person will probably notice the cage, and ask what is inside. It may be that they will also feel sufficient interest in me to inquire my price. If so, then please leave the arrangement of this matter again to me, simply saying that I cost a great deal of money and will declare my own price."

The fowler again acknowledged the wisdom of the parrot's counsel, and consented to follow it. And so on the following morning, a beautiful cage and cloth having been procured, the bird was put inside, and carried about by the fowler within the precincts of the palace-grounds.

Now the king of that country had several wives, but they were all barren except one, by whom a little daughter had been born to him. This daughter grew up to be so good and beautiful that His Majesty loved her very much. He cared not to be absent from her, and there was not a request of hers that he did not try to fulfil to the utmost of his power. One day she had expressed a wish to have a bird which could speak, and so thenceforth the king had inquired diligently for such a bird. The fowler's visit, therefore, was most opportune.

While the fowler was perambulating before the palace the chief *wazír* passed by. The fowler gave him a most profound *salám*. The parrot also gave him a *salám*, imagining that some great personage was near. When the *wazír* heard the *salám* from the cage, he was much surprised. "How strange!" he said. "Please, remove the cloth, that I may see the bird which can do this wonderful thing."

The fowler did so; and the *wazír* was more struck with the beauty of the parrot than with its cleverness, and offered to purchase it at any price. According to the previous arrangement the parrot at once named the price—"Eighteen thousand rupees."

"What! Eighteen thousand rupees?" said the astonished *wazír*.

"Yes; eighteen thousand rupees," the parrot again replied.

"Then I cannot buy you," said the *wazír*. "But my lord the king wishes to have a speaking bird like you; so you will please be carried to him."

The parrot consented; and so, on reaching the front entrance of the palace, the *wazír* took the cage and went inside with it. After making his obeisance he placed the cage before the king, saying that at last he thought His Majesty had obtained his long-felt desire. As soon as the cage was set before the king the bird most distinctly said, "*Salám*." This greatly astonished the king, who anxiously inquired whence the *wazír* had obtained such a clever and magnificent bird. "It is the very bird that I have been wanting for a long time," he added. "You must sell it to me. Ask what you like, and I will give it you."

The *wazír* replied, "It is not mine, O king. I met a poor fowler carrying it about the palace-grounds, and knowing that Your Majesty had need of such a bird I first tried to buy it; but finding that its price was more than I could afford, I ordered the man to bring it hither. With Your Majesty's leave I will call in the man."

The king ordered the fowler to be brought in, and when he appeared he asked him to sell the parrot. "Tell me its price and you shall have it," he said.

"My lord," answered the man tremblingly, "I cannot tell the worth of the bird. I only know that it was bought for a large sum of money. Let the king's will be. The bird will state its own worth."

Then the king turned towards the parrot and inquired its price; whereupon the parrot answered as before, "Eighteen thousand rupees!"

"Eighteen thousand rupees!" said the king, with a much astonished air. "Too much, too much. Surely you are joking with me."

He tried to bargain for a less sum, but the parrot was

as resolute concerning its price as the king was resolute concerning its purchase. Accordingly eighteen thousand rupees were paid to the fowler, and the parrot was carried in its beautiful cage to the king's only and beloved daughter.

The fowler was now a rich man. What a windfall! Eighteen thousand rupees all in one day! With what great joy he returned to his house, and how joyfully his family received him when they heard the glad news! After dinner—such a dinner as they had not eaten for a long time—they began to discuss plans for the future.

"What shall be done with these eighteen thousand rupees?" asked the fowler. "Shall we leave the country, the scene of so much sorrow and distress to us, and go to a fairer and better land? Or shall we remain here and spend our money in trading? Increasing in wealth and in honour we should forget our past troubles. Say, oh my wife and children, what shall we do?"

Thus were they engaged in conversation, when a great noise was suddenly heard in the yard, and loud above all sounded the voice of somebody shrieking out the fowler's name. A company of soldiers had arrived, who said that they had been sent by the king to summon the fowler to the palace. The poor man was terror-stricken. "My name! My name!" he cried. "The king sent for me? What does His Majesty require of me at this hour of the night? Perhaps he repents of his purchase, and wishes to take the money back again. Or it may be that the parrot has maligned my character. Ah me! ah me!"

But all his suspicions turned out to be wrong, for the king had summoned him in consequence of a conversation which His Majesty had just had with the parrot, wherein he had been informed of the bird's mission. He wished to order him, now that he had plenty of money, to abandon the cruel calling of a fowler, and to apply himself to trade and merchandise. The fowler readily consented, saying that this was his intention and that he would send his net and other things to the palace in testimony that he would not break his word. He then left, and as soon as he had gone the king issued a proclamation to the effect that no person should catch or kill birds throughout the whole of that kingdom, and that whosoever was discovered disobeying the royal mandate should be severely punished. Henceforth there was peace and contentment in the bird community of that kingdom. They flourished exceedingly, and their sweet songs filled the air all the day long.

Out of gratitude to the king the parrot decided to remain in the palace. He made himself so very agreeable that every member of the royal household fell in love with him, and especially the princess, whose whole time and thoughts the bird monopolised; so that she cared not to go to the king, her father, as aforetime, but was always talking and playing with the parrot, and saying, "Oh! what should I do if my pretty parrot died or flew away from me? Polly, you *do* love me, don't you? And you will *never* go away, will you? Oh, promise me truly that you will never leave me!"

Matters continuing thus, the king naturally felt annoyed, for he loved his daughter exceedingly, and did not like her whole time to be spent with the parrot. One afternoon he consulted some of his friends as to the right course to pursue. He did not wish, or rather he was afraid, to have the bird slain; but what was he to do? They advised him to order the bird to be brought to the Court, or to the garden, or wherever the king wished his daughter to come, for His Highness knew that wherever the parrot went there the princess would go too. The king was pleased with this advice, and at once sent a servant to bring the parrot to the Court.[6] Now, the parrot, as has been already mentioned, had the faculty of knowing all that was happening in the world, and used to tell his mistress any special news. Accordingly

[6] Cf. *Folk-Tales of Bengal*, p. 211.

he now explained to her the king's plan for getting his daughter to visit him again. "You had better go," continued the parrot. "Go immediately, and leave me here."

The princess did so. Half-way to the Court she met the king's messenger, and asked him what his errand was. He replied that he had been sent by the king to bring the parrot to the palace.

"Never mind," she said, "you need not go. I will make it all right with the king. Return with me. I am now going to His Majesty."

As soon as the princess had left to go to her father the parrot remembered its native place and old friends, and determined to see them once more, thinking it could return before the princess came back. So it pulled out its old and broken feathers, that it might look the more beautiful, threw them on the floor, and then started. It reached home safely, and was heartily welcomed by its relations and friends. They were all very glad to meet again, and had a lot to tell each other after so long an absence. They seemed hardly to have commenced conversation—so quickly did the hours pass by—when the falling shades of evening reminded the parrot that it was time to depart; and so, resisting all entreaties of its friends to stay, if only for an hour or so longer, it spread out its wings and flew away.

On its way back the parrot alighted in a garden which was by the sea-shore, where grew many rare and beautiful flowers. It plucked two of the most beautiful and returned to the princess. The princess had, however, come back from the Court long before, and finding that the parrot was not there, had become very anxious; and when, after a little while, she discovered some broken feathers lying on the ground, her grief knew no bounds. She thought that a cat had certainly entered the room and stolen her beautiful bird. After much weeping and lamentation she went to the king, told him her sad tale, and begged him to give orders that every cat found within the kingdom should be slain. Although the king cared nothing for the parrot, yet he was very desirous of pleasing his daughter and therefore he at once ordered the immediate execution of all the cats that could be found in his country. Hundreds of cats were killed before nightfall.[7]

The poor princess, however, got very little comfort out of this revenge. She returned to her room, shut the door, and wept until she had no more power to weep and could not bear it any longer. "My pretty Poll, my pretty Poll," she kept on saying in an agony of grief. "Why did I leave you? Oh! cruel, cruel, to have done this the very first time I was away from you!" Thus she mourned the loss of her pet companion. It was a long long while before she closed her eyes that night; and when sleep did come it came only for a short space. She soon awoke, and then, her thoughts naturally turning on her terrible bereavement, she got off her bed, and determined to put an end to her grief by hanging herself. She contrived to fasten a piece of cord to one of the beams of the ceiling, and having made a noose, was about to put it over her head, when the parrot flew in through the window! Another moment's delay and the bird would have found his mistress a corpse. What tongue can tell and whose pen can describe the astonishment of the one and the joy of the other when they thus met? The princess clasped the bird to her breast, and weeping floods of tears, explained how she had thought that it had been devoured by some cat, and on that account had prevailed on the king to sanction an order for the destruction of all the cats in the country; and then how she had felt so lonely and so miserable that she had fully resolved to kill herself, because she could not live without its company. The parrot was so touched with the princess's story that he almost forgot to ask her to hasten to the king and get him to revoke the cruel order concerning the innocent cats.

[7] Cf. *Folk-Tales of Bengal*, pp. 209–219.

For some time after this they both remained perfectly silent, lost in each other's joy. At length the parrot broke the silence. He told his mistress how he had felt constrained to leave her so abruptly and visit his home and people, also what he had heard from them and had seen on the way; and then he presented to her the two beautiful flowers which he had plucked from the garden by the sea. On seeing the beautiful flowers and inhaling their sweet perfume the princess fainted; she had never before seen flowers so lovely and of such delicious scent. When she came to her senses she went and showed them to the king. His Majesty and all the courtiers were greatly surprised when they saw them. Such magnificent flowers had never been seen or conceived of by them. Such splendid perfume too; it filled the whole palace, so that the attendants and servants living in distant apartments perceived it, and began to ask one another whence it was.

"How did you obtain these?" asked the king.

"The parrot gave them to me," replied the princess. "He said that they were plucked from the flowering trees in the garden of the daughter of the king of the fairies, which is by the sea-shore. There were twelve thousand of them in the garden, and each was worth twelve thousand rupees."

"True, true," remarked the king; "such flowers as these *must* be from heaven!"

Then the princess asked her father to send and get some of these flowers for her. Now this was a very difficult request. Nevertheless the king promised that he would try, and at once despatched messengers in search of them. After many days these messengers returned, saying that they were quite sure of never being able to procure the flowers. However, His Majesty was not going to abandon the search so readily. He ordered notices to be sent to the different kingdoms of the world asking if these flowers were to be met with anywhere, and promising that he would give his beautiful daughter in marriage to the person, whoever he might be, who could procure them for him. This was done; but years passed without any news of them.

Now, in former days there lived in the king's country a trader who was exceedingly wealthy, and who, on account of his immense wealth, was much honoured by the common folk. Flattery and adulation had made this trader very proud—so proud that he would never listen to any one, not even to the king. This proud man died, and owing to his not having any brothers or children his whole property reverted to the crown. It was a sad day for the trader's wife when her husband died. Poor woman! she was weak and sickly, and expecting soon to have a little child. She knew not what to do. However, work she must, if she did not wish to die; and so she went and hired herself to a farmer of that country.

In due time her child was born. His *qismat* was good, and he grew and waxed strong. When he was old enough to do some work the farmer sent him into the fields to tend the cattle. Day by day he found time, also, to go to school with the farmer's children; for he was a good boy, and wished to be wise and great. As his mother, being under the supposition that her child had been born under an unlucky star, had not given him a name, his schoolmates called him Khariá, because his head was covered with scabs.[8] The schoolmaster, however, soon discovered the boy's talents, and perceiving also that he was diligent in his studies and ambitious, he took special notice of him and taught him all he could. He gave him presents of books too, and Khariá soon became very clever and learned, and the envy of all the other boys.

One day it happened that, as Khariá was going on an errand for his master, the farmer, he met one of the messengers of the king who wished to get some more of the rare and beautiful flowers. "Whence come you?" he asked. "What have you come for? What is your name?"

[8] *Khur* is Kashmírí for the disease called scald-head (*favus*).

The messenger replied by putting the king's notice into his hand. Having perused it, Khariá said, "Give me some money for the expenses of the way, and I will obtain these flowers. Go back immediately to your royal master, and tell him to comfort his daughter with these words until I appear. Be not afraid that I will deceive you."

The messenger was much pleased with the boy's frank and ready manner; and giving him the necessary expenses and a specially sealed letter of the king, he hastened back to inform His Majesty of his success.

Khariá first went and told his mother what he was going to attempt. She begged him not to be so foolish, but he would not hear her. He then went to tell his master and his teacher, and taking leave of them, started on his journey. In two or three days he reached a jungle, where a very tall and grand-looking man met him. Catching hold of the tall man's hands, he said, "*Salám.*" The man returned the boy's *salám,* and asked him who he was, whence he came, and whither he was going. The boy told him everything, as he had told his mother and master and teacher, and kept nothing back from him. Then the grand tall man blessed him, prayed for him, and bade him depart in quest of the flowers. But the boy would not let go his hand until he had told him in what direction to go. Seeing that the boy was in earnest, and was a worthy boy, the grand tall man disclosed to him who he was, and how, by virtue of his great sanctity, he could obtain for him whatever he required.

"This is what I wanted from you," said Khariá, "for I could see that you were a very holy person and had all power. I pray you tell me whether I can get these flowers or not, what my future lot is, and what my name is."

The grand tall man answered, "My boy, you can get these flowers, your future is good, and your name is Gullálá Sháh."

Saying this, he placed his left hand on the boy's head,

and taking a hollow gourd filled with water, he threw its contents over him, when the scabs and all other defects in the boy's appearance disappeared, so that he was now very beautiful. As soon as he had done this the man finally told him to go; and as Khariá was leaving he again blessed him.

After many days Khariá arrived at a certain place, and took up his abode in the house of an old widow who lived there. He was very kind to the old woman, and used to give her food and in other ways help her. Every day he went for walks in and around the city, and constantly brought back with him some little present for the widow. One morning, as he was washing himself by the river-side, near the palace of the king of that country, the princess chanced to see him, and noticing that he was tall and handsome, she sent one of her attendants to call him, which was done. Khariá said that he would go, and was conducted to a certain spot in the palace-garden, which the princess had appointed. For many days they met together there, and the oftener they met the fonder they became of each other. At length the princess determined to marry Khariá, and went to her parents to obtain their consent. Of course the king and queen first wished to see and to know something of the young man, and so a message was despatched to him commanding him to appear at the royal Court. In a little while the king, seeing that he was good and clever, and worthy of becoming his son-in-law, married his daughter to him. It was a very grand wedding, and there was no stint of money or trouble. Every arrangement was on the most lavish scale, and everything seemed to pass off most happily. Gullálá Sháh—for this was the name by which he was now known—visited the *darbár* every day, and his words were always listened to with the greatest attention and respect. Through his efforts, also, many good and just laws were introduced and many old-established errors corrected. Thus the kingdom became the terror and avenger of all evil men, but the refuge and defender of all who wished for right.

One day Gullálá Sháh begged the king to excuse him from the *darbár*, as he wished to go a-shooting. The king readily assented, and ordered several soldiers and horses to attend him. About the middle of the day, when much excited by the chase, the horse on which Gullálá Sháh was mounted ran away. None of the other horses could keep pace with it, so fast did it gallop; and so Gullálá Sháh soon found himself alone and far out of reach of any help. At last the runaway horse suddenly stopped, for its legs had been fastened by an invisible chain. Perceiving that his horse was mysteriously bound, Gullálá Sháh dismounted, and taking his bow and arrow, climbed the mountain hard by, to see whether he could find anything to shoot there. A little way up he discovered a small pond, upon the banks of which grew a tree, then one mass of blossom. Under the shadow of this tree he sat to rest, and while he sat a monkey approached. He determined to shoot it, and so made ready his bow; but the monkey, guessing his intention, made a great rush and dived into the pond, much to the disappointment of Gullálá Sháh. He remained looking at the place where the monkey had disappeared, expecting every moment that it would appear again.

But lo and behold! presently a beautiful girl, wearing a costly necklace of pearls, came forth, and walking up to Gullálá Sháh, kissed him.[9] Gullálá Sháh was exceedingly astonished at this, but being very good and holy, he did not lose his presence of mind. He asked her who she was, and noticing that she hesitated to answer, he threatened to slay her if she did not tell him quickly. Being frightened, she said—

"My name is Pañj Phúl,[10] and my father is king of

[9] Not at all unfairylike procedure; cf. account of the "Fairy Princess Shâhpasand" in *Wide-Awake Stories*, p. 30.

[10] There does not appear to be the slightest connection between this part of the story and that of "Pánch Phúl Rání" in *Old Deccan Days*. Cf. *en passant* "*Panjphulan*," by Bhái Gopál Singh, a Panjábí poem.

this country, which is fairy-land. I have been good, and tried to do good, and everybody loves me. When I was very young my father intended to marry me to the son of his chief doorkeeper.[11] The hour was fixed and full preparations made, and but a few days remained before the wedding-day, when the chief doorkeeper's son went to play as usual with his companions. They played *Wazír Pádsháh*,[12] *i.e.*, one boy pretended to be the king, another pretended to be the *wazír*, and others took the part of other great officers in the state.

[11] In a native court the doorkeeper has considerable influence, inasmuch as he has it in his power to give or deny access to his chief. Those who have read Cunningham's *History of the Sikhs* will remember how Dhyán Singh, Ranjít Singh's doorkeeper, used the immense influence which this position gave him for advancing family interests. Dhyán Singh afterwards became a Rájá, and received Púnch as his principality.

[12] This game is also called *suhul*, and is very popular in Kashmír. It is generally played by four youngsters. Four little sticks are provided, off which the bark on one side is peeled. Any of the four children throw first. If one should throw these sticks, so that they all fall on the bark side, then he is appointed *pádsháh*, *i.e.*, king; but if not, then they all try and throw till some one finally succeeds. The next thing is to find out the *wazír*. He who throws the sticks so that one of them falls with the bark side up, but the other three with the peeled sides up, is appointed to this office. Then a *tsúr*, *i.e.*, a thief, has to be arranged. He who throws so that two of the sticks fall with the bark side upwards is proclaimed the thief. Lastly, a *said*, *i.e.*, an honest man, has to be found. This part he has to play, who throws the sticks so that three of them fall with the bark sides upwards. If it should happen that all four of them fall with the bark sides up then that thrower has to try again.

Pádsháh, *wazír*, *tsúr*, and *said* being known, the real play begins. The *tsúr*, thief, is brought before the king by the *wazír*, who says—

"*Pádsháh salámat!*
Duzd ámad"—

"O king, peace and health to you! Here is a thief."

The king replies, "*Av kujá ámad?*"—"Whence has he come?"

Then the *wazír* tells him the whole case, and punishment has to be inflicted on the criminal. This is the most amusing piece of the whole *tamáshá*.

"*Bidihed angálí Bangálí top*," says the king—"Give him Bangálí cannon." The *wazír* kicks the prisoner's backside.

Or the king says, "*Botanih anyus hún badal*"—"Bring a dog in his place from Ladák." The *wazír* takes the prisoner a short distance, and then holding him by the ear, pulls him back, while the prisoner barks like a dog.

Or the king says, "*Yindartul kadyus*"—"Take out the spindle." The *wazír* draws a line with his thumb-nail on the inside of the arm from the elbow-joint to the wrist, and then hits the arm over the line as hard as he can with the first and second fingers of the right hand. This is rather a painful punishment. There are many other words of punishment too numerous to mention here.

I notice an allusion to this game in the story of "Mahaushadha and Viśákhá," given in *Tibetan Tales from Indian Sources*, p. 135. Cf. also *Ardschi-Bord chichán* in Jülg's *Mongol, Märchensammlung*, Innsbruck, 1868, p. 197, *et seq.*; *Folk-Tales of Bengal*, p. 184; "Story of Ali Cogia" in *Arabian Nights*; *Kings of Kashmíra*, p. 38; and other tales in this collection.

Each one was supposed to talk and act according to his part in the play. That day the doorkeeper's son was voted king by his playmates, and sat in the royal place. While they were thus playing the real king's son passed by, and, seeing the state of the game, cursed the boy. 'Be degraded from fairy-land,' he said, 'and dwell among the common people.' On account of this curse the doorkeeper's son soon died, and was afterwards born among the common people.[13] A female companion told me of his death, on hearing of which I became very sad; for I loved the son of the doorkeeper, and am determined to marry nobody but him. The king and queen and others have tried hard to get me to change my mind, but I have remained steadfast. All my time has been spent in doing good and in interviewing holy men. To-day I came hither to worship. One day it happened that a very holy man arrived here, whom I loved very much, and I thought to have met him here again to-day. He seemed very pleased with me, and used to give me whatever I asked of him. Once I asked him to tell me how I could again see the doorkeeper's son, who had been born among the common people. He told me that he knew the lad, and that he was called Gullálá Sháh, and that I could see him if I was very careful to attend to his instructions. Of course I promised that I would be. 'Be careful,' he continued, 'and consider well, for the king will hinder you by strong charms and in other ways.' He then gave me a pearl necklace of such great virtue that no charms can affect the wearer, which I am to wear continually and guard patiently, if I would accomplish my purpose. After this I went back to my house. On the first opportunity I told my father of all that I had heard concerning Gullálá Sháh, and begged him to arrange for our wedding as soon as possible. The king looked very troubled when he heard this, and entreated me to think no more

[13] The universal belief in metempsychosis peeps out here.

about the young man, especially as he was now one of the common people. Such a thing as our marriage could not possibly be, as it would bring the whole of fairy-land into contempt. But I was resolute, and so the king spoke sharply to me, and I answered sharply in return, and left the palace in a great rage. This is my history. O friend, if you can do anything to help me to discover anything about Gullálá Sháh, do so I implore you, and I shall be obliged to you for ever."

Here was a strange coincidence! Gullálá Sháh told her who he was, and kissed her. She recognised him, and taking his hand, said, "I have found my long-lost beloved. With him let me ever dwell."

Holding each other's hands, they presently left the pond and came to the place where the horse was standing. Both mounted the horse, which was now quiet, and rode back to the attendants and the other horses, which the king had sent for an escort, and then returned to Gullálá Sháh's house.

On arrival Gullálá Sháh introduced Pañj Phúl to his other wife. The two princesses seemed glad to see one another, and for some time lived together most happily, until one day the first wife asked Pañj Phúl to give her the pearl necklace.[14] Pañj Phúl said that she could not do so, for it was the protector of her life. She could never take it off from her neck. The first wife again and again urged her request, and promised as beautiful and as costly a pearl necklace in exchange; or if Pañj Phúl did not care to give it or exchange it, she might lend it to her for a while. But Pañj Phúl was determined, and refused; nothing could persuade her to part with the pearl necklace for a moment. By reason of this the

[14] However difficult this may be to understand in the West, it is a very common characteristic of Eastern life. I know many families in which several wives live amicably together. Human nature, though, as a general rule, proves too strong for custom, and some petty cause, jealousy, or covetousness disturbs the peace of the household and now and again brings it to ruin. Concerning multiplication of wives, cf. *Dictionary of Kashmírí Proverbs*, p. 70.

first wife got very angry, and went and told Gullálá Sháh of their quarrel, and begged him to get the necklace, and he promised to try and do so. When Gullálá Sháh asked Pañj Phúl for the necklace she refused as before, saying that it contained the secret of her life, and was a charm to her against all dangers, sickness, and trials; deprived of it she might become sick and miserable, or be taken away from them and die.[15] However, Gullálá Sháh would not be denied, and so Pañj Phúl, for very love of him, handed it to him, and he gave it to his other wife.

Soon after this Pañj Phúl suddenly disappeared. On discovering this Gullálá Sháh and his first wife, together with all the household, mourned and wept. "What have we done?" cried they all. "For a trifle we have lost our lovely Pañj Phúl. How obedient she was to her husband! How unselfish in the house! How kind and loving to every one! Alas! alas! why did we this thing? We have caused the death of our darling!"

As for Gullálá Sháh, he knew not what to do for grief. He wept day and night. At last, thoroughly worn out and ill, he determined to leave the place, and to go and seek the flowers in search of which he commenced his wanderings. The king, seeing that he was getting weaker and thinner, consented, and gave him money for his journey.

Accordingly Gullálá Sháh started, and on the second day reached the mountain in fairy-land where he had first met Pañj Phúl. He climbed higher and higher, till he arrived at a certain path, along which he saw two men coming towards him. They happened to be two servants of the chief *wazír* of fairy-land. The *wazír* had no son to carry on his name, and so his wife had asked him to send men into the district with instructions to bring back with them such a youth as she could con-

15 Cf. "Story of Chandan Rájá" in *Old Deccan Days*, the authoress of which remarks:—"There are innumerable popular superstitions regarding the powers which can be conveyed in a charmed necklace; and it is a common belief that good and bad fortune, and life itself, can be made to depend on its being removed from the wearer's neck."

veniently adopt as her son. These men had been wandering everywhere, far and wide, and had not as yet met with a likely person. They were now starving and in great despair, but they dared not return to the *wazír* empty-handed. When they saw Gullálá Sháh their first thought was to eat him; but afterwards, seeing that he was clever and handsome, they decided to take him to the *wazír*. So Gullálá Sháh was seized and taken to the chief *wazír's* house in the fair city. The two servants pretended that he was the son of a fairy, who was a sister of the *wazír's* wife, though she did not know it. The chief *wazír*, his wife, and everybody who saw Gullálá Sháh were pleased with him, and therefore henceforth he abode in that house, and was everywhere recognised as the heir.

Every day the *wazír* attended the king's *darbár*, and in the evening, when he reached home, tired and weary from the day's business, he used to call his adopted son to him and pass the time in conversation. Hours and hours were thus occupied. Gullálá Sháh used to ask him the news of the *darbár*, and the chief *wazír* used to tell him everything. One evening, in the course of one of these long talks, the chief *wazír* told him that there had been great excitement in the *darbár* that day, as the king had been very angry with his daughter, Pañj Phul, who had formed an attachment for a person named Gullálá Sháh, one of the common people, and refused to be married to any other person. She had run away, and for a long time there were no tidings of her,—no doubt she had been trying to find that common man,—but the king had caused her to return by virtue of a most potent charm, and now a terrible punishment awaited her. Her body was to be turned into wood and placed publicly in a certain garden as a warning to other fairy daughters not to do likewise!

Hearing this, Gullálá Sháh experienced great difficulty in keeping his countenance. "Here, then, is Pañj Phúl!" he said within himself. "As soon as she gave up the pearl necklace she must have been brought back to her country, and now she is perhaps suffering the terrible consequences of my folly. Sorrow, a hundred sorrows!"

At length, however, he so far overcame his feelings as to ask the *wazír* if there were no means of saving Pañj Phúl from the dread sentence. The *wazír* said there were. If Gullálá Sháh could come, burn the wooden figure to ashes, throw the ashes into the pond in the midst of the garden where it was, then she would become her former self again.

Gullálá Sháh was very pleased when he heard this, and presently, wishing the *wazír* good-night, retired to his room. No sleep, however, closed his eyes. His mind was far too excited. As soon as he was quite sure that all the inmates of the house were fast asleep, he went forth secretly to Pañj Phúl's garden, burnt the wooden figure to ashes, and threw the ashes into the pond. Directly he did this, lo and behold! Pañj Phúl came forth, looking as he had seen her when she appeared out of the other pond on the mountain-side.

"My own dearest," said Gullálá Sháh, "how could I have been so stupidly wicked as to have caused you all this trial? Forgive me, and say that you will never leave me again. Come, we will wander away into unknown regions, whither the hand of your tyrannical father cannot reach you."

Pañj Phúl replied, "I forgive you, dear husband; but to go with you is not in my power, for my father has possession of me; without my charmed pearl necklace I cannot thwart him. Wherever I might wander, he would cause me to return from thence; and then my case would be worse than before. Now go, I beseech you, lest you also get harm; and pray that the king may have mercy on me, when he hears that I have been restored to life. Away quickly, my dearest, to a place safer for you than this."

Gullálá Sháh then told her all that had happened to

him—how he had wandered about in search of her, and was now the adopted son of the chief *wazír* of that country, who confided everything to him. He would see her again, he said, on going away; and even if the king still wished to punish her, he would get to know a remedy, and come and restore her.

The following morning, when the royal guard saw that Pañj Phúl was alive again, they went and told the king. His Majesty was greatly surprised, and sent for her. As soon as she appeared he said, "How is it that you have come again to trouble us? Be you a serpent, and find a home in yonder jungle," pointing in a certain direction where was a jungle, thick, intricate, and inhabited by wild beasts of various kinds. And it was so!

That evening, when the chief *wazír* returned to his house, Gullálá Sháh heard all that had happened. "Strange!" he said. "Can anything now be done for the princess? or must she for ever remain a serpent?"

"Yes, there is a remedy," replied the *wazír*. "If Gullálá Sháh could get to that jungle, dig a cave three yards deep and broad enough to admit two people, and make a covering with a hole in it for the mouth of the cave; and if after this he were to walk about the jungle calling, 'Pañj Phúl, Gullálá Sháh is here,' and then go back and shut himself up in the cave—if he were to strictly attend to all these directions, then Pañj Phúl, who is now a serpent, would find her way into the cave through the hole in the covering. And there is another thing, also, which he must remember to do, viz., to cut off as much of the snake as can enter in this way, chop it up into little pieces, carefully collect them, place them in a handkerchief, take them to the pond in the midst of Pañj Phúl's garden, and there throw them into the water. If all these instructions were carefully carried out Pañj Phúl would emerge thence in all her former beauty."

When he heard this Gullálá Sháh was much comforted. After a little more conversation he wished the minister good-night. No sleep, however, came to him. He was far too elated at the prospect of being able to restore his beloved to her former self and of seeing her again to wish for sleep. As soon as he knew for certain that the *wazír* and the others were fast asleep he left the house and went to the jungle. That night he only fixed on a place for the cave, and then returned to his room. On the following night, armed with pickaxe, crowbar, spade, and other necessary implements, he again visited the jungle and dug a cave. He also made a covering for the cave and a hole in the covering. He then went outside and called for Pañj Phúl. Pañj Phúl heard her name being called, and came in the form of a snake as soon as Gullálá Sháh had re-entered and shut himself into the cave. She wound the greater part of her body in through the hole in the covering, and Gullálá Sháh cut off as much of it as got inside the cave, and then chopped it up into small pieces. These he carefully gathered, and pushing back the covering took them with him to the pond in Pañj Phúl's garden, where he threw them into the water; and, just as the *wazír* had said, Pañj Phúl appeared in all her former beauty. Gullálá Sháh drew her to him and kissed her. They talked long and lovingly, until faint streaks of dawn warned them to make arrangements to leave the place. Neither of them wished to be separated from the other; but what were they to do? It was time for Gullálá Sháh to return to his home, if he did not wish the *wazír* to discover his absence; while Pañj Phúl could not leave the place. She tried to do so, but without avail; she was bound by the king's charm over her to remain there. And so they parted.

Gullálá Sháh hastened back to the *wazír's* house, and only just reached his room in time. Within an hour or so some of the poorer folk, going to their labours, passed by the place where Pañj Phúl was sitting. They were very much astonished at seeing her, and went and informed the king of the matter. When His Majesty heard the news he sent for the chief *wazír* to take counsel with him. "Do you not think," he said, "that Gullálá Sháh has been here and done this thing?"

"It is impossible," replied the *wazír*; "for, in the first place, how could he get here? and then, how could he, a common man, obtain this power? He must be great to have done this, and in favour with the gods—a thought not to be entertained for a moment."

Pañj Phúl was again summoned to the king, and this time was turned into a golden nail, which was immediately given to one of the attendants with instructions to hammer it into any boat[16] that chanced to be just then in course of construction. The attendant took the nail and fixed it into the first boat he saw. On reaching home the *wazír* bathed, and then called for Gullálá Sháh as usual, and told him all the news of the day. When he heard that the princess had been restored and again metamorphosed Gullálá Sháh assumed an expression of great surprise. "It is strange," he remarked, "that the king should have chosen a golden nail as the form into which to change her. Surely she can never again be restored from such a metamorphosis as this?"

"Oh yes, she can," said the *wazír*.

"How?" asked Gullálá Sháh.

"Well," replied the *wazír*, "if Gullálá Sháh could by any means arrive here and get into that boat, in one of the sides of which the golden nail is fixed, and could discover that nail, and then, having extracted it, were to file it small as powder, and throw the filings into the pond which is in the midst of Pañj Phúl's garden,—if he did all these things, then Pañj Phúl would return to her former shape and beauty; and if she was this time restored, then henceforth the king's charm would be powerless to do her harm. It would have expended itself."

This was enough. So presently, the hour being late,

[16] Meaning a Kashmírí river-boat.

the *wazír* and Gullálá Sháh went to their sleeping-rooms. When he heard of this radical cure Gullálá Sháh feigned no more than an ordinary interest, though in his heart he was inexpressibly glad. On reaching his room he said aloud, "Joy, joy, the time has come! I will go once more and restore my darling. Henceforth the charms of this hard, wicked father shall have no influence over her."

However, Gullálá Sháh did not immediately start. He thought it better to wait a while, until all excitement and interest about the princess had passed away. For several months he patiently waited, and then one day he asked the *wazír's* wife to allow him to go and visit certain places that he wished very much to see, and to get also the *wazír's* permission for the journey. He added that he was now of an age to take care of himself, and he did not like to hear only of the countries about which the *wazír*, his father, had so fully informed him. The *wazír's* wife was much pleased to notice this spirit in the youth, but she hesitated to give her sanction to the request, because the way to some of the places was exceedingly dangerous and the hardships unendurable; and especially so to one who had been brought up so gently as her adopted son. Gullálá Sháh was respectfully indignant at this reply. Drawing himself up to his full height, he said with intense earnestness, "What, my mother, shall the chief *wazír's* son be deterred by difficulties and hardships? A sorry youth I must be if such I show myself. Better far that I perish by them than that I should venture hereafter to attain to the post of chief *wazír* of this mighty and grand kingdom, as my father bids me do. Fear not, my mother, but let me go. However, if you have any talisman, I pray you give it me, for why should I unnecessarily suffer?"

Encouraged by her son's noble reply, the *wazír's* wife consented to his going, and gave him her signet-ring, saying, "Show this ring to the fire whenever you may be in any difficulty, and two *jinns* will appear and help you out of it. She gave him abundant money, also, for the expenses of the proposed journey. The *wazír*, too, was pleased when he heard from his wife of his son's enterprising and inquiring disposition, and acceded to his wishes.

As will be supposed, Gullálá Sháh started as quickly as possible. After travelling for some time, one day he found himself being paddled along in a river-boat, in which was the golden nail. His quick eye soon discovered it, though it was much tarnished and almost excluded from sight by a great beam that ran along the side of the boat. Disguising his real character, Gullálá Sháh begged the owner of the boat to make him one of his boat servants. The man agreed, and soon Gullálá Sháh was working the paddle as if he had been accustomed to that sort of thing all his life. Thus he continued for several weeks, until one day he told his master that he had had a dream during the night. In this dream two men appeared and pierced the bottom of the boat with spears, so that it was broken. "I know," he added, "the interpretation of dreams. Some enemy of yours has placed a charm here, and if that charm is allowed to remain it will sink the boat." The master of the boat was very frightened when he heard this, and entreated Gullálá Sháh to try and discover the malignant charm. Gullálá Sháh said that it was a very difficult task; nevertheless he would attempt it, if the owner of the boat would promise not to inform any one of the matter. The owner promised. Then Gullálá Sháh went to a lonely place and kindled a fire, and when the flames arose he showed them the signet-ring of the *wazír's* wife. Immediately two *jinns* appeared, ready to do whatever might be his bidding. Gullálá Sháh bade them bring the boat up on land. They obeyed, and then Gullálá Sháh pulled out the golden nail, after which he ordered the two *jinns* to put the boat back into the water. He now went and secretly showed the golden nail to his master. On seeing it the owner of the boat was greatly astonished, and thanked God for granting him such a useful and clever servant. Gullálá Sháh kept the golden nail by him, and in a little while, having assured his master that all would go well with the boat, he asked for leave of absence, which was readily granted. He then returned by the help of the charmed signet-ring to the house of his adopted father, the chief *wazír*. The *wazír's* wife only was at home, because it was the time of the *darbár*; and she welcomed him like a fond mother. Soon afterwards the *wazír* came home, and then there were great rejoicings in the house. The whole city, also, seemed interested, and accounts of Gullálá Sháh and his exploits, and the great trials and difficulties which he had overcome by virtue of the signet-ring, were upon the lips of every one.

In a day or two Gullálá Sháh rubbed the golden nail into the thinnest of filings, which he threw into the pond in the midst of Pañj Phúl's garden. No sooner was this done than Pañj Phúl became herself again and stepped out from the pond. They both kissed one another and cried, so glad were they to meet again. They told each other all they had experienced since they last met, and Pañj Phúl declared that now she could go with him wherever he wished, and advised him to wait there till she had been to her room (which had remained untouched since she last left it), and had taken such jewels and dresses, &c., as might prove of service to them on the way. Gullálá Sháh agreed, and Pañj Phúl went, and quickly returned with jewels and dresses of great worth.

Then they both turned their backs on the fairy city, and started on their journey. They walked fast and long before resting, until they arrived by a pond of water clear as crystal. Here they tarried a while and ate some food. While talking together Gullálá Sháh told Pañj Phúl of his great desire to get some of the beautiful flowers which grew in a certain garden on the sea-shore, This garden, he explained, contained twelve thousand flowering trees; each tree had been planted by a fairy princess, and was worth twelve thousand rupees. On hearing this Pañj Phúl said that she could obtain this desire for him, and any other desire that he might choose to prefer. But she only could get these flowers for him, for the princess of the fairy country where they grew had never shown herself to man, and therefore would not see him.

In a few days their wanderings brought them to the sea-shore, close by this wonderful garden. Here they hired a certain vessel which was anchored near, and as they sat on board that night Pañj Phúl gave Gullálá Sháh a beautiful pearl necklace, and told him to go immediately and hang it before the light of a lamp in a secluded room in the side of the vessel. She also told him to remain in that room. The good of this was, that several other beautiful pearl necklaces would be obtained by these means. Gullálá Sháh did as she had advised.

Meanwhile Pañj Phúl disguised herself in man's clothes, and pretended to be the servant of her husband. She then ordered the ship to be taken close to the garden of the fairy princess. On its arrival thither the princess's attendants came and ordered them to take the vessel away, because the princess wished the place to be kept strictly quiet and private, it being her wont to walk along just that part of the sea-shore. But the master of the vessel, Gullálá Sháh, and his sham servant, persisted in remaining, saying that they had many great and precious things on board, and so, from fear of thieves, had anchored the vessel in that place. They would not remove unless the king promised to refund them whatever losses they might suffer from thieves and such-like who would surely come and beset them in any other place. When the king heard this he gave them permission to tarry there for the night.

The following morning Pañj Phúl took some of the pearl necklaces, which had been made in the way just mentioned, and displayed them to view near to the princess's garden. Presently the princess's female attendants came down to the water to bathe. As soon as they saw Pañj Phúl they asked her who she was. She told them that she was the servant of a very wealthy trader who was on board the ship. He was exceedingly good, and had some very great treasures, especially some pearl necklaces, the most costly and beautiful in the whole world. When the attendants heard this they naturally desired to see these great treasures; and Pañj Phúl was only too ready to show them. At the sight of the beautiful pearls they were very much astonished, and entreated Pañj Phúl to allow them to be carried to their royal mistress. This also was readily granted. The princess admired them so much that she would not part with them, but told her attendants to inquire the price, and to get several more like them—as many as the merchant could spare. When these others arrived—a great pile altogether—the princess determined to go and see the merchant; "for," thought she, "he must be a very great man to possess all these costly things." Accordingly, closely veiled, she went to the ship, and arriving there, asked Pañj Phúl, the supposed servant, where his master's room was, as she herself wished to bargain with him for the pearls that she had selected.[17] Pañj Phúl was hoping for this, but she did not wish to betray any special interest in the matter, and so said that the princess could not see the trader, as he had performed a certain worship, and therefore could not see or talk with any woman.

"But why cannot I see the trader?" urged the princess. "I am a good woman, and have never seen a strange man. Surely he would not be defiled by my presence."

"He would not see you," answered Pañj Phúl. "If I took you to his room he would only be angry. He would never show himself to you."

On hearing this the princess became more desirous

17 Cf. *Grimm's Household Stories*, p. 84; "Faithful John," the which story, *en passant*, compare with that of "Phakir Chand," *Folk-Tales of Bengal*, pp. 17-52.

than ever of seeing this strange man. She would go alone, she said, and thus no responsibility would rest on Pañj Phúl. Pañj Phúl said nothing; so the princess went alone and knocked at the trader's door. He did not open it, but answered from within, "I care not to see any strange woman, and so cannot let you enter."

The princess, however, would not hear him. "What for?" she said. "I have never seen the face of a strange man. I am a good woman. Let me in. I am a good woman, and wish to be married to you. This only is my desire. Why should we not see one another?"

Being thus pressed, the trader opened the door, and they saw each other, and love came with the sight. They talked together for a long time, and the trader showed her all his treasures. Then the princess left, full of affection for the strange trader, and full of amazement at his great and exceeding treasure. As soon as she reached the palace she told the king where she had been and what she had seen, and how she had fallen in love with the man, and wished to be married to him. The king, being a very indulgent and good father, promised to see the man, and the next morning went for that purpose to the ship. When he saw the trader—how pleasant he was, and of such good speech, and so wise withal—he too accepted him in his heart, and on reaching home told his daughter so. The princess's joy was unbounded. How much she looked forward to the day! and what great excitement there was in the city at the thought of the approaching marriage! The wedding took place, and was celebrated with great grandeur, as befitted the rank and wealth of the king of fairy-land.

For some time Gullálá Sháh lived within the palace grounds and prospered exceedingly. However, he did not feel altogether satisfied; so one day he told the princess all about himself—why he had come there, and how he wished to get the flowers and return to his native country. The princess repeated everything to the king, and asked his permission to take the twelve thousand flowering trees and accompany her husband; and to this the king consented. Preparations for starting were at once commenced. Twelve thousand carts were got ready for the twelve thousand flowering trees, and other arrangements were made for the transport of the treasures that were given them by the king. An enormous company of troops and elephants, also, were placed at the disposal of the illustrious couple. At length the hour of departure arrived. It was a most sorrowful occasion, for they were both very much beloved.

They first visited that country where Gullálá Sháh got his first wife. The king was intensely glad to see him, and gave him a splendid house to live in, and all else that he required. Gullálá Sháh stayed there for a little while, and then, loaded with more presents, departed. They next went in the direction of Gullálá Sháh's own country. It was a long and difficult journey, but they all reached the city walls in safety. They pitched their camp just outside, thinking that so sudden an advent of such an immense company (several thousands in all, besides elephants, horses, and other beasts) would much inconvenience the people. When tidings of their coming reached the palace, the king was much frightened, and sent for his chief *wazír* and other advisers, to ask what he should do to appease this great king who had now arrived; "for surely," he said, "so great and powerful a king has come here on no other account than for war."

The chief *wazír* well considered the matter, and then replied, "O king, send, we pray you, your beautiful daughter, and let her arrange for peace. Who knows whether or not this great king will be captivated by her beauty, and so we be saved?"

"Alas! alas!" replied the king, "I have already given

away my daughter to the man who shall succeed in obtaining the flowering trees. Moreover, my daughter has refused several times to marry any man, no matter how great and wise he may be, except this person."

Thus were the king and his advisers occupied in conversation, when Gullálá Sháh, having arranged his camp for the night, took off his grand and princely clothes and put on the ragged garments of a beggar, and thus arrayed went forth into the city with the twelve thousand flowering trees. He ordered the drivers to take the carts straight to the palace, while he himself went on ahead. On arriving there he sent a message by the watchman to the king, saying, "Bid your master, the king, to command me, for I am come with the beautiful flowering trees from the garden of the king of the fairies."

Strange that this message should have been delivered just at the time when the king and his lords were talking about these flowers! But so it was. When he heard the words the king did not believe the watchman, but thought that he was mad. The *wazír* and other great officials present also thought that it was too strange to be true. However, His Majesty, in a jesting manner, bade the man to be brought in. Presently Gullálá Sháh appeared, clothed in rags, but bearing a sample of the beautiful flowers, which had been so much admired by the princess and all the royal family. True enough, there were the long-desired flowers, but the bearer of them was evidently of very mean origin—a dirty ragged beggar! The king placed his chin in the palm of his right hand, and fixed his eyes upon the carpet. Thus he remained for several minutes, perfectly silent. "Is this the man," he thought, "on whom I must bestow my beloved daughter? Surely the man will not presume to ask for this thing. I will handsomely reward him, and then let him go."

"Friend, what seek you?" he asked, looking up again. "Will you be a great *wazír* in the land, or do you wish for wealth? Say, and it shall be granted you."

"Let not the king be angry," replied the beggar; "I wish only for Your Majesty's daughter in marriage. In comparison with her, I esteem all honour and money as of little worth. I pray you, fulfil your promise to me."

The king answered, "Your request is your due; and far be it from me to break my promise by refusing it to you. Take my daughter; she is yours."

When all the lords and attendants, and even Gullálá Sháh himself, heard these words, they were astonished at the noble-mindedness of the king; for it would have been a small thing, nay, would have been accounted right and proper by nearly every one, if His Majesty had refused to gratify the beggar's desire.

Gullálá Sháh was bidden to go with the attendants to a certain grand house, and there reside for a few days, during which suitable garments would be provided for him and arrangements made for the nuptials. This done, the king and his *darbár* again conferred in council as to what was the best thing to be done under the present difficulties concerning the foreign powerful monarch, whose camp lay close to the walls of the city. They talked together for a long time; but eventually, nothing definite having been agreed to, the king dismissed the court, saying that he, attended only by his *wazír*, would visit this great king and inquire the reason of his coming. In the course of an hour the king and his *wazír*, with a few attendants, might have been seen pursuing their way with anxious countenances—more like pilgrims than a royal party—towards the great camp without the city.

Meanwhile Gullálá Sháh had succeeded in eluding his attendants, and, returning to his tent, had changed his clothes again. The king and the *wazír* did not recognise him when they were introduced. They were received with great ceremony; presents were offered, and the two visitors seated in state. Gullálá Sháh opened the conversation by inquiring all about the country and people. Then the king asked whence Gullálá Sháh had come, and why he had come. Gullálá Sháh then told him about himself, and how that he had come there in order to ask his (the king's) daughter in marriage.

"Sorrow, a hundred sorrows!" replied the king. "I have already promised my daughter to a certain beggar in consequence of a vow. Were it not so, there is none other whom I could prefer to thyself. Have pity on me, I beseech you, for it is with a sad heart I say this."

"Most noble, most righteous king!" replied Gullálá Sháh, "you have done well. Better that you should lose your life, your kingdom, your all, than that you should deny your word. Would that all the rulers of the earth were such as you are! Then would the people be happier, and righteousness and peace would fill the world. God has prospered you, O king, and He will yet prosper you. Only continue zealous for your people and faithful to your word. Know you now that the beggar whom you have just mentioned is none other than myself; and that I, also, am that same boy who was known to the people by the name of Khariá, whose father died without an heir, and therefore his wealth and property were appropriated by the crown; and whose mother, in consequence of this, sought for employment from a certain farmer. God was with me and prospered me exceedingly, so that I met with one of your messengers, who told me all about your wishes. After much travel, through which I have become learned, great, and rich, I have at last returned to your kingdom, bringing with me the flowering trees. I chose to appear with them first in beggar's clothes, that I might test your fidelity to your promise. You have been proved. Forgive me, I pray you, if I seemed to be wrong in this matter, and grant me your daughter in marriage." Saying these words, he caught hold of the king's hands and seated him by his side in the place of honour.

When the king heard the good news he was almost beside himself with gladness. "God be praised!" he said aloud, and clasped Gullálá Sháh to him in affectionate embrace. "Of course, I will give you my daughter,—but who am I, to promise this thing? Ask what you will, and you shall have it to the full extent of my power."

News of this meeting was at once conveyed to the princess, who would not believe it, until Gullálá Sháh himself appeared and declared it to her. In due time the wedding was celebrated with great *éclat*. Gullálá Sháh fixed his abode in that country, and lived most happily with his four princess wives, for Pañj Phûl had long ago reassumed her true character. He became increasingly popular and increasingly prosperous, and in a few years, on the death of the king, succeeded to the throne. Other countries were quickly conquered, and everything was managed with such skill and justice that soon Gullálá Sháh became the greatest king of those days. All nations did him homage, and all people respected him.

Some will, perhaps, think that Gullálá Sháh forgot his mother and relations in the time of his greatness; but it was not so. He found her out, and gave her a beautiful house to live in and a large number of servants to wait on her; he also inquired for those who had in any way helped her during her distress, and promoted them to offices of great honour. Thus did he live, universally just, loving, and good.

No wonder, then, that he became so popular! No wonder his kingdom waxed so great and strong! No wonder that when he died, at a ripe old age, there went up from all people, rich and poor, old and young, a great wail that seemed to rend the heavens![18]

18 Cf. Seventh story of *Madanakamárájankadai* (*Dravidian Nights*).

WHY THE FISH LAUGHED.[1]

As a certain fisherwoman passed by a palace crying her fish, the queen appeared at one of the windows and beckoned her to come near and show what she had. At that moment a very big fish jumped about in the bottom of the basket.

"Is it a male or a female?" inquired the queen. "I wish to purchase a female fish."

On hearing this the fish laughed aloud.

"It's a male," replied the fisherwoman, and proceeded on her rounds.

The queen returned to her room in a great rage; and on coming to see her in the evening, the king noticed that something had disturbed her.

"Are you indisposed?" he said.

"No; but I am very much annoyed at the strange behaviour of a fish. A woman brought me one to-day, and on my inquiring whether it was a male or female, the fish laughed most rudely."

"A fish laugh! Impossible! You must be dreaming."

"I am not a fool. I speak of what I have seen with my own eyes and have heard with my own ears."

"Passing strange! Be it so. I will inquire concerning it."

On the morrow the king repeated to his *wazír* what his wife had told him, and bade him investigate the matter, and be ready with a satisfactory answer within six months, on pain of death. The *wazír* promised to do

[1] Narrator's name, *Lassú*, a *zamíndár* in the village of Sonwár, near Srínagar.

his best, though he felt almost certain of failure. For five months he laboured indefatigably to find a reason for the laughter of the fish. He sought everywhere and from every one. The wise and learned, and they who were skilled in magic and in all manner of trickery, were consulted. Nobody, however, could explain the matter; and so he returned broken-hearted to his house, and began to arrange his affairs in prospect of certain death, for he had had sufficient experience of the king to know that His Majesty would not go back from his threat. Amongst other things, he advised his son to travel for a time, until the king's anger should have somewhat cooled.

The young fellow, who was both clever and handsome, started off whithersoever *qismat* might lead him. He had been gone some days, when he fell in with an old farmer, who also was on a journey to a certain village. Finding the old man very pleasant, he asked him if he might accompany him, professing to be on a visit to the same place. The old farmer agreed, and they walked along together. The day was hot, and the way was long and weary.

"Don't you think it would be pleasanter if you and I sometimes gave one another a lift?" said the youth.

"What a fool the man is!" thought the old farmer.

Presently they passed through a field of corn ready for the sickle, and looking like a sea of gold as it waved to and fro in the breeze.

"Is this eaten or not?" said the young man.

Not understanding his meaning, the old man replied, "I don't know."

After a little while the two travellers arrived at a big village, where the young man gave his companion a clasp-knife, and said, "Take this, friend, and get two horses with it; but mind and bring it back, for it is very precious."

The old man, looking half amused and half angry,

pushed back the knife, muttering something to the effect that his friend was either deluded or else trying to play the fool with him. The young man pretended not to notice his reply, and remained almost silent till they reached the city, a short distance outside which was the old farmer's house. They walked about the *bázár* and went to the mosque, but nobody saluted them or invited them to come in and rest.

"What a large cemetery!" exclaimed the young man.

"What does the man mean," thought the old farmer, "calling this largely populated city a cemetery?"

On leaving the city their way led through a cemetery where a few people were praying beside a grave and distributing *chapátís* and *kulchás* to passers-by, in the name of their beloved dead. They beckoned to the two travellers and gave them as much as they would.

"What a splendid city this is!" said the young man.

"Now, the man must surely be demented!" thought the old farmer. "I wonder what he will do next? He will be calling the land water, and the water land; and be speaking of light where there is darkness, and of darkness when it is light." However, he kept his thoughts to himself.

Presently they had to wade through a stream that ran along the edge of the cemetery. The water was rather deep, so the old farmer took off his shoes and *páijámas* and crossed over; but the young man waded through it with his shoes and *páijámas* on.

"Well! I never did see such a perfect fool, both in word and in deed," said the old man to himself.

However, he liked the fellow; and thinking that he would amuse his wife and daughter, he invited him to come and stay at his house as long as he had occasion to remain in the village.

"Thank you very much," the young man replied; "but let me first inquire, if you please, whether the beam of your house is strong."

The old farmer left him in despair, and entered his house laughing.

"There is a man in yonder field," he said, after returning their greetings. "He has come the greater part of the way with me, and I wanted him to put up here as long as he had to stay in this village. But the fellow is such a fool that I cannot make anything out of him. He wants to know if the beam of this house is all right.[2] The man must be mad!" and saying this, he burst into a fit of laughter.

"Father," said the farmer's daughter, who was a very sharp and wise girl, "this man, whosoever he is, is no fool, as you deem him. He only wishes to know if you can afford to entertain him."

"Oh! of course," replied the farmer. "I see. Well perhaps you can help me to solve some of his other mysteries. While we were walking together he asked whether he should carry me or I should carry him, as he thought that would be a pleasanter mode of proceeding."

"Most assuredly," said the girl. "He meant that one of you should tell a story to beguile the time."

"Oh yes. Well, we were passing through a corn-field, when he asked me whether it was eaten or not."

"And didn't you know the meaning of this, father? He simply wished to know if the man was in debt or not; because, if the owner of the field was in debt, then the produce of the field was as good as eaten to him; that is, it would have to go to his creditors."

"Yes, yes, yes; of course! Then, on entering a certain village, he bade me take his clasp-knife and get two horses with it, and bring back the knife again to him."

"Are not two stout sticks as good as two horses for helping one along on the road? He only asked you to

[2] *Virám karí chheyih dar?*—"Is your beam strong?"—is a Kashmírí saying, meaning, "Can you entertain me well? Can you make me comfortable?" Running along the upper storey of a Kashmírí house is a long strong beam called *narikot*, upon which the whole roof depends.

cut a couple of sticks and be careful not to lose his knife."

"I see," said the farmer. "While we were walking over the city we did not see anybody that we knew, and not a soul gave us a scrap of anything to eat, till we were passing the cemetery; but there some people called to us and put into our hands some *chapátís* and *kulchas*; so my companion called the city a cemetery, and the cemetery a city."

"This also is to be understood, father, if one thinks of the city as the place where everything is to be obtained, and of inhospitable people as worse than the dead. The city, though crowded with people, was as if dead, as far as you were concerned; while, in the cemetery, which is crowded with the dead, you were saluted by kind friends and provided with bread."

"True, true!" said the astonished farmer. "Then, just now, when we were crossing the stream, he waded it without taking off his shoes and *páijámas*."

"I admire his wisdom," replied the girl. "I have often thought how stupid people were to venture into that swiftly flowing stream and over those sharp stones with bare feet. The slightest stumble and they would fall, and be wetted from head to foot. This friend of yours is a most wise man. I should like to see him and speak to him."

"Very well," said the farmer; "I will go and find him, and bring him in."

"Tell him, father, that our beams are strong enough, and then he will come in. I'll send on ahead a present to the man, to show him that we can afford to have him for our guest."

Accordingly she called a servant and sent him to the young man with a present of a basin of *gyav*, twelve *chapátís*, and a jar of milk, and the following message:—O friend, the moon is full; twelve months make a year, and the sea is overflowing with water."

Half-way the bearer of this present and message met his little son, who, seeing what was in the basket, begged his father to give him some of the food. His father foolishly complied. Presently he saw the young man, and gave him the rest of the present and the message.

"Give your mistress my *salám*," he replied, "and tell her that the moon is new, and that I can only find eleven months in the year, and the sea is by no means full."

Not understanding the meaning of these words, the servant repeated them word for word, as he had heard them, to his mistress; and thus his theft was discovered, and he was severely punished. After a little while the young man appeared with the old farmer. Great attention was shown to him, and he was treated in every way as if he were the son of a great man, although his humble host knew nothing of his origin. At length he told them everything—about the laughing of the fish, his father's threatened execution, and his own banishment—and asked their advice as to what he should do.

"The laughing of the fish," said the girl, "which seems to have been the cause of all this trouble, indicates that there is a man in the palace of whom the king is not aware."

"Joy, joy!" exclaimed the *wazír's* son. "There is yet time for me to return and save my father from an ignominious and unjust death."

The following day he hastened back to his own country, taking with him the farmer's daughter. Immediately on arrival he ran to the palace and informed his father of what he had heard. The poor *wazír*, now almost dead from the expectation of death, was at once carried to the king, to whom he repeated the news that his son had just brought.

"Never!" said the king.

"But it must be so, Your Majesty," replied the *wazír*; "and in order to prove the truth of what I have heard, I pray you to call together all the female attendants in your palace, and order them to jump over a pit, which must be dug. The man will at once betray his sex in the trial."

The king had the pit dug, and commanded all the female servants belonging to the palace to try to jump it. All of them tried, but only one succeeded. That one was found to be a man!!

Thus was the queen satisfied, and the faithful old *wazír* saved.

Afterwards, as soon as arrangements could be made, the *wazír's* son married the old farmer's daughter;[3] and a most happy marriage it was.

[3] Cf. the Introduction to the *Sidat-sangárava*, p. ccxi.; also the *Kathá-saritságara*, in all the details given concerning Vararuchi; also the chapter on "Comparative Folk-Lore," p. 41 of vol. ii. of *The Orientalist; Tibetan Tales*, pp. 112, 113, 128–185. Similar incidents, also, are to be met with in a Lithuanian tale (Schleicher, No. I.), and in the tale of "The Husband of Aglaes" in *Gesta Romanorum*.

NÁGRAY AND HÍMÁL.[1]

ONCE upon a time there lived a poor bráhman of the name of Sodá Rám. His only possessions were a little tumble-down hut and an ill-tempered, selfish woman, whom he called his wife. This woman was a great trial to him. He did not so much mind his humble home. "Parameshwar has not given me a better," he used to say, "and who am I, to grumble at His will?" But constantly to endure the frowns and insults of this wretched woman, and sometimes to be beaten by her, when he had earned less than usual during the day, was too much for him. And so he decided to leave her. One morning he said to her, "My dear, I have heard that a certain king in Hindustán is giving away five *lachs* of rupees every day to the poor. I have determined to go and try to obtain some of these alms."

"All right," said the woman; "I shall not miss you."

The bráhman soon arranged his few things for the journey and started. He walked hard and fast that day, not stopping till he arrived at a certain wood, where he found a spring of pure, sweet water. Here he threw off his load and sat down to eat, and rest, and sleep. While he was sleeping a little serpent came out from the spring[2] and entered the bag, in which was the bráhman's

[1] Narrator's name, Pandit Shiva Rám of Bánah Mahal Srínagar.

[2] In the Valley there are a large number of small streams of water, to which a mysterious origin has been attributed by the people; generally a snake is believed to have its abode in or by the spring. A few miles beyond Pámpúr is one of these springs, close by which is a tank with a round building in the middle for the snake's abode. There is a spring on the *Takht* in Sulaimán, which is said to have been deserted by its snake.

food. By a strange coincidence the man then awoke, and saw the snake. "Oh! oh! What is this?" he exclaimed, and quickly closed the bag.

The thought occurred to him that perhaps it would be better to return to his wife and make her a present of the bag and its contents. "She will most certainly open it," he thought, "and then the serpent will spring out and bite her, and I shall be free." Happy in this thought, he rushed back to his hut, and shouting to his wife, said, "Oh, my dear wife, I was constrained to return. I could not leave you. Accept this present from my hand, and forgive me for ever thinking of going away."

The woman replied, "What is it? Where is it? How? Show it to me."

"No, not here," said the bráhman. "Come to the upper room, and there you shall see it."[3]

They both ascended the steps together; and when they had reached the top the bráhman gave her the bag, and told her to go inside the room and open it. She did so; and the snake, tired of imprisonment, sprang out, much to the astonishment and terror of the woman. She dropped the bag and rushed round the room in a most wild fashion, shrieking for her life. This continued for about ten minutes, when suddenly she beheld a light, as of the light of the moon, and a beautiful little boy appeared. On seeing this the woman was filled with joy and gladness. She shouted to her husband, who was standing outside holding fast the door, to come in and see the wonder; but he promptly declined, saying that he did not wish to be bitten. His wife called again and again; still he refused to enter. At last, however, prevailed on by the woman's glad voice, he opened the door a little, and peeping in, saw the wonderful thing. "It was no serpent that I shut up in the bag," he exclaimed, "but a beautiful boy." He was very glad, and kissed his wife and the child. Then and there the husband and wife

[3] Cf. *Tibetan Tales*, p. 148; also *Folk-Lore Journal*, vol. iv. p. 175.

were thoroughly reconciled to one another, and were very happy together.

From this time the bráhman was a very rich man. His heaven-born son grew more beautiful every day, and was named Nágray. Such was the boy's wisdom and understanding, that at the age of two years people supposed he was at least ten years old. No person in the whole country had either the skill or the confidence to attempt a discussion with him. Although he had never been taught like other children, yet he could speak and read all languages, and was well acquainted with all the sciences. This is accounted for by the fact that he was a heavenly boy.

One day, when Nágray had just passed his seventh birthday, he asked his adopted father if he might bathe in some pure spring. "It must be a very pure spring," he said, "otherwise I shall be defiled."

His father replied, "Yes; but there is not a good spring in the whole city, except one, which is in the garden of the daughter of the king; and that garden is so guarded by a high and strong fence that no person can enter it."

Nevertheless Nágray entreated his father to show him the way to this garden.

"Never," said the bráhman. "You could not get within; and if the king's soldiers saw us walking about the place without any object they would report us to His Majesty, and we both should be slain."

However, Nágray persisted, saying that he was a heavenly child, and could not be injured, till at length his father yielded.

When they arrived near the garden, Nágray, seeing how strongly it was protected, immediately began to search for some hole in the fence. A small hole was soon discovered. Nágray was much pleased at this, and transforming himself into a small serpent, crept into the garden. There he found the purest of springs, in which, after changing himself back into a beautiful boy, he quickly bathed. His coming, however, was noticed. The princess, who was sitting in the garden at the time, heard the splashing of the water, and sent one of her maids to inquire the reason. But when the maid arrived Nágray had resumed the form of a snake and disappeared.

A few days afterwards he returned to the garden and again began to bathe. The princess, whose name was Hímál, was sitting in the same place as before when Nágray came, and again heard the noise of the water. "Who is it," she said, "that so rudely dares to enter my garden and to bathe in my pool? Go and see." The maid went. But Nágray, knowing the mind of the princess, made haste and escaped; and so the maid came and found nothing, as before.

The third time that Nágray repeated his visit Hímál happened to be sitting near the spring, and saw distinctly the form and features of a most beautiful boy. She was entranced with the sight. Such a lovely creature she had never even heard of before. When the boy transformed himself into a serpent she ordered one of her maids to follow after it and see where it went. The maid obeyed, and returned and said that the serpent had reassumed the shape of a boy, and had entered the house of a bráhman called Sodá Rám, and she thought he was his son. Then Hímál thus soliloquised:—"This boy is of the highest caste, and is the same age as myself. He is beautiful, also, beyond description. Why should I not immediately go to my mother and ask her permission to be married to him?" Accordingly she went at once to her mother and told her all her mind—how she had seen the beautiful boy and had fallen in love with him, and that she was of full age and desired to be married.

The queen informed the king of this matter, and the king came to his daughter and said, "Precious sight of my eyes and delight of my heart, I have heard of your wish, and know many princes who would be very glad to be married to you. Select from among them whom you please, and I will arrange for the wedding."

Hímál answered, "O my father, I have seen a beautiful bráhman, whose father's name is Sodá Rám. I wish to be married to him."

When the king heard these words he became exceedingly angry, and said, "My foolish daughter, do you know what you are saying? Sodá Rám is only an ordinary bráhman. How can I degrade myself by giving my daughter in marriage to his son? This cannot be. Let me arrange for you. I will get for you one of the most beautiful, rich, and honourable princes in the world."

Hímál replied, "Nay, oh my father. What I have said, I have said. It does not matter to me whether Sodá Rám is rich or poor. To his son I have given my heart, and what more can I do?"

On this the king became more angry. He thought that the princess had certainly become mad. Some further conversation ensued, and then the king left. Eventually he was constrained by his daughter's entreaties, and one morning ordered Sodá Rám to be called.

When the bráhman heard the king's command he was filled with all sorts of fears as to what might be the reason of this summons. "Can His Majesty have discovered my son's constant visits to the princess's garden? or is he jealous of my wealth? What does he want with me?" Such were the questions occupying his mind when he was conducted before the king.

On seeing him His Majesty heaved a deep sigh. "Alas!" thought he, "whose son is this whom my daughter has chosen? How can I inform my *wazírs* and this man of her request? How they will laugh and jest about the affair! Ah me! sorry man that I am, what shall I do?" In a few minutes, when he had recovered possession of himself, he said to the bráhman, "I hear, O bráhman, that you have a very wise and beautiful son. Will you permit him to marry my daughter?"

The bráhman answered, "O king, you are great and noble in all your acts and wise in all your ways. It is a great blessing that you have spoken to me concerning this matter. I am your humble and obedient subject, and wish only your prosperity."

Then the king ordered the astrologers[4] to ascertain a good day for the wedding, and Sodá Rám returned to his house.

Poor man! he returned with mingled feelings of joy and sorrow. He was glad at the thought of the honour and respect paid to him by the king, but he was sorrowful at the prospect of the immense expense that the proposed marriage would entail upon him. "Whence can I obtain sufficient money to pay for such extravagances as the occasion will demand?" he said to himself.

On reaching home he told everything to his wife and son.

"Never mind," said the boy; "but go to the king and ask His Majesty's pleasure whether I shall come to him in humble state or with great pomp and show."

Sodá Rám was very much surprised at this reply. "Oh, my son," he said, "I am certain you will cause my death by the king's hand. I am rich, but what is my wealth in comparison with the resources of the king?"

The boy replied, "Did I not say, 'Be not anxious'? Believe me, my father, I have treasure which cannot be reckoned for value."

The following morning the bráhman went to the king, and was received most graciously. The king wished that the boy might come to the wedding in as great style as possible. Then the bráhman returned to his house in much fear and trembling, wondering how it would all come to pass.

On the day appointed for the wedding there was great stir and excitement throughout all the city. The people were dressed in their gayest clothes, and music and singing resounded on all sides. The king, too, had a grand

[4] Men who take up the science of the stars, especially with a view of being able to foretell future events, and the good and evil fortune likely to befall any man during his lifetime.

reception for the kings of other countries, and prepared a monster feast for all the people.

That morning the bráhman might have been seen sitting in his house, his face the very picture of grief and terror. He had not arranged anything; he had not even changed his ordinary clothes; because Nágray had thus advised him. At length, when only an hour remained before the appointed time, the boy said to him, "Come and behold my treasures." Then Nágray wrote a letter on paper and gave it to his father, saying, "Go to a certain spring and throw the paper into it, and return."[5] Sodá Rám did so, and on the way back, as he came near the house, he heard a great noise of trumpets and drums and fifes, and saw large numbers of soldiers prettily dressed, and horses richly caparisoned, and elephants loaded with treasures—gold, silver, and precious stones—and a most delicious perfume filled the air. He thought that some foreign potentate had come to do battle against the king, and was astonished beyond measure when he heard that the soldiers and elephants and horses were there in obedience to his son's orders.

Sodá Rám entered the house with a sigh of relief, and there he saw Nágray arraying himself in kinglike garments. Some beautiful garments were waiting for him also.

In due time, attended by a magnificent retinue, they both started for the palace. The king, viewing the immense procession from a little distance, said to his *wazírs*—"This cannot be Sodá Rám's son. There must be some mistake. This surely is some prince, or perhaps a god!"

His fears, however, were soon allayed by the sight of the bráhman and his beautiful son.

The marriage ceremony was conducted in a most magnificent manner, and everything went off most satisfactorily. As soon as the marriage was over, Nágray dismissed his retinue. He, however, remained in the palace. Every

[5] Cf. *Madanakamárájankadai*, pp. 74, 75.

day he attended *darbár*, and after a while the king granted him permission to build a palace for himself on the bank of the river.

. . . .

But Nágray had other wives besides Hímál, and these wives had become very much annoyed at his long absence from them, and had met together to decide what plans they should adopt for bringing back their husband. After much consideration one of the wives offered to undertake all the responsibility. She assumed the disguise of a witch and took with her some vessels of glass, of which such was the power, that if Nágray saw them he would at once remember his other wives and long to return to them. This woman went near Nágray's palace, and waited her opportunity. One day she met Hímál, and introducing herself as a glass-seller, offered to dispose of her precious wares very cheaply. Hímál saw the things and purchased a few of them. In the evening she showed her purchases to Nágray, who become very angry, and ordered her to break the glasses to pieces. "Never again listen to any of these creatures, and never again buy any of their things," he said. This most effectually crushed any hope that might have been lingering within the breast of the disguised serpent, and so she returned.

Another serpent from among his numerous wives then determined to try her plan. She disguised herself as a prostitute, and coming to Hímál, said, "O princess, I am a sweeper by caste. My husband, Nágray, has left me. Please tell me if you have seen or heard of him."

On hearing these words Hímál was very angry and said in a sharp manner, "Oh, is my husband a sweeper!"

The woman replied, "I do not know, I only want my husband. If you doubt your husband's caste, you can easily assure yourself by asking him to show you his caste by means of a spring. Let him throw himself into the water, and if he sinks, then know, O princess, that he is not a sweeper."

Hímál listened with intense excitement to the woman's answer, and directly the woman left she went to her husband and told him that she had heard that he was a sweeper, and not liking that such a vile report should spread, she wished him to go immediately to the spring and prove to her and everybody's satisfaction that this was not the case. When Nágray heard this he raved with passion, and sharply upbraided his wife for again listening to a poor, ignorant woman.

"I know," he said, "from whom you have got this tale. The woman is not a real human being. She is interested in my affairs, and wishes to accomplish our separation. Do not trust to these people."

Hímál replied, "I do not believe them, O my beloved, but do, please, show me your caste."

There was much further conversation, but although Nágray begged hard to be excused the trial, Hímál would not forego her wish, and eventually compelled him to fulfil it. In a little while they both wended their way together to the spring. On arrival Nágray descended, and no sooner did his feet touch the water than they were bound fast and firm with ropes, which the serpents had especially made for the occasion. Nágray at once knew that his feet were hopelessly bound, and that if he would escape from the water he must leave them behind. He told his wife so, but she persisted on waiting to the end. Very slowly but very surely Nágray descended lower and lower till the water reached his breast, then his shoulders, his neck, his mouth, his eyes, his forehead disappeared, till at last there was nothing left visible on the top of the water but his sacred tuft of hair. Now Hímál was satisfied and snatched at the tuft, hoping to pull her husband out of the water, but alas! only a few hairs remained in her hand. Thus Nágray was restored to his serpent wives, and Hímál was deprived of a beautiful, heavenly husband.

. . . .

Poor Hímál returned to the palace in a state of despair. But she could not live happily there, and soon left the place and built an immense caravanserai on the roadside. Here she spent most of her time and fortune in relieving the wants of the poor, who came in crowds every day and asked for alms in the name of Nágray.

One day, a long time afterwards, when she had almost exhausted her wealth and strength upon the multitudes of sick and distressed who flocked to her, an exceedingly poor man and a little girl, who appeared to be his daughter, came to the caravanserai. On seeing their poverty Hímál's heart was filled with pity for them.

"Come in," she said. "Would that I could help you, O poor man, but I have nothing left to me except this golden pestle and mortar. However, I will give you these. And then I will lie down and die. Ah me! I do not care to live."

The beggar and his daughter stayed that evening in the caravanserai, but before they departed the old man told the following story:—

"O princess, we two, my daughter and I, are always travelling hither and thither in search of food. Yesterday we reached a jungle, where we discovered a spring, and seeing that the water was pure and pleasant to the taste, we determined to spend the night by it. We slept in the hollow of a tree close by. As we lay awake looking at the stars, we heard a slight noise, and, turning round, saw a king attended by an immense army come forth from the spring.[6] When the last soldier had come out from the spring, preparations for dinner were commenced. Before dinner the king made a sacrifice. Then he and all his army sat down to eat. After dinner all the people, except the king, returned to the spring and disappeared. The king only remained, and he held a plateful of food in his hand. As soon as the army were out of sight, the king cried with a great voice, 'Is there any poor person here?'

[6] Cf. story of "The Base Friend" in this collection.

On hearing this we two went forward, and the king gave us the plate of food, saying, 'This is in foolish Hímál's name.' Then he, too, returned to the spring, and all was as before."

Hímál's state during the few minutes that were occupied in the narration of this story cannot be described. Her breath seemed to stop, her eyes almost started out of her head, her whole body was in a violent tremble. She knew not what she felt, or what she was doing or saying for very joy, because she was certain that this great king was none other than her own dear Nágray. She gave the golden pestle and mortar to the old beggar, and said, "O good man, this is your due. Now please do me a further kindness, and show me the spot where you witnessed this strange sight." Of course the old man, after receiving such a valuable gift, was only too glad to do anything for the princess, and at once rose up to guide her to the spring.

It was in the gloaming that Hímál and the beggars reached the place, and therefore they decided to pass the night there. The old man and the little girl were soon asleep, but Hímál had determined to keep awake all night to see if the king and his army would again visit the place. She was not disappointed. In the middle of the night, when all was quiet and still, Nágray and his host again appeared, and preparations were made for an immense dinner as before. After dinner the army returned, but the king remained. When every one had disappeared back again into the spring, the king cried as before, "Is there any poor person here?"

Hímál, seeing her husband alone and looking so grand and noble, could not refrain from running forward and seizing his hand. "O my beloved Nágray, I cannot live without you. Forgive me, love me, and come and live with me again," she said.

Nágray, apparently much surprised at this strange behaviour, replied, "I do not know you."

Hímál said, "Oh look upon me. See these eyes. Am I not your wife?"

Then Nágray, overcome with affection, recognised her; but he could not stay with her. "My serpent wives will not let me go," said he. "Depart now and I will come again in a month to see you."

But Hímál replied, "No, never. I cannot leave you. If you will not come with me, then I will go with you." Accordingly, Nágray was obliged to comply, but how to take his wife with him he did not know. This was a most difficult matter. At length, after much deliberation, he resolved to change her into a pebble, and carry her away with him in his pocket. In this way only could she accompany him to his abode in the spring, and be free from attacks of his other wives.

On reaching his home his serpent wives and family came to him and saluted him, but he noticed that there was something wrong, some secret which they had in their minds. He inquired what was the matter, and found that they had detected the smell of an earthly person on him, and therefore suspected that he had brought somebody from the outer regions into the spring. Nágray told them that they were quite correct in their suspicion, and that he would show the person to them, if they would promise to do her no harm. They promised, and so the pebble was taken out of its hiding-place and made to resume its original shape. When the serpent wives saw the beautiful young princess they envied her, and at once decided in their hearts to make her the general drudge. The work appointed to her was to boil the milk for the numerous children of the family. The custom was, when the milk was quite ready, to knock the pots, and then the children, hearing the sound, knew that their meal was ready and came to Hímál. Now Hímál was not quite *au fait* at her work, and so one day she knocked the pots while as yet the milk was steaming-hot. The little serpent children, supposing that all was ready, immediately rushed into the kitchen and drank up all the milk. But serpents cannot take hot milk with impunity, and therefore all the children died. Great was the grief of the bereaved mothers. The whole place was filled with their weepings and lamentations. When the serpents knew that their little ones had perished through the forgetfulness of Hímál, they went and bit her to death. Nágray soon heard of all that had happened, and was overwhelmed with grief.

At a convenient time he made a little bed for the corpse, and taking it up out of the spring placed it on a tree. Every day he visited the corpse and returned to the spring. One morning a very holy man passed by that way and noticed the bed among the branches. He climbed the tree to see what it was, and finding the dead body of a very beautiful woman lying on it, he unfixed it and brought it down. His soul was filled with pity for the young fair corpse, and he prayed to Náráyan to restore her life. His prayer was answered. Hímál became alive again and went with the holy man to his home.

When Nágray next visited the tree he saw that the corpse and the little bed had been taken away, and was very grieved. "Has any person stolen the body? or has Hímál come to life again and left me?" thought he. He at once commenced a search. He went everywhere looking for his beloved, till at last he called at the house of the holy man. Hímál happened to be asleep at the time of his visit, and therefore he resumed the form of a serpent, and going quietly to the bed coiled himself up there. While they were both thus lying on the bed together, the son of the holy man chanced to come in. This son was very fond of Hímál, and hoped to marry her. When he saw the serpent coiled up on the bed beside his beloved he was in great terror lest it should have bitten her. He immediately opened his knife and cut the serpent into two pieces. The noise woke Hímál. "Alas! alas! what have you done?" she cried. "You have slain my husband. My beloved Nágray is no more." That evening the corpse was burnt upon a pile of sandalwood, and Hímál, according to the custom of those days, lay down beside the corpse and was burned also.[7]

The holy man was terribly grieved at this sad sight. He went to the place of burning and collected the ashes of the two corpses. These he set before him and cried all day and night, and would not be comforted. Most fortunately it happened that Shiva and his wife Párvatí were sitting in the form of two birds on a branch of the tree under which the old man sat. They heard the holy man's cries, and decided to help him. Shiva said to his wife, "Behold this good man's grief. Oh that he knew the power that lies in those ashes! They have only to be thrown into the spring and the two persons will come to life again."[8] The holy man heard the bird say this and immediately went and threw the ashes into the spring. No sooner had he done this than Hímál and Nágray again appeared alive, and as well and as beautiful as ever.

Henceforth all was peace and happiness. They lived in a small house not far from the spring, and the holy man lived with them. Out of gratitude for his sympathy and respect for his goodness they would not let him go, but carefully attended to him up to the day of his death. And they were very much blessed in the deed.[9] [10]

[7] This inhuman practice was gradually put a stop to in Hindustán by Lord William Bentinck nearly sixty years ago. It lasted to a later date in Kashmír. Vigne was told that a *Sati* had never taken place here until the time of the Sikhs; that is, whilst it was in possession of the successive Muhammadan masters, who forbad the custom. Of course they were common enough during the time of its ancient Hindú dynasty.

[8] Cf. *Indian Fairy Tales*, pp. 5, 149, 182; *Old Deccan Days*, p. 74; *Wide-Awake Stories*, pp. 139, 176; *Folk-Tales of Bengal*, pp. 41, 135, 219; also stories of "Brave Princess," "Two Brothers," "Unjust King and Wicked Goldsmith," in this collection.

[9] Cf. *Indian Fairy Tales*, p. 78.

[10] This story has been put into Persian and Kashmírí verse. While I am correcting these proofs a Hindustání translation, entitled Hímál Nágarajan, by Pandit Hargopál Kol, reaches me. Nágray is one of the heroes of the valley. The Musalmáns claim him. They say that he was a Muhammadan, but fell in love with Hímál, and for a while pretended to be a bráhman. Amusing tales are told how the Musalmáns came with some soldiers and rescued Nágray's corpse from the funeral pyre and buried it, &c.

GLOSSARY

OF SUCH WORDS AS ARE NOT EXPLAINED IN THE BODY OF THIS BOOK.

Allah (*Alláh*), Musalmán word for God.
Almaira (also *almárí*), a chest of drawers, a book-stand.
Áná, the sixteenth part of a rupee.
Ashrafís (also *muhr*), a gold coin worth about a guinea and a half.
Bakhshish (also *bakshaish*), a gift, gratuity.
Baniyá (also *woni*), a shopkeeper, merchant.
Bázár (also *bazár*), a constant established market.
Bhagawant, a Hindú word for the Most High.
Bhút, a malignant spirit haunting cemeteries, lurking in trees, animating carcasses, and deluding or devouring human beings.
Bráhman, a Hindú of the highest caste. The priests are chosen from this caste.
Bráhmaní, the wife of a bráhman.
Chapátí, a thin cake of unleavened bread.
Chillam (also *chilam*), the part of the *huqqa* (pipe) in which the tobacco and charcoal is placed.
Coolie (*kúlí*), a labourer, a porter.
Dáí, a milk-nurse, midwife, lady's maid.
Darbár, hall of audience.
Dev, a demon.
Díwán, a minister or secretary.
Dulí (also *dolí*), a kind of sedan.
Gosáín, a Hindú saint or holy person.
Gyav, clarified butter.
Hakím, a native doctor in the general sense of the term.
Haram, the women's apartments, a seraglio.
Imám, a Musálman priest, leader in religious matters.
Indrasharájá, the god of firmament, personified atmosphere.
Jinn, a demon, an ogre.
Jogí, a Hindú ascetic.
Kamarband, a girdle, a long piece of cloth girt round the loins.
Kasába, a small red cap worn by Musálman women.
Kharwár, an ass load equal to 192 lbs.
Kotwál, the chief police officer in a district.

Kulícha (also *kulchá*), a kind of bread, biscuit.
Lach, one hundred thousand.
Maidán, a plain, an open field.
Malah, a Muhammadan teacher.
Melá, a religious fair.
Muhr, vide *ashrafí*.
Muqaddam, the headman of a village, an official.
Nách, a dance given by rich natives.
Náráyan, a Hindú name for the Deity.
Páijáma (also *Paijáma*), trowsers, long drawers.
Palanquin, a superior kind of sedan.
Pánsa, a copper coin, a farthing or a halfpenny.
Parameshwar, a Hindú word for God, the Almighty.
Pargana, an inferior division of a country, nearly equalling a barony.
Párvatí, the goddess Durgá, the wife of Shiva.
Parwána, an order, a warrant.
Paṭhán, an *Afghán*.
Patwárí, a village official, whose duty it is to keep an account of the various crops reared by the villagers.
Pír, a spiritual guide (Musalmán).
Píṭh, a stool, a seat.
Pújá, idol worshippers.
Puláv (also *piláv*), a kind of dish made of rice, spices, and flesh or fowl.
Puts, a long piece of cloth thrown over the head and allowed to hang down the back of the Musalmán woman ; the ordinary veil worn by Kashmírí females.
Qismat, fate.
Rákshasa, a demon, ogre.
Rakshasí, the female of *Rákshasa*.
Rání, a (Hindú) queen or princess.
Rishi (also *rikhi*), a sage, saint.
Rupee, a well-known silver coin so called worth at present about 1s. 5d. only.
Sáis (also *saís*), a groom.
Salám, the usual Musulmán salutation to a European.
Sers, the name of a weight of nearly 2 lbs. avoirdupois.
Shástras, Hindú religious books.
Shikár, hunting, game.
Shikárí, a hunter.
Shiva, a Hindú Deity.
Tamáshá, an entertainment, a spectacle.
Tsut, a loaf, bread.
Wazír, a minister of state.
Woni, a shopkeeper, merchant.
Zanána, a female—female apartments in a house.

INDEX.

PRINTED BY BALLANTYNE, HANSON AND CO.
EDINBURGH AND LONDON.

By the same Author.

Pp. viii.-263, 8vo, price 8s.

A DICTIONARY

OF

KASHMIRI PROVERBS AND SAYINGS.

(*EXPLAINED AND ILLUSTRATED FROM THE RICH AND INTERESTING FOLK-LORE OF THE VALLEY.*)

"The storehouse of facts here provided is one for which philologists and folk-lorists will have every reason to be grateful. . . . Most racy, amusing, and varied in interest. The whole of the book is very well worth reading. There must be a good deal of character in the average Kashmirian, and Mr. Knowles both a good and lucky observer."—*Saturday Review.*

"A genuine contribution to those folk-lore collections from India which are always welcome to students of nearly all sections of history; and Mr. Knowles has aided the student very learnedly and ably by his accumulation of folk-lore in illustration of the proverbial sayings. One cannot read these proverbs without at once detecting their primitive characteristics, and extracting from them some notion of the life of the people who use them—a fact which shows how faithful has been Mr. Knowles's method of work." —*Folk-Lore Journal.*

"The second edition, which we hope to see some day, for the work is well worthy of one. The book throughout shows that care and attention to details, which is in itself a proof that the general accuracy of the author may be taken on trust."—*The Indian Antiquary.*

"I have been much gratified by the perusal of your truly valuable work on the Proverbs of Kashmir. It entitles you to the gratitude of philologists, and it helps to save from oblivion the remnants of a most interesting language."—*Dr. Leitner, Vice-Chancellor of the Punjab University.*